On Gender, Labor, and Inequality

THE WORKING CLASS IN AMERICAN HISTORY

Editorial Advisors

James R. Barrett, Julie Greene, William P. Jones,
Alice Kessler-Harris, and Nelson Lichtenstein

A list of books in the series appears at the end of this book.

On Gender, Labor, and Inequality

RUTH MILKMAN

UNIVERSITY OF ILLINOIS PRESS
Urbana, Chicago, and Springfield

Library of Congress Cataloging-in-Publication Data
Names: Milkman, Ruth, 1954– author.
Title: On gender, labor, and inequality / Ruth Milkman.
Description: Urbana, Chicago : University of Illinois Press,
    2016. | Series: Working class in American history | Includes
    bibliographical references and index.
Identifiers: LCCN 2015046963 | ISBN 9780252040320 (hardback :
    alk. paper) | ISBN 9780252081774 (paperback : alk. paper)
Subjects: LCSH: Sex discrimination against women—United
    States--History—20th century. | Sexual division of labor—
    United States—History—20th century. | Women—
    Employment—United States—History—20th century. |
    Social classes—United States—History—20th century.
    | BISAC: SOCIAL SCIENCE / Gender Studies. | POLITICAL
    SCIENCE / Labor & Industrial Relations. | LANGUAGE ARTS &
    DISCIPLINES / Readers.
Classification: LCC HQ1237.5.U6 M55 2016 | DDC 305.420973—dc23
    LC record available at http://lccn.loc.gov/2015046963

Contents

Acknowledgments

This volume would not exist if not for the initiative of University of Illinois Press editor Laurie Matheson, who proposed the project to me over lunch several years ago and then patiently awaited its completion. My first book was published in the press's Working Class in American History series back in 1987, and I was delighted when Laurie suggested that my work might once again appear in that prized venue. Although I am a sociologist by profession, I have long been engaged in historical research, and it is an honor to have my work deemed worthy of historians' attention.

I am deeply indebted to the Radcliffe Institute at Harvard University, where I was privileged to receive a residential fellowship for the 2012–13 academic year. There I was lucky to work with three talented undergraduates who ably assisted me with the research for chapter 11 of this volume: Mariah Garcia, Barbara Halla, and Yekaterina Solovyova. Thanks also to Dorothy Sue Cobble, Cynthia Deitch, Linda Gordon, and Alice Kessler-Harris for comments on an earlier version of that chapter.

Many other teachers and colleagues, far too numerous to list here, contributed in myriad ways to the other ten chapters of the book, all of which were published previously in other venues, where my detailed acknowledgments also appear. But I do wish to extend special thanks to Dorothy Sue Cobble and Alice Kessler-Harris, both of whom reviewed the entire volume for the University of Illinois Press and made many helpful suggestions. I am grateful also to E. Tammy Kim for her thoughtful comments on an earlier version of the introduction. I acknowledge as well Rebecca Frazier at UCLA and Isaac Jabola-Carolus at the CUNY Graduate Center, both of whom cheerfully and meticulously assisted me in scanning and reformatting all the previously published chapters; Isaac also arranged reprint permissions on my behalf.

This book begins and ends with chapters on women and economic crises, a topic I first explored as an undergraduate; indeed, chapter 1 is based on my 1975 B.A. thesis on women in the Great Depression. Although I did not fully appreciate it at that time, I understand now that my lifelong interest in this topic stemmed directly from my own family history. My late mother, née Beatrice Mozon, was born into an immigrant family that prospered in the Brooklyn of the 1910s and 1920s, only to lose virtually everything in the 1929 crash. That trauma would haunt my mother for another seven decades, until her death in the very last week of the twentieth century. Although she did not live to see the Great Recession, nothing about it would have surprised her. No one did more to shape my intellectual trajectory or my worldview. This book is dedicated to her memory.

Abbreviations

ACLU	American Civil Liberties Union
ACW	Amalgamated Clothing Workers
AFL	American Federation of Labor
AFL-CIO	American Federation of Labor–Congress of Industrial Organizations
AFSCME	American Federation of State, County and Municipal Employees
AFT	American Federation of Teachers
BSOIW	International Association of Bridge, Structural, Ornamental and Reinforcing Iron Workers
CCPOA	California Correctional Peace Officers Association
CIO	Congress of Industrial Organizations (called the Committee for Industrial Organization from 1935–1937)
CNA	California Nurses Association
CSEA	California School Employees Association
CTA/NEA	California Teachers Association/National Education Association
CTW	Change to Win Federation
CWA	Communication Workers of America
EEOC	Equal Employment Opportunity Commission
FMLA	Family and Medical Leave Act
HERE	Hotel and Restaurant Employees Union

IAFF	International Association of Firefighters
IAM	International Association of Machinists
IATSE	International Association of Theatrical Stage Employees
IBEW	International Brotherhood of Electrical Workers
IBT	International Brotherhood of Teamsters
ILGWU	International Ladies' Garment Workers' Union
IUOE	International Union of Operating Engineers
IUPA	International Union of Police Associations
LIUNA	Laborers' International Union of North America
NAACP	National Association for the Advancement of Colored People
NLRB	National Labor Relations Board
NLU	National Labor Union
PDA	Pregnancy Discrimination Act
SDI	State Disability Insurance
SEIU	Service Employees International Union
SMWIA	Sheet Metal Workers' International Association
UA	United Association of Journeymen and Apprentices of the Plumbing, Pipefitting and Sprinkler Fitting Industry of the U.S. and Canada
UAW	United Automobile Workers
UBC	United Brotherhood of Carpenters and Joiners of America
UE	United Electrical Workers
UFCW	United Food and Commercial Workers International Union
UFW	United Farm Workers of America
UNITE	Union of Needletrades, Industrial, and Textile Employees
UNITE HERE	Union of Needletrades, Industrial, and Textile Employees–Hotel Employees and Restaurant Employees Union (formed by the merger of UNITE and HERE in 2004)
WMC	War Manpower Commission
WPB	War Production Board

On Gender, Labor, and Inequality

Introduction

The United States made substantial progress toward reducing gender inequality in the late twentieth century, not only thanks to the feminist movement of the 1960s and 1970s but also as an unintended consequence of the shift to a post-industrial economy. The gender gap in pay rates, for example, narrowed not only because unprecedented numbers of women gained entry to the elite professions and upper-level management starting in the 1970s, but also because real wages for male workers, especially those without a college education, fell sharply in that same period with de-industrialization and union decline. As manufacturing withered, the traditionally female-employing service sector expanded; surging demand for female labor, in turn, drew more and more married women and mothers into the workforce. By the twentieth century's end, women typically were employed outside the home throughout their adult lives, apart from brief interludes of full-time caregiving. They were far less likely to be economically dependent on men than their mothers and grandmothers had been. Their legal and social status had dramatically improved as well, and the idea that women and men should have equal opportunities in the labor market had won wide acceptance. Women workers continued to face serious problems, including sex discrimination in pay and promotions, sexual harassment, and the formidable challenges of balancing work and family commitments in a nation that famously lags behind its competitors in public provision for paid family leave and childcare. Still, by any standard, the situation has improved greatly since the 1970s.[1]

This improvement has not been evenly distributed across the female population, however. On the contrary, in precisely the same historical period during which gender inequalities declined dramatically—the 1970s through the early twenty-first century—class inequalities rapidly widened, with profound implications for women as well as men. Class inequalities *among women* are greater than ever before. Highly educated, upper-middle-class women—a group that is vastly overrepresented both in media depictions of women at work and in the wider political discourse about gender inequality—have far better opportunities than their counterparts in earlier generations did. Yet their experience is a world apart from that of the much larger numbers of women workers who struggle to make ends meet in poorly paid clerical, retail, restaurant, and hotel jobs; in hospitals and nursing homes; or as housekeepers, nannies, and homecare workers.

Many of those working women are paid at or just above the legal minimum wage; some—especially women of color and immigrants—earn even less because their employers routinely violate minimum wage, overtime, and other workplace laws. Although female managers and professionals typically work full time (or more than full time), many women in lower-level jobs are offered fewer hours than they would prefer, a problem compounded by unpredictable work schedules that play havoc with their family responsibilities. Millions of women are trapped in female-dominated clerical and service jobs that offer few if any opportunities for advancement, and in which employment itself is increasingly precarious. For them, bestselling books like Sheryl Sandberg's 2013 *Lean In*, which encourages women to be more assertive in the workplace, are of little relevance. Indeed, if women in lower-level jobs are foolhardy enough to follow such advice, they are more likely to be fired than to win a promotion or pay raise.[2]

The widening inequalities between women in managerial and professional jobs and those employed at lower levels of the labor market are further exacerbated by class-differentiated marriage and family arrangements. Most people marry or partner with those of a similar class status, a longstanding phenomenon that anthropologists call class endogamy. This multiplies the effects of rising class inequality: at one end of the spectrum are households with two well-paid professionals or managers, while at the other end households depend on one (in the case of one-parent families) or two far lower incomes. In addition, affluent, highly educated women are more likely to be married or in marriage-like relationships than are working-class women, and such relationships are typically more stable among the privileged. Women in managerial and professional jobs not only can more easily afford paid domestic help, but also are more likely to have access to paid sick days and paid parental leave than women in lower-level jobs. And families routinely reproduce class inequalities over the generations: affluent parents go to great lengths to ensure that their children—now daughters as well as sons—acquire the educational credentials that will secure them a privileged place in the labor market, similar to that of their parents, when they are grown.

Women of color are disproportionately likely to have been shut out of the gender revolution that transformed the United States during the late twentieth century. But class divisions have widened over recent decades within communities of color as well as among women. Although to a much lesser extent than among white women, unprecedented numbers of women of color have joined the privileged strata that benefited most from the reduction in gender inequality over recent decades. There is a literature on "the declining significance of race," starting with William Julius Wilson's 1980 book of that title.[3] More recently, public concern about growing class inequality has surged. Yet the rapid rise in "within-group" class inequalities among women has attracted much less attention.

This collection of essays interrogates the historical and contemporary intersections of class and gender inequalities in the U.S. labor market, as well as efforts to challenge those inequalities. The first four chapters focus on the 1930s and 1940s, the period of the "Great Compression," when class inequalities were on the decline. That era presents a striking contrast to the developments of the past half-century, which are the focus of the second half of the volume.

These essays span four decades of research, starting in the 1970s, when the study of gender and work was in its infancy. Over the decades since, sociologists, historians, and other feminist scholars have produced an enormous body of research on women's labor, past and present. I was fortunate to be among the pioneers in this field, and like many others at the time, my intellectual interests were firmly rooted in the social movements then flourishing both inside and outside the academy—especially the "second wave" of feminism that surged in the 1960s and 1970s. I was particularly influenced by what was then known as "socialist feminism," a second-wave theoretical perspective that understood the oppression of women to be inextricably intertwined with the dynamics of modern capitalism. Socialist-feminists elaborated a critique of traditional Marxism, which offered limited insight into "the woman question" but at the same time problematized "liberal feminism," with its narrow focus on expanding opportunities for women within the existing structure of capitalism. Class inequalities among women were far less pronounced in that period than they are today, but for socialist-feminists they (along with racial and ethnic inequalities) were centrally important.[4]

The first three chapters in this book are embedded in the debates that took place during this formative period in the history of feminist theory and explicitly reflect a socialist-feminist perspective. Some of the terminology as well as the broader theoretical orientation may seem quaint to uninitiated twenty-first-century readers. Yet in many ways the analytical framework and research agenda that socialist-feminists pioneered in the 1970s have become increasingly relevant over the decades since, as class inequalities have widened and as—especially since the 2008 financial crisis—interest in understanding the dynamics of capitalism has grown.

The widely discussed concept of "intersectionality," which emphasizes the interdependence of race, class, and gender (as well as other types of oppression), is itself an outgrowth of 1970s and 1980s socialist-feminist theory.[5] As a description of multiple oppressions operating simultaneously, the term is useful, yet it does not do much to *explain* the dynamics of the interrelationships among different forms of inequality. Moreover, most of those who invoke the term intersectionality devote far less attention to class inequalities among women than to racial inequalities and those based on sexual orientation. In contrast, the essays in this volume are concerned primarily with class and gender, and might be criticized for being insufficiently attentive to race and other inequalities. Yet they offer an important corrective to the many feminist conversations, including those framed in terms of intersectionality, in which class inequalities are totally ignored. As bell hooks put it, "Nowadays it is fashionable to talk about race or gender; the uncool subject is class."[6] Not coincidentally, the focus of several of the chapters that follow, namely the relationship of women workers to labor unions, is peripheral to the intersectionality literature as well.[7]

My own intellectual odyssey through this terrain began with a study of the impact of the 1930s economic crisis on women workers. As the child of Depression-generation parents, I grew up hearing countless stories about that era, and so it was surely no accident that it was the focus of my first serious research project, which became the first chapter in this volume. I began with the Marxist hypothesis that women were a "reserve army" of labor, pulled into the workforce during periods of economic expansion, and then expelled during economic downturns. However, as I began to investigate the history of women's work in the 1930s, I soon learned that this was not the case. Instead, I found that men had been more likely to lose their jobs than women during the Depression—exactly the opposite of what I had expected. The reason, I came to understand, was that the long-established pattern of job segregation by sex relegated women to segments of the labor market that were less vulnerable to economic downturns than the segments (especially manufacturing and construction) in which men predominated. Employers and workers alike saw the boundaries between "women's jobs" and "men's jobs" as permanent, so that substitution of male for female labor, or vice versa, was exceedingly rare.

As my own empirical research revealed that the hypothesis I had begun with was totally incorrect, I realized that being "wrong" was precisely what could lead to new insights. This was an intoxicating experience, and I was immediately hooked on evidence-based research. In addition, this first project led me to become fascinated with understanding the dynamics of job segregation by sex, which I now saw as the linchpin of gender inequality. I wanted to figure out *why* job segregation was such a persistent feature of the labor market. How could it be so resilient, even in the face of the deepest economic crisis of twentieth-century capitalism and despite widespread public hostility to women's employment during the Depression years?

That query soon led me to examine the history of women's work during World War II, the one time in U.S. history that large numbers of women had entered core industrial jobs, the monopolization of which by men in the preceding decade had led to higher male unemployment during the 1930s. I thought that by studying the incorporation of "Rosie the Riveter" and her sisters into the male preserve of basic manufacturing and their subsequent expulsion from it at the war's end, I might gain a deeper understanding of the dynamics of job segregation by sex. So I embarked on a study of the impact of World War II on what was the nation's largest industry at the time, automobile manufacturing.

As chapter 2 shows, my instinct that the war would offer a window into the dynamics of job segregation by sex was prescient, but not in quite the way I had expected. Once again, I was forced to abandon my preconceptions in the face of the evidence my research uncovered. I learned that while during the war years women did enter jobs that had been previously closed to them, employers did not hire them to work alongside men but instead created a new system of job segregation. Many jobs that had been exclusively male before the war were now reconfigured "for the duration" as distinct "male" and "female" positions. This was not difficult for managers to accomplish, since at the time the nation's factories were converting from making consumer products like automobiles and auto parts (none of which were manufactured during the war) to producing military goods such as jeeps, tanks, and airplanes. Thus, war factories did not eliminate job segregation by sex, even temporarily, but instead reproduced it in a new form. So once again my initial hypothesis—that job segregation had been dismantled during the war—was proved wrong, and once again that realization led me to some new insights.

Accompanying the economic upheavals of depression and war that marked the 1930s and 1940s was an equally dramatic labor movement upsurge, in which U.S. unions reached their peak level of power and influence. Chapter 3 was my first effort to explore the effects of union organization on women workers and job segregation. Although my main focus was on the 1930s and 1940s, I explored earlier developments in U.S. women's labor history as well, drawing on previous feminist scholarship that argued that trade unions' efforts to exclude women from membership had helped to consolidate patterns of job segregation by sex in the late nineteenth and early twentieth centuries. That earlier work did not examine the influence of the massive industrial unions that took shape in the late 1930s, however. Those unions had a more inclusive structure than the craft unions that dominated the earlier era, suggesting the possibility of an alternative outcome for women workers. As chapter 3 argues, the industrial unions had the potential to become an instrument to challenge job segregation by sex, especially in the period immediately after World War II, when women workers were pushed out of basic industry and into traditionally female sales, service, and clerical work. That pivotal opportunity was largely squandered, however, as the industrial unions seemed to have rarely challenged the reconstruction of the prewar sexual division of labor.

With this in mind, I set out to explore in more detail what happened at the end of the war. I began with the view that women had been pushed out of the "men's jobs" they had performed for the duration of the military conflict largely because male workers and their unions had insisted on restoring the prewar order. Here again I focus on the automobile industry, which in that period set the pattern for labor relations in the nation as a whole. As chapter 4 shows, once more my expectation proved incorrect. What I found was that the restoration of the prewar sexual division of labor was above all a *management* project. To be sure, unions and their male members collaborated with employers in restoring the prewar order, but it was the employers who directly controlled hiring policy and who therefore had far more influence on the outcome. From the perspective of managers and unionists alike, it was a foregone conclusion that the auto industry would revert to the prewar pattern of favoring men for all but a few marginal production jobs. Although the majority of women war workers themselves did want to make the wartime shift in the division of labor permanent, and some women unionists fought to do so, their influence was extremely limited. In addition, I found that while women workers were purged from auto industry and other "war jobs" that they had hoped to keep, most did not go "back to the home," contrary to popular belief, after the war ended. Most stayed in the workforce but found themselves newly restricted to traditionally female jobs, as the prewar pattern of job segregation was reconstructed.

This series of historical studies of the 1930s and 1940s not only reinforced my initial impression that job segregation by sex was the most important dimension of gender inequality, but it also exposed the importance of the cultural and ideological aspect of the gender division of labor. The notion that certain jobs were best suited to men and others to women was so hegemonic that job segregation by sex seemed "natural" to virtually everyone involved—even to women workers themselves. Once managers attached sex labels to particular jobs, those labels became naturalized in this way and thereafter were very difficult to change. Against that background, my attention was riveted by a legal controversy that surfaced in the early 1980s, when the giant retailer Sears Roebuck faced a class action sex-discrimination case brought by the U.S. Equal Employment Opportunity Commission (EEOC). In its defense, Sears contended that women simply were not interested in taking the better-paid commission sales jobs that were monopolized by men at Sears. But the EEOC argued that—just as I had found in the postwar auto industry—management's longstanding hiring policy was the key to explaining the allocation of commission jobs to men. Alice Kessler-Harris, then the nation's most prominent historian of women's labor, served as an expert witness for the EEOC and testified along these lines. But then Sears found an expert witness of its own, historian Rosalind Rosenberg, who deployed historical literature on "women's culture"—scholarship that emphasized the distinctive cultural meanings of paid work to women and men—to support Sears's claim that women did not want "men's jobs." This debate intersected with the question of whether feminists should insist on equal treatment for women and men at work or should instead take gender "difference" into account in crafting policies (especially on such matters as the treatment of pregnancy in the workplace). Chapter 5 analyzes the Sears controversy, which was hotly debated among feminist scholars at the time, in that context. It explores not only the dynamics of job segregation but also the social and cultural construction of boundaries between "male" and "female" work in the retail sector.

By the late 1980s many feminist scholars were enamored of post-structuralist theories, which had become increasingly influential in women's studies, especially among historians.[8] Although I eventually came to appreciate the contributions of those who adopted this perspective, initially I was deeply skeptical about the "cultural turn." It coincided with the Reagan-era right-wing ascendancy in the United States, and to me it felt like a retreat from the political concerns that had animated earlier feminist theory and had motivated my own research. Although I was well aware of the importance of analyzing the ideological and cultural aspects of job segregation by sex, I understood these in relation to the structural and material forces shaping gender and class inequalities—an approach that was anathema to post-structuralists. At this juncture my research focus gradually shifted to the highly unfashionable topic of labor and labor movements. Trade unions were facing formidable political attacks in the 1980s, just as women workers were finally becoming a substantial part of their membership. Among the studies I produced in that period were chapters 6, 7, and 8 in this volume, which interrogate the relationship of women to labor unions in the late-twentieth-century United States.[9]

Chapter 6 is the most theoretically driven of this triad, advancing a perspective rooted in sociological theories of organization. It argues that the characteristics of a labor union during the historical period in which it first takes shape tend to persist over time. Union growth in the United States has generally occurred in sharp spurts, rather than on an incremental basis, so that it is easy to identify distinct cohorts of unions, each formed in a different era of labor movement growth. Chapter 6 elaborates the enduring variations in gender arrangements among four such union cohorts: the craft-oriented trade unions originally formed in the late nineteenth and early twentieth centuries; the "new unions" that took shape in the clothing and textile industries in the 1910s; the industrial unions of the 1930s and 1940s; and, finally, the service- and public-sector unions that emerged in the 1960s and 1970s. Each of these four union cohorts had a different relationship to women workers, reflecting both their structural characteristics (for example, craft versus industrial unions) and the state of gender relations in the wider society at the time they first formed. Chapter 6 argues that this helps explain the wide variation in U.S. unions' relationships to women workers in the late twentieth century, as labor organizations tended to maintain the traditions shaped in their formative years.

Chapter 7 builds on this framework to interpret a range of empirical data on inter-union variations in female union membership and leadership, as well as variations in the extent and nature of attention to "women's issues" on the part of various unions. In addition, this chapter explores the dynamics of union organizing in the 1980s, finding that workplaces with large female majorities were the most readily organized in that period—as measured by the probability of winning National Labor Relations Board (NLRB) union representation elections. The chapter includes a quantitative analysis of NLRB election outcomes that demonstrates that workplaces with a gender-mixed labor force had the lowest win rates of all, while those with large male majorities had win rates in between the mixed and predominately female workplaces. This finding suggests that it may be easier to build union solidarity in the context of a gender-homogenous workforce. This chapter also examines the growing commitment in the 1970s and 1980s to gender equality issues and to incorporating women into positions of leadership on the part of some key unions, and shows that the most recently formed union cohorts are the most likely to adopt this agenda.

Chapter 8, the third in this set of studies of gender and unionism, focuses on the ways in which job segregation by sex is mirrored in the structure of organized labor. Some unions, most notably those in the building trades, are comprised almost entirely of male workers, reflecting the gender composition of employment in their traditional jurisdictions. Other unions, representing predominantly female fields like teaching and nursing, are composed mainly of women. Thus, the chapter argues, there are two separate worlds of unionism, one male and one female, each with a distinctive culture and political orientation. In the context of the continuing attacks on organized labor, which have sharply limited the possibilities of union growth, this sex-segregated structure has become even more deeply entrenched.

Chapters 9 and 10 turn to a different topic, namely the growth of inequalities among women in the late twentieth century. Chapter 9 focuses on paid domestic labor, an occupation that declined dramatically from the largest single female occupation in the late nineteenth century to a relatively small part of the workforce by the 1930s. That decline continued until the 1980s, when domestic labor suddenly began to expand again. This occupation has attracted a lot of attention from feminist scholars over the years, but as the chapter notes, most of that research is based on ethnographic or interview data. The literature focuses primarily on the interactions between domestics and their (typically female) employers, and on the racial and ethnic inequalities embedded in those interactions—given that women of color and immigrants make up the vast bulk of the paid domestic workforce, while employers are predominantly white. Chapter 9, which I co-authored with Ellen Reese and Benita Roth, argues that the microsociological orientation of this literature, as well as its focus on racial and ethnic divisions, has led it to overlook the importance of growing class inequality as a driver of employment growth in paid domestic labor. In a quantitative analysis of the hundred largest U.S. metropolitan areas, we show that the extent of income inequality is a highly significant factor shaping the size of the domestic service occupation (as a proportion of the overall female labor force). More generally, the chapter argues that widening class inequality, including inequality among women, is at the root of the expansion of employment in paid domestic work in the late twentieth century.

Chapter 10 also explores growing class inequalities among women but in a different context, namely that of work–family policy. The United States is famously exceptional in its minimal provision of family leave for workers who need to take time off to care for a new child or an ill family member. Only unpaid leave is mandated by federal law, and many workers are excluded from even that minimal protection. Less well known is the fact that access to paid family leave is far more widespread among managers and professionals than among lower-level workers. Low-wage workers cannot afford to take unpaid leave, and they rarely have access to employer-provided paid leave benefits, which are offered disproportionately to highly educated managers and professionals. In 2002 California passed a new law that promised to address this problem by creating a paid family leave program covering all private-sector employees in the state. As chapter 10 shows, this landmark law faced strong opposition from organized business, which denounced it as a "job killer." The advocates for paid leave built a broad coalition that prevailed despite the business campaign against the measure. However, the longstanding class disparities in access to paid family leave were only partially alleviated, because those who needed paid leave the most were the least likely to be aware of the state program.[10]

Although they treat very different subjects, chapters 9 and 10 both highlight the growing salience of class-based disparities among women in the late twentieth and early twenty-first centuries, a phenomenon that has not received as much attention as it should.[11] Chapter 11 once again highlights the importance of this issue, through a comparison of the gender dynamics of the Great Depression of the 1930s and those of the Great Recession associated with the 2008 financial crisis. Revisiting the topic of chapter 1, this closing chapter documents the many structural parallels between these two deep economic crises in regard to their effects on women, against the background of the massive changes in gender relations that occurred in the intervening decades. During the Great Recession, just as in the 1930s crisis, female unemployment increased less, and later, than male unemployment, because once again the predominantly male-employing construction and manufacturing sectors were most severely affected by the crisis. The two downturns had many other structural features in common as well, as chapter 11 documents. But whereas the Great Depression spurred a political transformation that led to a sharp reduction in economic inequality, accompanied by a dramatic upsurge in union organizing, neither of these developments took place after the 2008 crisis. Instead, inequalities between the haves and have-nots have continued to grow, and inequalities among women in particular have reached historically unprecedented levels.

The urgency of understanding the interactions between gender and class inequalities, and the relationship of both to the dynamics of capitalism, has never been greater. The feminist scholarship of the past half-century has offered rich insights into gender inequality, and those insights have made a difference not only in the academy but also in the larger society. Now it's time for our research to "bring class back in" and to extend the gender revolution to include not only the privileged elite but also the working-class majority.

Notes

1. For more details and documentation of the points in this paragraph and the next four, see chapter 11.

2. Sheryl Sandberg, *Lean In: Women, Work, and the Will to Lead* (New York: Knopf, 2013).

3. William Julius Wilson, *The Declining Significance of Race: Blacks and Changing American Institutions* (Chicago: University of Chicago Press, 1980).

4. For a detailed discussion of socialist-feminist theory that compares it with other schools of feminism in this period, see Alison Jaggar, *Feminist Politics and Human Nature* (New York: Rowman and Littlefield, 1983). Other influential socialist-feminist texts include Juliet

Mitchell, *Woman's Estate* (New York: Pantheon, 1972) and Zillah Eisenstein, *Capitalist Patriarchy and the Case for Socialist Feminism* (New York: Monthly Review, 1978).

5. Kimberle Crenshaw, "Mapping the Margins: Intersectionality, Identity Politics, and Violence against Women of Color," *Stanford Law Review* 43, no. 6 (1993): 1241–99.

6. See her book *Where We Stand: Class Matters* (New York: Routledge, 2000), vii.

7. Whereas feminist sociologists often frame their work in terms of intersectionality, this is less common among historians, who have produced most of the literature on women and the labor movement. See especially the writings of Alice Kessler-Harris and Dorothy Sue Cobble, as well as others cited in the chapters that follow.

8. Among them was the eminent historian Joan Wallach Scott, who wrote an extended critique of my analysis of the Sears case in chapter 5 (this volume) from that perspective. See Joan Wallach Scott, "The Sears Case," in her book, *Gender and the Politics of History* (New York: Columbia University Press, 1988), 167–77.

9. In this period I completed a series of books on other labor topics (which included some attention to gender but not as the central focus). See *Japan's California Factories: Labor Relations and Economic Globalization* (Los Angeles: UCLA Institute of Industrial Relations, 1991); *Farewell to the Factory: Auto Workers in the Late Twentieth Century* (Berkeley: University of California Press, 1997); and *L.A. Story: Immigrant Workers and the Future of the U.S. Labor Movement* (New York: Russell Sage Foundation, 2006).

10. California's paid family leave program is analyzed in much greater detail in the book I co-authored with Eileen Appelbaum, *Unfinished Business: Paid Family Leave in California and the Future of U.S. Work-Family Policy* (Ithaca, N.Y.: Cornell University Press, 2013).

11. Notable exceptions are Leslie McCall, "What Does Class Inequality among Women Look Like? A Comparison with Men and Families, 1970 to 2000," in *Social Class: How Does It Work?* edited by Annette Lareau and Dalton Conley (New York: Russell Sage Foundation, 2008), 293–325; and Dan Clawson and Naomi Gerstel, *Unequal Time: Gender, Class, and Family in Employment Schedules* (New York: Russell Sage Foundation, 2014).

Chapter 1

Women's Work and Economic Crisis

Some Lessons of the Great Depression

This chapter, although focusing on the experience of women workers during the Great Depression and World War II, also reflects the era in which it was written—the 1970s—when traditional family arrangements were still largely intact, and when the surge in labor force participation among mothers of young children and the entry of college-educated women into the elite professions was just beginning. Another crucial context for this chapter was the burgeoning of Marxist-feminist theory in the late 1960s and early 1970s: the argument here is deeply influenced by that literature but also presents a challenge to it. Originally published in 1976, this work was the first to critique the widely accepted precept that women workers were a "reserve army" of labor, pulled into the labor force during periods of economic expansion and then expelled during recessions or depressions. The central argument of this chapter is that job segregation by gender endures even during major economic upheavals like depressions and world wars. It shows that women were less likely to suffer unemployment than men during the Great Depression, contrary to what the "reserve army" theory suggests. However, women's unpaid work in the home did serve to absorb some of the economic pressures created by the most severe economic crisis of the twentieth century.

Introduction

In the course of capitalist development, women have come to play an increasingly important role in the sphere of paid labor, and yet participation in that sphere continues to be ideologically defined as "male." This disparity between the cultural definition of women and the reality of their material situation stems from a contradiction basic to the structure of capitalism. On the one hand, there is the continuing need for the family, particularly women's unpaid labor in it, and, on the other hand, the tendency for an increasing amount of human activity to be integrated into the sphere of commodity production in the course of economic growth.

The family lost its role as the primary unit of social production with the development of industrial capitalism, but as an institution it remains central to that form of economic organization, performing many vital functions. Women have been designated as the people responsible for the execution of these functions in the home. They provide a wide variety of personal services—preparing meals, cleaning the home, providing basic healthcare, and so forth. This work is necessary to the maintenance of the working ability, or labor power, of adult family members, and to the preparation of a new generation of workers. Women also do most of the family's buying, and the institution is the basic unit of commodity consumption. In addition, women instill in their children and maintain in their husbands the individualistic values basic to capitalist society, and they are responsible for emotionally and sexually maintaining their husbands. Family "life" is defined in direct opposition to work, as the one place where people can escape the "impersonal forces" of the economy. As wives and mothers, women are expected to absorb any tension generated by those forces. Finally, of course, they bear children, society's next generation of workers.

It is theoretically conceivable that all of the family's functions could be taken over by other institutions, and that the work involved, with the exception of childbearing, could be done by persons of either sex. However, there are a number of good reasons for preserving the present arrangement within the context of a capitalist society. First, the work done by women in the home retains a pre-capitalistic, wageless form, so that the costs of maintaining and reproducing its labor power are borne fully by the working class. Without families, adult men and women could probably fend for themselves, but the twenty-four-hours-a-day job of caring for young children would be very expensive if it were transformed into wage labor. Moreover, while it may be profitable for individual capitalists to hire waged workers to produce the essential personal services otherwise supplied by women in families as a "labor of love," this is not in the interests of the capitalist class as a whole, for wages must rise to cover the cost to the worker of such necessities.

Second, the small nuclear family is an optimal unit of consumption, generating much larger demand for household appliances, televisions, and so forth, than would obtain if housework and family activities were socialized. In addition, assigning women the responsibility for making the family into a "haven" from the frustrations of the world of work—at least for men—is tremendously accommodative to the needs of a society in which most jobs are inherently unsatisfying.

The family is, for all of these reasons, an important component of our economic system, and this is the material basis of the cultural definition of women as primarily wives and mothers. And yet, with economic development and growth, increasing numbers of women have entered the paid labor force, in a wide range of occupations. This, in women's real lives, has meant greater opportunity to receive pay for their labor, a development that threatens the culturally prescribed sexual division of labor assigning them the responsibility to work without pay to maintain their families.

There is, then, a real contradiction between the economy's need for women as unpaid family workers and its tendency to draw all available labor power, regardless of sex, into the sphere of production for profit. This creates a disjuncture between the ideology about sex roles, which continues to define women with reference to their family role, and the material reality of their increasing participation in the "male" sphere of paid production. As a result, as Juliet Mitchell has pointed out, women who work for pay tend nevertheless to view themselves as wives and mothers, not as "workers."

> Because the economic role of women is obscured (its cheapness obscures it) women workers do not have the pre-conditions of class consciousness. Their exploitation is invisible behind an ideology that masks the fact that they work at all—their work appears inessential.[1]

Because of this lack of class consciousness, Mitchell argued, the labor-market behavior of women is easily manipulated with changing economic conditions. She and other Marxist-feminists have argued that women function as a "reserve army" of labor power, to be drawn on in periods when labor is scarce and expelled in periods of labor surplus. Ideology, in this view, plays a crucial role, both perpetuating women's lack of class consciousness over the long term and propelling them in and out of the labor force in response to changing economic conditions.

Exponents of this "reserve army" theory agree, and the historical evidence is fairly clear, that in periods of economic expansion women do tend to enter the paid workforce. In periods of contraction, however, the situation of women is more problematic. On the one hand, as Mitchell suggests, "in times of economic recession and forced labour redundancy, women form a pool of cheap labour."[2] Since women work for lower wages than men, one might expect them to be the last to lose their jobs in a slump. On the other hand, this would violate the basic cultural prescription that, as Mitchell so strongly emphasizes, dictates that "woman's place" is in the home, that men are the "breadwinners." Reasoning on this basis, Margaret Benston, who also characterizes women as a "reserve army," has suggested that women tend to leave the labor market in a period of contraction.

> When there is less demand for labor . . . women become a surplus labor force—but one for which their husbands and not society are economically responsible. The "cult of the home" makes its reappearance during times of labor surplus and is used to channel women out of the market economy. This is relatively easy since the pervading ideology ensures that no one, man or woman, takes woman's participation in the labor force very seriously.[3]

This notion has gained wide currency—indeed, it has risen to the level of dogma—both in the women's movement and on the Left.

There are, then, contradictory arguments about women's labor force behavior in an economic contraction. If the Marxist concept of a "reserve army" of labor power is useful for analyzing the entrance of women into the paid workforce over the long term, Marxist-feminist applications of its converse do not tell us very much about their economic roles in a period of crisis. Those theoretical applications, moreover, are somewhat mechanistic and are insufficiently grounded in knowledge of history. This inquiry is an effort to remedy that through an analysis of the experience of women, both in the labor market and as unpaid family workers, during the Great Depression, the most severe economic crisis of the twentieth century. The experience of women during the period immediately following World War II will be considered also, as a contrasting case in which the "reserve army" theory is more useful.

The first part of this chapter analyzes the changes in women's paid employment patterns that resulted from the 1929 crash, in which I hope to demonstrate that the sex-typing of occupations created an inflexibility in the structure of the labor market that prevented the expulsion of women from it in the manner Benston suggests. It was not because of the fact that women's labor power is cheaper than men's, but rather because women's work is so rigidly sex-typed, that women enjoyed a measure of protection from unemployment in the Great Depression. It was the case, however, that women were urged to leave the paid labor force during the 1930s. That most of them did not suggests that ideological sex role prescriptions must be viewed not as determinant of but rather in constant interaction with behavior in analyzing women's experience during periods of economic crisis.

In the next part of the chapter, the focus of the discussion shifts to the impact of the economic crisis of the 1930s on women's economic role in the family—their unpaid work in the home. It is ironic that the Marxist-feminist discussion of women and economic crises has so far ignored this dimension of their experience, for it is a basic insight of Marxist-feminist theory as a whole that both paid work outside the home and unpaid work in it are crucial to women's experience in capitalist society. I will argue that in fact it was the work of women in the home, rather than their labor market participation, that was forced to "take up the slack" in the economy during this period of contraction.

After having considered the economic behavior of women in the 1930s, both in the labor market and in the home, and on this basis having rejected the "reserve army" theory, I will turn to a counterexample. The manner in which large numbers of women were drawn into the paid labor force during World War II, and their expulsion from it during the period of demobilization that followed, suggests that the "reserve army" theory does in fact have some explanatory power. I will argue, however, that the circumstances under which this occurred were highly peculiar and did not really constitute a "crisis," so that this case is not an adequate basis from which to generalize.

Unemployment of Women in the Great Depression

The Great Depression of the 1930s was the most severe economic contraction Americans experienced in the twentieth century. The official estimate of unemployment for 1933 was 25 percent (and the actual proportion of people who experienced economic deprivation was probably much larger).[4] Unfortunately, the only national unemployment data available for this period that are disaggregated by sex are those collected by the U.S. Census Bureau in 1930, when the proportion of all workers who had been laid off or fired and were seeking work was only 6.5 percent.[5] These early data are in several respects highly problematic and can by no means be assumed to be an accurate representation of the extent to which the nation's available labor power was unutilized in 1930. Nevertheless, for our purposes they are quite instructive.[6]

The April 1930 census found an unemployment rate of 4.7 percent for women, while that enumerated for men was 7.1 percent. There is some evidence that as the Depression deepened, the relative position of women grew somewhat worse, but the available data clearly indicate that, *insofar as their paid labor force participation was concerned, women were less affected than men by the contraction.*

This is precisely the opposite of what the "reserve army" theory about the relationship of women to economic fluctuations would lead one to expect. One might turn to an alternative hypothesis, reasoning that since women's labor power is sold at a cheaper price than that of men, they are the last to be fired during a period of worsening business conditions. While this interpretation may seem satisfactory for purposes of explaining the *aggregate* unemployment figures, an examination of the statistics on joblessness across the occupational structure suggests an altogether different explanation.

Table 1.1 shows sex differences in the 1930 unemployment rates for the broad set of occupational groups used by the Census Bureau at the time, and for a small selection of specific occupational groups characterized by high concentrations of workers of one sex. The table suggests that the female unemployment rate was lower than the male rate in 1930 *because the occupations in which women were concentrated, occupations sex-typed "female," contracted less than those in which men were concentrated.*

Indeed, there is substantial evidence that, accompanying the dramatic increases in the proportion of women in the paid workforce over the course of the twentieth century,[7] there has been a consistent pattern of labor market segregation by sex. Everyone "knows" that typists and nurses are women, while steelworkers and truck drivers—and bosses—are men. Statistically, gender segregation is an extraordinarily stable feature of the occupational structure. An analysis of the detailed occupational data in the decennial censuses taken between 1900 and 1960 has shown that the amount of job segregation by sex varies remarkably little, with no fluctuations related to the fact that decennial censuses occurred at many different points in the business cycle. In any of those seven census years, about two-thirds of the women in the paid labor force would have had to change their

Table 1.1. Employment and Unemployment, by Sex and Occupational Group, U.S., 1930

Occupational Group	Size[a]					Unemployment Rate[b]		
	Thousands	% of Total	% of All Female Workers	% of All Male Workers	Females as % of Total	Total	Female	Male
General Division of Occupations (U.S. Census Series)								
All occupations	48,830	100.0	100.0	100.0	22.0	6.5	4.7	7.1
Agriculture	10,472	21.4	8.5	25.1	8.7	1.4	1.2	1.4
Forestry & fishing	250	0.5	0.0	0.7	0.1	10.4	10.3	10.4
Extraction of minerals	984	2.0	0.0	2.6	0.1	17.8	13.8	17.8
Manufacturing and mechanical industry	14,111	28.9	17.5	32.1	13.4	12.8	9.7	13.2
Transportation and communication	3,843	7.9	2.6	9.4	7.3	7.3	2.5	7.7
Trade	6,081	12.5	9.0	13.4	15.8	3.7	4.4	3.6
Public service	856	1.8	0.2	2.2	2.1	3.5	1.6	3.5
Professional service	2,254	6.7	14.2	4.5	46.9	2.8	2.4	3.1
Domestic and personal services	4,952	10.1	29.6	4.7	64.2	4.9	4.6	5.5
Clerical occupations	4,025	8.2	18.5	5.4	49.4	4.3	3.8	4.7

Table 1.1 *continued*

Occupational Group	Size[a]					Unemployment Rate[b]		
	Thousands	% of Total	% of All Female Workers	% of All Male Workers	Females as % of Total	Total	Female	Male
Selected "pure" sex-typed occupational groups[c]								
Male								
Stenographers and typists	811	1.7	7.2	0.1	95.6	4.7	4.6	7.2
Laundresses and launderers[d]	361	0.7	3.3	0.0+	98.7	3.0	2.9	8.0
Trained nurses	294	0.6	2.7	0.0+	98.1	4.2	4.1	8.9
Housekeepers and stewards	257	0.5	2.2	0.1	92.1	3.1	2.8	7.1
Telephone operators	249	0.5	2.2	0.0+	94.6	2.5	2.5	2.7
Dressmakers and seamstresses[e]	156	0.3	1.5	0.0+	99.7	3.6	3.6	8.2
Midwives and nurses (not trained)	157	0.3	1.3	0.0+	91.2	12.0	12.4	7.4
Female								
Iron and steel industries[f]	1,314	2.7	0.7	3.3	5.4	12.9	8.9	13.1
Chauffeurs and truck and tractor drivers	972	2.0	0.0+	2.5	0.2	8.5	7.7	8.5
Carpenters	929	1.9	0.0+	2.4	0.0+	18.9	12.0	18.9
Machinists, millwrights, and toolmakers	761	1.6	0.0+	2.0	0.0+	9.0	5.0	9.0
Laborers, railroad	481	1.0	0.0+	1.3	0.7	8.9	4.0	8.9
Laborers, road and street	307	0.6	0.0+	0.8	0.0	13.4	12.8	13.5
Technical engineers	226	0.5	0.0+	0.6	0.0	3.6	2.7	3.6

[a] These data on the number of gainful workers in each occupational group, although collected after the onset of the Depression, approximate conditions before its onset, since people were asked to report their "normal" occupations to the census taker.

[b] This includes those workers enumerated in Unemployment Classes A and B as defined by the U.S. Census Bureau. Class A includes "Persons out of a job, able to work, and looking for a job." Class B includes "Persons having job, but on layoff without pay, excluding those sick or voluntarily idle." These two classes include almost all of the people counted as unemployed in the 1930 Census.

[c] These occupational groups were selected by the author from those in the most detailed occupational breakdown used in the 1930 Census of Unemployment, a breakdown comprised of approximately three hundred occupational groups. The selection was made according to two criteria: (1) a high degree (90 percent or more) of concentration of workers in the occupational group were members of one sex; and (2) the occupational group included at least one percent of all workers of that sex which predominated in it. All of the occupational groups sex-typed "female" and meeting these criteria are included in the table, and the seven largest of those sex-typed "male" were selected from a slightly larger set of occupational groups meeting these criteria.

[d] This occupational group excludes laundresses and launderers working in commercial laundries.

[e] This occupational group excludes dressmakers and seamstresses working in factories.

[f] Operatives and laborers (in iron and steel industries) have been aggregated here, although they are listed separately in the census table from which this one was made. This is appropriate since both occupational groups are overwhelmingly male in composition and both were similarly affected by the contraction.

Source: *15th Census of the U.S.*, 1930, Unemployment, vol. 2, pp. 13–18. (Totals and percentages were computed by the author.)

occupation in order for their distribution in the paid labor force to approximate that of men.[8]

This extraordinary phenomenon results from the fact that the increasing participation of women in the "male" sphere of paid work outside the home has been carefully delimited by an ideology linking that activity to their sex. The vast majority of women work in "women's jobs," occupations that frequently have some structural resemblance to their family role. They work in industries that produce commodities formerly manufactured by women in the home, such as clothing and processed food. In white-collar occupations, as secretaries, teachers, waitresses, nurses, and so forth, women perform such wifely and motherly functions as schedule management, ego-building, child socialization, cleaning up, caring for the ill, and serving as a sexual object. Even in instances where such structural resemblance to the traditional female role is absent, more often than not women's paid labor activity is sex-typed and set apart from that of men. The mere fact that a woman traditionally does a certain job is usually sufficient to stigmatize it as "women's work," to which members of the female sex are supposed to be "naturally" suited.[9] Occupations in the "female labor market" are also characterized by low status and pay relative to men's jobs,[10] reflecting the sexual inequality rooted in the family and basic to the organization of American society.[11]

The sex-typing of occupations does, in part, represent a cultural acknowledgment of the existence of wage-earning "*women* workers," and yet "workers" are clearly distinguished as a separate, male species. This helps to mediate the contradiction between the continuing need for women's unpaid work in the family and the tendency for women's work to be increasingly integrated into the sphere of paid production for profit. Sex-typing is an ideological mechanism which denies the existence of any conflict between women's family role and their role in paid labor, blithely labeling both "women's work."

But the contradiction has been reproduced in a new form in the workplace as more and more women have entered paid employment: occupational segregation along sex lines conflicts with the ideal of a fluid labor market that can be "rationally" shaped by the laws of supply and demand. It is this caste-like character of the female labor force that, ironically enough, prevented the automatic expulsion of women from the labor market during the economic contraction of the 1930s—despite the emergence of an ideology prescribing precisely that to ameliorate the unemployment situation. This dimension of women's role in paid labor, sex as caste, is a twist in the interaction of capitalism and patriarchy that the "reserve army" theory fails to capture in its full significance. And yet, sex-typing is the very essence of the blunting of women's consciousness of themselves as workers, which is the starting point of that theory.

Because of the rigidity of sex-typing, the occupational distribution of women before the 1929 crash (shown in the upper left portion of table 1.1) proved to be of great importance in determining the impact on women workers of the severe unemployment that followed. The "white collar" clerical, trade, and service occupations provided employment to more than half of all the women in the paid labor force at this time, while men predominated in the manufacturing sector. The "white collar" group was composed of the very occupations whose rapid expansion in the early part of the twentieth century had drawn many women into the paid labor force; their growth accounted for 85 percent of the rise in female labor force participation during the period between 1890 and 1930.[12] As women entered them, the new clerical, trade, and service occupations were typed "women's work" and became an essentially permanent part of the *female* labor market.[13] During the Great Depression, for reasons outside the scope of the present study, these predominantly "female" occupations declined less, and later, than the predominantly male manufacturing occupations. As a result, women suffered less than men from unemployment.

The examples of "pure" sex-typed occupational groups in the lower half of the table further illustrate how sex-typing protected women from differential unemployment. Although these occupations are in no way strictly representative of the labor market as a whole, they do hint at the structure of sexual segregation at a somewhat greater level of detail than in the broad occupational groupings and offer further support for the argument being made here.

It should be observed, however, that even in occupational groups sex-typed male, the unemployment rates of women were lower than those of men in the same occupation. This suggests that the overall gap between the male and female rates may have been somewhat less wide in actuality than the data indicate. One reason for this is that women were probably undercounted in the Census of Unemployment. To be counted as "unemployed" one must either have been temporarily laid off or have lost her/his job and be actively seeking another one. Young single women and, even more so, widows and divorced women would be those most likely to be self-supporting and therefore most likely to continue seeking work in spite of any difficulties. This would also be true of the majority of men in the labor force. Married women, in contrast, might be more easily discouraged if their husbands were employed and as a result might be undercounted in the official unemployment statistics. Indeed, those data indicate that women under twenty years old suffered the highest unemployment rates, and that there was a general decrease in frequency of unemployment with increasing age.[14] Furthermore, the recorded unemployment rate of married women was slightly lower than that of single women, while that of widowed and divorced women was highest of all.[15]

There are other factors as well that suggest that the gap in male and female unemployment rates may have been somewhat less wide than the data indicate. Women workers, both in hard times and in the best of times, suffer various forms of discrimination that increase the likelihood that they will be underemployed. They frequently work in highly seasonal industries and therefore have only irregular employment, being hired and fired in response to *short-term* industrial fluctuations.[16] Also, women work part time more frequently than men.[17] Thus there is characteristically a substantial amount of unrecorded underemployment among women, even in good times, and under depressed industrial conditions one would expect some increase in its frequency. To the extent that this was true in the 1930s, one might conclude that the "reserve army" theory is applicable to some sectors of the female labor market, but this was the case only because the "women's jobs" involved were volatile, *not because men replaced women in them*.[18]

There does seem to have been a gradual deterioration of women's situation relative to men's as the Depression deepened, however. Data collected in some states on an annual basis indicate a relative worsening of women's position over the course of the decade,[19] although when this change occurred and what its implications were for women in particular occupations cannot be gauged with any precision, since the federal government did not regularly collect unemployment data by sex in the 1930s.

The earliest set of reliable national data on sex differences in unemployment after 1930 is that in the U.S. Census of 1940.[20] The recovery that would accompany World War II had only begun, and 8.3 percent of the experienced labor force were still seeking work.[21] Another 4.9 percent were employed in public emergency work. The female unemployment rate was still lower than that of men, but the gap had narrowed somewhat: 8.6 percent of the experienced male labor force were unemployed in 1940, and 7.5 percent of the experienced female labor force were seeking work. The male unemployment rate was thus only 15 percent greater than the female unemployment rate, as compared with a differential of 49 percent in 1930. This is partly explained by the sex differential in public emergency work, which occupied 5.2 percent of the experienced male labor force but only 3.6 percent of the experienced female labor force in 1940. But even if persons doing public emergency work are counted as unemployed, the resulting male unemployment rate is only 24 percent above the female rate.[22]

One explanation for the deterioration of women's relative position in the unemployment rolls might be that large numbers of women previously engaged only in unpaid housework were forced to seek paid work during the Depression in efforts to compensate for the decline in family income resulting from the unemployment of male family members. Indeed, total female labor force participation rose in the period from 1930 to 1940 more than in any previous decade in the twentieth century. There were, moreover, declines in the participation of teenaged females and older women during this period so that the increased participation of women between twenty and sixty-five years old was even greater than the aggregate figures suggest.[23] There is also a vast amount of qualitative evidence supporting the hypothesis that many married women sought paid employment to compensate for their husbands' unemployment.[24]

If correct, this suggests that the fact that the unemployment rate of men was higher than that of women had only an indirect effect on the unemployment rate of women, insofar as the wives and daughters of unemployed men could find jobs more easily than they and were thus drawn into the labor market because of their declining family income. There is no evidence of any mobility from the male to the female labor market in the course of the Depression decade,[25] and the deterioration of women's relative position in the labor market seems to have been due primarily to increased competition among women for jobs in the female labor market. In fact, the degree of sex segregation within the occupational structure actually increased slightly between 1930 and 1940.[26]

Because the data on unemployment are so poor and so problematic, it is not possible to learn from them exactly what the relation of women to the labor market was in the Great Depression. But it is clear that the "reserve army" theory is not very useful for this purpose and that sex-typing is an extremely important factor.

Perhaps one reason that the "reserve army" theory has so seldom been questioned is that, on the ideological level, it was in fact the case that women were urged to return to the home during the 1930s. Male unionists and others frequently suggested that women were taking "men's jobs." Their entrance into the paid labor force in the previous years, these men argued, had produced a scarcity of jobs for men.[27] Disapproval of married women who worked was particularly fervent. The executive council of the American Federation of Labor urged that "married women whose husbands have permanent positions . . . should be discriminated against in the hiring of employees."[28] A 1936 Gallup poll indicated that most Americans agreed, 82 percent of those polled.[29]

Nor were these totally idle arguments. Discriminatory practices against married women were actually instituted in a number of cases. Many states reactivated old laws by means of which teachers and other female civil servants were dismissed upon marrying.[30] And yet, more and more married women were being forced into the labor market as unemployment struck their families. It was clearly better, in spite of the cultural sanctions that had emerged, to have what little income a woman could earn than no income at all in a household in which the male "breadwinner" was unemployed. As a result, it was not possible for ideological forces to successfully push women out of the labor market. Such behavior was in direct opposition to their material interests.

Nevertheless, the ideological condemnation of women's paid work did serve to diffuse people's discontent in the early 1930s. To the extent that women could be blamed for the economic crisis, attention was distracted from analyses that found its roots in the workings of capitalism. The number of people who actually thought that women had "caused" the crisis was in any case quite small, and women were not considered equally entitled to employment by large numbers of people. This was a less effective outlet for discontent but not altogether unlike what might have occurred if women had in fact transferred their jobs to men. Had that been the case, as the "reserve army" theory suggests, women would have "taken up the slack" in the economy quite directly. As it was, they generally retained their jobs, while on the cultural level some anger was directed at them rather than at those who controlled the society that could no longer provide jobs for those who sought them.

Making Ends Meet: The Unpaid Work of Women in the Great Depression

Perhaps the most important reason for the inadequacy of the "reserve army" theory is its failure to comprehend the primary importance of women's economic role in the family. Indeed, it is the economic need for their unpaid work in the home in which the caste-like structure of the female labor force, which is so basic to the experience of women during a crisis in their role as paid workers, first emerges. For this reason alone, it would be foolhardy to overlook the impact of economic crises on women's family role.

The productive activity of women in the home is accorded lower social status than any other occupation: housework is a "labor of love" in a society whose universal standard of value is money. Because it is not remunerated with a wage, housework does not directly produce surplus value. However, it does maintain and reproduce the ability of family members to work productively—their labor power—which they sell in the labor market for a wage.

The work involved in providing personal services has been greatly influenced by technological developments in the course of capitalist expansion, just as various productive activities that once engaged housewives—food processing, clothing manufacture, and so forth—have been increasingly integrated into the sphere of paid labor. Paralleling this process of the socialization of production is the transformation of the family from a unit of production into a unit of consumption. At the same time, other institutions have taken over some of the functions the family used to perform, like vocational training and the care of the aged. As this occurs, there is also a tendency toward nuclearization of the institution. All of these changes were well underway by 1930.

Within this general tendency for housework to become increasingly dependent on commodity production, at any one point in time there is a great deal of flexibility in the allocation of work between the home and the industrial workplace. During the Great Depression the long-term trends reversed themselves, and women's unpaid household production became more important than it had been in earlier years. In a sense, the family "took up the slack" in the economy during the 1930s.

People who were unemployed naturally turned to their families for support. The work of women in physically and psychologically maintaining their families became tremendously difficult as family incomes declined and the psychological stresses attending unemployment took their toll. Women showed amazing resourcefulness in coping with the crisis on the family level. They used a wide variety of strategies, generally turning back toward "traditional" forms of family organization.

The most immediate problem facing the family struck by unemployment was the material hardship created by their lowered income. Women cut back family expenditures in many areas. Typical strategies were moving to quarters with lower rent, having telephones removed, and denying themselves many purchased goods and services to which they had become accustomed in the prosperity of earlier years.[31] Clothing, prepared meals, domestic service, automobiles, magazine subscriptions, and amusements were among the many products and services that suffered declines in sales as optimists heralded the "live at home movement."[32]

Many women managed to approximate their families' prior standard of living despite lowered incomes by substituting their own labor for goods and services they had formerly purchased in the marketplace, reversing the trend toward increased consumption in the preceding decades. Home canning was so widespread that glass jar sales were greater in 1931 than at any other point in the preceding eleven years. There was a corresponding drop in sales of canned goods, which had doubled in the decade from 1919 to 1929.[33] Similarly, the 1930s saw a revival of home sewing. People who had never sewed before attended night-school classes to learn how to sew and remodel garments.[34]

Women's efforts to cut back family expenses by substituting their own labor for purchasable commodities represented only one set of alternatives in the struggle to make ends meet.[35] Many women engaged themselves in paid work in attempts to compensate for a reduction in family income. There was a revival of domestic industry: women took in laundry, ironing, and dressmaking; they baked cakes to sell; they took in boarders.[36] Everywhere there were signs in yards advertising household beauty parlors, cleaning and pressing enterprises, grocery stores, and the like.[37]

As well, women sought paid jobs outside their homes to increase the family income. They did this despite the strong cultural sanctions against married women working, sanctions that were strongly reinforced with the onset of mass unemployment. Women who thus defied the cultural prescription frequently justified their behavior as a response to the family emergency created by the unemployment of their husbands, and they generally planned to stop working for pay as soon as the situation improved.[38] The following case is representative:

> Until 1930 Mr. Fetter was able to support the family. After that date his earnings from irregular work were supplemented by his wife's earnings of $9.00 per week in a restaurant. Both husband and wife disliked to have the wife work, but there seemed no other solution of the economic problem.[39]

The last resort of families for whom none of these strategies succeeded—and there were many—was to go "on relief." Accepting this alternative, however, was widely viewed as an admission of failure of the family. Mr. Fetter's "reaction to the idea of relief was violent."[40] In another case study, a husband and wife expressed their reluctance to accept any government assistance: "We are able people; we must keep on our feet."[41] And in cases where the relief strategy was pursued, a great deal of resentment toward social service agencies was expressed. Experienced wives and mothers often felt, not without reason, that the social workers they dealt with were too young and naive to understand the costs involved in raising a large family.[42]

Added to the difficulties in maintaining families on a reduced income were the demands placed on the institution to reabsorb members who had been independent during the better times before the crash. Not only did unemployed husbands spend more time around the house, but old people, who frequently suffered from discrimination in employment, tended to "double up" with their sons' and daughters' families.[43] The younger generation was likely to be relatively better off in terms of employment but were less likely to have a securely owned dwelling. This strategy of pooling the resources of two generations represented a sharp break with the long-term trend toward nuclearization.

Youth, who also faced discrimination in the labor market, returned home during the Depression.[44] The dependence of this generation on the previous one caused delays, sometimes permanent ones, in new family formation. The marriage rate dropped sharply, from 10.1 marriages per thousand people in 1929 to 7.9, the low point in 1932.[45] In 1938 it was estimated that 1.5 million people had been forced to postpone marriage because of the economic depression.[46] Cohort data on ever-married rates reveal that many of these "postponements" were permanent. The proportion of single women (never married by 1970) aged twenty-five to thirty in 1935 is about 30 percent higher than the proportion in the cohort five years younger.[47] One spinster of this generation recalled:

> There were young men around when we were young. But they were supporting mothers.

It wasn't that we didn't have a chance. I was going with someone when the Depression hit. We probably would have gotten married. He was a commercial artist and had been doing very well. I remember the night he said, "They just laid off quite a few of the boys." It never occurred to him that he would be next. He was older than most of the others and very sure of himself. This was not the sort of thing that was going to happen to *him*. Suddenly he was laid off. It hit him like a ton of bricks. And he just disappeared.[48]

The material tasks of family maintenance became extraordinarily challenging during the 1930s, as women struggled to stretch a decreased income to maintain the members of their nuclear family and, in many cases, the younger and older generations as well. However, this was but one aspect of the increased importance of women's unpaid labor in the home during the Depression. The task of psychological maintenance was also made much more difficult in families affected by unemployment. The concrete fact of idleness, the stigma that generally accompanied it, and a multitude of side effects associated with the various strategies pursued to maintain the family materially placed enormous strains on the family as an emotional support system and on women's role in its maintenance.

Since his role as wage earner is often the basis of the father's status within the family, that status tends to be lowered by his unemployment. The man without a job in the 1930s often felt superfluous and frustrated, "because in his own estimation he fails to fulfill what is the central duty of his life, the very touchstone of his manhood—the role of family provider."[49] The strain attending unemployment was exacerbated in cases where other family members were earning money. A woman who replaced her husband as the "breadwinner" during the Depression recalls:

> In 1930, it was slack time. He didn't have a job, my husband. Even now, the painter's work is seasonal. So I went to work those times when he wasn't working, and he took care of the boy.
>
> Yah. He said he's walking upside-down, if you know what that means. (Laughs.) You start walking on the floor, and then you put yourself upside-down, how you feel. Because he couldn't provide for his family. Because when we got married, he actually said, "You're not gonna work."[50]

To say that the unemployed father lost status in the family would seem to imply that women who assumed the role of "provider" gained somehow. But such a role reversal was not a simple exchange of power. Women's responsibility for providing emotional support to family members was not diminished during this period. On the contrary, the reversal of roles made this task much more difficult, for an unemployed husband demanded more support than ever before. If there was any increased recognition of woman's economic role in the family, it did not represent a gain in status, for no one was comfortable with the new state of affairs, and the reversal of roles was resented by everyone involved.

The tension unemployment produced within the family was intensified by the downward mobility accompanying lowered family income. As the status of the family in the community dropped there appeared, alongside the tendency for families to strengthen their ties with relatives, a general decrease in social contacts outside the family circle. Lacking appropriate clothing and money for dues or donations, many families stopped attending church and dropped their club memberships. In addition, many had sacrificed their telephones and there was little money for carfare, so it was more difficult to socialize with friends.[51] People were ashamed of their lowered standard of living and hence reluctant to invite guests into their homes.[52]

Further pressures on the psychological balance of the family were exerted by the various strategies women pursued to maintain its members materially. The simple fact of decreased income increased family discord over financial matters,[53] and the crowding resulting from "doubling up," moving to less expensive quarters, or being unable to heat all the rooms in a house during the winter produced much friction among family members.[54] Moreover, they saw much more of each other than before, whether they wished to or not, simply because they were unemployed and spent more time at home.

Women in families affected by unemployment, then, were under pressure from all sides. Their responsibility to maintain their families materially and psychologically became much more difficult to fulfill. Sociologists who studied the impact of the Depression on families at the time noted that these strains generally resulted in an initial period of disorientation, which was ultimately resolved either through adjustment or "disintegration" of the family.[55] Whether or not a family was able to adjust to the new situation depended on a variety of factors, but on the whole, these studies showed that the impact of the crisis was to exaggerate previous family patterns. "Well-organized" families became more unified, while the problems of unstable families were accentuated.

Families that survived the crisis intact certainly were more "unified" in the sense that they spent more time together than before, but it is not clear that this choice was freely made or that families were newly prized by their members. Indeed, Lynds reported that "each family seems to wish wistfully that the depression had not happened to *it*, while at the same time feeling that the depression has in a vague general way 'been good for family life.'"[56] Families that broke under the strain did not always fall apart visibly. Although the frequency of desertion, the "poor man's divorce," rose, legal divorce was expensive, and its rate declined.[57]

There is scattered evidence that in some families the strain was manifested in a decline in sexual activity. The most common reason given for this was fear of unwanted pregnancy.[58] In a number of instances, however, women reported that they had lost respect for their unemployed husbands and could no longer love them as before.[59] A psychiatrist observed of a group of long-term unemployed miners:

> They hung around street corners in groups. They gave each other solace. They were loath to go home because they were indicted, as if it were their fault for being unemployed. A jobless man was a lazy good-for-nothing. The women punished the men for not bringing home the bacon, by withholding themselves sexually. . . . These men suffered from depression. They felt despised, they were ashamed of themselves. They cringed, they comforted one another. They avoided home.[60]

There must have been many cases like these, in which the family simply could not cope with all the strains which converged on it. The emergence of social services on a large scale during the later 1930s probably represented, at least in part, a response to these family failures and supplied a bolster to the institution. But what is far more remarkable than the record of failures is the extent to which families were able to successfully absorb all the new strains placed upon them.

In some cases there was organized resistance to the agents of dispossession. In the country, there were "ten cent sales," where neighbors would bid ridiculously low prices for a farmer's property that was being auctioned off by creditors trying to collect on a mortgage, and then return it all to the original owner.[61] In the city, people would move the furniture of an evicted family back into the tenement as soon as it had been put out in the street, to the despair of the landlord.[62]

While actions like these must often have represented the difference between survival and disintegration of a family, most families seem to have depended even more on their internal strengths. It was, to a great extent, women who took up the increased burdens involved in maintaining the family—indeed, this was their traditional responsibility. The importance of their contribution to family maintenance during the crisis was only seldom recognized, however. In Tillie Olsen's fictional portrayal of a family's efforts to cope with the crisis, for example, the husband appreciates his wife's contribution only after she is taken sick. "You useta be so smart with money—make it stretch like rubber. Now it's rent week and not a red cent in the house. I tell you we gotta make what I'm getting do."[63]

Some women were revitalized by the increased responsibility they acquired during the Depression. One woman's hypochondria disappeared with the crisis: "Now her mind is taken up with the problems of stretching her kitchen dollar further than ever and keeping the home up-to-date and clean without new furnishings and the help of a cleaning woman."[64] Another woman, a daughter, who would never have looked for paid work if not for the decline in her once-wealthy family's income, developed a whole new sense of self-respect from her experience as a wage earner. She recalled:

> Now it was necessary for me to make some money because the stepfather was drunk all the time and the father was pretending it hadn't happened. Having gone to a proper lady's finishing school, I didn't know how to do anything. I spoke a little bad French, and I knew enough to stand up when an older person came into the room. As far as anything else was concerned, I was unequipped.
>
> I heard there was a call for swimmers for a picture called *Footlight Parade*. At Warner Brothers. The first big aquacade picture. I went, terrified, tried out on the high-diving thing and won. I couldn't have been more stunned. I truly think this is where I got a life-long point of view: respect for those who *did*, no respect for those who *had* . . . just because their father had done something and they were sitting around.
>
> I loved the chorus girls who worked. I hated the extras who sat around and were paid while we were endangering our lives. I had a ball. It was the first time I was better than anybody at something. I gained a self-respect I'd never had.[65]

This kind of Depression experience was limited to women in privileged social groups, those who would otherwise have spent their lives as more or less leisured symbols of their father's or husband's status. Hard work was nothing new to working-class women, and their increased responsibilities could not have been welcomed so eagerly. For these women and their families, the experience of sex-role reversal—either a complete shifting of responsibility for earning money from husband to wife, or simply an increased reliance on the wife's unpaid work and her strategies for survival—was part of a very painful period in the family's history. The deviation from traditional sex roles was thus, to say the least, negatively reinforced by the accompanying experience of economic deprivation for most families.[66] It did not generally mean that the husband-wife relationship became more egalitarian in the long run; rather, the impact of the crisis was to define women in terms of the traditional female role even more rigidly than before.

Women "took up the slack" in the economy during the Great Depression, then, not by withdrawing from the paid labor force, as the "reserve army" theory suggests, but instead in their family role. There was an increased economic dependence on their unpaid household labor, reversing the pre-Depression trend toward increased use of consumer goods. The process of nuclearization, similarly, reversed itself, as the unemployed turned to their kin for help. The family's role in maintaining people psychologically also became more difficult for women to fulfill.

The traditional family role of women was reinforced because of its increased material importance during the 1930s, then, although women did not "return to the home" in the way the "reserve army" theory suggests. On the contrary, role reversals between husband and wife were common, and precisely because of the *negative* reinforcement given to sex role reversal which resulted from its origin in economic deprivation, traditional sex roles were reinforced.

Women's Place in the World War II Emergency

The Great Depression ended with a boom in the early 1940s, when U.S. involvement in World War II stimulated a tremendous amount of investment in war-related industrial production. The labor surplus of the Depression years rapidly disappeared, and soon the problem of unemployment was replaced by a severe shortage of labor power. All of this happened very fast, so that it is appropriate to describe the situation as a "crisis of expansion," a truly extraordinary kind of economic recovery.

Huge numbers of women were drawn out of their homes and into the paid labor force to meet the demand for workers. Many of them took "war jobs" in industries that produced military equipment or other war-related items, so that when the war ended, so did their jobs. Thus the "reserve army" theory, which, as we have seen, is quite inadequate for analyzing the experience of women during the contraction of the 1930s, fits their situation during the period of demobilization in the late 1940s rather well. Women were drawn into war production "for the duration," in many cases losing their jobs immediately upon the conclusion of hostilities. Most of them eventually found employment in the postwar years in traditional "women's jobs," so that their expulsion from the paid labor force was only temporary. Nevertheless, the war experience did demonstrate that women could, albeit under rather peculiar circumstances, function as a "reserve army" that was pulled in and then pushed out of the labor force in the way the usual formulation of the concept suggests.

The demand for female labor power created by the expansion of the American economy during World War II was of unprecedented magnitude. Between 1940 and the peak of war employment in 1944, the number of women in the paid labor force increased by more than six million, or 50 percent. The largest demand came from manufacturing industries, in which the number of women workers increased by 140 percent from 1940 to 1944, as can be seen in table 1.2. In industries producing directly for war purposes, the number of women workers rose by 460 percent. The female clerical labor force experienced a doubling in the same period. The only occupational group to experience a decrease in the number of women workers was domestic service.[67]

Sixty percent of the women who entered the labor market between 1940 and 1944 were thirty-five years old or older, and more than half of them were or

Table 1.2. Changes in Women's Employment, 1940–1944

Occupational Group	Women Employed (thousands)		
	1940	1944	% Change
All occupations[a]	11,140[b]	16,480	+48.0[b]
Professional and semiprofessional	1,470	1,490	+1.2
Proprietors, managers, and officials	420	650	+53.3
Clerical and kindred	2,370	4,380	+84.5
Sales	780	1,240	+58.4
Craftsmen, foremen [sic], operatives and laborers	2,250	4,920	+118.7
Domestic service	1,970	1,570	−20.4
Other service	1,260	1,650	+30.9
Farm workers	470	580	+18.6
Manufacturing, total[c]	2,320	5,590	+140.7
War industries—metal, chemicals, rubber	480	2,690	+462.7
Consumer industries—food, clothing, textiles, leathers	1,330	2,160	+62.6
Other industries	510	730	+42.6

[a] Totals do not add due to the failure to record the occupations of some workers.

[b] This takes no account of the women who in 1940 were unemployed or on emergency work, and who were thus technically part of the labor force. Their inclusion reduces the increase to about 36 percent.

[c] This classification is part of a Census breakdown by industry, altogether separate from the occupational breakdown given in its entirety in the first half of the table.

Source: Adapted from tables in U.S. Dept. of Labor, Women's Bureau, Special Bulletin No. 20, *Changes in Women's Employment during the War* (1914), pp. 9, 15.

had been married.[68] Although many of these women worked full time, the labor shortage also stimulated substantial efforts to provide part-time employment for women with heavy family responsibilities.[69] The first large-scale childcare programs were established (although these never met the huge demand). Lighting and other workplace amenities were improved in many plants as well, and employers redesigned the work process of many industrial jobs with women in mind, eliminating the need to lift heavy weights, for example. The motivation for all of this was, unmistakably, the need to maximize the efficiency of the new workers, who were difficult to recruit. Thus one government pamphlet distributed widely to employers, entitled *When You Hire Women*, pointed out that efficiency decreased after a point with longer hours, and that "harassed mothers make poor workers."[70]

Employers who offered women "men's" wages and working conditions could be assured of a labor supply, and during the war it was common for the government to assume the costs incurred in paying women high wages in war industries. Ostensibly because of the difficulties in estimating the costs of producing military items, which often underwent changes in design, government contracts often stipulated that the manufacturer would be reimbursed for all the costs of production plus a "fixed fee." The government thus took on all the risks of war production, and capitalists were guaranteed a profit.[71]

Even when the starting wages for women and men were equal, however, women rarely had equal opportunities for advancement.[72] Similarly, although women war workers often became members of unions, they frequently experienced differential treatment within the union structure. Many contracts provided that women and men be listed on separate seniority lists, and some stated outright that women's tenure in jobs previously held by men would be theirs "for the duration" only.[73]

This definition of women's war employment as temporary was not limited to unions but had been explicit in all of the propaganda issued by government and industry urging women to enter the paid labor force. The thrust of the appeal, indeed, was that women could do "their part" in the war effort by taking industrial jobs. The expectation that they would gracefully withdraw from "men's jobs" when the war ended and the rightful owners reappeared on the scene was clear from the first.

Moreover, during World War II, jobs that had previously had all the attributes of "men's work" suddenly acquired a new femininity and glamour. There was an unrelenting effort to reconcile the traditional image of women with their new role. It was suggested, for example, that an overhead crane operated "just like a gigantic clothes wringer" and that the winding of wire spools was very much like crocheting.[74] A pamphlet emphasizing the importance of safety caps for women machine operators to prevent industrial accidents showed pictures of pretty women dressed in the twelve available styles of head covering.[75] A 1943 advertisement in *Fortune* for an iron works company showed a photograph of a woman worker operating a steel-cutting machine with this caption:

> Tailor-made suit cut to Axis size! . . . Skillful Van Dorn Seamstress, with scissors of oxyacetylene, cloth of bullet-proof steel, and pattern shaped to our enemy's downfall![76]

The women who took war jobs were not allowed to forget their sex for a moment. They were not to be viewed as war workers but as *women* war workers performing "men's jobs" "for the duration" of the war emergency. Media images of these women almost invariably contained allusions to their sexuality. An article on "Girl Pilots" in *Life*, for example, quips:

> Girls are very serious about their chance to fly for the Army at Avenger Field, even when it means giving up nail polish, beauty parlors and dates for a regimented 22½ weeks. . . . They each have on the G.I. coveralls, called zoot suits in Avenger Field lingo, that are regulation uniform for all working hours. Though suits are not very glamorous, the girls like their comfort and freedom.[77]

Many women war workers reported similar attitudes being expressed by their male co-workers. One personal account, for example, noted:

> At times it gets to be a pain in the neck when the man who is supposed to show you work stops showing it to you because you have nicely but firmly asked him to keep his hands on his own knees; or when you have refused a date with someone and ever since then he has done everything in his power to make your work more difficult. . . . Somehow we'll have to make them understand that we are not very much interested in their strapping virility. That the display of their physique and the lure of their prowess leaves us cold. That although they have certainly convinced us that they are men and we are women, we'd really rather get on with our work.[78]

Women were laid off in huge numbers immediately after the war ended. As industrial plants reconverted to consumer-oriented production they returned to their prewar male work force. In January 1946 the number of women in the labor force was four million less than at the 1944 peak, and only two million more than in 1940.[79] The most dramatic decline was in durable goods manufacturing, the sector where most of the high-paying "war jobs" had been located. The employment of women in these industries declined by 1.5 million between the 1944 peak and January 1946.[80]

Despite the fact that the nation had been well prepared ideologically for this eventuality, women themselves resisted the notion that they were working only "for the duration." Most insisted that they would remain in the paid labor force after the war. Although at the beginning of the war, polls had indicated that 95 percent of the women who were new entrants to the labor force expected to quit after the war,[81] the Women's Bureau survey of thirteen thousand women war workers in 1944–45 found that three out of every four wanted to continue working after the war ended.[82] Moreover, the older women who had made up so large a portion of the new recruits to the labor force planned to stay there: 81 percent of the women who were age forty-five or older said that they intended to remain in the paid work force.[83]

Women not only seemed to enjoy working, but they also had strong material incentives to continue to do so in a period of high inflation. The case of Alma is perhaps representative of the general feeling of women at the close of hostilities:

> Alma goes to work because she wants to go to work. She wants to go now and she wants to keep going when the war is over. Alma's had a taste of LIFE. She's poked her head out into the once-man's World . . . Of course, all the Almas haven't thought through why they want to work after the war or how it's going to be possible. But they have gone far enough to know that they can do whatever is required in a machine shop. They've had the pleasure of feeling money in their pockets—money they've earned themselves.[84]

And yet, the material fact of "reconversion" peacetime production would force the withdrawal of many women from the labor force. They were eventually reintegrated, not in the heavy industry "war jobs" but rather in the white-collar and service occupations that had been part of the female labor force before the war and that continued to expand in the postwar years. While women's penetration into "men's jobs" with high status and pay during the war years proved ephemeral, then, their increased presence in the paid labor force would be duplicated in later years.

The experience of World War II demonstrates that women could function as a "reserve army" to meet the economy's needs in a crisis of expansion. Had a depression followed the war—an eventuality widely feared at the time—women would almost certainly not have re-entered the paid labor force as easily as they did in the period of expansion that followed the initial postwar contraction. And yet, the war-induced labor shortage that drew women into paid employment was of an extraordinary type. The jobs created by the boom in industrial production for military purposes were, by definition, temporary, whereas in other periods of expansion the jobs women took became integral parts of the occupational structure. This difference was crucial, for it meant that in the contraction of "reconversion" that followed the war boom, the jobs women had were essentially eliminated from the occupational structure. This was most unlikely to occur in a depression following a "normal" period of economic growth, so that the demobilization experience can only be regarded as atypical.

Epilogue and Conclusion

There have been numerous economic crises in the twentieth century, of which the Great Depression was of exceptional intensity. Yet precisely for that reason, it is a particularly revealing case for the study of the impact of economic crises on women's lives. Its analysis allows us to critically evaluate the "reserve army" theory, the major focus of discussion on this question to date.

In order to understand the implications of the experience of women in the 1930s for the present, however, it is necessary to look more closely at the changes that have occurred in the intervening decades. The most important trends were the acceleration of the rate of increase in female labor force participation and the resulting intensification of the contradiction between this tendency and the continuing need for the family.

In 1940, 26 percent of American women of working age were in the paid labor force. By 1970 that figure had risen to 40 percent. Accompanying this dramatic increase in the size of the female labor force has been an important change in its composition. The labor force participation rate of married women rose from 15 percent to 39 percent during the same period, and that of women aged twenty-five to forty-four rose from 31 percent to 48 percent.[85] This represents a major change in the typical life-cycle pattern of female labor force participation and a new relationship between women's role and their role in paid labor. While in the early part of the twentieth century, the normal pattern for middle-class women was to leave the labor force when they became wives and mothers, in the 1970s it was becoming common for women of both the middle and working classes to work for pay at virtually every point in their life cycles.

Accompanying this development has been a remarkable change in the *male* labor force participation rate. As table 1.3 shows, while the labor market participation of women rose in the postwar decades, there was a major *decline* in that of men. Until the late 1960s the decline in the male rate was at least partly due to the fact that men went to school longer, but the fact that the rate for men aged twenty-five to sixty-four also decreased, although less rapidly, indicates that this was a more basic trend.[86] Indeed, this is the age group of men most likely to be in the labor force if employment is available to them. Since this is also the age group in which female labor force participation has expanded most rapidly, the ratio of women to men in the labor force, within that age bracket alone, increased steadily from .37 in 1950 to .54 in 1973. This is almost exactly parallel to the changes in the ratio of women to men among labor force participants of all ages, suggesting that the trend among the "hard core" of the male labor force is representative of the overall situation.

Table 1.3. Labor Force Participation Rates,[a] by Sex and Age, for Persons 16 Years and Older, Selected Years, 1950–1973

Year	Males				Females				Female/Male ×100	
	Total	16–24	25–64	65+	Total	16–24	25–64	65+	Total	25–64
1950	86.8	79.3	94.8	45.8	33.9	44.0	35.1	9.7	39.1	37.0
1953	86.9	80.2	95.8	41.6	34.5	42.9	40.1	10.0	39.7	41.9
1956	86.3	78.9	95.8	40.0	36.9	44.5	39.9	10.9	42.8	41.6
1959	84.5	75.5	95.4	34.2	37.2	41.9	41.3	10.2	44.0	43.3
1962	82.8	73.8	94.9	30.3	38.0	43.4	42.4	9.9	45.9	44.7
1965	81.5	72.3	94.5	27.9	39.3	44.1	44.4	10.0	48.2	47.0
1968	81.2	73.0	94.0	27.3	41.6	48.6	46.8	9.6	51.2	49.8
1970	80.6	73.4	93.4	26.8	43.4	51.3	48.6	9.7	53.8	52.0
1973	79.5	74.5	91.8	22.8	44.7	55.0	49.9	8.9	56.2	54.3

[a] Defined as "percent of noninstitutional population in the labor force."
Source: Computed from U.S. Departments of Labor and H.E.W., Manpower Report of the President (1974), pp. 254–55. This data is from the Current Population Survey, a series that has somewhat different statistics than the decennial censuses for the years involved.

The explanation for this seems to be that the economic expansion of the post-war period has been in occupational groups that were early sex typed "female": clerical, service, and sales jobs. Once these jobs were established as "women's work," employers had little motivation to hire men to fill them. Thus the demand for labor in the postwar period was largely a demand for *female* labor power, and older and married women responded to the demand.[87]

Rough indicators of the demand for male and female labor power can be derived from the broad occupational groupings used by the Census Bureau. Throughout the period since World War II, nearly half of all male workers were blue collar workers, while only about 15 percent of female workers were in this group. Similarly, about half of all female workers during this period were in clerical or service (other than private household) jobs, and only about 15 percent of all male workers were in these groups. Between 1958 and 1973, the proportion of blue-collar workers formed of all gainfully employed persons dropped slightly, from 37 to 35 percent, while the proportion of clerical and service workers grew from 23 to 29 percent.[88]

Female labor force participation, for reasons that are not altogether clear, has been increasing faster than the number of available "women's jobs," so that the female labor market has become "overcrowded."[89] The unemployment rate of women has been higher than that of men throughout the postwar period, and the gap has widened over time. In 1950 the unemployment rate of men was 5.1 percent and that of women 5.8 percent. In 1973 that of men was 4.1 percent and that of women 6.0 percent.[90]

The accelerating integration of female labor power into paid production in the years since World War II has not left the family unaffected. Wives and mothers who work for pay have increasingly come to depend on consumer goods and services in maintaining their families. While the much-vaunted affluence of this period has been disproportionately enjoyed by those women whose husbands earn enough to allow them to remain outside the labor force for most of their lives, clearly many mass-produced household "conveniences" have become widely available.

Even more striking in its effect on women's home responsibilities is the drop in the birth rate since 1957, and the tendency for women to stop bearing children at a much younger age than formerly.[91] The period of their lifetime devoted to maternity in relation to their life expectancy has fallen rapidly. By the late 1960s, more than half of all American mothers had had their *last* child by the time they reached their thirtieth birthday. This is a very important change: the maternal role by which women have traditionally been defined was reduced to less than a seventh of their average lifespan, so that the longest phase of the female life cycle followed family completion.[92]

Thus as women's role in the paid labor force has come to take up a longer period of their lives, their family role has yielded more and more of its direct production functions to the sphere of commodity production, while the reproduction of children, the one commodity that this society still inevitably depends on women to produce, takes up a much shorter period of their lives.

All of these changes, combined with the increase in female labor force participation, have made it somewhat easier for women to exist outside the institution of marriage. It is true that the family as an institution and women's work within it continues to be economically essential, as has been emphasized repeatedly here. Also, women continue to experience discrimination in wages, and this still makes it very difficult for them to survive without having the additional source of income that accompanies marriage. And yet, the situation of women is significantly different in this regard from what is was in the early part of the century, when the vast majority of women who worked for pay left the labor force when they married and had children, never to return. The woman in a dual-worker family, even though her contribution to family income is much less than her husband's, can, simply because she has some independent income, more easily choose to strike out on her own than her grandmother, who was totally dependent on her husband's support, could have done.

Indeed, there was a dramatic increase in the number of women who have established single-person households over the postwar years.[93] The divorce rate (per thousand women under age forty-five) increased by two-thirds between the mid-1950s and 1970, while the remarriage rate (per thousand divorced or widowed women under age fifty-five) rose by about one-third during the same period.[94] Yet the degree to which traditional sexually stratified family patterns have persisted is as remarkable as the signs of pressure on the family as an institution. Because women's paid employment continued to be sex-typed, so thoroughly linked to their sexuality and to their family role in its cultural definition, their increased labor force participation has made only a slight difference in their family role. Sex-typing, based on the assumption that women's labor force role is "secondary," insured that they would earn less than men, rendering marriage to a man with greater earning power more attractive. Sex-typing also tended to suppress women's consciousness of their actual power as wage workers.

It is not surprising, then, that in the years after World War II, the rapid increase in female labor force participation, which represented such an unprecedented threat to the perpetuation of a family structure in which women have heavy unpaid responsibilities, was accompanied by an intensification of the ideology that said that their "place" was in the home. This cultural current, which Betty Friedan called "the feminine mystique" in the 1960s,[95] was nothing new in the history of America, but the extent to which it diverged from the reality and the possibility of women's lives was much greater than at any previous point. Women were working outside their homes, and they could choose not to live the "mystique" to a greater degree than ever before.

Just as in the 1930s and 1940s, when, as we have seen, women did not passively conform to ideological forces that pressured them to enter and leave the labor force, so, too, in the 1960s women actively resisted the revival of the mystique. The women's movement of that period presented a strong challenge to the system of occupational segregation and to the notion that women's primary role is that of wife and mother, and was an important force to be reckoned with.

In the years since World War II, then, female labor force participation has increased, intensifying the contradiction between women's paid work and family roles. Traditional sex-role ideology has at the same time become more essential to the perpetuation of the family, and yet there has also been an increase in political resistance to that ideology.

Notes

An earlier version of this chapter was published in *The Review of Radical Political Economics* in 1976. It is reprinted here with permission from Sage Publications.

1. Juliet Mitchell, *Woman's Estate* (New York: Vintage, 1971), 139.

2. Ibid., 124.

3. Margaret Benston, "The Political Economy of Women's Liberation," *Monthly Review* 21 (1969); reprinted in *From Feminism to Liberation*, edited by Edith Hoshino Altbach (Cambridge, Mass.: Schenkman Publishing Co., 1971), 206.

4. U.S. Census Bureau, *Historical Statistics of the U.S.* (1960), 73.

5. The only reliable national data that exist for the entire period are those in the 1930 and 1940 censuses. See U.S. Census Bureau, *Historical Statistics of the U.S.* (1960), 73. The 1933 figure cited here and the other official annual unemployment statistics are interpolations made using the decennial census figures as "benchmarks." Moreover, unemployment is calculated as a residual, that is, the difference between the estimated size of the civilian labor force and that of the employed population. Nor were data for these items collected directly in the decade of the 1930s. Rather, they were estimated later with the use of a variety of sources. For details see Stanley Lebergott, "Labor Force, Employment, and Unemployment, 1929–39: Estimating Methods," *Monthly Labor Review* 67, no. 1 (July 1948), 50–53. (Adjustments were made in the 1930 census data to make them comparable with those collected on a monthly basis by the Bureau of Labor Statistics beginning in the 1940s; the official revised figure for 1930 is 8.7 percent.)

The situation in regard to data on sex differences in unemployment is even worse. Because the nature of the relationship of female labor force participation to economic fluctuations is even today only dimly understood, it is impossible to interpolate from the decennial census data that are available. This is of course a severe limitation to the present study.

Annual data on sex differences in unemployment were collected for a small number of states. Most of this information is unpublished, however, although it is described in a few published sources and will be used to support the argument made here. See R. R. Lutz and Louise Patterson, *Women Workers and Labor Supply* (New York: National Industrial Conference Board Studies, No. 220, 1936); U.S. Women's Bureau Bulletin No. 159, *Trends in the Employment of Women, 1928–1936* (1938).

6. U.S. Census Bureau, *Historical Statistics*, 71–72. Also see chapter 1 of Valerie Kincade Oppenheimer, *The Female Labor Force in the U.S.* (Berkeley: University of California Population Monograph Series, No. 5, 1970) for an excellent discussion.

7. Twenty percent of all women fourteen years old and older were in the paid labor force in 1900, and by 1970 this figure had risen to 40 percent. Increasing female labor force participation is a secular trend, which registered little variation in response to the contraction of the 1930s.

8. Edward Gross, "Plus Ca Change . . . ? The Sexual Structure of Occupations Over Time," *Social Problems* 16, no. 2 (Fall 1968): 198–208.

9. It is virtually impossible to determine precisely what proportion of the jobs women hold are sex-typed in this manner. It seems reasonable to assume that occupations with extremely high concentrations of workers of one sex (such as those in the lower half of table 1.1) are of this character. But since the government's occupational statistics are not designed for the purpose of facilitating analysis of this dimension of the occupational structure, even the most detailed breakdowns offered by them frequently group together two or more occupations that are sex-typed differently. Thus while it is likely that the degree to which the labor market is sexually segregated is even greater than the study of the 1900–1960 decennial census data cited above indicates, it is not possible to gauge the actual extent of sex-typing from currently available data.

10. For discussion see chapter 3 of Oppenheimer, *Female Labor Force*. Data on sex differentials in pay are fragmentary. Some good collections of tables can be found in: U.S. Women's Bureau Bulletin No. 155, *Women in the Economy of the U.S.A.* (1937), 46–76, and U.S. Women's Bureau Bulletin No. 294, *1969 Handbook on Women Workers*, 132–38.

11. Even in the relatively infrequent cases where women do the same jobs as men, they almost invariably receive less pay. A study by the U.S. Bureau of Labor found only eight hundred cases in a 1895–96 sample of 150,000 workers, in which men and women were in the same job classifications. In six hundred of these cases the men earned more, by an average of about one-third. See Robert W. Smuts, *Women and Work in America* (New York: Schoken, 1959), 91. Cases of "equal work" are still quite rare, but the most cursory examination of earnings by sex across the decennial census's detailed occupational classification shows that women still earn much less than men when they do equivalent work. Male sociologists, for example, earned 65 percent more than their female counterparts in 1970 (computed from U.S. Census Bureau, *1970 Census of Population*, vol. PC(2)-7A, 1).

It is often suggested that economic discrimination of this type and differential treatment generally (including sex-typing) are justifiable because of differences in the "costs" of hiring men and women. Studies that control for such cost differentials, however, clearly show that only a fraction of the earnings gap can be so accounted for. For a review of this literature, see Beth Niemi and Cynthia Lloyd, "Sex Differentials in Earnings and Unemployment Rates," *Feminist Studies* 2, nos. 2–3 (1975): 194–201. There are some sex differences in absenteeism and turnover rates in aggregated data, but if one examines instead the rates for men and women with similar occupational characteristics, the differences almost completely disappear. See U.S. Women's Bureau, "Facts About Women's Absenteeism and Labor Turnover," (August 1969), reprinted in *Woman in a Man-Made World: A Socio-Economic Handbook*, edited by Nona Glazer-Malbin and Helen Youngelson Waehrer (New York: Rand McNally, 1972), 265–71. Absenteeism seems to be a result of discrimination, not a cause. It is closely associated with lack of qualifications, which in turn is related to lack of responsibilities at work, absence of promotion prospects, and low wages. See Evelyne Sullerot, *Woman, Society, and Change* (New York: McGraw-Hill World University Library, 1971), 183. These are typical characteristics of occupations that are sex-typed "female." A skilled woman worker with responsibility on the job, however, does not stay away from it any more often than a man in a similar position.

12. Lutz and Patterson, *Women Workers and Labor Supply*, 19.

13. For an excellent discussion of this process as it affected clerical workers, see Margery Davies, "Woman's Place Is at the Typewriter: The Feminization of the Clerical Labor Force," *Radical America* 8, no. 4 (August 1974).

14. Computed from U.S. Census Bureau, *15th Census of the U.S.*, 1930, *Unemployment*, vol. 2, 280–81.

15. Computed from *15th Census of the U.S.*, 1930, *Unemployment*, vol. 2, 344, and *15th Census of the U.S.*, 1930, *Population*, vol. 5, 276.

16. For data on this phenomenon in the early 1930s see U.S. Women's Bureau Bulletin No. 113, *Employment Fluctuations and Unemployment of Women, Certain Indications from Various Sources, 1928–31* (1938).

17. The extent to which this may have been ignored in unemployment statistics is phenomenal. One study found that in 1932, only 4 percent of the women surveyed in South Bend, Indiana—95 percent of whom were "normally" employed full time in manufacturing jobs—had full-time work. However, almost three-fifths of them were reported as "employed" in the Indiana unemployment statistics. U.S. Women's Bureau Bulletin No. 108, *The Effects of the Depression on Wage Earners' Families: A Second Survey of South Bend* (1936), 19.

18. It is possible that in some "mixed" occupations men actually did replace women to some extent. Given the high degree of sex-typing evident even in the poor data that are available (as discussed above), however, it seems likely that such replacement was the exception rather than the rule. A few studies of the question done during the 1930s reflected an understanding of this. See, for example, Lutz and Patterson, *Women Workers and Labor Supply*; Women's Bureau Bulletin No. 159, *Trends in the Employment of Women*; and Marguerite Thibert, "The Economic Depression and the Employment of Women," *International Labor Review* 27, nos. 4–5 (April and May 1933): 443–70, 620–830.

We can understand this intuitively by noting that even unemployed men tend to be extremely reluctant to take a job as a secretary—"that's women's work." Nor will the average secretary be likely to voluntarily give up her job in a time of economic hardship.

19. Lutz and Patterson, *Women Workers and Labor Supply*; Women's Bureau Bulletin No. 159, *Trends in the Employment of Women*; also see William H. Chafe, *The American Woman: Her Changing Social, Economic, and Political Role, 1920–1970* (New York: Oxford University Press, 1972), 270.

20. The U.S. Census Bureau did conduct a *Census of Partial Employment, Unemployment and Occupations* in 1937. It found a *higher* unemployment rate for women than for men, 14.9 percent and 13.9 percent, respectively. Registration of unemployment status was voluntary in this enumeration, intensifying the general tendency for women to be undercounted. A special "Enumerative Check Census" was conducted by the U.S. Census Bureau in the same year for a smaller sample in an effort to correct for this. It found that actually the unemployment rates of both men and women were much higher than the original data indicated, although women were undercounted to a greater extent than men. The revised figures were 18.6 percent for men and 24.6 percent for women.

However, both the first enumeration and the revisions have been widely discredited. Stanley Lebergott of the U.S. Bureau of Labor Statistics, in an extensive retrospective analysis of all the available data on unemployment in the 1930s (the analysis upon which the current official government figures are based), found that the 1937 census data were methodologically unsound and noted that they were inconsistent with virtually all other available evidence in their findings on sex differences in unemployment. U.S. Bureau of the Census, *Census of Partial Employment, Unemployment, and Occupations, 1937;* vol. 1:17 has the data from the first voluntary registration enumeration; vol. 4:9 has those for the enumerative check census. Reasons for the official rejection of the 1937 census are mentioned in Lebergott, "Labor Force," 62.

21. This differs from what is now the official unemployment figure for 1940, which is 14.6 percent (including public emergency workers). As in the case of the 1930 census data, adjustments were made in the 1940 census data to render them comparable with the unemployment statistics collected on a monthly basis by the U.S. Bureau of Labor Statistics beginning in the mid-1940s. For details, see Lebergott, "Labor Force."

22. All statistics in this paragraph are from U.S. Census Bureau, *16th Census of the U.S., 1940, Population,* vol. 3: 10.

23. Male labor force participation declined between 1930 and 1940, but this was largely due to decreases in the participation of teenaged and retirement-aged males. The labor force participation rate of males ages twenty-five to sixty-four changed insignificantly. U.S. Census Bureau, *Historical Statistics,* 71.

24. See for examples the case studies in Ruth S. Cavan and Katherine H. Ranck, *The Family and the Depression: A Study of One Hundred Chicago Families* (Chicago: University of Chicago Press, 1938) and in Mirra Komarovsky, *The Unemployed Man and His Family: The Effect of Unemployment upon the Status of the Man in Fifty-Nine Families* (New York: Dryden, 1940).

25. There is substantial evidence, on the other hand, of widespread downward mobility within the female labor market. Women who were unemployed were evidently willing, after a certain point, to seek work in an occupation different from their former one, even when this meant a cut in status and/or pay. Data on this point are scattered. Figures from a Pennsylvania employment office show that the proportion of women seeking jobs as service workers and in sales occupations in 1936 was substantially larger than the proportion of women in those occupational groups in 1930. See U.S. Women's Bureau Bulletin No. 155, *Women in the Economy,* 37. Another interesting study with data on downward mobility is

Pennsylvania Department of Labor and Industry, Bureau of Women and Children, *Women Workers after a Plant Shutdown*, Special Bulletin No. 36 (Harrisburg, 1933). For discussion on how the upgrading of educational requirements of teachers and nurses displaced women into occupations of lower status, see Smuts, *Women and Work*, 103–4. Men probably experienced a similar pattern of downward mobility in the 1930s, and in light of this it is all the more surprising that they did not replace women to any significant extent.

26. Gross, "Plus Ca Change."

27. Caroline Bird, *The Invisible Scar* (New York: McKay, 1966), 56–58.

28. Chafe, *American Woman*, 108.

29. Oppenheimer, *Female Labor Force*, 44.

30. Smuts, *Women and Work*, 145.

31. Cavan and Ranck, *Family and the Depression*, 1.

32. Dixon Wecter, *The Age of the Great Depression, 1929–41* (Chicago: Quadrangle, 1948), 26; Winona L. Morgan, *The Family Meets the Depression: A Study of a Group of Highly Selected Families* (Minneapolis: University of Minnesota Press, 1939), 22.

33. Cecile Tipton LaFollette, *A Study of the Problems of 652 Gainfully Employed Married Women Homemakers*, Contributions to Education No. 619 (New York: Teachers College, Columbia University, 1934), 95–96.

34. Ibid., 102.

35. Another strategy was that of going back to the land. Actually, most farmers had lived in poverty even during the "prosperous" 1920s, but this fact was evidently not widely appreciated, for in the early 1930s, the flow of people from farms to cities slowed and then actually reversed itself for the first time since records of internal migration had been kept. By 1935, two million people were living on farms who had not been there five years before. See Wecter, *Age of the Great Depression*, 133. This strategy had an understandable appeal at a time when fear of starvation was realistic and widespread.

36. Cavan and Ranck, *Family and the Depression*, 82; Wecter, *Age of the Great Depression*, 26.

37. Robert S. Lynd and Helen Merrell Lynd, *Middletown in Transition: A Study in Cultural Conflicts* (New York: Harcourt Brace and World, 1937).

38. Cavan and Ranck, *Family and the Depression*, 83.

39. Ibid., 57.

40. Ibid., 57.

41. Ibid., 56.

42. Ibid., 159.

43. Wecter, *Age of the Great Depression*, 29; Glen H. Elder, *Children of the Great Depression: Social Change in Life Experience* (Chicago: University of Chicago Press, 1974).

44. As far as I am aware, data on school retention rates for the 1930s are not available by sex. However, a study based on data on the postwar business cycles found that teenage boys accelerate their school-leaving in times of prosperity, while girls tend to do so in times of depression. Since girls are more productive at home in hard times, the logic runs, they leave school and devote their energy to helping their mothers to carry the increased burden of housework during depressions. Boys, in contrast, decide when to leave school according to

their opportunities for paid employment and thus go to school longer during hard times. It seems plausible that this would hold for the 1930s also. See Linda Nasif Edwards, "School Retention of Teenagers over the Business Cycle," *Journal of Human Resources* 11, no. 2 (Spring 1976): 200–208; see also Wecter, *Age of the Great Depression*, 29, who argues that youth returned home during the 1930s.

45. U.S. Census Bureau, *Historical Statistics*, 30.

46. Wecter, *Age of the Great Depression*, 199.

47. Paul C. Glick and Arthur J. Norton, "Perspectives on the Recent Upturn in Divorce and Remarriage," *Demography* 10, no. 3 (August 1973): 305.

48. Studs Terkel, ed., *Hard Times: An Oral History of the Great Depression* (New York: Avon, 1970), 447.

49. Komarovsky, *Unemployed Man*, 74.

50. Terkel, *Hard Times*, 191.

51. Cavan and Ranck, *Family and the Depression*, 86.

52. Morgan, *Family Meets the Depression*, 46.

53. Ibid., 21.

54. Cavan and Ranck, *Family and the Depression*, 86.

55. See Cavan and Ranck, *Family and the Depression*; Komarovsky, *Unemployed Man*; and Robert Cooley Angell, *The Family Encounters the Depression* (New York: Scribner's, 1936).

56. Lynd and Lynd, *Middletown in Transition*, 146.

57. Wecter, *Age of the Great Depression*, 198.

58. The birth rate dropped from 21.3 live births per thousand population in 1930 to 18.4 in 1933. U.S. Census Bureau, *Historical Statistics*, 23.

59. Komarovsky, *Unemployed Man*, 130.

60. Terkel, *Hard Times*, 229.

61. Ibid., 248.

62. Ibid., 248; also see Gladys L. Palmer and Andria Taylor Hourwich, *A Scrapbook of the American Labor Movement* (New York: Affiliated Summer Schools for Women Workers in Industry, 1931–32).

63. Tillie Olsen, *Yonnodio from the Thirties* (Delacorte / Lawrence, 1974), 81.

64. Angell, *Family Encounters the Depression*, 124–25.

65. Terkel, *Hard Times*, 127.

66. This inference is supported by Elder's finding that females who were adolescents during the Depression years (born 1920–21) were more likely to marry early if their families of orientation experienced deprivation (defined as a loss in family income of 35 percent or greater) during the 1930s. These women also showed a marked preference for the domestic role over any alternative one. See Elder, *Children of the Great Depression*, 214–15. Aggregate cohort data shows that daughters born in the late depression years—roughly parallel to the daughters of the women in Elder's cohort—have the highest proportion "ever married" on record. See Glick and Norton, "Perspectives on the Recent Upturn," 305.

67. This was due to the unfavorable comparison between domestic work and other occupations in which there were openings. There was a great deal of upward occupational mobility during the 1940s. Women left occupations with low status and pay, such as service and sales

jobs, for new opportunities in war industries, which offered better pay and working conditions. Movement out of service employment was so pronounced that there were many shortages in provision of services. In 1942, for example, six hundred laundries closed because of their inability to recruit workers. International Labor Office, *The War and Women's Employment: The Experience of the United Kingdom and the United States* (Montreal, 1946), 212.

There was also a great deal of geographical mobility, for war production was not evenly distributed across the country but, on the contrary, centered in a relatively small number of urban areas. Many women migrated from areas outlying the war production centers in response to the spectacular demand for their labor power. See Women's Bureau Bulletin No. 209, *Women Workers in Ten War Production Areas and their Postwar Employment Plans* (1946).

These mobility patterns completely reversed those that had characterized the Depression years, when most occupational mobility had been forced and in a downward direction and geographical mobility had been from urban to rural areas. See Wecter, *Age of the Great Depression*, 130. The mobility that was possible for women, moreover, was no longer limited to the female labor market, for the heavy industrial "war jobs" that accounted for the largest single part of the increased employment of women—jobs in aircraft assembly, shipbuilding, ammunition manufacturing, and steel—had traditionally been sex-typed male. See Women's Bureau Special Bulletin No. 20, *Changes in Women's Employment during the War* (1944) for discussion.

68. U.S. Women's Bureau Bulletin No. 211, *Employment of Women in the Early Postwar Period, with Background of Prewar and War Data* (1946), 7, 10.

69. U.S. Women's Bureau Special Bulletin No. 13, *Part-Time Employment of Women in Wartime* (June 1943).

70. U.S. Women's Bureau Special Bulletin No. 14, *When You Hire Women* (1944), 18.

71. Richard Polenberg, *War and Society: The United States, 1941–1945* (Philadelphia: Lippincott, 1972), 12–13.

72. International Labour Office, *War and Women's Employment*, 214.

73. U.S. Women's Bureau Special Bulletin No. 18, *A Preview as to Women Workers in Transition from War to Peace* (1944), 13.

74. Chafe, *American Woman*, 138–39.

75. U.S. Women's Bureau Special Bulletin No. 9, *Safety Caps for Women Machine Operators*, supplementary folder.

76. *Fortune* 27, no. 2 (February 1943): 37.

77. "Girl Pilots: Air Force Trains Them at Avenger Field, Texas," *Life* 15, no. 3 (July 19, 1943): 75–76.

78. Josephine von Miklos, *I Took a War Job* (New York: Simon and Schuster, 1943), 188–89.

79. U.S. Women's Bureau Bulletin No. 211, *Employment of Women*, 2.

80. Sheila Tobias and Lisa Anderson, "What Really Happened to Rosie the Riveter? Demobilization and the Female Labor Force, 1944–47," Module 9 (New York: MSS Modular Publications, 1974), 9.

81. J. E. Trey, "Women in the War Economy—World War II," *Review of Radical Political Economics* 4 (July 1972), 47.

82. U.S. Women's Bureau Bulletin No. 209, *Women Workers*, 4.

83. U.S. Women's Bureau Bulletin No. 211, *Employment of Women*, 8.

84. Elizabeth Hawes, "Woman War Worker: A Case History," *New York Times Magazine* (December 21, 1943): 21.

85. U.S. Census Bureau, *Historical Statistics*, 71–72; 1970 U.S. Census Bureau, *1970 Census of Population*, 68–69.

86. Ginzberg pointed out the salience of the "elongation of the educational cycle" in 1968, just before the labor force participation of males aged sixteen to twenty-four began to rise again. He suggested also that part of the decline was due to the buildup of the armed forces in the postwar period, since this reduced the number of men in the labor force. See Eli Ginzburg, "Paycheck and Apron—Revolution in Womanpower," *Industrial Relations: A Journal of Economy and Society* 7, no. 3 (May 1968): 196. However, the data in table 1.3 include persons in the armed forces and yet show a persistent decline in male labor force participation. Even if that decline can be explained by external factors, the change in the relationship between male and female rates is a highly significant one.

87. Oppenheimer, *Female Labor Force*, 97, 102.

88. U.S. Departments of H.E.W. and Labor, *Manpower Report of the President* (1974), 268.

89. See Barbara Bergmann, "Labor Turnover, Segmentation, and Rates of Unemployment: A Simulation-Theoretic Approach," University of Maryland Project on the Economics of Discrimination, mimeo, August 1973.

90. A full set of data on this topic can be found in the table in Niemi and Lloyd, "Sex Differentials," 194–201.

91. Ginzberg, "Paycheck and Apron," 198.

92. Evelyne Sullerot, *Woman, Society, and Change* (McGraw-Hill World University Library, 1971), 74–75.

93. Frances E. Kobrin, "The Primary Individual and the Family: Changes in Living Arrangements in the United States since 1940," *Journal of Marriage and Family* 38, no. 2 (May 1976): 233–39.

94. Glick and Norton, "Perspectives on the Recent Upturn."

95. Betty Freidan, *The Feminine Mystique* (New York: Dell, 1963).

Chapter 2

Redefining "Women's Work"

*The Sexual Division of Labor in the Auto Industry
during World War II*

This chapter examines the process through which new patterns of job segregation by sex were constructed in the auto industry during World War II. Its analysis complicates the conventional narrative that women entered "men's jobs" during the war years, disrupting the longstanding pattern of job segregation. Instead, new patterns of job segregation developed within what had previously been a sector of the industrial economy nearly monopolized by men. The World War II era offers a magnified view of the continual process of establishing boundaries between "women's work" and "men's work." The chapter shows how and why this unfolded in the course of the war mobilization, documenting the ways in which employers, unions, and workers themselves participated in the reproduction of job segregation by sex in this unique historical context. It shows that although Rosie the Riveter held what had previously been a "man's job" for the duration of the war, she typically worked in an all-female job classification. Rather than integrating women workers throughout the production process, auto industry employers systematically reconfigured the gender division of labor as they converted their factories from consumer automotive production to manufacturing war material. They did incorporate women into the industry's ranks but at the same time went to great lengths to preserve job segregation by sex. They developed elaborate cultural justifications for this practice by highlighting parallels between women's wartime jobs in the factory and their traditional work in the home. Auto workers and their union struggled with management over these issues, as the chapter also shows, but such struggles focused on preserving hard-won standards of pay and seniority rather than challenging job segregation by sex.

Introduction

Feminists have deliberately idealized the experience of women workers during World War II, challenging the ideology of "woman's place" that obliterated women's wartime contribution to industrial production from public memory. The stunning imagery of female strength and versatility captured in photographs of women industrial workers in the 1940s has become a mainstay of "feminist realism." Ultimately, our vision of social change encompasses more than securing equal access for women to alienating jobs in capitalist industry: work itself must be fundamentally transformed—for both women and men. But so long as women workers are excluded from basic industry and ghettoized in low-status, poorly paid jobs, the woman war worker will remain a resonant symbol.

A closer look at the actual experience of women industrial workers during the war years, however, suggests that the retrospective feminist construction of their place in history is apocryphal. Women were hired to do "men's jobs" during the war on a scale unparalleled before or since, but this was in no way the result of a feminist campaign. In basic industries like auto manufacturing, employers were initially quite resistant to the idea of hiring women for war work. They did so only when the supply of male labor had been completely exhausted because of military conscription, on the one hand, and the rapid expansion of demand for labor to produce military hardware, on the other. It was not a change in management beliefs about women's capabilities in industry that led to their incorporation into jobs previously considered suitable only for men; rather, the male labor shortage during the war years led to the change in management's beliefs.

Once women were drawn upon to meet the need for labor in war-bloated "heavy" industries, moreover, they were not randomly incorporated into "men's jobs" as vacancies occurred. Instead, *new* patterns of occupational segregation by sex were established "for the duration" within sectors of the economy previously monopolized by men. So Rosie the Riveter did a "man's job," but more often than not she worked in a predominantly female department or job classification.[1]

The wartime experience of women in industry is a fruitful object of feminist analysis, then, but for reasons opposite to those generally presumed. The economic mobilization led to a shift in the location of the boundaries between "men's" and "women's" work, not the elimination of those boundaries. The persistence of segregation during the war, in the face of a massive influx of women into the labor force and a dramatic upheaval in the previously established sexual division of labor, poses quite starkly the fundamental problem of explaining how and why job segregation by sex has been maintained and reproduced over and over again throughout the history of capitalist development.[2]

The underlying forces that continually reproduce segregation within the supposedly "impersonal" wage labor market remain obscure if the problem is approached at the level of the individual employer or firm. Once women have been introduced into the paid labor force at a lower cost than men, one would expect that the relentless efforts of capital to maximize profits would lead employers to substitute women for men whenever possible, at least until the costs of female and male labor power are equalized. It appears quite irrational for management to differentiate rigidly between women and men workers, as if they were truly non-interchangeable sources of labor power. But the ideology of sex-typing and the job segregation it legitimates do serve the class interest of capital, despite the countervailing pressures impinging on individual capital.

Collectively, capital benefits from the existence of gender divisions within the working class in that they—like racial and other intraclass cleavages—foster political disunity within what might otherwise be a stronger source of opposition to capital.[3] In addition, and crucially, segregation by sex within the wage labor market helps to secure the daily and generational reproduction of the working class through the unpaid household labor of women, by denying female workers a living wage, and by maintaining their economic dependence on men and on families. At the same time, the sexual division of labor in the household is exactly what constitutes women as a source of "cheap" and expendable labor to begin with.[4]

Not only collective capital but also male workers benefit from job segregation by sex, at least in the short term. Not only do men receive higher wages than women within the wage labor market, but the concentration of women in poorly paid, insecure jobs ensures that women will perform personal services for men in the household even if these women also work for pay. While capital, not the male workforce, generally controls the process of job definition and allocation, insofar as men mobilize themselves to maintain the subordination of women within the wage labor market, the interest of collective capital in a gender-segregated labor market is reinforced.[5]

But if male workers pursued their *class* interest, rather than seeking to maintain their position as a privileged gender, they would mobilize *against* job segregation by sex. Male workers have a class interest in working-class unity. Job segregation by sex, even as it reinforces male power over women, threatens at the same time to undercut the bargaining power of male labor vis-à-vis capital, precisely because of the "cheapness" of female labor. In short, the class interest and what might be called the gender interest of male workers directly conflict with one another. Historically, the apparent domination of men's gender interest over their class interest in shaping their relationship to job segregation by sex must be explained, not presumed from the outset as inevitable or "given." It is crucial to understand the specific historical conditions under which male workers' class interests might predominate over their gender interests, if we are to have any hope of successfully eliminating job segregation.

Unions, which historically have been disproportionately controlled by men, have often served to maintain the gender privileges of their male members. But there are also historical instances in which the class interest of male workers instead has prevailed in the policy and practice of unions. For example, fear of female substitution, jeopardizing the labor market position of male workers, may lead male-dominated unions to struggle for equality between women and men in the labor market, in spite of the immediate benefits the male gender enjoys as a result of job segregation.

For the class interest of male workers to prevail over their gender interest in a sustained way, however, an oppositional ideology must be generated that challenges the legitimacy of the elaborate and deeply rooted ideology of gender division. The most thoroughgoing such oppositional ideology, namely, feminism, has had limited influence on the American labor movement. But there have been moments in the history of industrial unionism when an ideological commitment to nondiscrimination and class unity has galvanized male workers and their organizations to struggle against rather than for job segregation.

Failing this, the interest of collective capital is reinforced by the gender interest of male workers in job segregation by sex and its rationalizing ideology of occupational sex-typing. Both these interests are served by the maintenance of the family as an institution of social reproduction based on unpaid female labor. Women's participation in wage labor on equal terms with men would ultimately undermine the unequal sexual division of labor in the household. Access to an individual wage, even on terms unequal to men, erodes the structure of women's economic dependence on men and on families. This is precisely why, rather than disappearing as women's labor force participation increases, occupational sex-typing persists and indeed becomes ever more important: it constructs women's "primary" commitment as devotion to home and family, whether or not they also work for pay.

This interdependence between the circumscribed roles of women in the family and in the labor market, which has been observed in a wide range of circumstances by feminist scholars, helps to explain the particular case of the reconstruction of job segregation by sex within the mobilized economy of the early 1940s. During the World War II years, married women and mothers poured into the labor force in massive numbers for the first time, posing an unprecedented threat to family stability.[6] Thus, far from being rendered unnecessary by the exigencies of the war emergency, job segregation was more crucial than ever before at this juncture.

The sex-typing of the jobs newly opened to women "for the duration" reconciled women's new economic situation with their traditional position as guardians of the hearth. This was manifested in the pervasive wartime propaganda image of "woman's place" on the nation's production lines, which portrayed women's war work in industry as a temporary extension of domesticity.

The World War II experience not only reveals the resilience of the structure of job segregation by sex and of the general ideology of sexual division that legitimates it, but it also renders transparent the specific *idiom* of sex-typing, which is flexibly applied to whatever jobs women and men happen to be doing. Jobs that had previously been cast in terms suggestive of the very quintessence of masculinity were suddenly endowed with femininity and glamour "for the duration." The propaganda newsreel *Glamour Girls of '43*, for example, suggested:

> Instead of cutting the lines of a dress, this woman cuts the pattern of aircraft parts. Instead of baking cake, this woman is cooking gears to reduce the tension in the gears after use. . . . They are taking to welding as if the rod were a needle and the metal a length of cloth to be sewn. After a short apprenticeship, this woman can operate a drill press just as easily as a juice extractor in her own kitchen. And a lathe will hold no more terrors for her than an electric washing machine.[7]

Virtually any job could be labeled as "woman's work" in this way.

Idioms of sex-typing are unified in the global presumption that "men's work" and "women's work" are fundamentally distinct, but they also vary among sectors of the economy, specific industries, and even individual firms. In "pink collar" service and clerical sector jobs, the skills and capacities presumed to be developed by wives and mothers, such as nurturance, solicitousness to emotional and sexual needs, and skill in providing personal services, are the central reference point of the idiom of sex-typing. Sex segregation in the manufacturing sector speaks a different language, rooted less in women's family role than in their real or imagined biological characteristics. No one pretends that being nurturant or knowing how to make a good cup of coffee are important qualifications for "female" factory jobs. Here the idiom centers on such qualities as manual dexterity, attention to detail, ability to tolerate monotony, and women's relative lack of physical strength. Analogies to domestic labor are present in both the pink-collar and blue-collar idioms, but the physical tasks comprising housework are paramount in descriptions of women's manual labor outside the home, rather than the psychological tasks emphasized in relation to women's paid "mental" work.

If the underlying logic of job segregation by sex is rooted in the collective interest of capital, reinforced by the gender interest of male workers, in preserving the sexual division of labor within the family, this still does not adequately explain the specific location of women in the wage labor force at a given point in time. Once established, idioms linking women's paid and unpaid work tend to acquire a certain ideological stability, in the form of "tradition." In practice, such "traditions" often guide the actual hiring and placement policies pursued by management. Yet, as suggested by the flexibility with which the idiom was readjusted during the war, the ideological construction of the sexual division of labor obscures the economic and political forces that help shape the particular configurations of sex-specific employment.

Employers must take account of a range of economic considerations in their hiring decisions: not only the available supplies of female and male labor and their relative costs, but also such factors as the proportion of a firm's capital outlays made up by wages or the ease with which labor costs can be passed on to consumers. There are also political constraints that limit, or potentially limit, management's freedom in allocating jobs to women and men. For example, the greater the actual or anticipated male resistance to feminization, the less likely an employer may be to attempt it. Managerial initiatives affecting the sexual division of labor may become objects of political struggle for women and/or men workers, especially when the sex-specific supply-and-demand equilibrium in a labor market is disrupted—which occurs quite regularly in a dynamic capitalist economy. Usually, these struggles are over marginal changes in the sexual division of labor, but there are times when more dramatic shifts in the structure of the labor market take place, presenting political opportunities for a broader challenge to the sexual division of wage labor as a whole. The large-scale economic dislocations associated with the mobilization for World War II and the subsequent postwar reconversion presented one such historical opportunity.

The rest of this chapter explores the dynamics of job segregation by sex in the automotive industry during the 1940s. It examines how the idiom of sex-typing was implemented and readjusted in the face of a dramatic change in the economic constraints on the sexual division of labor, and the ensuing political struggles over the redefinition of the boundaries between "women's work" and "men's work." The upheaval in the sexual division of labor precipitated by the wartime mobilization was particularly dramatic in basic manufacturing industries such as auto. While women's labor force participation increased by 50 percent in the economy as a whole between 1940 and 1944, in heavy "war industries" the number of women rose 460 percent during that period, and in the auto industry the increase was an astounding 600 percent.[8] Clearly the auto industry was by no means typical of the economy as a whole in regard to the changes that occurred in the sexual division of labor. Yet precisely because the shifts in the position of women were so extensive and so rapid, the auto industry experience is especially revealing. It offers a magnified view of the reproduction of job segregation by sex, a process that is always occurring.

Politically, the situation in the auto industry in the 1940s is also of special interest. The young auto workers' union, the United Automobile Workers—Congress of Industrial Organizations (UAW-CIO), was the largest union in the country during the war, boasting more than one million members in 1945, 28 percent of whom were female.[9] It was also one of the most progressive unions on questions of discrimination—although this was saying very little, and there were certainly instances of UAW–management collusion at the expense of women workers. Still, in the absence of an organized feminist movement during this period, the UAW became a crucial avenue for political challenges to management on sexual division of labor issues. The union set up a Women's Bureau in 1944, and prior to that it was instrumental in several precedent-setting cases involving the issue of "equal pay for equal work." The auto industry was highly unusual in this respect as well, but here again its very atypicality is illuminating: it suggests the limits and possibilities of political challenges to the managerial construction of the sexual division of labor in this period.

"Women's Work" in the Prewar Auto Industry

Automotive manufacturing relied overwhelmingly on male workers in the years before World War II, with women accounting for less than one-tenth of the industry's labor force throughout that period. The revolutionary organization of production around the moving assembly line laid the basis for auto's development as a high-wage, capital-intensive industry in which employers had relatively little incentive to substitute female labor for its more expensive male equivalent. Women auto workers were concentrated in a relatively small number of jobs and in particular branches of the industry, consistent with the broader pattern of job segregation by sex found throughout the nation's economy. Although small numbers of women could be found scattered through many departments of the plants, they were clustered primarily in the upholstery or "cut-and-sew" divisions of body plants and in small-parts assembly.[10]

Although women auto workers earned wages higher than those available in most other fields of female employment, throughout the industry women's wages were far below men's. In 1925 the average hourly earnings of female workers in the auto industry were forty-seven cents, compared with a seventy-three-cent average for men.[11] Although there were occasional incidents of women being substituted for men, and at lower pay, what is much more striking is that management was never particularly interested in pursuing a policy of large-scale feminization. The supreme lever of control over labor in the industry was machinery, and especially the assembly line—centerpiece of the Fordist revolution. Mechanization was carried forward to such a degree that wages became a relatively small component of costs. The announcement of the legendary Five-Dollar Day by the Ford Motor Company in 1914 quickly established the industry's reputation as a *high-wage* industry. Under these conditions, female substitution had little to recommend it.[12]

Jobs were clearly defined as "male" or "female" during this period, with none of the subtlety with which segregation by sex would later come to be disguised in the face of challenges to the legitimacy of discrimination. "It is customary," wrote one authoritative commentator on labor relations in the auto industry in 1940, "for management to draw a sharp line of demarcation between male and female occupations."[13] Even the aggregate data on the occupational distribution of women through the industry in this period reveal a high degree of sex segregation. A 1925 government survey of motor vehicle manufacturing found women in only twenty-two of the 110 occupational groups enumerated for the industry, and more than two-thirds of the women were working in just four of these classifications. When a similar survey was conducted fifteen years later, the situation was virtually unchanged. Women were found in but fifteen of the 84 job categories listed in 1940, with 72 percent of them clustered in the four largest occupations.[14]

The idiom in which the sexual division of labor in the prewar auto industry was cast emphasized the suitability of women for "light" or "delicate" work in accounting for their concentration in particular job classifications. "In finishing, polishing, and upholstery, where much hand work is required," wrote one observer in 1929, "they [women] are considered fast workers." In another typical rendition, it was suggested that women were especially well represented in the parts branch of this industry "since they are adept at assembly of light units."[15] These were the characteristics associated with "women's work" in the manufacturing sector generally, in the prevailing idiom of sex-typing: "light," "repetitive" work, demanding manual "dexterity."

Yet the actual sexual division of labor in the prewar auto industry bore at best a limited relationship to such factors. The majority of jobs done by both women and men in the industry were repetitive operations, and most required some degree of manual "dexterity." There were also some "women's jobs" that required substantial physical exertion. And firms varied to some degree in the ways in which they constructed the sexual division of labor, despite an overall similarity in the organization of production. It seems that whatever jobs women were assigned to in a given plant came to be viewed as requiring a feminine touch, although exactly the same positions might be deemed suited only for men elsewhere in the industry. Thus in 1926 the *Wall Street Journal* reported that women crane operators at the Hudson Motor Company who lifted motors and carried them to the chassis were "more sensitive and accurate than men," while at other auto firms this was an exclusively male occupation.[16]

Once firmly established, the sexual division of labor in the auto industry remained remarkably stable during the years before the war. Even during the economic depression of the 1930s, when the auto industry underwent a severe profitability crisis, there was surprisingly little change in the sexual division of labor. Although there were occasional efforts to substitute women for men to save on labor costs, in general the ideology of sexual division reigned supreme even in the face of the extraordinary economic circumstances of the Depression decade. While the incentive for substituting female labor for male was more compelling than it had been previously, so was the social ideology that decried the employment of women so long as men were unemployed. The ideology of the "family wage," together with the established idiom of sex-typing, continued to set limits on the extent to which employers would attempt female substitution during the depression.

The 1930s brought a political transformation to the auto industry as well as changed economic circumstances. In the second half of the decade, management's recognition of the UAW profoundly altered the character of labor relations in the auto industry, where unions had never been able to establish a foothold before. For the UAW, as for other CIO unions in this period, it followed from the logic of industrial unionism that the minority of women production workers should be organized along with the much more numerous male workforce. The CIO had a serious commitment to opposing all forms of employment discrimination, although it lacked any special commitment to challenging sexual inequality as such. This reflected the weakness of feminism in the interwar period, as well as the hardy tradition of male domination within the labor movement itself. Women auto workers still benefited enormously from unionization. Women's average hourly wages in the industry jumped from fifty-four cents in 1936 to sixty-five cents two years later, while men's rose from eighty-one to ninety-eight cents over the same period.[17] And the institutionalization of seniority systems gave women workers some protection from sexual favoritism and sexual harassment for the first time, although frequently there were separate seniority lists for women and men.[18] Yet the UAW's main concern in this period was with consolidating its organizational gains generally, and issues concerning women specifically were rather low on its list of priorities. In the 1930s the union never mounted a serious challenge to the sexual division of labor in industry or to the pervasive social ideology of "woman's place" that supplied it with such a compelling rationale.

Indeed, to the degree that the UAW became involved in conflicts with management affecting the sexual division of labor at all, the primary result was the consolidation of the existing pattern of female employment, not the dissolution of the boundaries between "women's work" and "men's work." When management did attempt female substitution, male workers could now resist it more effectively than before the introduction of collective bargaining. Sex differentials in wages and separate seniority systems, established by management in the pre-union era, were now institutionalized in many local contracts. Although the principle of nondiscrimination embedded in the new industrial unionism provided the basis for a challenge to sex discrimination, it would be many years before such a struggle materialized.

During the 1930s, then, the auto industry remained predominantly male with a clearly demarcated "woman's place" in its various divisions, essentially unchanged in this respect from the non-union era. It was not the political forces unleashed with unionization but the economic impact of World War II that exploded the traditional sexual division of labor in the auto industry.

Redefining "Women's Work" in the Wartime Auto Industry

The immediate effect of U.S. entry into World War II on the auto industry was a complete shutdown of production. Consumer production of cars and trucks was banned shortly after Pearl Harbor, and in February 1942 the last car rolled off the assembly line. There followed massive layoffs of auto workers, as the industry retooled for war production, and "conversion unemployment" was particularly pronounced among women auto workers. The number and proportion of women in the industry therefore dropped in the first part of 1942, but this was followed by a sudden rise in the representation of women as demand for labor outstripped the available supply of men. As table 2.1 shows, in April 1942 only one of every twenty auto production workers was a woman; eighteen months later, one out of four workers in the industry's plants was female.[19]

Table 2.1. Female and Total Employment in the Automobile Industry, 1940–1947

Month/Year	All Production Workers	Female Production Workers	Percent Female
October 1940	533,300	30,400	5.7
April 1941	585,200	31,600	5.4
October 1941	577,500	28,300	4.9
April 1942	429,200	20,600	4.8
October 1942	576,000	69,700	12.1
April 1943	670,200	121,300	18.1
October 1943	775,900	199,400	25.7
April 1944	746,000	185,000	24.8
April 1945	706,000	158,000	22.4
August 1945 (VJ Day)	577,000	101,600	17.6
April 1946	646,000	61,400	9.5
April 1947	807,000	76,700	9.5

Source: U.S. Department of Labor, Bureau of Labor Statistics, *Women in Factories*, mimeo. (1947), 6–7.

Initially, women war workers in the auto industry were employed only in jobs that had long before been established within the industry as "women's work." Although a U.S. Employment Service survey of war work in early 1942 found that women could capably perform the tasks required in 80 percent of job classifications, UAW woman-employing plants showed women in only 28 percent of the classifications, on average, in July of that year. "The chief classifications on which they were employed," the UAW reported, "were assembly, inspection, drill press, punch press, sewing machines, filing, and packing."[20] Such positions had long before been associated with women.

Even as the supply of male labor was being depleted, auto employers were loath to forsake their prewar hiring preference for white male workers. "As long as the employers can hire men," Ernest Kanzler, the head of the Detroit office of the War Production Board (WPB) pointed out in 1942, "they don't talk about hiring women." Ultimately the federal government intervened, setting male employment ceilings and giving the War Manpower Commission (WMC) the power to enforce them. "Over our strenuous objections," Detroit WMC director Edward Cushman recalls, "the Ford Motor Company began hiring 17, 18 and 19 year old men. And we kept drafting them."[21] Women, as well as blacks and other industrial minorities, were only incorporated into the automotive labor force when there was no longer any possibility of continuing to hire white men.

Management foot-dragging applied doubly to black women. "The [black] men are o.k. on unskilled jobs," reported one government representative, summarizing the attitude of auto industry employers toward black workers in mid-1943, "but the women are a drug [sic] on the market." Geraldine Bledsoe of the U.S. Employment Service in Detroit complained publicly in October 1942 that more than one thousand black women had completed vocational training courses, "and yet they go day after day to the plants and are turned down." By mid-1943 the WMC estimated that twenty-eight thousand black women were available for war work in Detroit, but that most war plants would employ them only as janitors, matrons, and government inspectors. By the war's end, Detroit auto plants had hired black women in substantial numbers, but this was only after all other sources of labor had been fully exhausted.[22]

The auto firms had always actively recruited male labor from the South, and they continued to do so during the mobilization period. But Detroit, where the vast bulk of the industry's production took place, could not accommodate male in-migrants and their families on the scale that the rapid wartime expansion of the industry would have required. Housing and transportation facilities were limited, and with wartime restrictions on construction and rationing of scarce materials, the deficit could not be met. Moreover, the entire nation was facing a male labor shortage. It was these circumstances that generated government pressure on the auto firms to hire women. The WPB threatened to withhold additional war contracts from Detroit manufacturers and even to remove existing contracts if in-migration to the Motor City was not stemmed. The alternative to continued in-migration, the WPB urged in mid-1942, was recruiting women for war work:

> The recruitment of local women who are not now in the labor market is free from the disadvantages or limitations of the other methods of meeting the labor deficit. Local women workers will not require new housing, transportation or other facilities. They do not create a possible future relief burden. Each woman who is recruited will reduce the necessary in-migration correspondingly and thus reduce or eliminate the need for transferring contracts elsewhere.[23]

The government pressured the auto firms to hire women but made no effort whatsoever to influence their placement within the industry once management let them into the factory gates. The U.S. Employment Service routinely filled employer job openings that called for specific numbers of women and men, and while ceilings were imposed on the number of men who could be allocated to each plant, employers had a free hand in placing women and men in particular jobs within this constraint.[24] Although the UAW sometimes contested the sexual division of labor after the fact, the initial decisions about where to place women within the plant job structure were left entirely to management.

Women were not evenly distributed through the various jobs available in the war plants but were hired into specific classifications that management deemed "suitable" for women and were excluded from other kinds of jobs. Sometimes management conducted special surveys to determine the sexual division of labor in a plant; probably more often such decisions were made on a less systematic basis by individual supervisors.[25] Although data on the distribution of women throughout the various job classifications in the wartime auto industry are sketchy, there is no mistaking the persistence of job segregation by sex. A 1943 government survey of the industry's Detroit plants, for example, found more than one-half of the women workers clustered in only five of seventy-two job classifications. Only 11 percent of the men were employed in these five occupations.[26]

Job segregation by sex was explicitly acknowledged in many automotive plants during the war. In 45 percent of the plants with sexually mixed workforces responding to a survey conducted in mid-1944 by the UAW Women's Bureau, jobs were formally set up on a "male" and "female" basis.[27] And it is extremely unlikely that women were more fully integrated into the range of job classifications in the other 55 percent. A case in point is the Ford River Rouge plant. The available data do not offer a very detailed breakdown, yet a great deal of segregation is apparent. In December 1943, when women's employment in the industry was at its wartime peak, women made up 16 percent of the work force at the Rouge plant. More than one-half of the occupational groups listed in the company's internal factory count included women, but 62 percent of the women workers were clustered in just twenty of the 416 job categories. And nearly two-thirds of the job groups were at least 90 percent male.[28]

Management was quick to offer a rationale for the concentration of women in certain kinds of jobs and their exclusion from others, just as it had done in the prewar period. "Womanpower differs from manpower as oil fuel differs from coal," proclaimed the trade journal *Automotive War Production* in October 1943, "and an understanding of the characteristics of the energy involved was needed for obtaining best results." Although it was being applied to a larger and quite different set of jobs, the basic characterization of women's abilities and limitations was familiar. "On certain kinds of operations—the very ones requiring high manipulative skill—women were found to be a whole lot quicker and more efficient than men," reported the article.

> Engineering womanpower means realizing fully that women are not only different from men in such things as lifting power and arm reach—but in many other ways that pertain to their physiological and their social functions. To understand these things does not mean to exclude women *from the jobs for which they are peculiarly adapted,* and where they can help to win this war. It merely means using them as women, and not as men.[29]

Repeatedly highlighted was the lesser physical strength of the average woman worker. "Woman isn't just a 'smaller man,'" the industry's organ pointed out.

> Compensations in production processes must be made to allow for the fact that the average woman is only 35 per cent muscle in comparison to the average man's 41 per cent. Moreover, industrial studies have shown that only 54 per cent of woman's weight is strength, as against man's 87 per cent, and that the hand squeeze of the average woman exerts only 48 pounds of pressure, against man's 81 pounds.[30]

This emphasis on the physical limitations of women workers had a dual character. Not only did it provide a justification for the sexual division of labor, but it also served as the basis for increased mechanization and work simplification. "To adjust women's jobs to such [physical] differences, automotive plants have added more mechanical aids such as conveyors, chain hoists and load lifters." Although production technology was already quite advanced in auto relative to other industries, the pace of change accelerated during the war period. This was due at least as much to the combined impact of the labor shortage and the opportunity to introduce new technology at government expense as to the desire to make jobs easier for female workers, but the latter was particularly stressed by the industry's spokespersons.[31]

There was a contradiction in the management literature on women's war work. It simultaneously emphasized the fact that "women are being trained in skills that were considered exclusively in man's domain" and highlighted their special suitability for "delicate war jobs."[32] The link between these two seemingly conflicting kinds of statements was made primarily through analogies between "women's work" in the home and in the war plants. "Why should men, who from childhood on never so much as sewed on buttons," inquired one manager, "be expected to handle delicate instruments better than women who have plied embroidery needles, knitting needles and darning needles all their lives?"[33]

Glamor was a related theme in the idiom through which women's war work was demarcated as female. As if calculated to assure women—and men—that war work need not involve a loss of femininity, depictions of women's new work roles were constantly overlaid with allusions to their stylish dress and attractive appearance. "A pretty young inspector in blue slacks pushes a gauge—a cylindrical plug with a diamond-pointed push-button on its side—through the shaft's hollow chamber," was a typical rendition.[34] Such statements, like the housework analogies, effectively reconciled woman's position in what had previously been "men's jobs" with traditional images of femininity.

Ultimately, what lay behind the mixed message that war jobs were at once "men's" and "women's" jobs was an unambiguous point: women *could* do "men's work," but they were only expected to do it temporarily. The ideological definition of women's war work explicitly included the provision that they would gracefully withdraw from their "men's jobs" when the war ended and the rightful owners returned.

Women, as everyone knew, were in heavy industry "for the duration." This theme would become much more prominent in the immediate aftermath of the war, but it was a constant undercurrent from the beginning. Women had always been stereotyped as temporary workers in any case, and the sex-typing of jobs prior to the war had helped to ensure that even if they were gainfully employed, women would continue to view themselves as women first, workers second. Now this aspect of the relationship between women and paid work took on new importance, because the reserves of "woman-power" drawn on by the war industries included married women, and even mothers of young children, in unprecedented numbers. A study by the Automotive Council for War Production noted that of twelve thousand women employed during the war by one large automotive firm in Detroit, 40 percent were married with children, and another 28 percent were married without children. Another study by the WPB in 1943 also found that 40 percent of the 150,000 women war workers employed in Detroit were mothers. "With the existing prejudice against employing women over forty, the overwhelming majority of these women workers are young mothers with children under 16."[35]

This was exactly the group of women least likely to have been employed in the prewar years. "In this time of pressure for added labor supply," the U.S. Women's Bureau reported, "the married women for the first time in this country's history exceeded single women in the employed group."[36] The representation of married women in the auto industry was especially large, probably due to the vigorous effort to recruit local female labor in Detroit. Some firms went so far as to make a deliberate effort to recruit the wives and daughters of men whom they had employed prior to the war. The Detroit Vickers aircraft plant, for example, had a policy of hiring "members of men's families who have gone to forces so that when these men come back there will be less of a problem in getting the women out of the jobs to give them back to the men."[37]

This dramatic rise in employment of married women in the war mobilization period raised the longstanding tension between women's commitment to marriage and family and their status as individual members of the paid workforce to a qualitatively different level. Prior to the war, unmarried women, young wives with no children, and self-supporting widowed, divorced, and separated women had made up the bulk of the female labor force. With the inclusion of married women and mothers in this group during wartime, the ideology of occupational sex-typing that linked women's roles in the family and in paid work, far from disintegrating under the impact of the war emergency, was infused with new energy.

The wartime idiom of job segregation by sex combined such familiar prewar themes as women's dexterity and lack of physical strength with a new emphasis on the value of women's multivaried experience doing housework and an unrelenting glamorization of their new work roles. That the construction of a "woman's place" in the wartime auto industry was achieved so quickly and effectively owed much to the power of this elaborate ideology of occupational sex labeling. Although the initiative came from management, neither unions nor rank-and-file workers—of either gender—offered much resistance to the *general* principle of differentiation of jobs into "female" and "male" categories. Nor was the idiom of "woman's place" in the war effort ever frontally challenged. There was a great deal of conflict, however, over the location of the boundaries between the female and male labor markets within the wartime auto industry, and over wage differentials between these newly constituted markets.

Ambiguity and Labor–Management Conflict over "Women's Work"

"Will you please advise me on our particular job as to what is considered as major assembly and what is considered as minor assembly?" inquired the president of UAW Local 249 of Mauro Garcia, an international representative of the union's Ford Department, in July 1943. "We cannot agree down here [Kansas City, Missouri] as to where we should draw the line. . . . Also, what is considered a light drill press and what is considered a heavy drill press?" Garcia in turn wrote to the Ford Motor Company's Rate Department with the same questions, saying, "I do not know what method you use in determining these classifications."[38]

This is one example of a dilemma that pervaded the auto industry, and other war industries as well, in the aftermath of conversion. How to go about classifying the new sets of jobs that had come into existence "for the duration" was ambiguous not only for management but also for workers themselves—both female and male. There was, of course, some resemblance between many of the new war jobs and their predecessors in the peacetime auto industry, but the conversion process, with its attendant technological changes, and the dramatic shifts in the composition of the labor force combined to create tremendous disarray in what had before the war been a relatively stable system of job organization. Although in this example the issue of gender was not explicitly broached, distinctions like "heavy" and "light," or "major" and "minor," more often than not coincided with the sexual division of labor in this period. The problem of ambiguity in job classifications was not limited to the dilemma of where to assign sex labels, but this issue was central to the more general case illustrated here. It is also clear from this example that the UAW viewed these matters as management's province, at least initially.

Not only in classification systems but also in actual job content, "heavy" and "light" tended to differentiate women's and men's jobs. Yet where the line should be drawn between the two was always ambiguous, and its arbitrariness—along with that of the accompanying wage differentials—became completely transparent in this period. "Except that there is a division as to what's heavy and what's light, there's no difference in men [sic] and women's jobs," Irene Young remarked at a UAW Women's Conference in February 1942.

> This is a carry-over from procedure they have had years ago. They just decide what our [sic] women's jobs and what are men's jobs. Men get all the way from ten to 20¢ more on the same job. We have many women doing similar types of work—I have seen a lot of men working alongside women and getting more pay for the same work. It is that sort of thing that has caused a certain amount of the split between women and men.[39]

Moreover, Young pointed out, there were many women in the plants whose jobs were physically taxing, protective legislation notwithstanding. "We have today any number of women who are doing heavy work, who lack safety devices," she said.

> I've worked in any number of plants in Detroit where women worked on high production rates and lifted and were forced to carry packs of stock. They were forced to do this if they were to make a decent day's wage. This kind of hard work they were under for years. . . . The plant where I am from, all of our stock had to be gotten out of box trucks. It necessitated leaning over and pulling and hauling on box trucks.[40]

Eleanor Brenthal, another delegate at the conference, explained that women often accepted such working conditions because they feared that their very right to employment was at stake. "Women are to blame in some cases," she said. "We decided this work was very heavy. When the shop committee came to agree that this work was too hard for us, we denied it. We were afraid that if we couldn't do this particular heavy work . . . we'd be put out on the street. We said we agreed to do that work, but it was too heavy." Clearly women's placement in the industry's labor force was by no means consistently linked to their physique—and Brenthal for one would have been more satisfied if it had been. "Someone should point out to us just what work we are suited for," she concluded.[41]

Young and Brenthal were speaking on the basis of their prewar experience in the auto industry. But it was obvious to everyone at the conference that the war presented a situation where such problems would be compounded. Many delegates expressed uncertainty as to which jobs were suited for women. "How would you determine whether a job was too difficult?" Bernice Cut wanted to know. "If they asked me to work on a lathe machine—would you label that as a man's job?" another delegate inquired. Yet a third woman pointed out, "Some of our sisters are stronger than others—they could handle jobs that would about kill some of our other sisters in one or two days. How will we manage to distinguish this?"[42]

In response to such comments as these, UAW Secretary-Treasurer George Addes articulated the union's policy on this issue at the conference. He said:

> First of all under this program you train the women for a particular job and machine. If said employer should assign women to jobs that are strenuous, too difficult because of the heaviness of the work, or materials that are detrimental, then it becomes a problem for the local union negotiating committee and the management to determine the type of work they should be placed on for the time being. Of course, when the male help is gone and these jobs must be filled it must be decided which jobs women are capable of performing—the jobs must be classified.[43]

Again, it was the union's official policy to leave initial decisions on such matters to management and then to negotiate any necessary adjustments. None of the women at the conference objected to the idea of using some system of job classification arrived at in this way—on the contrary, they hoped it might protect them from assignment to overly strenuous jobs. Evidence that such abuses had occurred in the prewar period only served to reinforce the women's support for a more systematic classification of jobs.

This view, however, soon proved naive. The union historically had developed other principles of job assignment that conflicted with the notion that women should be placed on the lighter jobs. There were numerous charges that management was manipulating the sexual division of labor in the mobilization period in ways calculated to undermine the seniority-based job preference rights of the prewar (that is, predominantly male) labor force. George Romney, testifying before the U.S. Senate hearings on "Manpower Problems in Detroit" in 1945 in his capacity as head of the Automotive Council for War Production, cited such a case:

> On September 13, 1943, company Y tried to discontinue the placement of men on jobs that women would be able to handle. Since that date, the company has tried on numerous occasions to effect this policy but each attempt has been met by positive union resistance. On May 26, 1944, a survey of the company's plants revealed that over 400 jobs then being held by men could be performed by women. Again the management requested, and the union refused, the replacement of these men by women, even though the management offered to guarantee the rates of the men so transferred.... To date the union has not granted such approval.
>
> The types of jobs to be vacated by men and filled by women were varied, but all were considered to be light enough for women to fill. The union's reasons for not granting approvals seemed to be that the men, for the most part, had worked long periods of time to acquire these lighter jobs, and did not feel that they should be removed from them just so the jobs could be filled by women.[44]

There were also numerous grievances of this sort filed by the UAW against General Motors (GM) in late 1943 and early 1944. "When female employees were brought into the plant and assigned to various jobs," according to the umpire's summary of one set of such grievances concerning the Chevrolet Gear and Axle Plant,

> complaints arose from the male employees who were on the so-called "waiting lists" pending possible promotion to higher rated classifications. These male employees complained that the placing of women in the jobs above them in rate prevented the male employees from gaining the promotions to which they would ordinarily have been entitled.[45]

What provoked these union challenges was not a belief that the idiom of sex-typing (on which all parties seemed to agree) had been incorrectly applied. Rather, the central concern was that management was undercutting the seniority principle as a factor in job placement. Thus the evolution of the sexual division of labor in the war years became entangled with political and economic conflicts that involved a range of other issues. The ways in which management, the union, and rank-and-file workers defined and sought to advance their respective interests in relation to the sexual division of labor were determined in the larger context of labor relations and shop floor politics.

What was the role in these struggles of the women workers whose position in the auto industry was directly affected by their outcomes? Many of the key wartime conflicts over the sexual division of labor took place before many women had even entered the auto industry and were essentially fought out between male workers and management. The new women workers, most of whom had no factory or union experience, scarcely had time to get their bearings, much less develop the political resources they needed to participate effectively in struggles over job classification, during the short period when the wartime sexual division of labor was established. Those women who did take an active role at this stage were the minority with prewar experience in the industry and the union, but they were rarely able to mobilize other women into an effective constituency.

For the majority of the new women auto workers, the chance to work in a unionized basic industry, in virtually any job category, meant an enormous improvement in their economic circumstances. For example, 68 percent of the women employed at the Ford Willow Run bomber plant earned at least three times as much in their war jobs than in their prewar jobs, while this was true for fewer than 15 percent of the men.[46] This dramatic improvement in their wages was not the result of any political effort on the part of the women who got war jobs in the auto industry, but it reflected the historical development of the industry as one paying relatively high wages. Under such circumstances, it is not surprising that most women were relatively indifferent to their placement within what was for them a completely new and unfamiliar system of job classification.

As chapter 4 in this volume shows, the situation would be very different in the immediate postwar period, when the gains women had made in the war years were directly threatened. Women would be the protagonists in the battles that ensued over the sexual division of labor in the course of postwar reconversion. But during the mobilization period, the struggles were generally waged between management and the predominantly male prewar labor force, and the interests of women workers lacked any politically effective vehicle for their expression.

The explicit struggles waged by the UAW (generally on behalf of its prewar, predominantly male membership), in opposition to managerial initiatives affecting the sexual division of labor, effectively incorporated the interests of men into the process of defining boundaries between "women's work" and "men's work." In addition, the ways in which management initially constructed the wartime sexual division of labor reflected the differential in political power between the sexes, and the anticipation that any opposition to the specific pattern of job placement by sex would come from men rather than from women. Thus, beneath the idiomatic construction of the sexual division of labor in terms of "heavy" and "light" jobs and so forth, a set of principles can be discerned according to which the allocation of jobs by gender was organized. In the wartime auto industry, women were excluded from positions where they supervised men or directly preceded them in the flow of work. Indeed, this was the case throughout the economy, and not only during the war: job segregation coincides with a *gender hierarchy* within the labor market.[47]

Management, then, controls the day-to-day process of assigning women and men to jobs, but it does so with a view to minimizing friction within the workforce that might potentially disrupt social relations among workers and impede the smooth flow of production. That women were relatively powerless within the auto industry during the mobilization period meant that management had an interest in constructing hierarchies within the internal labor market to coincide with this gender difference in power. It was only when management failed to do so that the political dimension of the sexual division of labor took the form of explicit struggle, as in the instances previously described.

But what are the interests of men vis-à-vis the sexual division of labor in industry? On the one hand, they benefit from sexual inequality in wages and from male monopolies of positions of power within the shops, in that this reinforces their power as a gender, both in the workplace and in the family. On the other hand, as workers, men have an interest in unity with women workers vis-à-vis capital. The ideology of industrial unionism and the principle of nondiscrimination that it includes reflects this latter interest. The political posture of male auto workers and of the UAW in the 1940s in relation to the sexual division of labor vacillated between these two opposing sets of interests and indeed shifted quite markedly as the particular circumstances facing the auto industry were altered by the exigencies of the mobilization for war.

The Variability of Male Interests: From Exclusion to "Equal Pay"

On the eve of U.S. entry into the war, in October 1941, there was a strike at a newly built defense plant owned by the Kelsey-Hayes Wheel Company in Plymouth, Michigan. Although it took place before anyone could fully comprehend the unprecedented scale on which female labor would have to be incorporated into the auto industry, this strike already posed the key issues that would have to be confronted in establishing the wartime sexual division of labor. "The issue, raised in its present form for the first time since defense production got under way," commented *Business Week*, "promises to become one of the most dangerous and troublesome ones Washington will have to meet."[48]

The two-day work stoppage was the culmination of a conflict between the company and the union that had been the subject of negotiations for some weeks prior to the October 28 walkout. On October 15 the UAW had filed a strike notice against Kelsey-Hayes demanding a wage increase and "the removal of all girl employees from machine work which, it [the UAW] contends, is a man's job." Negotiations over these issues were continuing when workers, after discovering that two women had been hired on the night shift, walked out at midnight in protest because the company had agreed to hire no more women pending the outcome of the negotiations. Significantly, "the strikers had no objection to women being hired, ordinarily on other jobs in the plant." But because women in the plant received a maximum of eighty-five cents per hour, while men earned one dollar per hour, "workers feared the company would replace men with women workers in order to reduce labor expenses."[49]

The strike was successful. The union and the company settled upon the following working arrangement:

> It was agreed by the Company that girls would not be used on any Screw Machine Operations, nor would they be used on Profiling operations. The Company would use them, however, on Filing wherever possible, on Inspection (Bench) where they can be utilized, and on small assemblies wherever they can be utilized. Female employees at no time will exceed 25% of the total.[50]

Thus the main object of the walkout was achieved: the exclusion of women from "men's jobs." The union did not object to women being employed at lower wage rates than men's, providing they were confined to "women's jobs," as stipulated in this agreement. Indeed, the maximum pay rates negotiated for the female job classifications established after the strike were eighty-eight cents for women with two years' seniority or more, and eighty-five cents for those with less than two years. Men's maximum rates under the new agreement, in contrast, ranged from $1.01 to $1.13 in the various classifications they occupied.[51]

In this case, the effect of the union's action in clarifying and then enforcing the system of job segregation by sex is obvious, but the circumstances behind the strike make the matter more complex. In the face of a shortage of male labor, management sought to take advantage of the lower wages historically paid to women by breaking down the existing pattern of job segregation by sex. It was this assault on their own wage standards that provoked the strike in defense of the extant sexual division of labor. The immediate point of contention in the dispute, in short, was wage rates, not the pros and cons of job segregation, and yet because it was so tightly intertwined with the wage issue, the sexual division of labor was directly shaped by the outcome.

The demand to exclude women from what had previously been regarded by everyone as male job classifications was male labor's first line of defense in the mobilization period—as it had been in many earlier historical episodes of this type, particularly in the craft union era. After the no-strike pledge, there were wildcat strike actions opposing the hiring of women, and although their illegal status gave them a different character, such strikes expressed the same impulse as the officially sanctioned strikes such as at Kelsey-Hayes.[52] And there were other ways to pursue the objective of excluding women from particular jobs besides going on strike—notably, refusing to break in new workers properly or actively obstructing their work.

The various exclusionary tactics male auto workers employed, while at times successful in the short term (as at Kelsey-Hayes), became less and less viable as the rising demand for labor and the rapid exhaustion of the male labor supply forced a break with the old sexual division of labor. Once it became clear that resistance to the inclusion of women in the industry's male preserves was doomed to failure, a new set of tactics emerged. These were of two basic types. First, the union undertook various efforts to ensure that women's employment in "men's jobs" would be limited to the period of the war emergency—by such means as separate seniority lists, special agreements providing for the integration of women "for the duration" only, or by giving the newly hired workers "trainee" status, with limited seniority rights. Such arrangements would affect the sexual division of labor in the industry in the postwar period but not during the war. It was the second set of tactics that had the greatest impact on the wartime sexual division of labor: the various efforts to protect the wages and working conditions won in the prewar period from managerial attacks that sought to take advantage of the upheaval in the sexual division of labor to erode labor's past gains.

Job classification grievances like those already mentioned, protesting the transfer of women into highly rated "light" jobs that had been previously reserved for high-seniority men, were one important form of this second type of struggle. But once the exclusionary impulse of the transition was abandoned, the demand for "equal pay for equal work" became the central focus of the struggles shaping the wartime sexual division of labor. This demand was not a new one in the 1940s—it had been the UAW's standard defense against the actual or potential replacement of men with women. But before the war, actual incidents of such replacement had been relatively rare. It was only with the disruption of the sexual division of labor in the mobilization period that the union's longstanding fears of large-scale female replacement really materialized. Worse, there was every reason to fear that any wage cuts made while women occupied any given position would affect men after the war, when the job reverted to them. And the wartime wage freeze meant that equal pay demands were one of the few avenues of any kind for the pursuit of substantial wage increases.

Some companies readily agreed to adopt a policy of equal rates for women, without a protracted struggle (though perhaps in anticipation of one if women were paid less on "men's jobs"). Ford's recruitment handbills for the giant Willow Run bomber plant advertised the firm's policy: "Women paid same rates as men," and Ford as well as Studebaker and Vultee signed national contracts with the UAW that had equal pay clauses.[53] Because a great deal of war production was done under "cost-plus" war contracts, under which the wage bill was passed directly on to the government, and because the expectation was that women's war jobs would revert to men after the war in any event, "equal pay for equal work" was a sensible policy for many managements.

But there were also numerous disputes over the question of equal pay in the wartime auto industry. The most important was a WLB case the UAW brought against GM in 1942. The board's decision in this case was widely regarded as a milestone in the development of government policy on the issue, and it firmly established the equal pay principle in WLB practice. "Wages should be paid to female employees on the principle of equal pay for equal work," the September 26, 1942, WLB decision stated. "There should be no discrimination between employees whose production is substantially the same on comparable jobs." The WLB ordered GM and the UAW to include an equal pay clause in their contract as well, and they did so.[54]

Subsequently, however, major disputes developed over the implementation of the equal pay principle as embodied in the contract, and when negotiations failed to resolve the matter, the UAW requested arbitration in June 1943. At three GM plants, hearings were held before WLB arbitrator William Simkin, who issued a decision on July 31, which was later sustained by the National WLB. The issue in this case, typical of equal pay disputes, was whether jobs being done by women were "comparable in quantity and quality" to those jobs done by men. The union contended that the jobs in question were new ones, established in the conversion period, and were comparable to jobs previously performed by men. The company, in contrast, insisted that the jobs were of the sort that had always been "women's jobs," although due to the peculiar circumstances of the conversion period some of them had been performed by men during a brief "experimental" period. In all three plants, there had been local wage agreements that included female job classifications explicitly designated as such prior to the initial WLB ruling in September 1942, and the issue now was whether or not the various war jobs being performed by women fit into those female classifications.

Simkin baldly acknowledged the ambiguity surrounding the assignment of sex labels to the jobs in question in a section of his decision, aptly titled, "WOMAN'S JOB OR MAN'S JOB?" He noted that "exact and certain allocation of a specific operation to a given type is by no means easy."[55] But ultimately he accepted, at least in part, the arguments put forward by GM that detailed why all the jobs in question were appropriate for women and distinct from the "men's jobs" to which the union insisted they were comparable. GM's case was cast entirely in terms of the idiom of job segregation by sex, emphasizing that women did physically "light" work and had fewer responsibilities than men, as well as insisting that most of women's war jobs resembled their prewar jobs. Typical was the statement that "it is not possible to assign to a woman all the duties that over a period of time can be assigned to a male janitor because of her physical capacity. Often the janitors are called on to do heavy work such as moving furniture."[56]

The arbitrator ruled that not only were the existing wage differentials too wide to be justified by the variation in content between "men's" and "women's" jobs, but they also perpetuated what had been sex differentials in wages in a new, if thinly disguised form: as differentials between "light" and "heavy" work. "The only solution consistent with the 'equal pay' clause [in the union contract]," the decision stated, "is to wipe out the sex designation of the . . . jobs and establish . . . rates for various types of work which reflect only the type of work performed."[57] The detailed opinion issued by the Regional WLB drew out the implications of this ruling even more sharply:

> Under the principle of equal pay for equal work, sex differentials are no longer proper. The principle . . . however, is consistent with differences in rates which are based upon differences in job content. It is upon this basis that the arbitrator *substituted* for the classifications "Inspection—Receiving—Male" and "Inspection—Receiving—Female" the classifications of "Inspection—Receiving—Heavy" and "Inspection—Receiving—Light" and fixed the rate for the former at $1.14 per hour and for the latter at $1.04 per hour. Roughly, the new classification "Inspection—Receiving—Heavy" corresponds to the former classification "Inspection—Receiving—Male" and the "Inspection—Receiving—Light" to the former classification "Inspection—Receiving—Female." *Rates of each classification imply whether the employees are men or women.*[58]

Thus was the sexual division of labor recodified "for the duration."

The primary motive behind the UAW's opposition to distinctions between "heavy" and "light," or "men's" and "women's" work, was its concern about the postwar implications of cases like this for men's wages. The union's position, however, amounted to advocating the abolition of the sexual division of labor in the job categories at issue, in sharp contrast to the stance it had adopted in situations like the 1941 Kelsey-Hayes strike. There it had been the company that purported to be interested in eliminating the sexual division of labor (although without altering wage differentials). The shift in the form of what was essentially a struggle—in both instances—between management and the union over the wage bill thus reversed the "interests" of each, in relation to the sexual division of labor. In both instances, as well, male auto workers had an interest in perpetuating women's subordination in industry so as to preserve men's power as a *gender* both inside the wage economy and in the family. The crucial difference was that, in the Kelsey-Hayes case, fear of permanent displacement generated an exclusionary impulse to preserve the male monopoly of the bulk of the jobs. By contrast, during the war, when women's presence in the industry was unavoidable, the same employment insecurity led men to define their interest as residing in the elimination of sex discrimination in wages. These examples illustrate the variability of male workers' interests under different sets of circumstances. The gender interests of male workers, rather than being located outside the wage labor market and inexorably transcending the forces operating within it, could either prevail over or be subsumed by the class interests of male workers in challenging sex discrimination. Struggles between male workers and management could thus work for or against women workers, according to the particular situation.

But if the demand for equal pay challenged wage discrimination by sex, it did so in a very limited way. The very formulation of the issue as "equal pay for equal work" precluded from the outset the general equalization of work between women and men. The struggle was explicitly confined to determining whether women within a relatively small spectrum of occupational categories were indeed engaged in "men's work," or work similar enough to "men's work" to merit similar compensation. Although the ensuing debate revealed the arbitrary aspect of the sex labeling of jobs, at the same time it reinforced the legitimacy of the sexual division of labor as a whole. Indeed, the previously established pattern of job segregation was elevated into the reference point for determining the legitimacy of particular claims for equal pay, at the margin between "women's" and "men's" jobs. A more radical formulation of the issue, as in the struggles being waged today for "equal pay for comparable worth," would not only challenge the pay rates of those jobs at the margin but would also put forth a critique of the entire structure of job segregation and the systematic undervaluing of women's work.[59] Although it certainly benefited those women employed at the margin, the UAW's more narrow formulation of the issue offered no possibility of fundamentally altering the sexual division in paid work.

Conclusion

The changes in the sexual division of labor in the auto industry during the mobilization for World War II illustrate how job segregation by sex can be reproduced in the face of dramatic changes in the economic setting. Although neither the war period nor the auto industry experience is typical in women's labor history, that job segregation was reconstituted under such extreme circumstances—in a high-wage industry and in a situation in which women's incorporation into basic industry's workforce was construed as temporary—suggests the resilience of the ideology of sex-typing and the job segregation it enforces. The auto industry experience during this period reveals the ways in which that ideology, as constrained by a particular set of economic exigencies and political forces, provided the basis for automotive management to construct a new sexual division of labor "for the duration."

In the absence of an organized feminist movement or consciousness, the only vehicle for political struggle over the sexual division of labor in this period was the labor movement. The UAW did challenge managerial initiatives in this area during the mobilization, most important in the form of demands for "equal pay for equal work." Here the conflict was essentially between male auto workers and management, as women were new to both the industry and the union and were not yet a politically effective force. In addition, just securing access to "men's jobs" in the auto plants brought such a dramatic improvement in women workers' status and pay that the sexual division of labor within the wartime industry understandably did not preoccupy them.

During the postwar reconversion, when these gains were threatened and when women had accumulated some political experience, they would mobilize in opposition to management's effort to return to the prewar sexual division of labor in the auto industry. In the mobilization period, however, women and men alike generally accepted as legitimate the overall idiom of the sexual division of labor in that industry. The struggles that took place focused on where the boundaries between women's and men's work should be drawn, without questioning the existence of such boundaries, as the equal pay example well illustrates. Ultimately, then, despite the dramatic upheaval in women's position in the workforce during the war, the ideology of sex-typing retained its power for both workers and management in the auto industry. In the absence of either a more fully developed class consciousness or a feminist movement, there was no political basis for a sustained challenge to job segregation and the ideology of gender division that underpins it. Rather than romanticizing the wartime experience of women workers, then, we need to specify the kind of consciousness, of both class and gender, that might make it possible to dismantle the sexual division of paid labor and to transform work itself.

Notes

This chapter was originally published in *Feminist Studies* 8, no. 2 (1982): 337–72. Reprinted with permission.

1. Karen Skold has documented the wartime pattern of job segregation by sex in the shipbuilding industry in her article "The Job He Left Behind: Women and Shipyard Workers in Portland, Oregon during World War II," in *Women, War, and Revolution,* edited by Carol R. Berkin and Clara M. Lovett (New York: Holmes, Meier, 1980). Evidence is offered below for the automotive industry case. For a more detailed account of the situation in the auto industry as well as documentation of wartime job segregation in the electrical manufacturing industry, see Ruth Milkman, *Gender at Work: The Dynamics of Job Segregation by Sex during World War II* (Urbana: University of Illinois Press, 1987).

2. To be sure, the existence of a clearly defined sexual division of labor is not peculiar to capitalist societies—quite the contrary. Yet the persistence and reproduction of job segregation within capitalist relations of production presents a distinct theoretical problem—and an especially paradoxical one. Indeed, the development of capitalism was expected by friend and foe alike eventually to eliminate such "ascriptive" characteristics as sex (and race) from the process of allocating people to places within the social division of labor and above all in the wage labor market. Both Karl Marx and Max Weber predicted this in the nineteenth century, and the same expectation has been expressed by many twentieth-century Marxist writers and by mainstream social scientists. Today it is impossible to defend the view that capitalism is incompatible with a rigid sexual division of labor outside the home. Such a thesis is instantly falsified by even a superficial glance at the situation in the United States and other advanced capitalist countries. Yet an adequate theoretical account of the continuous reproduction of job segregation by sex in capitalist societies has yet to be developed. The perspective frequently put forward by Marxist-feminist theorists—that male domination exists as a "system," usually called "patriarchy," which is separate from and preceded capitalism, and is theoretically irreducible to it—while a possible starting point for such a theory, by itself, offers no way out. This simply presumes the persistence of gender inequality within capitalism in general, and the capitalist labor market in particular, rather than *explaining why* it persists, which is hardly self-evident.

3. This consideration is highlighted in the literature on "labor market segmentation" developed by Marxist economists. See, for example, Richard Edwards, Michael Reich, and David Gordon, eds., *Labor Market Segmentation* (Lexington, Mass.: Heath, 1975), especially the introduction. However, this literature fails to distinguish between the class interests of capital and the interests of individual capital, missing a critical aspect of the problem altogether.

4. This dynamic has been discussed extensively in Marxist-feminist literature. See especially Veronica Beechey, "Some Notes on Female Wage Labour in Capitalist Production," *Capital and Class* 3 (Autumn 1977): 45–66; and Heidi Hartmann, "Capitalism, Patriarchy, and Job Segregation by Sex" in *Women and the Workplace: The Implications of Occupational Segregation,* edited by Martha Blaxall and Barbara Reagan (Chicago: University of Chicago Press, 1976).

5. This is the main emphasis in Hartmann, "Capitalism, Patriarchy, and Job Segregation." She neglects, however, to consider the potential for class interests prevailing over gender

interests for male workers, as discussed below. Instead, she asserts the supremacy of the interests of "men as men" in maintaining a gender-stratified labor market, and she takes this to be a primary underpinning of job segregation. This is a specific version of the problem discussed more generally in note 2.

6. The war years produced a "family crisis" with many parallels to that of our own time and aroused many of the same concerns among contemporaries. This is discussed indirectly in Karen Anderson, *Wartime Women: Sex Roles, Family Relations and the Status of Women in World War II* (Westport, Conn.: Greenwood, 1981), chap. 3.

7. The transcript of this newsreel was made available to me by the Rosie the Riveter Film Project, Emeryville, California. Additional examples of the wartime idiom are cited below.

8. U.S. Department of Labor, Women's Bureau, *Changes in Women's Employment During the War*, Special Bulletin No. 20 (1944), 15; and U.S. Department of Labor, Bureau of Labor Statistics, *Women in Factories* (1947), 7.

9. U.S. Department of Labor, Women's Bureau, *Women Union Leaders Speak* (1945), mimeo., 32.

10. Statistics on the representation of women in the auto industry for this period are scattered and not entirely consistent. The 1930 census reported that women were 7 percent of all workers employed by the industry, and the 1940 census enumeration produced a figure of 9 percent. U.S. Department of Commerce, Bureau of the Census, *Fifteenth Census of the United States, 1930: Population*, 5: 468; and *Sixteenth Census of the United States, 1940: Population*, 3: 180. William McPherson reported in 1940 that women made up about 5 percent of the wage earners in auto assembly plants, about 10 percent of those in body plants, and about 20 percent of those in parts plants. See his *Labor Relations in the Automobile Industry* (Washington: Brookings Institute, 1940), 8–9.

11. U.S. Department of Labor, Bureau of Labor Statistics, *Wages and Hours of Labor in the Motor Vehicle Industry: 1925*, Bulletin No. 438 (1927), 2–3.

12. Even in the Depression decade, when wage cuts were endemic throughout the economy, the weekly earnings of auto factory workers averaged 24 percent above the average for all manufacturing industry. See Andrew T. Court, *Men, Methods and Machines in Automobile Manufacturing* (Detroit: Auto Manufacturers' Association, 1939), 9. For discussion of Fordism, see Keith Sward, *The Legend of Henry Ford* (New York: Rinehart, 1948); and Martha May, "The Historical Problem of the Family Wage: The Ford Motor Company and the Five Dollar Day," in *Feminist Studies* 8, no. 2 (1982).

13. McPherson, *Labor Relations in the Automobile Industry*, 83.

14. Computed from data in Bureau of Labor Statistics, *Wages and Hours of Labor*, 2–3; and U.S. Department of Labor, Bureau of Labor Statistics, *Wage Structure of the Motor-Vehicle Industry*, Bulletin No. 706 (1942), 23–24. In 1925, 11 percent of the male workers were in the four classifications employing the most women; while in 1940 fewer than 10 percent of the men were in the four largest female job categories. In both years, women were 2.5 percent of the work force in the motor vehicle plants surveyed.

15. Robert W. Dunn, *Labor and Automobiles* (New York: International, 1929), 74; William McPherson, "Automobiles," in *How Collective Bargaining Works*, edited by Harry A. Millis (New York: Twentieth Century Fund, 1942), 576.

16. *Wall Street Journal*, November 22, 1926, cited in Dunn, *Labor and Automobiles*, 74. For evidence that this was generally an exclusively male occupation, see Bureau of Labor Statistics, *Wages and Hours of Labor*.

17. "Annual Averages of Hourly and Weekly Earnings and Average Hours per Week for Male and Female Wage Earners in the Automobile Industry," June 28, 1944, in UAW Research Department Collection, Wayne State University Archives of Labor History and Urban Affairs, Detroit, Michigan (hereafter cited as WSUA), box 10, folder 10–19: "Employment, Detroit, 1941–1947."

18. See U.S. Department of Labor, Bureau of Labor Statistics, "Seniority in the Automobile Industry," by Jonas Silver and Everett Kassalow (1944), mimeo., 25–27.

19. On conversion, see Barton J. Bernstein, "The Automobile Industry and the Coming of the Second World War," *Southwestern Social Science Quarterly* 47 (June 1966): 22–33; and Alan Clive, *State of War: Michigan in World War II* (Ann Arbor: University of Michigan Press, 1979), 18–42.

20. "Women in War Industries," *UAW Research Report* 2 (September 1942), 1.

21. "Meeting for Discussion on Labor Supply and Future Labor Requirements," June 26, 1942, Detroit, Michigan, pp. 30–31 of transcript, in Records of the War Production Board—Record Group 179, National Archives (henceforth RG 179-NA), box 1016, folder: "241.11R Labor-Women-Recruiting Drive"; Edward Cushman interview with the writer, June 25, 1981, Detroit, Michigan.

22. Memorandum from Anthony Luchek to Joseph D. Keenan, July 14, 1943, "Degree of Utilization of Negro Workers . . .," in RG 179-NA, box 1017, folder: "241.3 Labor Negroes"; "Women Seek Factory Jobs," *Detroit News*, October 26, 1942, in UAW Public Relations Department Collection, WSUA, box 14, folder: "Women." Black employment in the Detroit auto industry rose from about 4 percent in the prewar period to 15 percent of the labor force in 1945. See Robert Weaver, *Negro Labor: A National Problem* (New York: Harcourt, Brace, and World, 1946), 285; August Meier and Elliott Rudwick, *Black Detroit and the Rise of the UAW* (New York: Oxford University Press, 1979), 213.

23. On prewar recruitment by auto firms, see Blanche Bernstein, "Hiring Policies in the Automobile Industry," Works Projects Association National Research Project (1937), marked "not for publication," copy in the W. Ellison Chalmers Collection, WSUA, box 1. On wartime migration and the problems associated with it, see Clive, *State of War*, 94–95, 172. The government report cited is an "Outline of Proposed Drive to Recruit Women for War Work in Wayne County Area," attached to memorandum from Ernest Kanzler to John L. Lovett, July 3, 1942, in RG 179-NA, box 1016, folder: "241.11R Labor-Women-Recruiting Drive."

24. U.S. Congress, Senate, *Manpower Problems in Detroit*, Hearings before a Special Committee Investigating the National Defense Program, 79th Cong., 1st Session, March 9–13, 1945, pp. 13534, 13638.

25. Reference to such a survey designed "to determine those operations, which were suitable for female operators" is made on pp. 2–3 of the Summary Brief Submitted by Buick Motor Division, Melrose Park, General Motors Corp., In the Matter of GM-Buick, Melrose Park, Ill., and UAW, June 14, 1943, pp. 2–3, in Walter Reuther Collection, WSUA, box 20, folder: "WLB, GM Women's Rates." A survey of this type was also conducted at Willow

Run; see the section on "Training of Women" in Willow Run Bomber Plant, Record of War Effort, vol. 2, pt. 2, January–December 1942, Ford Motor Company (notebook), p. 30, La Croix Collection, Acc. 435, Ford Archives, box 15.

26. Computed from data in U.S. Department of Labor, Bureau of Labor Statistics, Division of Wage Analysis, Regional Office No. 8-A, Detroit, Michigan, December 3, 1943, Serial No. 8-A-16, "Metalworking Establishments, Detroit, Michigan, Labor Market Area, Straight-Time Average Hourly Earnings, Selected Occupations, July 1943," mimeo. Copy in UAW Research Department Collection, WSUA, box 28, folder: "Wage Rates (Detroit) Bureau of Labor Statistics, 1943–5." Women were 22 percent of the labor force surveyed here. If these data are compared to those in the 1940 Bureau of Labor Statistics survey cited in note 10, the degree of segregation by sex in the auto industry during the war is put into better perspective. In 1940, women were only 2.5 percent of the labor force, and two occupational groups accounted for one-half of the women in the industry. In 1943 five groups accounted for 51 percent of the women, which, given the much greater representation of women in the auto workforce, does not indicate a significant decline in the degree of segregation.

27. Computed by the author from the survey questionnaires (unprocessed) in the UAW War Policy Division-Women's Bureau Collection, WSUA, series I, box 5, folders 5-10, 5-11, and 5-12.

28. Computed by the author from "Ford Motor Company-Rouge Plant, Factory Count, December 14, 1943." This is one of several years' worth of weekly "Factory Counts" in Acc. 732, Ford Archives, box 1.

29. "Engineers of Womanpower," *Automotive War Production* 2 (October 1943): 4–5 (emphasis added). This magazine was published monthly, starting in March 1942, by the Automotive Council for War Production.

30. "Provisions in Plants for Physical Differences Enable Women to Handle Variety of War Jobs," *Automotive War Production* 2 (September 1943): 7.

31. Ibid. Also see "Technological Advances in Automotive Plants Help to Combat Growing Manpower Crisis," *Automotive War Production* 2 (September 1943): 3; and "Automotive Industry Reducing War Costs through Improved Production Techniques," *Automotive War Production* 2 (March 1943): 3.

32. "Women Work for Victory," *Automotive War Production* 1 (November 1942): 4; "Engineers of Womanpower," 4.

33. "Engineers of Womanpower," 4.

34. "Engineers of Womanpower," 4.

35. "New Workers," *Manpower Reports No. 10* (published by the Manpower Division, Automotive Council for War Production), 4; and "Problems of Women War Workers in Detroit," August 20, 1943, p. 2, by Anne Gould of the Office of Labor Production of the War Production Board, in RG 179-NA, box 203, folder: "035.606 Service Trades Division, WPB Functions."

36. Women's Bureau, *Changes in Women's Employment*, 18.

37. "Report of Mrs. Betty Sturges Finan on Cleveland Detroit Trip, February 9–17 (1943) Inclusive," 3–4, in Records of the War Manpower Commission-Record Group 211, National Archives, box 977, series 137, folder: "Consultants-Betty Sturges Finan." See also

the discussion of this in Helen Baker, *Women in War Industries* (Princeton, N.J.: Princeton University Press, 1942), 15.

38. Gene Minshall to Mauro Garcia, July 29, 1943; Mauro Garcia to DeWitt Patterson, August 9, 1943, in UAW Ford Department Collection, WSUA, box 13, folder: "Patterson, DeWitt, Ford Motor (Rouge)."

39. Transcript of February 7, 1942, Women's Conference, Detroit, Michigan, p. 27, in UAW War Policy Division-Victor Reuther Collection, WSUA, box 2, folder: "Conferences."

40. Ibid., 24.

41. Ibid., 26.

42. Ibid., 23.

43. Ibid.

44. *Manpower Problems in Detroit*, Hearings, 13595. See also Example No. 29, pp. 13594–95, for another example of this type of controversy.

45. Umpire Decision No. C-139, November 29, 1943, "Hiring of Women," *Decisions of the Impartial Umpire Under the October 19, 1942 Agreement between General Motors Corporation and the International Union, United Automobile, Aircraft and Agricultural Implement Workers of America-Congress of Industrial Organizations*, vol. 1 (privately published, Detroit: General Motors Corporation and United Automobile Workers), 465–67.

46. "Work and Wage Experience of Willow Run Workers," *Monthly Labor Review* 61 (December 1945): 1086.

47. I have not uncovered evidence of this specific to the auto industry, but the wartime literature on managerial policy toward women war workers generally is replete with insistences that women make "poor supervisors" and the like. See, for example, American Management Association, *Supervision of Women on Production Jobs: A Study of Management's Problems and Practices in Handling Female Personnel*, Special Research Report No. 2 (New York: AMA, 1943). For a general discussion of this issue, see also Joan Acker and Donald R. Van Houten, "Differential Recruitment and Control: The Sex Structuring of Organizations," *Administrative Science Quarterly* 19 (June 1974): 152–63.

48. "Labor 'Dilution,'" *Business Week*, No. 636 (November 8, 1941): 59.

49. "Strike is Threatened at Kelsey Hayes Plant," *Detroit News*, October 28, 1941; "Workers Reject Plea for Truce," *Detroit News*, October 29, 1941, both in Joe Brown Collection, WSUA, Scrapbook No. 21, p. 85.

50. "Clarification of Female Work," November 5, 1941, enclosed in letter from Caroline Manning, Industrial Supervisor with the U.S. Department of Labor, Women's Bureau to J. H. Wishart, Research Director, UAW-CIO, November 17, 1941, in UAW War Policy Division-Victor Reuther Collection, WSUA, box 11, folder: "U.S. Dept. of Labor."

51. Kelsey Hayes-Plymouth Plant, Productive Rates," November 5, 1941, UAW Research Department Collection, WSUA, box 9, folder: "Dept. of Labor, U.S., 1940–2."

52. See Nelson Lichtenstein, *Labor's War at Home: The CIO in World War II* (New York: Cambridge University Press, 1982).

53. "Sample handbill announcing arrival of company employment representatives to interview recruits for Willow Run," in *Willow Run Bomber Plant: Record of War Effort* 2, notebook 2, p. 8, La Croix Collection, Ace. 435, Ford Archives, box 15; "History of the Support of the

Equal Pay Principle by Official Federal, State, and International Action, and by Unions and Management," Exhibit A submitted by Frieda Miller of the Women's Bureau, in U.S. Congress, Senate, *Equal Pay for Equal Work for Women*, Hearings on S. 1178, Senate Subcommittee of a Committee of Education and Labor, 79th Congress, 1st Session, October 29, 30, and 31, 1945, p. 34.

54. Bureau of National Affairs, *War Labor Reports* 3, pp. 355–56. For discussion and analysis of this and other equal pay decisions, see National War Labor Board, *The Termination Report: Industrial Disputes and Wage Stabilization in Wartime*, January 12, 1942–December 31, 1945, pp. 290–97; Ella J. Polinsky, *National War Labor Board Policy on Equal Pay for Equal Work for Women*, National War Labor Board, Program Appraisal and Research Division, Research and Statistics Report No. 32 (Washington, D.C., 1945).

55. "Arbitrator's Decision-Women's Rates at Buick Division-Melrose Park, Ill.; Buick Division-Flint, Mich.; Chevrolet Division-Bay City, Mich.," In the Matter of General Motors Corporation and United Automobile, Aircraft and Agricultural Implement Workers of America-C.I.O., Case No. 125, July 31, 1943, pp. 5–6, in UAW Research Department Collection, WSUA, box 32, folder: "Women-Statistics and NWLB Cases 1943–5."

56. "Summary Brief Submitted by Buick Motor Division, Melrose Park, General Motors Corporation," In the Matter of General Motors Corporation, Buick Motor Division, Melrose Park, Ill., and International Union, United Automobile, Aircraft and Agricultural Implement Workers of America, C.I.O., June 14, 1943, pp. 7, 8, and 12, in Walter Reuther Collection, WSUA, box 20, folder: "WLB, GM Women's Rates," and "Summary Brief Submitted by Buick Motor Division, Flint, Michigan, General Motors Corporation," In the Matter of General Motors Corporation, Buick Motor Division, Flint, Mich., and International Union, United Automobile, Aircraft and Agricultural Implement Workers of America, C.I.O., June 17, 1943, pp. 11, 14, in Walter Reuther Collection, WSUA, box 47, folder: "WLB, GM Women's Rates." These five examples are only a small selection from the many such contained in the two briefs.

57. "Arbitrator's Decision-Women's Rates," 6.

58. "Opinion Explaining Directive Order," NWLB Region XI, Case 125, stamped October 9, 1943, in Walter Reuther Collection, WSUA, box 47, folder: "WLB-GM Women's Rates" (emphasis added).

59. This more radical formulation of the equal pay issue did emerge in the 1940s, but not in the auto industry. The United Electrical Workers Union did bring a case to the War Labor Board against General Electric and Westinghouse in 1945, which foreshadowed the "comparable worth" strategy being pursued by feminists in the labor movement today. The case may be found in *War Labor Reports* 28, pp. 666–92. For discussion, see Milkman, *Gender at Work*, 77–83.

Chapter 3

Organizing the Sexual Division of Labor

Historical Perspectives on "Women's Work"
and the American Labor Movement

This chapter examines the changing relationship of women workers to labor unions in two formative periods of U.S. history. The first period is the late nineteenth and early twentieth centuries, when the American Federation of Labor (AFL) dominated the labor movement; the second is the period from 1935 to 1955, when the Congress of Industrial Organizations (CIO) existed as an independent entity (it merged with the AFL in 1955) and when unions experienced their most rapid growth. In both periods the labor movement showed little interest in recruiting women into its ranks. As a result, few women enjoyed the benefits associated with union organization—except during World War II, when women were employed on a massive scale in the very industries that the CIO had organized in the 1930s, which had been male-dominated at the time. The chapter's central argument is that in both periods trade unions played a critical role in the formation of the sexual division of labor. In the first period, many AFL unions excluded women workers from their ranks and thus barred them from the workforce of the trades they represented. The CIO unions were not exclusionary in this way, but in the period immediately following World War II they failed to protect women war workers in basic industry who wanted to keep their jobs.

As the American labor movement took shape in the course of the nineteenth century, there was considerable struggle over how best to relate to women workers. Some unionists argued that women should be organized together with men to prevent them from undercutting established wage races, while others maintained that the same end could best be achieved through excluding women from unions entirely. The resolution of this question in an exclusionary direction with the ascendancy of the craft-unionist American Federation of Labor (AFL) in the late nineteenth century had critical implications for both the labor movement and the structure of sexual segregation within the labor market.

The success of AFL unions in excluding women, as well as people of color, from craft occupations contributed to the consolidation of the sexual division of paid work. To be sure, there had been a sexual division of labor throughout American history. But the period of AFL hegemony was one of enormous economic expansion and major occupational shifts. With the development of monopoly capitalism, many skilled crafts were broken down into unskilled and semi-skilled jobs, and at the same time the information and distribution needs of the new large corporations led to rapid expansion of the "white collar" clerical and sales sectors. Why were workers of all races and sexes not distributed more or less evenly through the occupational structure as the demand for labor grew? This was in fact what many nineteenth-century commentators, Marx among them, expected—and it was something the craft unions feared and sought to prevent.

Thus it is not sufficient to point to the fact that women are concentrated in occupations that have historically been peripheral to the main thrust of union organizing in order to explain their low level of representation in labor unions for most of U.S. history. To do so is to take as given precisely what has to be explained. Indeed, the history of women's relationship to unions suggests that the line of causality may run in the opposite direction: that the exclusion of women from unions is an important part of the explanation for their concentration in unorganized sectors of the economy.

The AFL's role in shaping patterns of occupational segregation by sex in the late nineteenth and early twentieth centuries stemmed partly from its weakness in the face of an employers' open-shop offensive and chronically high levels of unemployment. Nevertheless, exclusionary union policies significantly affected the organization of the sexual division of labor, and established what would prove to be a hardy tradition within the labor movement of collusion in the perpetuation of sexual inequality in the labor market.

A second crucial period saw the occupational structure and the distribution of women through it change dramatically. In the early 1940s the labor shortages associated with economic mobilization for World War II opened up large numbers of "men's jobs" in heavy industry to women. Significantly, this took place immediately *after* a shift within the labor movement away from the craft organizations of the AFL with the rise of the rival unions of the CIO. While exclusionism was built into the logic of craft unionism, the opposite was true of the new industrial unionism of this period—at least in theory. Indeed, the CIO's challenge to the existing boundaries of trade union organization in the late 1930s immediately reopened the question of the appropriate stance of unions toward women workers, which the triumph of the AFL half a century before had seemingly laid to rest.

Although large numbers of women moved into heavily unionized basic industries during World War II and the number of women union members increased dramatically, the prewar status quo was quickly re-established with the conclusion of hostilities abroad. Women were rapidly pushed back into the ghettoes of clerical and service work. And the labor movement in the demobilization period was instrumental in reconstructing the nearly impermeable barriers between the male and female labor markets that AFL exclusionism had helped to establish in an earlier era.

The massive increases in female labor force participation in the postwar decades greatly exceeded those in the AFL period. While the proportion of adult women in the paid labor force had grown from 18 percent in 1890 to 26 percent in 1940, it skyrocketed to 35 percent in 1955 and continued to rise for the rest of the twentieth century.[1] It was also during and after World War II that older and married women were drawn into paid employment in large numbers for the first time. Yet in those years the majority of jobs enjoying union representation remained male monopolies, even as women poured into the rapidly expanding clerical and service sectors, which remained largely unorganized and poorly paid.

That organizational failure stems from policies established during World War II and the demobilization period, when the labor movement gained a stronger position than it had ever enjoyed before, with more than 80 percent of the workforce in the basic manufacturing industries in its ranks. The war period offered an unprecedented opportunity to incorporate large numbers of women workers into the unions on a permanent basis and to break down job segregation by sex. That the labor movement lost that opportunity has been costly both to women workers and to the unions themselves.

Theories of Occupational Segregation by Sex

The role of unions in the formation of labor-market boundaries between "women's work" and "men's work" is not seriously considered in either of the two major sets of explanations for the sex-typing of occupations: those put forth within Marxist-feminist theory, on the one hand, and those developed as part of "labor market segmentation" theory, on the other. Both these literatures focus on the functions and consequences of occupational segregation by sex for the capitalist economy and generally neglect to explore the process by which it was originally established and the ways in which it is maintained. As a result, the historical importance of the differential access of men and women workers to the political and economic power union membership carries with it has generally been overlooked.[2]

Marxist-feminist analyses of sex-typing point to the ways in which it ensures that women stay in their "place" as unpaid family workers, even if they also work for pay outside the home. Predicated on the importance of housework in capitalist reproduction, this approach explains sex segregation in the paid labor force as deriving indirectly from the organization of domestic life. The notion is that the work women do outside the home is modeled after their work inside it: in industries like food and clothing, women produce goods they formerly manufactured at home; in "white collar" jobs, women, as secretaries, teachers, waitresses, and nurses, perform the wife-and-mother-like tasks of schedule management, socializing children, cleaning up, caring for the ill, and managing emotional stress. Moreover, as proponents of this view point out, whether or not there is a clear parallel to domestic labor in the content of their paid work, women workers are still viewed not as "workers" but as "women"—women who happen to be working. Occupational sex-typing is the institutionalized expression of this ideology and helps to blunt and distort women's consciousness of themselves as workers while keeping them in low-paying jobs and thus still dependent on men and on families.[3]

In contrast, "labor market segmentation" theorists claim that sex-typing, as well as occupational segregation along racial lines, is functional under capitalism because it makes for disunity within an otherwise increasingly homogeneous labor force. While careful to note that both sexual and racial oppression antedate the development of capitalism, these analysts ultimately explain the persistence of labor-market segregation along the lines of these pre-existing divisions in terms of the need of capital for control over labor.

There is a general correspondence, in this view, between the racial and sexual cleavages in the labor market and the cleavage between stable, high-paying "primary" jobs (in oligopolistic firms) and "secondary" jobs with high turnover and low wages (in the competitive sectors of the economy). The "primary" sector is further divided into two segments: the predominantly white and male "independent primary" group of professional, managerial, and technical jobs, and the semi-skilled (blue and white collar) "subordinate primary" segment, which has a racially and sexually mixed workforce. This theoretical framework does not attempt to explain occupational segregation by sex as a distinct phenomenon, but sees it as one of several cleavages that divide the working class in advanced capitalist society.[4]

Both analyses offer important insights into sex-typing, but neither adequately explains the location of women workers in particular places in the occupational structure. Of the two, the Marxist-feminist perspective is better able to account for the specificity of women's situation. For although it accurately describes both sex-typing and race-typing, labor-market segmentation theory conceives of women and racial minorities as an undifferentiated group, together composing the "secondary" (and part of the "subordinate primary") labor market. This approach fails to account for the fact that particular jobs within the "secondary" labor market are exclusively assigned to white women, and others to black men. And the allocation of positions within the sexually and racially mixed "subordinate primary" sector—for example, the fact that women (increasingly a multiracial group of women) occupy the vast majority of clerical positions in oligopolistic firms—is left completely mysterious.

By focusing on the critical interconnection between the family and women's paid work, the Marxist-feminist discussion has been able to go much further, and yet ultimately it also fails to solve the problem. For the link between women's domestic labor and their wage labor, to which Marxist-feminists attribute the allocation of women to specific jobs, is actually an ideological link. There is nothing intrinsically "feminine" about the jobs women do as wage-workers—even if one were to assume (erroneously) that women's domestic labor is in some sense "feminine." There is an arbitrariness in occupational sex-typing: "A job that is clearly and exclusively women's work in one factory, town, or region may be just as clearly and exclusively men's work in another factory, town, or region."[5]

Even more compelling evidence that the sex-labeling of jobs is a fundamentally ideological phenomenon is supplied by the experience of women workers during World War II, when industrial jobs that had previously been performed exclusively by men were suddenly endowed with femininity and glamour "for the duration" of the war. The analogy between domestic labor and whatever women happen to be doing for pay proved sufficiently flexible to be extended to what had previously been the most "masculine" of jobs. An outdoor billboard encouraging women to take war jobs in 1943, for example, read:

> "What Job is mine on the Victory Line?"
> If you've sewed on buttons, or made buttonholes, on a machine, you can learn to do spot welding on airplane parts.
> If you've used an electric mixer in your kitchen, you can learn to run a drill press.
> If you've followed recipes exactly in making cakes, you can learn to load shell.[6]

Thus the process of sex-typing centers on the construction of analogies between the tasks women's paid jobs involve and domestic labor. The latter includes such an endless variety of tasks that this is never very difficult. That sex-typing is "merely" ideology, however, does not mean that it is unimportant. On the contrary, as Marxist-feminist writers have repeatedly emphasized, sex-typing as ideology plays a critical role in shaping women's consciousness and in ensuring that women identify primarily as mothers, wives, daughters, or lovers—whether or not they work for pay. But while this may tell us something about why women stay in families, like "labor market segmentation" theory it ultimately cannot explain why some jobs are sex-typed "female" and others "male"—much less why sex-typing varies regionally and over time.

Theories of labor market segmentation do suggest why certain jobs are allocated to certain kinds of workers—if not to women specifically, at least to the larger group of workers in the "secondary" labor market. It is capital (and its representatives) that acts, in response to labor militancy, to "divide and conquer the work force." Employers did this in the late nineteenth century, when labor was becoming "increasingly homogeneous and proletarian in character," by constructing internal labor markets that, among other things, limited promotion opportunities to white males. Furthermore, "employers quite consciously exploited race, ethnic, and sex antagonisms in order to undercut unionism and to break strikes."[7]

In this view, there is nothing problematic about employers' interest in a divided labor force or about workers' interest in a unified one. The assumption that capital is the primary beneficiary of "divisions" in the labor force is embedded in the language that these writers use—"segmentation," "divisions in the working class," and other terms suggesting a neutral separation between groups of workers that is imposed from above. Yet, while workers *as a class* do have an interest in building united opposition to capital, *individual* workers who derive immediate benefits from the segmentation of the labor market may want to protect their relative privilege. Indeed, even if the links between labor market position and skin color or gender are entirely ideological, racial and sexual "divisions" in the labor market may be jealously guarded by the workers who benefit from them once they are established. Moreover, to the extent that sex and race are linked to differentials in social position outside the capitalist labor market prior to its ascendancy, the more privileged groups may be instrumental in establishing the old differentials in the new context.

Similarly, employers have contradictory interests. On the one hand, *as a class* they benefit from a divided labor force. Different fractions of capital can be played off against one another to weaken the working class as a whole, and this task is made easier if the divisions coincide with pre-existing sexual and racial antagonisms. Employers also benefit as a class from a divided labor force in that they are provided with a supply of "cheap" labor. On the other hand, rigid sex- and race-typing of jobs may create difficulties for individual employers in obtaining the labor supplies they require at minimal costs, precisely because wage differentials are a key underpinning of occupational segregation.

What becomes critical, then, is how the contradictory interests of workers and employers, as individuals and as classes, are expressed and organized at particular historical junctures, as well as the interaction between them. To explain occupational segregation by race and sex, it is necessary to examine the structure of these interests—both in labor-management struggles in particular firms and industries, and in the broader state arena. Labor market segmentation theories, instead, assume precisely what needs to be explained.

The character of union organization, particularly the orientation toward the various "segments" of the labor force, thus requires serious attention. Heidi Hartmann has begun to examine this aspect of the problem and indeed has brought it to the center of her analysis of occupational segregation by sex. Although writing from a Marxist-feminist perspective, she abandons the emphasis on the ideological aspect of sex-typing, which is the main concern of much of the earlier Marxist-feminist literature. She is also writing explicitly in reaction to labor market segmentation theory and takes particularly strong exception to that theory's assumption that all workers have an interest in working-class unity. On the contrary, Hartmann argues, male workers have a material interest in perpetuating job segregation by sex because it enforces lower wages for women's employment and thus keeps them dependent on men by encouraging marriage. Thus, she suggests, the interests of male workers do not oppose but rather reinforce the interests of capital in a sexually segmented labor force. The error of the segmentation theorists, for Hartmann, is that they "ignore the role of men—ordinary men, men as men, men as workers—in maintaining women's inferiority in the labor market."[8]

She goes on to suggest that patriarchal social relations, and especially the structure of the family, not only give men particular interests "as men" but also endow them with greater organizational resources than women with which to achieve those interests.[9] As evidence, she points to the historical record of efforts by male organizations like guilds, professional organizations, and especially unions, to limit women's labor market opportunities.

Hartmann's attention to the role of unions and her critique of labor market segmentation theory is a major advance over most previous writings on this subject. However, her argument in some ways reproduces the problems of the segmentation theories she criticizes. She argues that male workers have given, immutable interests and does not examine the ambivalent character of those interests or the process by which they come into being. Hartmann does bolster her contention that male workers inevitably have interests opposed to those of female workers by pointing to the divergent positions of men and women in the family—certainly a logical place to search for what is specific to the situation of women workers.

Yet even when gender inequality in the family is taken into account, it is by no means self-evident that it is in the interest of "men as men, men as workers" to enforce women's dependence on them by thwarting their labor market opportunities, nor is it obvious that this is *not* in the interest of women. Indeed, Jane Humphries persuasively argues precisely the opposite—that working-class women and men, at least in the early stages of capitalist development, shared an interest in the struggle for a "family wage" that would permit one wage worker to support his (!) family.[10] It is not necessary to agree with Humphries to recognize that the point is a debatable one: that the interests of male workers are much more fluid and complex, and the relationship between their family position and their interests as workers more ambiguous, than Hartmann's argument would suggest.

The fact that at various times and places labor organizations dominated by men have taken the position that women ought to have the same labor market opportunities as men, and made some efforts to realize that goal, also raises questions about Hartmann's analysis. She is correct in identifying the dominant historical pattern as one of labor union hostility to women workers and in pointing to the significance of this for patterns of job segregation by sex. But it would be more fruitful to examine the conditions under which this is (or is not) the case than to invoke the interests of "men as men" as an explanation of the apparently dominant pattern while asserting the latter's inevitability. Different men may have different interests under different conditions—and moreover, women might behave quite similarly to men on those occasions, however rare, when they find themselves in similar structural positions.

To explain how the interests of men are shaped under varying sets of conditions, Hartmann would have to return to the question of ideology. While sex segregation cannot be adequately explained in terms of analogies between domestic labor and the character of women's paid work, the broader ideology of "woman's place" in which such analogies are rooted is central to understanding the role of men in the kinds of struggles Hartmann discusses. That broader ideology is the terrain on which the interests of "men as men" are formed, under certain conditions—while a very different ideology, and a different set of conditions would cause the shared class interests of men and women to prevail. Hartmann ultimately substitutes a more crudely economistic explanation for the earlier Marxist-feminist account and thereby misses the significance of ideology and the ideological struggle entirely.

In short, instead of examining the forces contributing to (and those working against) the reproduction of "patriarchy" in the course of the development of capitalism, Hartmann assumes that the interest men have in preserving it is sufficient to ensure its survival. This leads her to miss the contingent aspect of the role of unions in shaping occupational segregation by sex and the consequent need to account for it in terms that go beyond blanket references to the interests of "men as men" or to "patriarchy."

What follows attempts to develop such an account of the role of unions in shaping the sexual division of labor in the United States from the late nineteenth century to the post–World War II period. This is only one component of the establishment and reproduction of occupational segregation by sex. A fuller account

would also have to consider the effect of women's family position on their relationship to the paid labor market, as well as the role of capital, itself complex and
often fractionalized, in shaping the sexual division of paid labor. But analyzing the
forces shaping the relationship of women to the labor movement is an essential
part of the larger project of theorizing job segregation by sex—and one that so
far has received relatively little attention.[11]

The Working-Class Family, Deskilling, and Women's Employment

There was a clear (and unequal) sexual division of labor within the American
economy from the earliest period. But this did not mean that its reconstitution
inside the labor market that emerged with capitalist development was inevitable.
On the contrary, in completely reorganizing social production, capitalist industrialization posed a direct challenge to the traditional sexual division of labor.[12] What
should constitute "women's work," and indeed, whether or not such a category
should continue to exist in the new economic structure, became the object of
struggle, both between men and women and between workers and employers.

The first factory workers in the United States were women and children, mostly
farmers' daughters who were recruited to work in the New England cotton mills.
But as capitalist development drew more and more types of production out of the
home and into the workshop or factory, young women were soon outnumbered
in the ranks of industrial wage workers by adult men. Married women avoided
joining their husbands in the ranks of wage laborers and generally did so only if
their husbands' earnings were completely inadequate for family support.[13] Such
circumstances were undesirable from the point of view of wives as well as husbands, and indeed the introduction of married women workers into the wage
labor force was perceived by both men and women as a capitalist assault on the
working-class family.

The desire to defend the family pattern in which the male was the sole
"breadwinner"—a desire that bourgeois ideology about the family bolstered—
became a key source of working-class resistance to the employment of married
women. In 1835, for example, the Philadelphia Trades Union warned against the
growth in female employment:

> Oppose this with all your mind and with all your strength, for it will prove our
> ruin. We must strive to obtain sufficient remuneration for our labor to keep
> the wives and daughters and sisters of our people at home. . . . Avoid by every
> means the bringing of female labor into competition with ours. That cormo-
> rant capital will have every man, woman, and child to toil; but let us exert our
> faculties to oppose its designs.[14]

Here the main enemy is identified not as women but capital, yet the effective aim is to exclude women not only from the unions but also from the labor force itself.

Opposition to female employment was also rooted in another factor. The introduction of women into a trade often coincided with the introduction of machinery and the elimination of traditional skills. Unskilled, underpaid women, like people of color, were often used as strikebreakers when skilled workers protested the introduction of machinery. This practice created bitter resentment toward women workers (and blacks), despite the fact that white men probably were hired as strikebreakers in the majority of cases.[15] More generally, craftsmen perceived the deterioration in their standard of living and working conditions as a direct result of the influx of cheap, unskilled labor into industry.[16]

Efforts to exclude women were most vigorous in trades they were just beginning to enter and in which men had predominated for some time. In industries where it was clear that women had become a permanent part of the labor force, so that excluding them was a hopeless endeavor, male unionists often encouraged the organization of women in order to prevent a general lowering of wages. Yet even in such instances, men who supported the unionization of women workers, like those who sought to exclude them, held a strong conviction that the presence of women in the wage labor force was undesirable. Thus the committee on female labor in the National Trades Union, which recommended in 1836 that craft unions include women in their organizations to prevent "ruinous competition," explained its position as follows: "We must first curb the excess before we destroy the evil."[17] This orientation was carried to its logical extreme by the president of the Philadelphia Trades Assembly, William English, who sympathetically suggested to the women workers who were members of that organization, in 1835:

> You can not recede from labor all at once, for then you would have no means of subsistence; but you can form . . . a female trades' union, and a formidable one it would be, too. When that is done you can raise the wages of your several productions, and thus live on less labor . . . and the less you do the more there will be for the men to do, and the better they will be paid for doing it, and, *ultimately, you will be what you ought to be, free from the performance of that kind of labor which was designed for man alone to perform.*[18]

This view was not peculiar to male trade unionists but rather reflected the ideology about "woman's place" that was generally accepted (by both men and women) at this time. In contrast to the colonial period, when women, married or single, were expected to work and idleness was considered sinful, by the mid-nineteenth century idleness had become the hallmark of "true womanhood."[19]

This ideology shaped the substantial working-class opposition to the use of women's labor in factories, an opposition that emerged from the struggle for a "family wage" on the one hand, and for the protection of traditional craft skills on the other, against the tendencies within capitalist development to erode both. Resistance to the employment of married women was especially strong and was relatively successful. Throughout the nineteenth century the vast majority of women in the labor force were single, widowed, or divorced, and as late as 1900, only 14 percent of those females ten years old or older who were gainfully employed were married. However, the broader opposition to female employment, like the attempts to prevent the introduction of machinery, was generally ineffective, partly because of the existence of chronic labor shortages in the course of the economic expansion during and after the Civil War. Throughout the second half of the century, women were substantially represented among manufacturing workers, accounting for about 20 percent of the workforce.[20]

The logic of opposition to the introduction of women into industry began to falter as the hope of completely excluding them from the wage labor force receded. Consequently, there was much debate within the late-nineteenth-century labor movement over the question of female labor. This was one aspect of the broader issue of the appropriate relationship between the trade unions and the growing number of unskilled workers. Two distinct tendencies within the labor movement advocated directly opposing policies in this area. The local and national trade unions were organized on a craft basis and limited membership to skilled workers, which meant that all but a few women were automatically excluded. These unions, which later coalesced into the AFL, coexisted with a quite different kind of labor organization that was committed to organizing unskilled as well as skilled workers and that actively encouraged the unionization of women. This was the orientation of the National Labor Union and, later, of the Knights of Labor.

The philosophy of unionism that informed the exclusionary outlook of the first tendency was predicated on a notion of "skill" as the basis of trade union membership. Given employers' dependence on the extensive knowledge of the labor process that union members possessed, this approach sought to restrict access to that knowledge as much as possible in order to enforce their wage scales. They did so primarily by means of union-controlled apprenticeship systems, and by collective resistance to employers' efforts to hire untrained or partially trained workers at rates below the union scale.

To the extent that women became "rats" (workers who accepted pay rates below union scale), skilled workers' antagonism was inherent in the logic of craft unionism. At the same time, the exclusion of women from the union apprenticeship system, which typically limited entry to the sons of craftsmen, meant that women were unable to find employment in the organized trades except as partially trained workers who could not obtain union rates.

The craft unions, moreover, saw organizing women as a hopeless endeavor. Because female workers were unskilled and, in most cases, single women who expected to leave the paid workforce when they married, they could not be expected to develop any real commitment to work or to trade union organization. Yet women workers themselves recognized that the only means by which they could improve their bargaining position in the labor market was to organize themselves into unions. They were excluded from most of the men's unions but did build independent women's unions and separate locals affiliated with men's unions. Women organized successfully in industrial fields in which they were numerous—textiles, the needle trades, laundries, and shoemaking—and also in some trades in which they were a small minority, most importantly among cigar making and printing.[21]

However, these efforts were ignored by the craft unions, which persisted in building their strategy on control over skill even as machinery was being introduced into industry after industry and the proportion of the labor force made up of unskilled workers was growing. These developments made skill an increasingly precarious basis for organization. This would not prove decisive for some time, however, and meanwhile, if craft unions were increasingly inadequate for representing the interests of the working class as a whole, they often did succeed in establishing high wage scales for their members and retained substantial strength in many industries.

The second tendency within the labor movement during this period, however, discarded skill as a criterion for membership and strongly encouraged the unionization of women. The National Labor Union (NLU) and the Knights of Labor were committed to building broad organizations of all working people, explicitly including both women and black workers. This organizational goal stemmed from a broader ideological commitment rooted in the reform tradition of American labor. Both the NLU and the Knights sought to establish a classless "cooperative commonwealth" in which all persons would be producers, combining both worker and employer roles into one. This project was to be realized through the organization of a political party based in the laboring class, which was defined to include everyone involved in productive activity, be they petty entrepreneurs, wage workers, or housewives. Only bankers, lawyers, gamblers, and other such nonproducers were excluded from this definition.[22]

The NLU was primarily a political organization. Although it supported independent efforts to organize women workers, it made no direct contribution to that process. But the "Noble and Holy Order of the Knights of Labor" carried on the commitment to the organization of the unskilled with far greater practical effect. Founded in 1869 as a tiny secret society of craft workers, it grew very rapidly after 1881, when it became a public organization, and by the mid-1880s it was the largest labor organization in the nation, with between six hundred thousand and one million members at its peak in 1886.

In 1881, the same year it became a public organization, the Knights of Labor began to admit women to membership, and it systematically recruited them from that point on. By 1886 women made up about 8 percent or 9 percent of the membership. They were organized into 192 separate women's locals, about half of which were "mixed" (including workers from various trades) and the rest composed of women working in one industry. Ultimately, more women became members of the Knights than had ever been part of any one labor organization. While only a small proportion of the women in the nation's paid workforce were members, and few women were in official leadership positions, the Knights' organizing strategy was conducive to the organization of women workers because of its emphasis on unity between skilled and unskilled workers.[23]

However, craft unions had always been a major component of the Knights, and its attempts to foster labor solidarity typically took the form of building unity between the local trade assemblies of skilled workers and the "mixed" assemblies, not of merging them into one body. As industrial capitalism became more solidly rooted and hopes for the construction of the cooperative commonwealth withered, the Knights' rank-and-file membership became increasingly concerned with their immediate practical problems as workers. The failure of the organization's leadership to respond to this shift, combined with the energetic employers' offensive in the aftermath of the Haymarket affair, led to the rapid decline of the organization. Between 1886 and 1888, the Knights lost a full two-thirds of its membership. Many of the trade assemblies within the organization left for the AFL after its founding in 1886, and the new federation quickly rose to occupy a dominant position in the labor movement.

In contrast to the Knights, with their interest in political action and social change, the AFL was dominated by elements advocating disengagement from the political arena and a more concentrated pursuit of the immediate economic interests of its members—what came to be called "pure and simple unionism." Moreover, the federation was dominated from the outset by trade unions of skilled workers, which had long practiced exclusionary policies toward women. These became increasingly characteristic of the AFL as time passed, and the promise that the Knights of Labor had held forth of organizing women workers receded as it disintegrated and the AFL's strength grew.

The AFL and Women Workers

The American Federation of Labor dominated the American labor movement during a critical period in the shaping of women's relationship to the economy. Between 1890 and 1930 the number of employed women nearly tripled, and the proportion of women in the labor force grew from 18 percent to 24 percent.[24]

Eighty-five percent of the total rise in female labor force participation in this period is accounted for by the growth of female employment in "white collar" occupations, and by 1930 more than half of all women wage-earners were in clerical, sales, or service jobs.[25] Previously, both clerical and sales work had characteristically been done by men, and only now were such jobs typed as "women's work." Women became so heavily concentrated in these areas of the labor market, rather than being more evenly distributed through it, partly because employment in these fields was expanding so rapidly in response to the needs of the new giant corporations for recordkeeping and distribution.

After the demise of the Knights of Labor in the late 1880s, the labor movement at first grew slowly, mainly because of the economic depression of the 1890s. Then, however, membership picked up quite dramatically, particularly in unions affiliated with the AFL. Between 1897 and 1904, the number of trade union members more than quadrupled, and between 1900 and 1904 the AFL alone tripled in size. After that, however, there was little progress, and as a result of an open-shop drive by employers the unions actually lost members. Unionization levels soared upward again in the 1910s, however, especially during the war, and reached a peak of over five million, 17.5 percent of the labor force, in 1920. After the war, the labor movement again suffered a serious decline, losing about half of its membership between 1920 and 1933.[26]

The AFL consistently included 75 percent to 80 percent of all union members within its ranks in the first three decades of the twentieth century.[27] And no organization had as great an influence on the sexual division of labor. In the early years of the federation's existence, official AFL statements consistently encouraged the trade unions affiliated with it to organize women workers, and in 1890 a committee on women's work was appointed to facilitate this process.[28] Women could become members of the federation either by joining the unions already affiliated with it or by organizing their own separate unions. Any group of seven or more workers could form a local union and obtain a charter from the AFL as a Federal Labor Union. Such locals were affiliated directly to the federation and thereby offered a means of organizing to unskilled workers and others who were unable to join any of the established national unions. Since most women workers were unskilled and therefore ineligible for membership in the craft unions that made up the bulk of the AFL, to the extent that they became part of the federation it was primarily by this route.[29]

There seemed to be good cause for optimism about the future of relations between women workers and the AFL in the early years. The federation's 1891 convention went so far as to endorse women's suffrage, and Samuel Gompers spoke frequently in these years of "the identity of the interests of the wage-earning masses." Recognizing that women workers could often not be effectively organized by men, he appointed a series of female organizers in the 1890s, although their appointments were brief and they had only minimal support from the federation's executive council.[30]

The AFL's competition with the Knights of Labor for the allegiance of workers seems to account for its relatively progressive stance and practices on the question of labor solidarity, with regard to women as well as other groups of unskilled workers. By the turn of the century, however, the Knights no longer posed a threat, and the craft-unionist forces within the AFL pushed the organization in the exclusionary direction it subsequently pursued. By 1900, women who organized themselves and sought membership in unions affiliated with the AFL were regularly turned away.[31]

AFL leaders pointed to Federal Labor Unions whenever the growing exclusionism of the federation came under attack. Gompers once called the Federal Labor Unions "a splendid haven of protection [for] . . . the unskilled." Yet in reality they functioned primarily as recruiting grounds for the craft unions. In localities where there was an insufficient number of workers in a trade to form a local craft union, a mixed Federal Labor Union would be granted a charter, but as it grew larger the skilled workers in each trade would be recruited into the appropriate craft union, leaving the unskilled workers isolated. The Federal Labor Unions themselves repeatedly urged the AFL to allow them to function permanently as mixed organizations of skilled and unskilled workers, but this was consistently refused due to the opposition of the craft unions. The Federal Labor Unions therefore never constituted more than 6.4 percent of the AFL's membership, and their strength dropped from that level in 1902 to only 1.3 percent in 1910.[32]

Theoretically, women working in organized trades could become affiliated with the existing national unions that in all but a few cases represented skilled male workers in their trades. Some unions, including the Barbers, the Engravers, the Switchmen, and the Molders, had constitutions that explicitly barred women from membership.[33] The Molders went further and imposed a fine on members who taught women workers any aspect of the molding trade, with the objective of restricting "the further employment of women labor in union core rooms and foundries, and eventually the elimination of such labor in all foundries."[34]

Even when the official policies of national unions appeared favorable to the organization of women, it was not unusual for the local unions affiliated with them to disregard these policies and deny admission to female applicants. But in most AFL unions women were excluded by more subtle means. One of the most common indirect mechanisms was the institution of high initiation fees and dues, ostensibly to give the unions a firm financial foundation. That aim was reasonable enough, yet because women earned, on the average, half of what men did, few among them could afford to pay the fees and dues required.[35] The unions were generally insensitive to this aspect of their financial policies. Some unions did offer lower dues to women members, but more often than not this practice was used to justify policies that perpetuated the prevailing sex differentials in wages, excluded women from the best-paid jobs in the trade, and denied them some of the benefits of union membership that men enjoyed.[36] Under such circumstances lowered dues were a mixed blessing.

Another widespread policy that excluded many women from unions was the perpetuation of the long apprenticeship requirements traditionally associated with skilled trades. The AFL unions typically chose to maintain such requirements even when jobs had already been considerably deskilled so that the actual training periods necessary were relatively short. Some unions went further and required women to pass special examinations in order to gain admission.[37]

Even if they could overcome such hurdles, women wage workers were more likely than men to have family responsibilities, which made it difficult for them to be active in union affairs in an era when broad social norms still discouraged female involvement in public affairs. The unions did little to help overcome these problems, and indeed many union practices compounded them. Union meetings were typically held in unkempt halls in back of saloons or in otherwise questionable locations, and they all too often began and ended late in the evening. Another problem was that most paid organizers were men. Little was done to remedy this problem, although it was widely recognized. The AFL employed a grand total of thirty-eight female organizers in the forty years between 1886 and 1926, and most held their posts for very short terms.[38]

On numerous occasions women workers organized themselves only to find that they were not welcome in the union that represented the men of their trade, and then sought admission to the AFL by requesting a charter from the national office as a Federal Labor Union. The AFL leadership refused to issue such charters whenever the craft union that had been granted jurisdiction in that trade expressed opposition to the existence of a separate women's local—even when the cause for the request was the refusal of that same union to admit women to its ranks. This was justified in terms of the principle of "craft autonomy" and its corollary, the need to respect the jurisdictional boundaries of each craft.[39]

Given the multifaceted hostility of AFL unions toward women workers, it is not surprising that the proportion of union members within the female workforce remained small throughout this period. Between 1900 and 1910 the proportion of women who were organized into unions actually declined, from 3.3 percent to a low of 1.5 percent.[40] Table 3.1 shows the situation in 1920, the high-water mark of the AFL period, when 6.6 percent of all women in the nonagricultural labor force were union members. It is striking that a full 43 percent of the four hundred thousand women union members in 1920 were in the garment industry, and

Table 3.1. Nonagricultural Wage Earners and Unionization Levels, by Sex, 1920

Part A: Manufacturing Industries	% of Women Wage-Earners in Manufacturing	% of All Workers Unionized	% of Men Workers Unionized	% of Women Workers Unionized	% of All Unionized Women
Chemical and allied industries	1	0.2	0.2	—	—
Clay, glass, and stone	1	22	22	9	4
Clothing industries	23	58	77	46	43
Food and kindred products	6	19	23	6	1
Iron and steel industries	5	29	29	1	0.1
Leather industries	6	29	25	43	10
Lumber and furniture industries	2	18	19	—	—
Metal industries, except iron and steel	4	13	16	—	—
Paper and pulp industries	3	8	10	1	0.1
Printing and publishing	3	50	55	25	3
Textile industries	29	15	18	12	14
Cigar and tobacco industries	6	29	48	13	3
Other	10	1	1	2	1
All manufacturing industries	100	23	24	18	79

Part B: Other Sectors	% of Women Wage-Earners	% of All Workers Unionized	% of Men Workers Unionized	% of Women Workers Unionized	% of All Unionized Women
Mining	—	41	41	—	—
Transportation	3	37	40	6	3
Building trades	—	26	26	—	—
Trade	8	1	1	0.5	1
Clerical	20	8	13	3	10
Professional and semi-professional	15	5	9	2	4
Public service	—	7	8	—	—
Domestic and personal services	30	4	10	0.6	3
All industries (including manufacturing)	100	21	26	7	100

Source: Compiled from Leo Wolman, *Growth of American Trade Unions, 1880–1923* (New York: National Bureau of Economic Research, 1924), 85, 105, 137–45.

another 14 percent were textile workers. The AFL unions in these two industries were both quite unusual in that they included both skilled and unskilled workers, yet the impetus toward such de facto industrial unionism had come from forces outside the AFL. In the case of the garment workers, it was the 1909–1910 "Uprising of the Twenty Thousand," a strike led by rank-and-file women workers that the leaders of the AFL-affiliated International Ladies' Garment Workers' Union initially opposed. Similarly, the IWW-led textile strikes, especially the 1912 Lawrence strike, galvanized the AFL into organizing along industrial lines in the textile industry.

Even in these two industries, unionization among male workers greatly exceeded that among their female counterparts in 1920. And as table 3.1 clearly shows, this was the case in the vast majority of industries.[41] The fact that in the two industries with the greatest concentration of female employment large numbers of women *were* successfully organized suggests that there was substantially greater potential for organizing working women than the AFL unions were prepared to acknowledge.[42] Between 1895 and 1905, a total of eighty-three strikes occurred that were conducted entirely by women workers—a tiny proportion of the nearly sixteen thousand strikes that took place during that time and yet a significant one under the circumstances.[43]

When women workers organized themselves in this period, they generally turned toward industrial forms of organization, since they were not welcome in most of the craft unions and as unskilled workers they could not organize autonomously along craft lines. So, for example, a study of women in San Francisco trade unions conducted in 1913 found that "the laundry workers employed in garment factories belong to the union of garment workers and all women who work in binderies are included in one union instead of being divided according to occupation as is common elsewhere."[44]

While women persisted in efforts to organize themselves, the AFL continued to view them as "unorganizable." They were unskilled, temporary workers, it was argued, who were looking forward to marrying out of the labor force, not taking action to improve their situation within it. And besides, the federation's leaders exclaimed repeatedly, women really did not belong in the labor force at all. "The demand for female labor is an insidious assault upon the home," an official of the Boston Central Labor Union declared in 1897. "It is the knife of the assassin, aimed at the family circle."[45] AFL president Gompers stated in 1905 that "in our time ... there is no necessity for the wife contributing to the support of the family by working ... the wife as a wage-earner is a disadvantage economically considered, and socially is unnecessary." Some union leaders went so far as to suggest that not only industrial work but also trade union membership itself might "unsex women and make them masculine."[46]

The AFL in this way uncritically adopted the ideology of "woman's place" prevalent in the larger society. But it would be wrong to assume that had women received the full support of the AFL in their organizing efforts, they would have achieved a unionization level comparable to men's. The family situation of women and the ideology that proclaimed its centrality for women's lives as paid workers were far from imaginary impediments to the organization of women. Minimally, any successful struggle to organize women had first to challenge the ideology of "woman's place"—a problem that did not arise in organizing men.

Instead, the AFL adopted that ideology in defense of its policies, which undermined women's organizing efforts and excluded them from the most desirable, highest-paid jobs in industry. In addition to resisting any efforts by employers to place women in such positions, AFL unions were firm advocates of protective legislation, restricting the hours and conditions under which women could work.

The unions' arguments in favor of such legislation tended to take the form of appeals to enlightened self-interest, as for example when one AFL spokesman asked, "Women may be adults, and why should we class them as children? Because it is to the interest of all of us that female labor should be limited so as not to injure the motherhood and family life of a nation."[47] But the exclusionary aspect of the craft unions' advocacy of protective legislation was often clear, as when the Wisconsin Federation of Labor resolved to press for legislation to keep women out of the polishing and buffing trades, or when the Building Trades Material Council of Chicago asked the state factory inspectors to bar women from the trades it represented on the grounds that the work was unhealthy. That the AFL did not advocate protective legislation regulating the hours and working conditions of men as well as women is revealing in this regard.[48]

To be sure, women workers themselves, and others genuinely concerned about their welfare, often supported the drive for protective legislation. The hostility of the craft unions toward organizing women often made it extremely difficult to win better working conditions through unionization, and in such situations protective legislation was the best alternative open to them.[49] But for the craft unions it was often one more way to make use of the prevailing ideology of "woman's place" in order to protect their members' narrow interests.

From the point of view of the AFL leadership, an exclusionary policy toward women workers was less a product of ideology about woman's place than a logical consequence of the organization's broader commitment to craft unionism. To them, any inclusive form of unionism was anathema—simply the "old K. of L. idea," the unsoundness of which was proved to their satisfaction by the demise of that organization.[50] Advocates of craft unionism made it clear that their primary concern was the protection of the interests of skilled workers, despite the fact that this group was a shrinking minority within the workforce. Since most women were not skilled workers, it was patently obvious to any good craft unionist that women did not belong in his organization. And this was true regardless of his personal views about the range of activities appropriate for women in general. While the prevailing ideology of "woman's place" was a tool ready at hand with which half of the potential competitors for the positions of the skilled workers could be eliminated at one stroke, that ideology was not the root cause of the AFL's exclusionary policies. Other unskilled workers were, indeed, viewed as "unorganizable" in much the same way as women.

Thus the fact that craft unionism dominated the American labor movement during the early twentieth century was of enormous significance. Industrial unionism in itself never guarantees that unions will fight for equality between men and women in the labor market. But craft unionism is predicated upon a logic that militates against any efforts to achieve that goal. Bonds of skill had been the main basis of unionism throughout the nineteenth century. While by the period of AFL hegemony they had weakened greatly, the federation was able to achieve a degree of organizational stability that had eluded its craft union predecessors. Perhaps it was the combination of backward-looking modes of resistance and fragile organizational power that made for the rigidity of the AFL's stance toward women workers.

Another reason for the AFL's inflexibility and exclusionism was the defensive position it was forced to assume in the face of frequent employer attacks on the unions it comprised—attacks that frequently went hand in hand with the deskilling of jobs. The unionized proportion of the labor force, even in the skilled trades, was relatively low throughout this period. The "pure and simple unionism" that the AFL embraced can be viewed as a pragmatic, short-term strategy adopted by the unions from a position of weakness at a time when their main priority was to build lasting organizations where and when they could.[51]

Nevertheless, the AFL's failure to unionize the growing numbers of working women together with their male counterparts significantly affected the organization of the sexual division of labor within the blue-collar sector of the occupational structure during this period, as the many examples already reviewed suggest. It had another equally important, if less direct, consequence: namely, to push more and more women in the labor force into clerical, sales, and service jobs. These were and would long remain prototypical "women's occupations," and their feminization occurred in the very period when the AFL dominated the labor movement.

The AFL argued that women's position in the paid labor force—namely, their concentration in white-collar and unskilled blue-collar jobs—made them "unorganizable." But the craft unions' exclusionary policies were critical in preventing women's integration into the most easily organized sectors of the occupational structure: the skilled crafts. Thus the "unorganizability" argument became a self-fulfilling prophecy.

While the craft unions kept women out of certain jobs, they did not really determine which jobs women ultimately got. Some women continued to hold unskilled industrial jobs, as did black and immigrant workers, but this category did not account for many of the women who joined the labor force during this period, the vast majority of whom found employment in clerical, sales, and service work.

Feminization in both the blue- and white-collar sectors of the labor market thus occurred largely by default in these years, as the AFL unions reserved the choice jobs for their white male members and left the other fields to women, immigrants, and people of color. There was also a sexual division of labor within the unorganized sectors of the labor market that the AFL's actions cannot account for. It is conceivable, however, that had these areas of employment been organized, unions might have been instrumental in either preserving or altering the sexual division of labor in each of them, and that analysis of informal levels of organization and struggle might indeed help to account for the actual outcomes.

In this period, the trade unions, which could have been an instrument with which working men and women might have forged a united opposition to their employers, became instead a weapon with which white male workers defended their relatively privileged position within the working class against their increasingly numerous female counterparts. Unions were not the only force underpinning occupational segregation by sex, but as Theresa Wolfson pointed out in her 1926 study, *The Woman Worker and the Trade Union*, they constituted "the more flexible instrument":

> It may be considered presumptuous to suggest that industry shall change its habits, slough off traditions concerning jobs, and distribute them among workers regardless of sex—in order that women may be organised into trade unions. It seems easier to point out that the union—the more flexible instrument and primarily a functional organ purporting to serve the interests of all workers—must change its form. The union, if it would organise unskilled workers, either women or men, must adopt a structure which does not emphasize skill and crafts but admits every worker in the industry.[52]

A decade later the industrial unionism Wolfson advocated would come to the forefront of the labor movement with the formation of the CIO, opening up a new era for women workers within the labor movement.

Women in the Years of the Early CIO

The formation of the Committee for Industrial Organization (later called the Congress of Industrial Organizations) in 1935 led to a substantial improvement in the relationship of women workers to the labor movement. The CIO was committed to organizing the mass-production industries of the nation along industrial lines, regardless of skill, race, and sex differentials. By the end of the 1930s, largely through its efforts, eight hundred thousand women had been organized into labor unions. This was a 300 percent increase over female union membership ten years earlier, and double the 1920 figure, which had been the high point of women's unionization in the AFL years.[53]

The change in the orientation of the labor movement that took place in the 1930s is often overstated, however. The dramatic rise of the CIO did lead to a sharp increase in unionization among both male and female workers. But while it revitalized the labor movement, the industrial unionism advocated by John L. Lewis and the other founders of the CIO was in many ways akin to the "pure and simple unionism" of the craft-dominated AFL. Communists and other leftists were actively involved in union organizing in the CIO, but the leaders of the movement to organize the mass-production industries had immediate, pragmatic goals, and saw unionization as an end in itself.[54] While some of them did see unionization as part of a larger program of social change, that program was limited and involved no special commitment to the struggle against sexual inequality in the labor market.

The situation in the 1930s was in any case not particularly auspicious in this regard. The feminist movement had all but disappeared with the passage of the Nineteenth Amendment in 1920, and its remnants were seriously divided. Moreover, job segregation along sex lines had been firmly established within the industrial economy earlier in the century, and the Depression offered little scope for a widening of the labor market opportunities open to women. Those union organizers with an interest in eliminating sex-based inequities within the working class thus confronted enormous difficulties.

Although female union membership rose significantly in the late 1930s, sex discrimination persisted within the ranks of the labor movement. Women were still thought of by most unionists as temporary workers, and collective bargaining agreements frequently provided for unequal pay and separate seniority lists for women. One male picket line depicted in the *C.I.O. News* displayed signs reading "Restore Our Manhood: We Receive Girls' Wages." And women were almost entirely absent from the leadership of the labor movement, even where they made up a large proportion of an organization's membership. For example, there was only one woman among the twenty-four people on the ILGWU executive board in 1940, despite the fact that three-fourths of the union's members were female.[55]

Women won enormous praise from the CIO for their support work in the ladies' auxiliaries, and indeed the female contribution to the organizing efforts of their husbands, fathers, and sons was often critical. But these efforts were rarely reciprocated, for organizing women as paid workers was simply not a priority for the labor movement in the 1930s. While the structural logic of craft unionism that had been so critical in shaping the AFL's relationship to women workers was absent in the CIO, most of the women who became members of unions in the 1930s were either organized because they were employed in an industry (often predominantly male) that was seen as strategic to the industrial union movement in some larger sense, or as a result of special, local efforts by left women, women union organizers, or reformers. It is ironic that Woody Guthrie's popular song "Union Maids," originally written in 1940, later became a mainstay of the romanticization of women's relationship to the 1930s labor movement. The last verse, which was generally omitted from later renditions of the song, conveys all too accurately the view of "woman's place" in the labor movement that prevailed within the CIO:

> You gals who want to be free, just take a tip from me
> > Get you a man who's a union man
> > And join the ladies' auxiliary.
> Married life ain't hard when you've got a union card
> > A union man has a happy life
> > When he's got a union wife.[56]

Most production workers in the industries the CIO sought to organize in the 1930s were men. No serious attempts were made by any of the major CIO unions in this period to organize office workers, the vast majority of them female. Since the CIO wanted its strong unions to have primary jurisdiction over the clericals in their respective industries, it went so far as to discourage CIO white-collar unions from organizing these clerical workers. The result was that in both the steel and auto industries, the CIO unions bargained away the contract rights of clericals and tolerated the wage cuts, layoffs, and speed-ups to which office workers in those industries were then subjected.[57]

There were some successful attempts to organize women workers and to speak to their special needs.[58] But these small, local, and usually isolated efforts were peripheral to the main work of the CIO. In sharp contrast to the thinking that had guided the craft unions, the logic of industrial unionism mandated the organization of all workers in an industry, regardless of skill, race, or sex. Equally important, it pointed toward the systematic narrowing, and ultimately the eradication, of inequalities in wages and working conditions imposed on different sectors of the labor force. With the emergence of the CIO, then, the potential for the development of a labor movement committed to the elimination of sexual inequality in the workplace made its first appearance. Yet this potential was unlikely to be realized so long as the unions were still struggling for a secure foothold in a stagnating economy, and so long as consciousness about women's oppression

101

remained at a low ebb both in the labor movement and in the larger society. Under these conditions, and burdened as it was with the tradition established in the labor movement by the AFL, the CIO failed to challenge sexual inequality in the labor market in any systematic way.

With the coming of World War II, however, the situation changed significantly. The full employment economy made it possible for the industrial unions to consolidate their organizational gains. At the same time, there was a huge rise in female labor force participation, accompanied by a drastic shift in the sexual division of paid work. In this context, the structural features of the CIO that facilitated the incorporation of women workers took on new significance. While in the 1930s the fact that women were poorly represented in the basic industries that were the CIO's organizing focus had meant that the increase in their unionization rate was modest, in the 1940s the demand for "womanpower" pulled women into the strongholds of the CIO.

More than six million women entered the paid labor force between 1940 and 1944, a 50 percent increase. In manufacturing, the rise was a disproportionately large 140 percent, and the most dramatic gains were in the "war industries" such as metals, chemicals, and rubber. This industry group, which corresponded roughly to the basic industries the CIO had organized in the 1930s, registered an enormous 460 percent gain in female employment.[59] The percentage of women among production workers in the iron and steel industries grew from 7 percent in 1940 to 22 percent in 1944, while in auto it jumped from 6 percent to 24 percent in the same period.[60]

This same labor-shortage situation also brought stability to the still-precarious industrial unions. In the first year of war-stimulated economic growth (1940–1941), CIO membership jumped from 1.35 million to 2.85 million. More workers struck in 1941 than in 1937, the explosive year when the initial impact of the CIO organizing drives had made itself felt.[61] By 1945 total labor union membership was almost at the fifteen million mark, an increase of 65 percent over the 1940 level.[62] Women were 9.4 percent of all union members in 1940 and 21.8 percent four years later.[63]

The no-strike pledge that the labor movement entered into during the war brought an end to the 1941 strike wave. In exchange, the unions won a measure of security in the form of "maintenance of membership," which consolidated the organizational gains of the years preceding Pearl Harbor. As it emerged from a series of decisions by the War Labor Board, which had been set up under state auspices immediately after Pearl Harbor to mediate labor disputes once the unions agreed to abandon the strike weapon, the maintenance-of-membership formula provided that workers who were union members at the time a contract was signed were required to remain members and continue to pay dues until they left their jobs or the union contract came up for renewal. Since few workers made use of the "escape clause" that allowed them to withdraw from the union during the first fifteen days of their employment under jurisdiction of a union contract, the maintenance-of-membership compromise was very similar in its practical effect on union stability to the union shop that the labor movement had initially sought from the War Labor Board.[64] By 1945 there were 3.7 million manufacturing workers covered by maintenance-of-membership clauses, 46 percent of all manufacturing workers under union agreements. The number of workers covered by the closed or union shop also grew during the war years, under agreements reached between employers and unions without WLB intervention. By 1945, 87 percent of all unionized manufacturing workers were covered by closed-shop, union-shop, or maintenance-of-membership agreements.[65]

Many of the women who became union members during the war thus did so automatically, and not as a result of any special organizational efforts to attract them. Yet the dramatic changes in the sexual composition of the industrial labor force that the war economy produced led unions to be more interested in including women. By the end of the war, all AFL and CIO unions were free of restrictions barring women from membership, and only one, the International Brotherhood of Bookbinders, had separate women's locals, which had been commonplace in the prewar years. Female union membership climbed to an estimated 3 million to 3.5 million at the peak of war employment in 1944. While this was only between 15 percent and 20 percent of all women in the labor force at that time, it was an unprecedented achievement.[66]

Women's representation in staff positions also increased, especially on the local level. Only one union, the United Federal Workers, had a woman president, and only a small number of women were found on the national executive boards—although more than had held such positions previously. At lower levels, as organizers, department heads, business agents, and shop stewards, women were better represented, though never in proportion to their share of the unions' total membership. The most impressive but unfortunately quite atypical case was the United Electrical Workers (UE), which had an organizing staff of which women made up more than one-third in 1944—almost matching the 40 percent of the UE's membership that was female.[67]

Women union leaders were often influential in developing and pressing for special programs to meet the needs of women workers, some of which were set up by unions during the war years. In other cases the women unionists' ideas were too far ahead of what they could actually persuade the predominantly male leadership to implement.[68] But largely thanks to their female leaders, some unions, notably the United Automobile Workers, did make special efforts to aid their female members. Many unions sought to provide childcare and other community services for women workers, and several negotiated contracts providing for maternity leave without loss of seniority for their female members. By the end of the war most unions had endorsed the idea of "the rate for the job," or equal pay for equal work. There were even occasional efforts to confront the reality of unequal work by seeking to narrow or eliminate sex differentials in wages between "men's" and "women's" jobs, as when the UE negotiated a contract with Westinghouse in 1942 that provided for a wage increase to be applied to women's jobs exclusively.[69]

The labor movement's solid support for equal pay during the war stands out as the most positive area in its relationship to women workers. But the issue was complex and involved much more than an abstract commitment to nondiscrimination. Union support for the "rate for the job" developed in a context where it was clear that large numbers of women would be entering "men's jobs," at least for the duration of the war. Moreover, many employers took advantage of the changeover to reorganize the labor process and to increase the ratio of unskilled and semiskilled to skilled positions. The combination of the substitution of women for men and deskilling in war industries was a clear threat to the wage standards that the industrial unions had fought so hard for in the 1930s, and insisting on equal pay for women was the main strategy for defending those standards.

In this regard the case of a strike that took place in Detroit just a month before Pearl Harbor is revealing. The UAW struck a newly established machine-gun plant owned by the Kelsey-Hayes Wheel Company when the firm, expanding its workforce, hired women at eighty-five cents an hour, which was fifteen cents less than the rate the men who struck received. The strikers' demand was that women be removed from all machine jobs in the plant.[70] Before Pearl Harbor and the massive mobilization of women into the workforce, this exclusionary strategy appeared viable. But it soon became clear that women were going to enter the industrial labor force, in just such jobs as these, and that the unions' strategy would have to accommodate that.

After the UAW, reversing the position it had taken in the Kelsey-Hayes strike, brought a case for "equal pay for comparable quantity and quality of work" against General Motors before the War Labor Board, the government threw its support behind the "rate for the job" idea.[71] Employers, desperately recruiting female workers and treated to cost-plus contracts under which the government picked up the costs of labor, materials, and plant equipment "plus" a guaranteed profit, had little reason to oppose demands for equal pay. The industrial unions quickly embraced the equal pay demand, and gradually even the most recalcitrant craft unions abandoned their exclusionary policies in favor of this position, recognizing that at this juncture, "nondiscrimination" best served their interests.

Union support for equal pay was given further impetus by the government's wage stabilization policies, which limited across-the-board wage increases to the

Little Steel formula *except* in cases where increases were necessary to "correct inequities."[72] This "loophole" in the government's wage-control policies played an important role in channeling unions' wage demands toward the elimination of differentials. Under these conditions, the demand for equal pay was not only nominally endorsed, but efforts to narrow sex differentials in wages were seriously pursued by many unions.

Although equal pay policies were written into many union contracts and were backed by the government even where the union did not take up the issue in collective bargaining, the gains made in this area were limited. While cases of men and women doing identical work, side by side, at different rates of pay were often corrected, the far more common situation, involving slightly different jobs requiring "comparable quality and quantity of work," was less readily identified. Wage differentials between jobs were, in practice, attacked only rarely, and the system of job classification by sex was almost never challenged. A department within a plant that employed predominantly women might well continue to pay lower wages than a traditionally male department with slightly different jobs of the same skill level.[73] A 1944 study covering twenty-five industries found that men's hourly earnings were 50 percent higher than women's, and 20 percent higher on unskilled jobs. Of eighty union contracts covering seventy-five thousand women, only one-third had the same entrance rates for men and women.[74]

There was great variation from industry to industry and from shop to shop in the extent to which equal pay standards were enforced and in the degree of tolerance for evasions. But in spite of all the limitations, the war period opened up more high-paying jobs to women than they had ever had access to before. Large numbers of women were integrated into what had been exclusively male preserves. The full employment economy meant that the competition over jobs that had in earlier years led unions to adopt exclusionary policies for reasons of expediency vanished as the state and employers tried to recruit women, blacks, and other racial minorities, the blind and disabled, and anyone else they could reach, into the paid labor force.

Not only were women integrated into what had previously been "men's jobs," but they were organized into unions to an unprecedented degree, and the unions had come out in strong support, self-serving as it may have been, of their rights to equal pay. There were certainly many instances of discriminatory treatment toward women, but wartime conditions had nevertheless transformed women's relationship both to paid work and to the organized labor movement. The possibility, indeed the partial reality, of eliminating job segregation by sex appeared to exist for the first time in the twentieth century.

But this situation was the peculiar product of wartime conditions. What would happen to the women war workers when peace returned? The seniority issue was of critical importance here. As the unions recognized, in this area the interests of the prewar male labor force and those of women "war workers" did not coincide, as they had on the equal pay issue. Rather, the hard-won seniority rights of the male workers who were drafted into the military were directly threatened by the influx of new workers into industry, among whom women figured prominently. In the absence of full employment—and fears of a return to the high unemployment levels of the thirties were widespread—it was unclear how to prevent different groups of workers from being pitted against one another over the seniority issue after the war.

Women unionists understood the significance of the seniority issue in shaping the future relationship of women to the labor movement during the war years. In one union, rather than promoting equal seniority rights on the abstract grounds of social progress, the women successfully argued, "If men are now going to tell the women members that when cutbacks come, this will be at the expense of the women, the women will say, 'We want to leave the union now.'"[75] Indeed, the resolution of the seniority issue in the aftermath of the war would have enormous consequences, not only for the future relationship of women to the unions, but also for their "place" in the labor market as a whole.

Demobilization, Women Workers, and the Postwar Labor Movement

As the war drew to a close and the process of economic reconversion got under-way, the organized labor movement pressed for full-employment legislation in anticipation of a rise in unemployment. But Congress passed only a severely weakened version of this labor program in the Employment Act of 1946, which ultimately did nothing to prevent the massive layoffs that came immediately after the war. Women received 60 percent of the layoff notices issued in the first months after the war. They were laid off at a rate 75 percent higher than that of men.[76] The question of women's seniority rights now came to the fore.

Sixty percent of the women who were employed as "war workers" had been gainfully employed before Pearl Harbor, though few of them had been employed before 1941 in the well-paid, unionized industrial jobs the war opened up to them. A U.S. Women's Bureau survey of thirteen thousand women war workers in such jobs in 1944–1945 found that 75 percent of them wanted to keep their jobs after the war ended.[77] Women workers expected to be laid off in disproportionate numbers from their new jobs in accordance with their generally lower seniority. They neither demanded nor expected preferential treatment, but they did think that they deserved the same protection as men, so that returning veterans would displace workers of either sex only if they had accumulated greater seniority.

106

Thus women often expected to be rehired along with men of equivalent seniority status once the plants they had worked in during the war were reconverted
to postwar consumer goods production. For a variety of reasons, however, this
rarely occurred.

In some cases, union contracts provided specifically for separate seniority lists
for men and women workers. This practice had been widespread in the 1930s and
was endowed with new legitimacy in the war period because of the ideology that
women war workers were interested in working "for the duration" only.[78]

Women union leaders and others with a special interest in the effect of seniority rules on women workers had strongly opposed separate seniority lists during the war years and urged the elimination from union contracts of all forms,
of discrimination by sex or marital status in regard to job security rights. They
argued also for plant-wide rather than departmental seniority systems, anticipating reconversion situations in which women's departments might be eliminated
entirely even if the women had higher seniority than men in other departments.[79]

The effort to establish nondiscriminatory seniority systems enjoyed considerable success. A 1945 Women's Bureau survey of union contracts covering seventy-
five thousand women workers in a midwestern war-industry area found that four-
fifths of the contracts provided for plant-wide rather than departmental seniority.
Separate seniority lists for women were written into only one-fifth of the contracts
sampled. The most interesting finding of the survey was that in plants where no
women were on the bargaining, grievance, or shop committees, three-fourths of
the contracts included in the survey provided for separate seniority lists.[80]

The thorny issue of veterans' seniority rights further complicated matters.
Many unions negotiated contract provisions granting veterans who came back
to work in their prewar jobs seniority for the period of their military service as
well as the tenure they had accumulated before the war. To the extent that unions
negotiated such veterans' rights, workers of either sex who were newly employed
during the war under the contracts involved were automatically denied the job
security rights they would otherwise have enjoyed. And yet there was ample justification for veterans' protection in light of the hardships of military service these
workers had undergone, and contract provisions granting them special seniority
rights were seen as legitimate even by those nonveterans, both men and women,
who were adversely affected by them.

But when the wartime gains the unions had made came under a wide-ranging
political attack, the veterans' rights issue emerged as an important terrain of
struggle. The Selective Service Act of 1940 had guaranteed veterans seniority
for the years during which they had been employed before the war, but beyond
that the law was ambiguous.[81] The director of the Selective Service, Lewis B.
Hershey, predicated his actions on what came to be called the "super-seniority"

interpretation of the act. He argued that it guaranteed veterans an absolute right to reinstatement in their former positions (or comparable ones) and protection from layoff for a year thereafter, regardless of how the prewar seniority status of the veteran compared to the seniority accumulated by a nonveteran he might displace. Under this interpretation, a veteran who had worked two years for a company and then served four years in the military could displace a worker with twenty years' seniority.

Unionists strongly objected to this reading of the law, not only because it played havoc with the seniority principle but also because it encouraged veterans to look to the government rather than to organized labor for protection. The unions strongly supported special seniority rights for veterans but saw Hershey's interpretation of the law as an effort to divide veterans from other workers. Thus they urged veterans to reject the temporary, one-year guarantee the government proffered in favor of permanent seniority protection that took the special situation of veterans into account, backed by a union contract rather than by the force of law.

In a 1946 case, the U.S. Supreme Court sided with the labor movement in rejecting the "super-seniority" argument. However, individual employers and unions remained free to make contractual agreements on the issue, and some of the most progressive unions pursued their own versions of "super-seniority" in collective bargaining. The UAW developed a "Model Veteran's Seniority Clause," which was written into contracts with Chrysler, North American Aviation, and Mack Truck, among others, by 1946. It granted seniority equal to the time spent in military service both to veterans previously employed by a company *and to those newly hired* after their discharge from the military. The UE negotiated a similar clause in at least one of its contracts, with the additional proviso that all newly employed veterans would rank junior to those veterans employed by the company prior to entering the military.[82]

The labor movement was aware of the potential impact of the treatment of veterans. *Ammunition*, the organ of the UAW's Education Department, stated the position clearly:

> Should veterans without seniority be given jobs over women who have seniority rights in UAW plants?
>
> Here is Jimmy Smith, he's just 22 and a veteran of two years in the Pacific. He's had miscellaneous jobs before he went into service—delivery jobs, drug and grocery store clerking—but no re-employment rights to a job he's interested in. He's hired at X auto plant, simply because he's a veteran. When he goes to work he cuts out Alice Jones who was next on the seniority list. With three and a half years in X plant Alice, who was laid off the day after V-J day,

has exhausted her unemployment compensation and needs a job desperately
... she's got two children to support.

Should Alice Jones be responsible for providing Jimmy Smith with a job?
The UAW *says no.*

... No individual worker or groups of workers should be expected to give
up their jobs so that another group might work. It's not Alice's responsibility to go hungry and let her children suffer to provide Jimmy with a job. It's
management's responsibility to provide jobs, and if free enterprise fails then
it's government's job to see that every citizen able and willing to work has an
opportunity for a useful job at decent wages.[83]

Under the UAW's model veteran's seniority clause, Alice Jones had more
seniority than Jimmy Smith, and in this respect the union's policy was consistent. But in the many cases where a veteran's time in the military exceeded the
period a woman had worked in the plant, the woman would in fact be bumped.
The labor movement clearly would have preferred a full employment situation,
but with the failure of the legislative campaign on that issue, the reality was that
veterans and women workers were pitted against one another, and ultimately the
gains that had been made by women during the war years were eroded.

Women, like other workers, did support the special seniority rights unions
won for veterans and did not view them as discriminatory in the way separate
seniority lists and departmental seniority systems clearly were. And while under
the circumstances it was inevitable that women would bear the brunt of the initial layoffs, with the postwar industrial expansion women should have eventually
been reintegrated into the labor force of the industries that had employed them
as "war workers" if they were gradually recalled according to seniority. Furthermore, if the seniority systems were followed correctly, women would have gotten
back into the same high-paying "men's jobs" they had held during the war, rather
than being incorporated into the postwar labor force exclusively in "female" job
classifications.

In fact, there were frequent abuses of women's formal seniority rights even
in cases where unions had negotiated contracts that were nondiscriminatory.
Many contracts that did not provide for separate seniority lists or any of the other
blatantly discriminatory forms of seniority allowed the perpetuation of job classification systems that differentiated between men's and women's jobs and then
granted men categorical bumping rights over women filling jobs designated as
"male." Women had no protection against this unless their contracts had both
plant-wide seniority provisions *and* explicit nondiscrimination clauses or unless
the contracts specified that there be no job classifications by sex. However, the
absence of such classifications was exceptional at this time. Protective legislation,

which had been eased in many states due to the wartime labor shortages, frequently became the mechanism by which jobs that women had performed quite adequately during the war, and wanted to keep, were reclassified as "men's jobs."[84]

Managers could and often did reclassify jobs arbitrarily in the course of postwar reconversion. The fragmentary evidence makes it difficult to disentangle the extent to which unions, especially on the local level, initiated such job reclassifications. What is indisputable is that union-management collusion in this area was common in the postwar period. While many national union leaders proclaimed support for the principles of nondiscrimination, they rarely exerted themselves on behalf of the women among their members who were directly affected by layoffs. Things were far worse on the local level, where the official position of the Internationals on seniority issues, however progressive, was often rejected outright.

The UAW, well known for its progressive policies on women's rights to job protection, did more than the average labor organization to protect women's seniority rights. At its 1946 convention the UAW adopted a resolution affirming the union's unequivocal support for "Protection of Women's Rights in the Auto Industry," which laid out a detailed model policy on equal pay, seniority, and other basic issues. However, there was no provision for penalizing locals that violated the terms of the resolution.

Subsequently, many UAW locals continued to negotiate contracts that openly discriminated against women. Even where contracts did provide women with adequate formal protection against discrimination, their efficacy depended entirely on the vigilance and enforcement efforts of local unions. Many shop stewards simply ignored inequities or failed to pursue women's grievances. The membership of one large local, where men outnumbered women by a ratio of 50 to 1, voted—in direct opposition to the national UAW guidelines, which prohibited discrimination based on marital status as well as sex—to force women workers to resign when they married. An extreme case of discrimination on the local level involved four women workers who were suspended from the UAW in January 1947 because they did not receive "men's pay" while working on a "man's job." At least one of the women had filed a grievance about the matter, but that did not stop the local from punishing her and the other three victims of this wage discrimination rather than coming to their support.[85] In other cases, UAW locals addressed the grievances of women members more adequately.

The immediate postwar period provided the industrial unions organized in the 1930s with an unprecedented opportunity to act as the force challenging the sexual division of labor within their jurisdictions and to preserve and deepen the gains women had made as a result of the wartime labor shortage in the postwar years. By instead acting to exclude women and colluding with managerial efforts to do so, the CIO unions violated their own principles of industrial unionism and lost an opportunity unlike any before or since to organize work on a sex-blind basis. Never since have the industrial unions been in as strong a position as they enjoyed in 1946, when between 80 percent and 100 percent of the workforce in such industries as aircraft, auto, electrical machinery, meatpacking, rubber, ship-building, and steel were under union agreements.[86]

Women did re-enter the paid labor force after the postwar layoffs, although relatively few were able to get their old jobs back. They flocked instead to the expanding clerical, sales, and service sectors of the economy. Women made up 25 percent of all production workers in manufacturing industry in 1940, and 33 percent at the peak of war employment in 1944, but only 27 percent in 1950. The small net gain was smaller than the general rise in the proportion women made up of the labor force as a whole, which grew from 25 percent in 1940 to 29 percent in 1950. But in clerical work women increased their share from 53 percent to 59 percent over the decade from 1940 to 1950, in sales work from 28 percent to 39 percent, and in service work from 40 percent to 45 percent.[87] As in the early twentieth century, these unorganized "white collar" sectors absorbed the large numbers of women entering the economy, once this basic pattern of sex-typing was re-established in the demobilization period. While craft exclusionism had been instrumental in the earlier period, now the failure of unions to protect women's seniority was critical in consolidating this pattern.

The reasons for that failure were rooted in the particular conditions of the postwar period, and not in structural imperatives of the unions (at least for the industrial unions). The simple fact that the transition to a peacetime economy involved the elimination of many jobs and a vast overhauling of the nation's entire economy made it much more difficult for women to hold on to the gains they had made. And that the ideology had emphasized from the outset that women's relationship to "war work" was a temporary one did not help matters.

In addition, there was the political situation of the labor movement in the postwar period. The no-strike pledge was no more, and the efforts of unions to decrease unemployment and to win higher wages for their members, who had endured rapid inflation under wage controls during the war, involved them in a major offensive against the nation's corporations. The postwar strike wave resulted in a rash of anti-labor legislation, exemplified by the 1947 Taft-Hartley Act. Much of the postwar period's militancy was rooted in the same fears of unemployment that led many local unions to deny seniority rights to women. And the bitter factionalism that wracked the labor movement at this time led to increased tolerance by the top-level leadership of discriminatory tendencies on the local level. Contenders for union leadership had to consolidate their support among rank-and-file members, and the fight for equal treatment of the sexes was far too low a priority on which to risk losing that support.

All these factors were important, but the most basic reason for the unions' failure to protect the rights of their female members was that the link between the unions and the women workers who were part of them had never been a very strong one. Huge numbers of women had become union members during the war, but because of the maintenance-of-membership agreements, the unions had not had to speak to the special needs of their female constituency in order to keep their allegiance. And few unions made any serious attempt to address the needs of women workers. The distance between the unions and the rank-and-file women in them was further widened by the family responsibilities of many women members, which were further intensified by the special hardships (for example, rationing) of wartime. That a solid link between the labor movement and the unions' female membership was never forged during the war years, in short, meant that the bonds that did exist could easily be broken under the pressures of postwar economic and political conditions. Thus the prewar sexual division of labor was firmly re-established in the demobilization period, just as women's attachment to the paid labor force was increasing.

Conclusion

There were two critical periods in the development of women's current relationship to the paid labor market in the United States. The first was the early twentieth century, when the clerical, sales, and service sectors expanded and absorbed large numbers of women, establishing a basic pattern of job segregation by sex that would endure for many decades. The period immediately following World War II is of comparable significance. The war disrupted the sexual division of paid work established earlier in the century, absorbing large numbers of women into the industrial jobs that had been most rigidly sex-typed as "male" in previous years. But after the war, the pattern of occupational segregation by sex that had prevailed earlier in the century was re-established.

In both periods, the organized labor movement failed to respond proactively to the changes that were occurring in the economy. The AFL continued to predicate its strategy on control over skills in the very period when deskilling was eroding the basis of this approach. The labor movement shifted toward industrial unionism in the 1930s but continued to focus its organizing efforts on blue-collar production jobs in the postwar years, precisely when the tertiary sector of the economy was expanding most dramatically. In both periods, the labor movement's failure to organize women workers and to challenge the system of job classification by sex had negative consequences both for the strength of organized labor and for the growing numbers of women workers.

Labor unions cannot be held fully responsible for the establishment and maintenance of the sexual division of labor, particularly in the United States, where they have never included even a majority of workers. But the organized labor movement in both of these periods was situated in a crucial arena of struggle within which the contemporary pattern of sex-typing was shaped.

Organized labor is weaker today than at any time since the early 1930s, but the erosion of the bargain between labor and management struck in the expansionary postwar period, in which economic benefits were traded for a "hands off" approach to management prerogatives, has forced even the most conservative labor leaders to search for new directions. In that context, the long history of union participation in the construction and reproduction of job segregation by sex does not preclude the possibility that a renewed labor movement could take a leading role in seeking to eradicate sexual inequality at work.

Notes

The chapter was originally published in *Socialist Review* no. 49 (1980): 95–150. It is reprinted here with permission from Taylor and Francis, www.tandfonline.com.

1. U.S. Census Bureau, *Historical Statistics of the U.S.* (1960), 71.

2. Heidi Hartmann's work is a noteworthy exception but has theoretical problems of its own to which I will return. See her "Capitalism, Patriarchy, and Job Segregation by Sex," in *Women and the Workplace: The Implications of Occupational Segregation*, edited by Martha Blaxall and Barbara Reagan (Chicago: University of Chicago Press, 1976), 137–69.

3. See for example Paddy Quick, "Women's Work," *Review of Radical Political Economics* 4, no. 3 (Summer 1972): 2–19; Juliet Mitchell, *Woman's Estate* (New York: Vintage, 1971), especially 144; and Margaret Benston, "The Political Economy of Women's Liberation," *Monthly Review* 21 (1969): 13–28.

4. Richard Edwards, in his *Contested Terrain: The Transformation of the Workplace in the Twentieth Century* (New York: Basic, 1979), especially chaps. 9 and 10. Also see Richard C. Edwards, Michael Reich, and David M. Gordon, eds., *Labor Market Segmentation* (Lexington, Mass.: Heath, 1975), the introduction to which summarizes this theoretical framework; and chapter 4 of David Gordon's *Theories of Poverty and Underemployment* (Lexington, Mass.: Heath, 1972). The fullest effort to argue that the situation of women in the labor market is best explained by segmentation theory is R. D. Barron and G. M. Norris, "Sexual Divisions and the Dual Labour Market," in *Dependence and Exploitation in Work and Marriage*, edited by Diana Leonard Barker and Sheila Allen, 47–69 (New York: Longman, 1976), which examines the British case.

5. Mary Stevenson, "Women's Wages and Job Segregation," in *Labor Market Segmentation*, edited by Richard C. Edwards, Michael Reich, and David M. Gordon (Lexington, Mass.: Heath, 1975), 245–46. See also National Manpower Council, *Womanpower* (New York: Columbia University Press, 1957), 82.

6. Eve Lapin, *Mothers in Overalls* (New York: Workers Library, 1943), cited in *America's Working Women*, edited by Rosalyn Baxandall, Linda Gordon, and Susan Reverby (New York: Vintage, 1976), 284.

7. Edwards, Reich, and Gordon, *Labor Market Segmentation*, xii–xiv.

8. Hartmann, "Capitalism, Patriarchy, and Job Segregation," 139. Many of the criticisms of Hartmann that follow apply as well to Edna Bonacich's "split labor market" theory. While

Bonacich is concerned primarily with racial divisions in the workforce and does not enter into any detailed discussion of job segregation by sex, her characterization of the relationship between "higher paid labor" and "cheaper labor" is strikingly similar to Hartmann's view of the relationship between male and female workers. Patriarchy, or for that matter "given" racial interests, is not the starting point for Bonacich, as it is for Hartmann, but both make similar assumptions about the resources and interests of "higher paid" or male labor. See Edna Bonacich, "A Theory of Ethnic Antagonism: The Split Labor Market," *American Sociological Review* 37, no. 5 (October 1972): 547–59. It is telling that in this initial formulation of her theory, Bonacich does not recognize the *possibility* of a cross-race alliance forming among workers, although she does incorporate this possible "outcome" into later expositions of the split-labor-market theory, starting with "Abolition, the Extension of Slavery, and the Position of Free Blacks: A Study of Split Labor Markets in the United States, 1830–1863," *American Journal of Sociology* 81, no. 3 (November 1975): 601–28.

9. Hartmann, "Capitalism, Patriarchy, and Job Segregation," 152.

10. Jane Humphries, "The Working Class Family, Women's Liberation, and Class Struggle: The Case of Nineteenth-Century British History," *Review of Radical Political Economy* 9, no. 3 (Fall 1977): 25–41.

11. There are, of course, exceptions, such as Hartmann, "Capitalism, Patriarchy, and Job Segregation," and Alice Kessler-Harris's work, especially her "'Where Are the Organized Women Workers?'" *Feminist Studies* 3, no. 1–2 (Fall 1975): 92–110. For an insightful discussion of some reasons socialist feminists, whom one might expect to have explored this issue, have been loath to do so, see Carol Hatch, "Socialist Feminism and the Workplace," *Socialist Review* 47 (September–October 1979): 119–30.

12. Marx predicted that sexual distinctions would disappear entirely from the division of labor as a result of this transformation. See *Capital* (New York: International, 1967), 1:394–402.

13. See Mary P. Ryan, *Womanhood in Africa: From Colonial Times to the Present* (New York: New Viewpoints, 1975), especially 210–12.

14. John B. Andrews and W. D. P. Bliss, *History of Women in Trade Unions*, vol. 10 of Senate Document no. 645, "Report on Condition of Woman and Child Wage-Earners in the United States" (61st Congress, 2nd Session, Washington, D.C., 1911), p. 47. Humphries, "The Working Class Family," extensively documents this for nineteenth-century Britain and offers an insightful discussion. This analysis is not necessarily inconsistent with Neil Smelser's argument in his *Social Change in the Industrial Revolution* (Chicago: University of Chicago Press, 1959) about the efforts of families, at least in the British cotton industry, to preserve the family as a unit of production in the early nineteenth century. Rather, the struggle for a family wage would seem to characterize a slightly later period, after the breakup of families within the industrial labor market was an accomplished fact. Smelser focuses on efforts to limit child labor more than on female labor, but his argument does support the view that seeking a family wage constituted a defense of the working-class family—Humphries's argument. In any case, the pattern of preservation of the family unit within factory employment that figures so prominently in Smelser's account of the British cotton industry was probably less common in early American capitalism. While some factories did employ whole families

in the nineteenth century, especially immigrant families, most married women remained outside the factory labor force.

15. See Sterling D. Spero and Abram L. Harris, *The Black Worker: The Negro and the Labor Movement* (New York: Atheneum, 1971; first published 1931), 131.

16. A useful theoretical discussion of the relationship between deskilling and women's employment in early capitalism is Veronica Beechey, "Some Notes on Female Wage Labour in Capitalist Production," *Capital and Class*, no. 3 (Autumn 1977): especially 54–56.

17. Andrews and Bliss, *History*, 47–48.

18. Ibid., 48. Emphasis added.

19. See Barbara Welter, "The Cult of True Womanhood: 1820–1860," *American Quarterly* 18, no. 2, part 1 (Summer 1966): 151–74.

20. Helen L. Sumner, *History of Women in Industry in the United States*, vol. 9 of Senate Document no. 645, "Report on Condition of Woman and Child Wage-Earners in the United States" (61st Congress, 2nd Session, Washington, D.C., 1910), pp. 248–49.

21. Andrews and Bliss, *History*, 91ff.

22. Gerald N. Grob, *Workers and Utopia: A Study of Ideological Conflict in the American Labor Movement 1865–1900* (Evanston, Ill: Northwestern University Press, 1961).

23. See Barbara M. Wertheimer, *We Were There: The Story of Working Women in America* (New York: Pantheon, 1977), 180–91; and Philip S. Foner, *Women and the American Labor Movement* (New York: Free Press, 1979), 185–212.

24. U.S. Bureau of the Census, *Historical Statistics of the U.S., Colonial Times to 1957*, 71.

25. R. R. Lutz and Louise Patterson, *Women Workers and Labor Supply*, National Industrial Conference Board Studies no. 220 (New York: National Industrial Conference Board, 1936), 19; *15th Census of the U.S., 1930, Population*, 5:39.

26. Leo Wolman, *Ebb and Flow in Trade Unionism* (New York: National Bureau of Economic Research, 1936), 16, 116, 138–39.

27. Ibid., 139–40.

28. Andrews and Bliss, *History*, 155–56.

29. Philip S. Foner, *History of The Labor Movement in the United States*, vol. 2 (New York: International, 1955), 143, 189–90.

30. Foner, *Labor Movement*, vol. 2, 184–85, 190–91, 193–94; Andrews and Bliss, *History*, 156.

31. Foner, *Labor Movement*, vol. 2, 186–87, 194, 205, 345–68.

32. Foner, *Labor Movement*, vol. 3 (1964), 198–99.

33. See the list in Theresa Wolfson, *The Woman Worker and the Trade Unions* (New York: International, 1926), 75.

34. Cited in Foner, *Labor Movement*, vol. 3, 226. Also see Wolfson, *Woman Worker*, 75–76.

35. Foner, *Labor Movement*, vol. 3, 222, 227.

36. Wolfson, *Woman Worker*, 81–89.

37. Foner, *Labor Movement*, vol. 2, 365.

38. Wolfson, *Woman Worker*, 104, 140–41, 166–68.

39. Foner, *Labor Movement*, vol. 2, 365.

40. Andrews and Bliss, *History*, 138; Leo Wolman, *The Growth of American Trade Unions, 1880–1923* (New York: National Bureau of Economic Research, 1924), 105.

41. The only exception is the "leather industries" group. This can be accounted for by three factors: (1) the long tradition of self-organization among women shoe workers; (2) the fact that women shoe workers were often skilled workers; (3) the fact that, while the percentage of women organized in the industry is higher than that of men, the absolute number of male union members (71,600) is nearly double that of female members within this industry group. In other words, there were relatively few women in the industry at this point, but a relatively high number of them were unionized.

42. Alice Kessler-Harris has pointed to another indication of this unrealized potential, namely, the fact that there were dramatic year-to-year fluctuations in the proportion of working women who were unionized during the years when the AFL dominated the labor movement. See Kessler-Harris, "Organized Women Workers," 92–93.

43. Women were involved in 1,262 of the 15,726 strikes that occurred during that period, yet in all but 83 of these strikes male workers were concerned as well. Andrews and Bliss, *History*, 204.

44. Lillian Ruth Mathews, *Women in Trade Unions in San Francisco*, University of California Publications in Economics, vol. 3, no. 1 (Berkeley: University of California Press, 1913), 93.

45. Edward O'Donnell, "Women as Breadwinners: The Error of the Age," *American Federationist* 4 (October 1897), cited in Kessler-Harris, "Organized Women Workers," 97.

46. See Foner, *Labor Movement*, vol. 3, 224.

47. Kessler-Harris, "Organized Women Workers," 101, citing the *American Federationist* 7 (April 1900).

48. Elizabeth F. Baker, *Protective Labor Legislation* (New York: Columbia University Press, 1925), 144, 446; Foner, *Labor Movement*, vol. 3, 224.

49. See Kessler-Harris, "Organized Women Workers," 101.

50. Foner, *Labor Movement*, vol. 3, 196–97.

51. For unionization levels, see table 3.1, and Wolman, *Growth*, 82–96, 137–61. For discussion of the logic behind the pragmatism of the AFL, see John R. Commons, "Karl Marx and Samuel Gompers," *Political Science Quarterly* 41, no. 2 (June 1926): 281–86.

52. Wolfson, *Woman Worker*, 99–100.

53. Gladys Dickason, "Women in Labor Unions," *Annals of the American Academy of Political and Social Science* 251 (May 1947): 71.

54. See David Brody, "The Emergence of Mass-Production Unionism," in *Change and Continuity in Twentieth Century America*, edited by John Braeman, Robert H. Bremner, and Everett Walters (Columbus: Ohio State University Press, 1964), 221–62.

55. William H. Chafe, *The American Woman: Her Changing Social, Economic, and Political Role, 1920–1970* (New York: Oxford University Press, 1972), 86; Sharon Hartman Strom, "'We're No Kitty Foyles': Organizing Office Workers for the Congress of Industrial Organization, 1937–1950," in *Women, Work and Protest: A Century of U.S. Women's Labor History*, edited by Ruth Milkman (New York: Routledge and Kegan Paul, 1985), 206–34.

56. Brochure accompanying the phonograph record *Talking Union*, Pete Seeger and the Almanac Singers, Folkways Records, pp. 3, 6.

57. Strom, "'We're No Kitty Foyles,'" discusses this. The subject arose at the UAW'S 1946 convention, where one delegate remarked in the course of debate over a resolution urging

the organization of white-collar workers: "I recall that in the original Ford contract the payroll department was organized and then it was cancelled out of the contract, due to some finagling. I would like to know, if this resolution passes and the payroll department and all other departments such as that department come under the jurisdiction of the Union, could that be done without violating the present contract? . . . I only want to mention that because I recall at one time the members of the payroll department picketed the members of the International Union for being sold out." See *Proceedings of the Tenth Convention of the United Automobile, Aircraft, and Agricultural Implement Workers of America* (UAW-CIO), March 23–31, 1946, p. 41.

58. Strom, "'We're No Kitty Foyles,'" recounts numerous examples of this for white-collar work. Also see the oral history of "Stella Nowicki" in Alice Lynd and Staughton Lynd, *Rank and File* (Boston: Beacon, 1973), 67–88.

59. U.S. Department of Labor, Women's Bureau, *Changes in Women's Employment during the War*, Special Bulletin no. 20 (June 1944), 15.

60. U.S. Department of Labor, Bureau of Labor Statistics, *Women in Factories* (Washington, 1947), 6–7.

61. Walter Galenson, *The CIO Challenge to the AFL* (Cambridge, Mass.: Harvard University Press, 1960), 587, 604.

62. U.S. Department of Labor, Bureau of Labor Statistics, *Brief History of the American Labor Movement*, Bulletin No. 1000 (1976), 52.

63. Dickason, "Women in Labor Unions," 71.

64. Joel Seidman, *American Labor from Defense to Reconversion* (Chicago: University of Chicago Press, 1953), 91–108; Nelson Lichtenstein, *Labor's War at Home: The CIO in World War II* (New York: Cambridge University Press, 1982), pp. 192–223.

65. "Extent of Collective Bargaining and Union Recognition, 1945," Bulletin No. 865 of the U.S. Bureau of Labor Statistics (Washington, D.C.: 1946), 5.

66. Dickason, "Women in Labor Unions," 71–72; Labor Research Association, *Labor Fact Book 7* (New York: International, 1945), 70. These two sources provide estimates of women's union membership in this period; precise figures are unavailable.

67. See *Labor Fact Book 7*, 70–71; and "Women Take Posts as Union Leaders," *New York Times*, February 5, 1943.

68. For example, see the discussions at the April 1945 Conference of Trade Union Women and Women's Bureau (sponsored by the U.S. Department of Labor), summarized in the pamphlet "Women Union Leaders Speak" (Washington, D.C.: 1945), especially 8–25.

69. Dickason, "Women in Labor Unions," 73–74.

70. "Labor 'Dilution,'" *Business Week*, November 8, 1941, 59–60; and Lichtenstein, *Labor's War at Home*, 223–24.

71. Dickason, "Women in Labor Unions," 73.

72. Seidman, *American Labor*, 109–16.

73. "Women Union Leaders Speak," 15.

74. "Rate for the Job," U.S. Women's Bureau pamphlet, Union Series, no. 2 (1945).

75. "Women Union Leaders Speak," 10.

76. Chafe, *American Woman*, 180.

77. *Changes in Women's Employment during the War*, 6; U.S. Women's Bureau, Bulletin No. 209, *Women Workers in Ten War Production Areas and Their Postwar Employment Plans* (1946), 4.

78. "Seniority Status of Women in Unions in War Plants," U.S. Women's Bureau pamphlet, Union Series, no. 1 (1945); Sheila Tobias and Lisa Anderson, "What Really Happened to Rosie the Riveter: Demobilization and the Female Labor Force, 1944–47," Module 9 (MMS Modular Publications, 1973), 20–25.

79. "Seniority Status of Women"; "Women Union Leaders Speak," 8–12.

80. "Seniority Status of Women."

81. Robert P. Brecht, "Collective Bargaining and Re-employment of Veterans," *Annals of the American Academy of Political and Social Science* 227 (May 1943): 94–103.

82. Seidman, *American Labor*, 231–32; UAW-CIO, *Ammunition* 4, no. 4 (April 1946): 23; *U.E. News* 8, no. 1 (5 January 1946): 10.

83. UAW-CIO, *Ammunition* 4, no. 2 (February 1946): 20. Emphasis in the original.

84. Tobias and Anderson, "What Really Happened to Rosie the Riveter," 12–26; Lyn Goldfarb, *Separate and Unequal: Discrimination against Women Workers after World War II (The U.A.W., 1944–54)*, Union for Radical Political Economics pamphlet (Washington, D.C.: 1976).

85. See the many examples cited in Goldfarb, *Separate and Unequal*, 30–39.

86. U.S. Department of Labor, Bureau of Labor Statistics, *Extent of Collective Bargaining and Union Recognition*, Bulletin no. 909 (1946), 2.

87. *Women in Factories*, 5; and U.S. Women's Bureau, *Handbook of Women Workers*, 1969, table 40.

Chapter 4

Rosie the Riveter Revisited

*Management's Postwar Purge
of Women Automobile Workers*

*Whereas Chapter 3 focused on the ways in which labor unions contributed to the
historical formation of the gender division of labor and to patterns of job segregation
by sex, this chapter argues that employers played a far more important role. Through
a case study of the auto industry during the period of postwar reconversion following
World War II, the vital importance of hiring policy comes to the fore. A closer examination of this case reveals that, given the continuing expansion of employment in the
auto industry and the high turnover that has always characterized auto production
jobs, the industry could have retained all of the women it had employed during the
war and still have been able to hire vast numbers of veterans. Indeed, while the representation of women in the industry declined precipitously after 1945, that of black
workers—who, like women, had been minimally employed in auto production prior
to the war—continued to rise, especially in the Detroit area. Unions collaborated with
management in purging women from the industry, but management was the far more
powerful actor in this drama.*

A vital question facing historians of American women's labor involves the defemi-
nization of basic industry at the end of World War II. The economic mobilization
for war dramatized the possibility of employing women in "men's jobs" on an
unprecedented scale and seemed to throw into question the sexual division of
paid labor as a whole. Yet, in the course of postwar reconversion, women were
systematically purged from their wartime jobs, and the prewar sexual division of

labor in manufacturing was effectively reconstructed. The automobile industry is a prominent case in point. At the peak of wartime employment, women workers accounted for more than one-fourth of the labor force in auto; by September 1945, a month after V-J Day, the female share of employment in the industry had dropped below 10 percent, where it would remain for many years to come.[1]

The key question is why women were not retained in the postwar years, despite the success with which they were integrated into the production workforce of industries like auto during the war. This is a specific—and extreme—version of a more general problem, namely, why the sexual division of labor, as it has developed historically within and between industries, has been so resistant to change. Despite the rapid growth of female labor force participation over the postwar decades and despite the fact that the resurgence of feminism has undermined the legitimacy of sex discrimination in the labor market, occupational segregation by sex and the wage inequality that accompanies it have remained a highly salient feature of the U.S. labor market.

Several careful studies have considered the critical moment in women's labor history immediately following the end of World War II. Most have focused on the auto industry, primarily on the failure of the United Auto Workers (UAW) to protect women's employment rights in the aftermath of the war. The scholarship of Sheila Tobias and Lisa Anderson, Lyn Goldfarb, and Nancy Gabin has demonstrated that, although women workers overwhelmingly wanted to stay in "men's jobs" in auto after the war, the UAW colluded in the purge of women from the industry. Despite an official union policy in support of women's seniority rights, the UAW did little to protect women's jobs, especially at the local level. And, in many instances, the union actively supported excluding women from postwar employment in the auto industry.[2]

This body of research has greatly deepened historians' understanding of the complex relationship between women and industrial unions in the 1940s. However, this body of scholarship does not adequately explain the exclusion of women from the postwar auto industry. And, because it focuses primarily on the role of the union, this literature is in some respects misleading. I argue here that, although it is true that the UAW colluded with management and that effective union resistance to the policy of purging women from the postwar workforce might have altered the situation, to understand why the postwar sexual division of labor in auto took the form it did, one must look to *management* first and foremost. The central question is: Why was management so intent on excluding women from postwar employment in the first place? During the war, women auto workers won enormous praise for their performance from all sides. Why should employers have been so reluctant to retain them after the war? Given the historical "cheapness" of female labor, management's postwar policy seems especially paradoxical.

This chapter analyzes the postwar shift in the sexual division of labor in the auto industry, giving center stage to the policy and practice of automotive management and placing the UAW's role in a broader perspective. Although I am most concerned with the 1940s, the first section begins with a discussion of the formation of the sexual division of labor in the prewar auto industry. This is crucial for the analysis of postwar developments, because the logic of the managerial policy that excluded women from automotive employment in the reconversion period in many respects recapitulated that which shaped the industry's sexual division of labor in the early twentieth century. Ever since the rise of Ford's mass-production system and the introduction of the famous five-dollar day in 1914, auto had been a high-wage industry. Moreover, high wages have always been central to the Fordist system of control over labor. Under these circumstances, automotive management never had much incentive to substitute female for male labor, despite the relatively low wages of the former; thus, the vast majority of jobs in the industry were sex-typed as "men's work" from the outset. Females entered the industry in large numbers during World War II, and then only in the face of an extraordinary shortage of male labor. Moreover, the mobilization of female labor during the war emergency only temporarily disrupted the sexual division of labor in the industry. Indeed, for management, the exclusion of women workers from postwar employment in auto was a foregone conclusion.

But what about the seniority system institutionalized in UAW contracts in the years immediately preceding the war? The previously mentioned studies focus on the union's failure to protect women's seniority rights and presume that the seniority system was the main determinant of whether women workers hired in wartime would be retained after the war. However, as I argue in the second section of this chapter, seniority was actually of secondary importance in the immediate postwar period because the industry expanded very rapidly and turnover rates were extremely high. Even with the large influx of returning veterans, who held a special seniority status, large numbers of vacancies in the industry's workforce could have been filled by women, had management cared to hire them. In sharp contrast to their policy toward women, automotive employers did hire large numbers of blacks in the postwar era, dramatically departing from prewar practice. Therefore, management's hiring policies were the critical determinant of the composition of the auto industry's postwar labor force. The UAW's failure to fight on behalf of women's postwar employment rights and the opposition to women's inclusion in the postwar labor force, which this failure suggested, were important insofar as they reinforced management's position. This is where studies of the UAW's role are relevant, but the union's ambivalent stance was only one reason management never seriously considered permanently institutionalizing the changes in hiring policy that the war had forced upon them.

Fordism and the Sexual Division of Labor in Auto

The historic structure of the auto industry and the character of its labor process were the most important reasons that female substitution was not an attractive option for automotive management in the immediate postwar period. The Fordist revolution, which had organized mass production around the moving assembly line, laid the basis for automobile manufacturing to develop as a high-wage, capital-intensive industry; thus, employers had little incentive to substitute female labor for its more expensive male equivalent. Despite the fact that the obstacles to female substitution were minimal in the early days—auto was a rapidly expanding and completely new industry with no tradition of union organization and no history of sex-stereotyped jobs—management showed negligible interest in employing women workers.

Because they have historically been performed by men, production jobs in the auto industry are frequently described as "heavy," neatly reversing the actual line of causality. In fact, the need for workers capable of great physical exertion was eliminated early in the history of the industry, given mechanization and streamlined organization of production. Henry Ford wrote in 1922: "The rank and file of men come to us unskilled. They do not have to be able-bodied men. We have jobs that require great physical strength although they are rapidly lessening; we have other jobs that require no strength whatsoever—jobs which, as far as strength is concerned, might be attended to by a child of three."[3] Similarly, in a 1924 essay on the auto industry Charles Reitell observed that

> quickly—overnight as it were—the machine, gigantic, complex and intricate, has removed the need of muscle and brawn. As Frederick W. Taylor put it, "The gorilla types are no more needed." Instead we have a greater demand for nervous and mental activities such as watchfulness, quick judgements, dexterity, guidance, ability and lastly a nervous endurance to carry through dull, monotonous, fatiguing rhythmic operations.[4]

These were precisely the characteristics of manufacturing jobs commonly thought to be most appropriate for women workers in the early part of the century, according to the prevailing stereotypes. So one might have expected management, as ever eager to maximize profits, to have had an enormous incentive to utilize the ample supplies of "cheap labor" available in the female population of this period. However, this did not occur. Women remained a tiny minority of the auto manufacturing labor force throughout the pre–World War II period. They were employed mostly in parts plants and in the "cut-and-sew" (upholstery) departments of body plants. Although occasionally women were substituted for men, and at lower pay, management's apparent disinterest in any serious effort at large-scale feminization is far more striking.[5]

A crucial difference between the auto industry and those manufacturing industries employing large numbers of women at low wages in this period is that in auto, the supreme lever of control over the workforce was a *high-wage* policy, the magic of the Fordist revolution. Mechanization was carried forward to such a great extent that wages became a relatively small component of costs. "Machinery," proclaimed Henry Ford, "is the new Messiah."[6] The industry quickly gained a reputation for good pay after the famous 1914 announcement of the five-dollar day by the Ford Motor Company, then the largest firm in the industry. Ford had pioneered in the development of control over labor through the use of the moving assembly line, an innovation that spread rapidly throughout the industry along with the high wages it made possible.

Relative to other branches of manufacturing, pay rates were high in the auto industry after 1914. Even during the Depression, when wage cuts were endemic throughout the economy, the weekly earnings of auto workers were 24 percent above the comparable average for all manufacturing.[7] Women auto workers earned substantially less than men, generally about two-thirds as much (on an hourly basis) in the prewar era.[8] Yet management did not seek to depress wage costs by substituting women for men in auto, even during the severe profitability crisis of the 1930s.

Most women employed in auto manufacturing were engaged in the production of auto parts. Unlike the rest of the auto industry, parts manufacturing had many characteristics of the secondary sector of the economy.[9] Machine pacing was used far less extensively, and piece rates—the standard form of wage payment in the heavily female "sweated" manufacturing industries of the day—remained the predominant form of wage payment as late as 1950. The auto parts industry was also relatively competitive and included some notorious sweatshop operations like Briggs, where women's labor was used quite extensively and wage rates were reported to be as low as four cents per hour in the 1930s.[10] But this was atypical. In the major auto firms the predominant policy was to pay high wages in exchange for subordination to the machine-paced organization of production. In fact, thanks to the "new Messiah," even the five-dollar day was an economizing measure. The combination of dramatically lowered turnover rates and the extra production extracted by means of the speed-up meant Ford workers produced more per dollar of wages after the implementation of the five-dollar day than before. Ford himself justifiably called it "one of the finest cost-cutting moves we ever made."[11]

That classic comment captures the essence of management strategy at Ford, a model for the auto industry generally. There was no incentive to seek supplies of cheap female labor in this situation. On the contrary, Ford, and the other auto firms as well, were in a position to offer their predominantly male workforce pay rates approximating a "family wage," an ideal with great resonance in the early-twentieth-century working-class community. In his 1924 autobiography, Ford explicitly embraced the concept:

> If only the man himself were concerned, the cost of his maintenance and the profit he ought to have would be a simple matter. But he is not just an individual. He is a citizen, contributing to the welfare of the nation. He is a householder. He is perhaps a father with children who must be reared to usefulness on what he is able to earn.... The man does the work in the shop, but his wife does the work in the home. The shop must pay them both.... Otherwise, we have the hideous prospect of little children and their mothers being forced out to work.[12]

Among other things, this supplied the rationale for excluding those few females who did work for Ford from the much-lauded five-dollar day. Ford himself told the U.S. Commission on Industrial Relations in 1916 that only one-tenth of the women in his employ received the five-dollar minimum.[13]

Once the auto industry's basic pattern of employment by sex had been established, with men in the vast majority of jobs and women concentrated in small parts production and in cut-and-sew operations, the sexual division of labor proved extraordinarily stable. As is the case throughout the economy, once an auto production job came to be ideologically labeled male or female, the demand for labor to fill it tended to expand or contract in a sex-specific manner, barring major disruptions of labor supply or a basic restructuring of the labor process itself. In day-to-day managerial practice, the established system of sex labeling guided decisions as to whether to hire a male or female in each job opening. Thus, auto employers—and auto workers as well—came to view certain jobs as quintessentially male and others (a far more limited group) as suitable for women. Neither the 1921 recession, the Great Depression, nor the rise of industrial unionism significantly altered the sexual division of labor in auto; it remained unchanged throughout the prewar era.

Even during World War II, employers were initially quite resistant to the idea of hiring women for war jobs in auto plants. They did so only when military conscription had exhausted the supply of male labor in an era of rapidly increasing war production. The federal government intervened in 1942, setting male employment ceilings and giving the War Manpower Commission the power to enforce them.[14] The results were quite dramatic: the proportion of women employed in the auto industry swelled from only 5 percent just before Pearl Harbor to 25 percent two years later.[15]

Once it became clear that there was no alternative, managerial attitudes about the employment of women in production jobs seemed to shift dramatically. As early as June 1942, George Romney, then head of the Automotive Council for War Production, reported to a meeting of automotive managers and government planners on wartime labor-supply problems that "the consciousness of the capability of women is growing all through the [auto] industry." He recounted a conversation at another meeting of automotive employers, held a short time earlier, where the topic of women's employment had been discussed: "One of the fellows said, 'Where will we have any use for men? Why should there be any men?' One fellow said, 'At least one thing a man can still do better than a woman, and that is being a father.' That is where they wound up in their discussion."[16] During the war, numerous testimonials from management conceded that women's production record exceeded that of men on the same or similar jobs.[17] For example, women hired to do "men's jobs" at the four largest plants of the Ford Motor Company "job for job . . . out-produced the men in most cases," according to a 1943 report.[18]

Despite this general enthusiasm for the performance of women war workers, wage differentials between the sexes did not disappear during the war years—a consideration one might expect, given the glowing praise for the performance of women war workers, to have generated some management interest in retaining women permanently in the kinds of jobs they held during the war emergency. The UAW, to be sure, contested wage discrimination, rather successfully, in a series of "equal pay for equal work" cases before the War Labor Board. Although sex differentials in pay in the auto industry were narrowed considerably following these struggles, they were not fully eliminated. In August 1944, women's average straight-time hourly wage in Michigan's auto plants was 90 percent of the male average.[19]

Employers claimed extra costs associated with the employment of women, particularly in previously all-male plants. UAW president R. J. Thomas, questioned at a 1945 Senate hearing about auto industry employers' reluctance to hire women for postwar jobs, summarized the prevailing view:

> Managements have told us some of the reasons. First is that as you know on most jobs equal rates are paid for equal jobs today. . . . Management doesn't want to pay women equal rates with men. Not only that but in many of these plants additional facilities have to be put in, such as toilet facilities to take care of women. More space has to be taken to give an opportunity of changing clothes and more safety measures have to be instituted. I think it is pretty well recognized that it is an additional expense to a management to have women.[20]

This was an accurate report of the reasons auto managers themselves adduced for their reluctance to employ women; however, it seems unsatisfactory when considered alongside other economic factors. Despite equal pay provisions, women's wages were lower than men's in many instances, and few had "equal jobs," even during the war, as job segregation by sex persisted within the war economy.[21] As for the costs of maintaining special "facilities" for women, these were installed largely at government expense during the war; they could hardly have been a major financial consideration in any event. Surely sex differentials in pay would have outweighed any expense firms would incur in maintaining such facilities. Indeed, if only the obvious, direct economic costs and benefits to the auto corporations of female employment were taken into account, one might expect management to have consistently discriminated *in favor of* women and against men in postwar layoffs and rehiring. Particularly in view of the vigorous efforts of employers to increase labor productivity in the reconversion period, management should have preferred to retain women permanently in the "men's jobs" they had just demonstrated their capabilities to perform.[22]

However, in the aftermath of the war, just as in the early development of the industry, automotive employers ignored the opportunity to feminize the work-force. Indeed, in the massive layoffs immediately following the end of the war, women were thrown out of work at a rate nearly double that for men in the manufacturing sector as a whole. The disparity was even greater in auto and other "heavy" industries that had employed very few women in the prewar period. In the month following V-J Day, there was a precipitous drop in women's share of the automotive workforce, from 18 percent in August 1945 to 10 percent in September.[23] The dramatic wartime employment gains of women in the industry were thus rolled back even more rapidly than they had been made. As postwar hiring resumed, it became clear that auto would once again rely on an overwhelmingly male labor force. Wage levels remained high, even increasing during the postwar years. As in the prewar era, management's efforts to boost productivity focused on tightening control over labor, not on reducing pay levels.[24] Management continued to nourish the basic conviction, historically rooted in the logic of Ford-ism—as operative in the postwar situation as in the prewar environment—that women were simply not suitable for employment in automotive production jobs. Employers saw the successful performance of women war workers as, at best, a fortunate outcome of an experiment in which they had participated with great trepidation and only because there had been no alternative. Women had performed better than anyone had expected during the war, true enough, but now the emergency was over, and men's jobs were men's jobs once again.

Seniority, the UAW, and Reconversion Hiring Policy

Studies of the impact of the postwar transition on women auto workers have focused primarily on the issue of women's seniority rights and the role of the UAW. Source materials available on this aspect of the problem are far more extensive than those regarding the role of management; perhaps this accounts for the detailed attention the seniority issue has received in the pioneering work of Tobias and Anderson, Goldfarb, and Gabin.

Their starting point is the observation that women's departure from the automotive labor force, contrary to popular belief at the time, was not voluntary. In fact, the overwhelming majority of women working in the industry during the war intended not only to continue working after the war but to stay in the same type of work. Eighty-five percent of the women war workers responding to a 1944 UAW survey wanted to remain in the labor force after the war, and almost all of them preferred to continue doing factory work. Another survey conducted by the U.S. Women's Bureau at about the same time found that 78 percent of women workers in Detroit planned to continue working after the war and that 85 percent of the Motor City's female factory workers planned to remain in manufacturing. These preferences persisted in the immediate aftermath of the war. In July 1946 the Detroit office of the U.S. Employment Service had nearly twice as many applications on file for semiskilled and unskilled manufacturing jobs from women as from returning male veterans, but the applicants for clerical and service work included a higher proportion of veterans than of women. Although officials alerted automakers and other manufacturing employers to the availability of women for the factory jobs being spurned by men, the demand for workers in auto remained overwhelmingly male.[25]

This situation presented the UAW with a serious dilemma. After the war ended, the full employment economy, the crucial precondition for female incorporation into "men's jobs" in industry in the first place, could no longer be sustained. As a result, women war workers now directly competed for jobs with their male counterparts—a problem intensified by the influx of large numbers of returning veterans into the industrial labor force. Moreover, fear of a return to the high unemployment levels of the Depression years after the war was widespread, especially among workers in durable-goods industries like auto, always particularly sensitive to cyclical economic changes. This situation produced considerable hostility toward women.

In the late 1930s the fledgling UAW had fought long and hard for the establishment of seniority systems to distribute employment equitably in just such situations as this. During the war, it was already obvious that postwar demobilization would bring the first real test of the seniority principle. At the same time, the UAW's commitment to eliminate all forms of discrimination provided an opening for women union activists to work toward the equalization of seniority rights. They pursued this goal energetically and relatively successfully. By the end of the war, the UAW's official policy stance was that women should enjoy the same seniority rights as men. Locals were urged to eliminate separate women's seniority lists and other sex-discriminatory contract provisions, and many did so.[26]

However, in the absence of full employment, the principle of seniority, even if properly enforced, had mixed implications for women war workers. Because their employment gains were so recent, concentrated in the three-year period of war production, the "last hired, first fired" principle embedded in the seniority system meant women would be laid off in disproportionate numbers. Indeed, this was the basis for the argument against strict seniority systems advanced in the 1970s and 1980s by advocates of affirmative action for women and other industrial minorities; however, this view did not enjoy much credibility in the 1940s. Female union activists concerned about women's postwar employment pressed not for preferential treatment for women but simply for the enforcement of the limited seniority rights women war workers already had.[27]

But preferential treatment was widely advocated for one group of workers: returning veterans. Popular appreciation of the hardships of military service thoroughly legitimized the idea that veterans should not be further penalized for their absence from the labor market during the war, and UAW contracts granted seniority equal to the time spent in military service to veterans previously employed by an auto company as well as to those newly hired after their military discharge.[28] At the same time, the union, wary of the potential division between veterans and other workers, strongly opposed so-called super-seniority rights for veterans, which would have given them preferential status over virtually all other workers.[29] To this extent, the UAW's official policy unambiguously protected women's seniority rights, limited as they were.

Official union policies were one thing, but their enforcement was another matter altogether, as feminist scholars have pointed out. There was tremendous ambivalence about women's rights to postwar jobs in industry on the part of both UAW leaders and the rank and file, despite the union's formal opposition to sex discrimination. Internal battles over women's seniority rights raged within the UAW, and all too often the union's practice was inconsistent with its official policy. Separate women's seniority lists remained in effect at the war's end in some locals, although in many others women activists had succeeded in eliminating them during the war. There were other blatantly discriminatory arrangements as well. The national General Motors contract, for example, provided that women employed on "men's jobs" during the war would accumulate temporary seniority, applicable "for the duration only."[30]

In many plants, women *did* have equal seniority rights according to the contract, and the main problem was lack of enforcement. As postwar production resumed and hiring increased, many complained that women war workers were not being recalled according to seniority, in violation of contract provisions. The situation Ida Griggs of UAW Local 306 described to the union's 1946 convention is representative:

> In our plant, and I guess it is the same in most plants, we have women laid off with seniority . . . and every day they hire in new men off the street. They hire men there, they say, to do the heavy work. The women do light work. During

the war they didn't care what kind of work we did, and still we have to work on hard jobs now, and some of the men with lesser seniority get the small jobs.[31]

Explicit job classification by sex was still prevalent at this time; thus, management had only to reclassify jobs in the course of postwar reconversion—from female to male, or from light to heavy—in order to justify not recalling women. Protective legislation, temporarily eased during the war, now became another mechanism by which jobs that women had performed quite adequately during the war, and wanted to keep, were reclassified as "men's jobs."[32]

Previous scholarship offers extensive documentation of the UAW's failure to challenge management in these practices, as well as many instances of explicit union collusion with management in purging women from the industry's labor force. We also know, thanks to this literature, that women workers themselves valiantly sought to defend their seniority rights, even in the face of united opposition from both management and their male co-workers. In the rare cases where their protests were effective and women were ultimately rehired, management proved unrelenting in its determination to oust them from the plants. Those who returned to work under these conditions were subjected to various forms of managerial harassment. "They'd hassle them by putting them on the broom—as it was called—janitorial [work]," recalled Mildred Jeffrey, the head of the UAW Women's Bureau at the time. "They'd hassle them by putting them on night shift or afternoon shift, or just putting them on one job after another. Say, 'do this,' and then in the same day, move them to two or three different jobs, giving them very hard jobs."[33]

It is indisputable that the seniority system was stacked against women, even where nominally nondiscriminatory, and that women war workers' seniority rights, limited as they were, were honored more in the breach than in the observance. However, the seniority system and the UAW's failure to protect women's limited job rights still do not *explain* the virtual absence of women in the postwar auto labor force. The problem is that this line of argument ignores management's crucial role in shaping the postwar sexual division of labor. Far more important than the seniority system, properly enforced or not, in determining the composition of the future labor force in auto was hiring policy. Here, managerial control was virtually complete. So many new workers were hired in the industry after the war that seniority lists were of marginal significance. Contrary to general expectations, the postwar years saw enormous expansion in the auto industry, after a relatively brief interlude of reconversion unemployment. The postwar boom was based on a vast consumer demand for automobiles, as a result of both the unavailability of cars during the war and the general prosperity of the period. By 1947 the number of production workers in the nation's auto factories already exceeded that at the peak of war employment.[34]

Postwar expansion in the auto industry was so massive that even the dramatic influx of veterans, with their preferential seniority status, left plenty of room for recalling women war workers with seniority and even hiring additional women workers. In addition to the rapid postwar expansion of employment in the industry, the emigration of large numbers of war workers (mostly male) from war-production centers along with high attrition meant that the composition of the postwar labor force was shaped primarily by hiring policies.

Between December 1945 and July 1946 veterans constituted on the average 47 percent of all workers hired in the auto industry. By mid-1946 they made up fully 23 percent of the workforce in automobile factories.[35] But this high rate of veteran entry into the industry reflected employers' preference for young male workers, not seniority. "Employers in the auto industry prefer white males, between 20 and 25, weighing over 150 pounds and in good physical condition," the U.S. Women's Bureau reported in July 1946.[36] These were precisely the characteristics the military had sought in conscripting soldiers, and so it is hardly surprising that veterans were hired in large numbers. Andrew Court, a labor relations executive at General Motors at the time, recalled that the 1945–1946 strike against GM increased the representation of veterans in the firm's workforce:

> There was a lot of moaning and groaning about the strike, but really it was one of the best things that happened to our labor supply. We lost people we'd hired during the war who were not as desirable as the GI's. They went somewhere else and didn't come back after the strike, and it was settled when the GI's were coming back, so we had a fairly good supply of young, vigorous, fairly adequate men. A few years later they made a study, and General Motors got "all A's" for having hired so many GI's, and this was the reason.[37]

Most veterans who found postwar employment in the auto plants were young men who had not worked in the industry before; thus, even when granted seniority credit for their time in the military, few had greater seniority status than the women whose wartime "service" had been in war jobs rather than in the armed forces. Only about 20 percent of all returning World War II veterans nationally were entitled to re-employment rights.[38] That those veterans without formal re-employment rights got a seniority bonus meant that employers' preference for them did affect the seniority system, but this was offset by other factors.

Women war workers had at least as much seniority as most of the veterans. Turnover rates among the latter were high, with quits alone averaging 5.4 percent monthly between December 1945 and July 1946.[39] Nonveterans, especially migrants, also left the industry in droves at this time. Between 100,000 and 150,000 people left Michigan between V-J Day and mid-September 1946 alone, many of them southerners returning home. Men predominated in this group.[40] Although the number of veterans with substantial seniority in the auto industry cannot be precisely determined, it can be estimated for the immediate postwar period at a maximum of 100,000.[41] But in the twenty months between V-J Day and April 1947 alone, total employment in auto rose by more than twice that figure—230,000.[42] The high rate of veterans' employment in the auto industry reflected employers' hiring preferences, but it cannot explain the exclusion of women from the postwar labor force.

Perhaps the most convincing evidence that women's low seniority standing was not the cause of their poor postwar representation among auto workers is the comparison of the effects of reconversion on women with those on black workers in the industry. Like women, black workers as a group had relatively low seniority standing at the conclusion of the war. They, too, had first entered the auto industry in large numbers during the war mobilization period. The proportion of blacks in Detroit's automotive plants rose from 5.5 percent in May 1942 to 15 percent by the spring of 1945. Black workers gained access to semiskilled auto jobs on a significant scale for the first time during the war years, in a process paralleling the expansion in the number of jobs open to women.[43]

The experiences of these two groups, so similar during the war, diverged sharply with reconversion to consumer automobile production. While women were ousted from their new positions in the industry at the end of the war, and in most cases not recalled, blacks were more fortunate. "Once the painful transition to peacetime was over," Meier and Rudwick conclude, "blacks found that they retained the foothold in semi-skilled machine production and assembly-line work which they had won during the war."[44] Data on black employment in individual auto firms confirm this. The proportion of blacks in Chrysler's production workforce actually rose just after the war, from 15 percent in 1945 to 17 percent in 1946, in stark contrast to the "exodus" of women from the industry. By 1960 blacks were 26 percent of the labor force in Chrysler's Detroit plants and 23 percent of GM's production workforce in that city. Ford, the one auto manufacturer that had employed blacks in significant numbers before the war, also increased its black employment in the postwar years; by 1960 blacks made up more than 40 percent of the production workforce at the huge River Rouge plant.[45]

This divergence between the experience of women and blacks can be understood only in the context of management's hiring policies. The female proportion of the workforce might have been marginally greater in the postwar years if the UAW had more effectively defended women's seniority rights. But given the high turnover rates for all auto workers and the vast postwar expansion of the industry, even if the UAW had secured the reinstatement of every woman war worker, there would still have been a sharp decline in female representation in the industry's labor force, unless additional women were added as well. Only an insistence on sex-blind hiring policy—which the UAW had no means to enforce—could have substantially altered the situation.

But why was postwar hiring policy different for blacks vis-à-vis women? In the prewar period, management's lack of interest in hiring blacks—like women, a source of "cheap labor"—for auto production jobs had the same basis as its disinterest in feminization. Both were by-products of the industry's general regime of labor discipline, to which high wages were central. And, again paralleling the case of women, racial stereotypes rationalized and legitimized racially exclusive hiring. Yet by the late 1940s, at least in the North, race discrimination had already lost some of its former legitimacy. A large and vital civil rights movement enjoyed substantial UAW support, and management might have expected vigorous protests if it pursued racially discriminatory employment policies.[46]

When blacks were first hired in large numbers in Detroit's auto factories during the period of economic mobilization, there had been considerable opposition among white workers, most dramatically expressed in the numerous "hate strikes" that erupted in the plants and in the "race riot" of the summer of 1943.[47] But by the end of the war there was no longer any legitimate basis for excluding blacks from postwar jobs in the Detroit auto industry. During the war, Detroit had become a major center of the civil rights movement. The Motor City had the largest branch of the National Association for the Advancement of Colored People (NAACP) of any city in the nation, with a membership of twenty thousand by 1943. And the UAW had developed into a strong ally of the NAACP and other civil rights groups. Although discrimination persisted in the auto industry regarding promotion of blacks to the elite skilled trades, no one contested their claim to semiskilled jobs.[48]

The sharp regional variations in patterns of racial hiring within the auto industry suggest the critical importance of the legitimacy or illegitimacy of racial exclusion in shaping employment policies. The proportion of blacks in Detroit's auto plants rose quite dramatically in the 1940s and 1950s, reaching well over 25 percent of the production workforce by 1960, but in the United States as a whole the percentage of nonwhite workers in the auto industry grew much more modestly, from 4 percent in 1940 to only 9 percent in 1960. The national figures reflect the continuing practice of excluding blacks from employment in southern plants. As a manager at a GM plant in Atlanta told the *Wall Street Journal* in 1957, "When we moved into the South, we agreed to abide by local custom and not hire Negroes for production work. This is no time for social reforming and we're not about to try it."[49]

The situation of women auto workers was quite different from that of northern blacks. The incorporation of women into the industry provoked no riots or "hate strikes," precisely because female employment was explicitly understood as a temporary expedient "for the duration" of the war. There was no parallel expectation regarding black men, whose interests were aggressively defended by a growing interracial constituency of liberals, unionists, and civil rights supporters throughout the North. Although women war workers wanted to remain in the auto industry, their preferences seemed to have little social or political legitimacy. No popular consciousness of women's job rights emerged at this critical juncture when the sexual division of labor that would characterize the entire postwar period was crystallizing. Unlike race discrimination, which might have been politically and socially costly, management could rely on minimal resistance, either from women themselves or from the UAW, to purging women from the auto workforce in the war's aftermath.

Although there were some protests against postwar sex discrimination, these were both rare and generally unsuccessful.[50] At best, they secured postwar employment for small groups of women war workers with contractual seniority rights. Demanding that management also refrain from discriminating against women in hiring new workers, once the seniority lists were exhausted in the course of postwar expansion, was never "on the agenda." But this is precisely what would have been required for women to maintain their wartime gains in the industry.

Instead, the typical pattern was collusion between male workers and management in excluding women from postwar employment. This was due not only to the general cultural setting but also to the particular structural features of the auto industry. The response of male workers to the postwar transition was quite different in some other industries. In electrical manufacturing, for example, the same fear of unemployment that led to union collusion with management's violation of women auto workers' seniority rights produced strikingly opposite results. In the electrical case, it was impossible to think of excluding women from employment; the industry had been one-third female even before the war. Instead, male workers responded to the wartime upheaval in the sexual division of labor (and the anticipated postwar upheaval as well) by fighting against sex discrimination and challenging the whole system of job segregation by sex in a struggle for equal pay for jobs of comparable worth. As in auto, the goal was to decrease the likelihood of permanent (in other words, postwar) female substitution. Because auto management had never seriously attempted to replace men with women, except, of course, during the war emergency, the UAW had little incentive to protest hiring policy; in electrical manufacturing, management's extensive use of female labor generated a radical challenge to sex discrimination in the form of a comparable worth demand. In this way, management policy not only shaped the sexual composition of the labor force in each industry but also profoundly influenced the character of labor struggles over women's position.[51]

If management ever seriously considered the permanent substitution of women for men in the postwar auto industry—and no evidence suggesting that has been uncovered—there would have been good reason to anticipate protest from male workers. Minimally, management could have anticipated a postwar fight for equal pay for equal work for women, if postwar hiring had not been exclusively male. More generally, in view of the widespread fear of unemployment in the demobilization period, auto industry managers might reasonably have expected that any effort on their part to renege on the wartime assurances that women were in "men's jobs" only "for the duration" would have precipitated considerable resistance from men.[52] Thus, the UAW's role was not the only, or even the primary, cause of the postwar expulsion of women workers from the auto industry; but it did reinforce the managerial logic of reconstructing the prewar sexual division of labor.

Conclusion

The primary determinant of the postwar sexual division of labor in the auto industry was management's preference for male workers. Historically rooted in the logic of Fordism, as it shaped the industry's structure in the early twentieth century, the sexual division of auto production work became such a permanent characteristic of the industry that even the dramatic transformation of the war years had no lasting impact. The UAW's failure to challenge the sexual division of labor in the immediate aftermath of the war served to reinforce management's policy. But that failure was also a product of the policy, for the history of predominantly male employment in auto itself defined the possibilities for struggle over "woman's place" in the industry.

Except for the brief interlude during World War II, women have always remained a small minority among auto production workers. Even in the 1970s, when the proportion of women in the industry's blue-collar workforce increased slightly, the changes were quite modest, particularly given the dramatic rise in U.S. female labor force participation in that decade. The effect of the women's movement of the late 1960s and 1970s on auto employment in some respects paralleled the effect of the civil rights movement in the 1940s; however, since there was no comparable expansion of employment in the 1970s, the scale of change was far smaller. Gains made through affirmative action were significantly eroded after 1978, when women's employment peaked, as a result of plant closings and layoffs.[53] In general, the continuity of the sexual division of labor in the auto industry is far more striking than the changes that have occurred. The reconstruction of the prewar situation in the aftermath of World War II is but the most extreme instance of that broad continuity, rooted in the structural characteristics of the industry and its labor process.

Notes

This chapter was originally published in *On the Line: Essays in the History of Auto Work*, edited by Nelson Lichtenstein and Stephen Meyer (Urbana: University of Illinois Press, 1989).

1. U.S. Department of Labor, Bureau of Labor Statistics, *Women in Factories*, mimeo., August 1947, 7.

2. Sheila Tobias and Lisa Anderson, "What Really Happened to Rosie the Riveter? Demobilization and the Female Labor Force, 1944–47," Module 9 (New York: MSS Modular Publications, 1974), 1–36; Lyn Goldfarb, *Separated and Unequal: Discrimination against Women Workers after World War II (The U.A.W., 1944–1954)* (Washington, D.C.: Union for Radical Political Economics, 1976); and Nancy Gabin, "Women Workers and the UAW in the Post-World War II Period: 1945–1954," *Labor History* 21, no. 1 (Winter 1979–1980): 5–30.

3. Henry Ford, in collaboration with Samuel Crowther, *My Life and Work* (Garden City, N.J.: Doubleday, 1923), 79.

4. Charles Reitell, "Machinery and Its Effects upon the Workers in the Automotive Industry," *Annals of the American Academy of Political and Social Science* 116 (1924): 43.

5. Examples of substitution are noted in Robert W. Dunn, *Labor and Automobiles* (New York: International, 1929), 73, 76; and in William H. McPherson, *Labor Relations in the Automobile Industry* (Washington, D.C.: Brookings Institute, 1940), 8–9.

6. Keith Sward, *The Legend of Henry Ford* (New York: Rinehart, 1948), 1.

7. Andrew T. Court, *Men, Methods and Machines in Automobile Manufacturing* (New York: Automobile Manufacturers Association, 1939), 9.

8. In 1925, women auto workers averaged 47 cents per hour, compared with 73 cents for men in the industry. Similarly, in April 1934, women averaged 52 cents an hour in auto factory jobs, compared with 73 cents for men. A third survey in September 1934 found average earnings of 54 cents for women and 75 cents for men. (All three sets of figures exclude auto-parts plants, where wages were substantially lower for workers of both sexes.) See U.S. Department of Labor, Bureau of Labor Statistics, Bulletin no. 438, *Wages and Hours of Labor in the Motor Vehicle Industry: 1925* (1927), 2–3; and N. A. Tolles and M. W. La Fever, "Wages, Hours, Employment and Annual Earnings in the Motor-Vehicle Industry, 1934," *Monthly Labor Review* 42, no. 3 (March 1936): 527.

Despite these differentials, a U.S. Women's Bureau survey of Flint, Michigan, in 1925 found that the $20.10 per week women averaged in that city's auto industry (and this did include workers at parts plants) was more than they were paid in any other type of work. See U.S. Women's Bureau, Bulletin no. 67, *Women Workers in Flint, Michigan* (1929), 19.

9. As I have argued elsewhere, dual-labor-market theory has many deficiencies in regard to its propositions about the sexual division of labor. But the distinction between primary and secondary economic locations does seem useful here. For a critique of the overall framework as applied to gender, see Ruth Milkman, *Gender at Work: The Dynamics of Job Segregation by Sex during World War II* (Urbana: University of Illinois Press, 1987), chap. 1.

10. "Automotive Parts; Wage Structure, March-April 1950," *Monthly Labor Review* 72, no. 1 (January 1951): 37; Robert Blauner, *Alienation and Freedom* (Chicago: University of Chicago Press, 1964), 89–92; William McPherson, "Automobiles," in *How Collective Bargaining Works*, edited by Harry A. Millis, 611–12 (New York: Twentieth Century Fund, 1942); Philip

S. Foner, *Women and the American Labor Movement: From World War II to the Present* (New York: Free Press, 1980), 260, 270.

11. Sward, *Legend of Henry Ford*, 56.

12. Ford, *My Life and Work*, 128. See also Martha May, "The Historical Problem of the Family Wage: The Ford Motor Company and the Five Dollar Day," *Feminist Studies* 8, no. 2 (Summer 1982): 399–424.

13. U.S. Commission on Industrial Relations, Industrial Relations, vol. 8, *Final Report and Testimony* (1916), 7637.

14. "Meeting for Discussion of Labor Supply and Future Labor Requirements," June 26, 1942, Detroit, Michigan, 23–35 of transcript, in folder: "241.11R Labor-Women-Recruiting Drive," box 1016, Records of the War Production Board, RG 179, National Archives; interview with Edward Cushman, former head of the War Manpower Commission's Detroit office, Detroit, June 25, 1981. See also chap. 2, this volume.

15. U.S. Bureau of Labor Statistics, *Women in Factories.*

16. "Meeting for Discussion of Labor Supply," 30–31 of transcript.

17. National Industrial Conference Board, *Wartime Pay of Women in Industry*, NICH Studies in Personnel Policy, no. 58 (1943), 27.

18. "Women Outdoing Men, Ford Survey Reveals," *New York Daily News*, September 8, 1943.

19. "Women's Rates Advance," *UAW Research Report* 4, no. 9 (October–November 1944): 4. For discussion of the equal pay struggles, see Milkman, *Gender at Work*, chap. 5.

20. U.S. Senate Hearings before a Special Committee Investigating the National Defense Program, *Manpower Problems in Detroit*, 79th Congress, 1st Session, March 9–13, 1945, pp. 13112–13.

21. See Milkman, *Gender at Work.*

22. Howell John Harris, *The Right to Manage: Industrial Relations Policies of American Business in the 1940s* (Madison: University of Wisconsin Press, 1982), 66–67, 91–93.

23. U.S. Bureau of Labor Statistics, *Women in Factories.* (The August figure of 18 percent was well below the wartime peak of 26 percent female.)

24. This is the main thesis of Harris, *The Right to Manage.*

25. U.S. Women's Bureau, Bulletin no. 209, *Women Workers in Ten War Production Areas and Their Postwar Employment Plans* (1946), 31, 42; "Women's Postwar Plans," *UAW Research Report* 4, no. 3 (March 1944): 3; Karen Anderson, *Wartime Women: Sex Roles, Family Relations, and the Status of Women in World War II* (Westport, Conn.: Greenwood, 1981), 170–71.

26. "Policy on Women's Seniority Problems," *UAW-CIO Ammunition* 2, no. 3 (March 1944): 13; "Women in Trade Unions during the War Period," p. 10 of draft report, in box 1351, Records of the U.S. Women's Bureau, RG 86, National Archives.

27. For a representative statement, see the National Women's Trade Union League pamphlet, *Action Needed: Postwar Jobs for Women* (1944), 11–12. See also sources cited in note 2.

28. The UAW had a "Model Veterans' Seniority Clause," written into contracts with Chrysler, North American Aviation, and Mack Truck, among others, by 1946. See *UAW-CIO Ammunition* 4, no. 6 (April 1946): 23.

29. Robert P. Brecht, "Collective Bargaining and Re-employment of Veterans," *Annals of the American Academy of Political and Social Science* 227 (May 1943): 94–103; Joel Seidman, *American Labor from Defense to Reconversion* (Chicago: University of Chicago Press, 1953), 231–32.

30. For discussion, see sources cited in note 2.

31. *Proceedings of the 10th Convention of the United Automobile, Aircraft and Agricultural Implement Workers of America (UAW-CIO)*, March 23–31, 1946, p. 53.

32. For discussion, see sources cited in note 2.

33. Mildred Jeffrey, oral history, "The Twentieth-Century Trade Union Woman: Vehicle for Social Change—Oral History Project," pp. 63–64 of transcript. For other examples of this sort of harassment, see William Oliver, "Report on Employees Laid Off from the Bomber Project, Highland Park Plant (Johnson's Division)," February 9, 1945, in folder: "William Oliver Reports," box 16, UAW Ford Department Collection, Wayne State University Archives of Labor History and Urban Affairs (hereafter ALHUA); Jennie Lee Murphy and Minnie P. Sowell to Thomas I. Starling, April 13, 1946, in folder: "Ford Dept., 1946–47," box 23, Walter Reuther Collection, ALHUA. Many additional examples of this phenomenon could be cited.

34. U.S. Bureau of Labor Statistics, *Women in Factories*. Regarding the universal expectation of postwar depression, see Harris, *Right to Manage*, 129.

35. The figure of 47 percent is the mean of the percentages for each of the eight months from December 1945 to July 1946; it does not reflect monthly variations in hiring rates. See "Veterans Return to the Nation's Factories," *Monthly Labor Review* 63, no. 6 (December 1946): 924–34.

36. "Recent Trends Affecting the Employment of Women in Automobile Manufacturing in Detroit," July 26, 1946, in folder: "247 Michigan Dept. of Labor," box 1290, Records of the U.S. Women's Bureau, RG 86, National Archives.

37. Interview with Andrew Court, Detroit, Michigan, June 25, 1981.

38. This is Alan Clive's estimate in his *State of War: Michigan in World War II* (Ann Arbor: University of Michigan Press, 1979), 216. David Ross also emphasizes the limited reemployment rights of veterans in *Preparing for Ulysses: Politics and Veterans during World War II* (New York: Columbia University Press, 1969), esp. 157.

39. "Veterans Return to the Nation's Factories."

40. Olga S. Halsey, "Women Workers and Unemployment Insurance since V-J Day," *Social Security Bulletin* 9, no. 6 (June 1946): 4.

41. Unfortunately, detailed statistics on the long-term postwar employment situation of veterans are not available for individual industries. However, existing aggregate data are suggestive. A special survey of veterans by the U.S. Census Bureau conducted in October 1955 found that ten years after the end of World War II, 28.5 percent of all veterans were employed in manufacturing jobs; 60 percent of these veterans were younger than age thirty-five in 1955. (The survey included both Korean War and World War II veterans, but the latter made up 85 percent of the total of 21 million veterans in the United States in 1955.)

Of the six million veterans employed in manufacturing jobs in 1955, five million were World War II veterans. About two million of these were thirty-five years old or older in 1955. In 1947 the auto industry employed 5 percent of all manufacturing workers; if we assume that auto also employed 5 percent of the veterans in manufacturing, we can estimate that one hundred thousand veterans over age twenty-five worked in auto in 1945. This is surely a maximum figure, since veterans' turnover was high and auto firms were known to discriminate against older workers of both sexes. Also, Korean War veterans were probably disproportionately represented in the under-thirty-five age group in the 1955 census. For the figures on veterans, see *Readjustment Benefits: General Survey and Appraisal. A Report on Veterans' Benefits in the United States by the President's Commission on Veterans' Pensions* (House Committee Print No. 289, for the use of the House Committee on Veterans' Affairs, Staff Report No. IX, Part A, 84th Congress, 2d Session, September, 1956), p. 276. The 5 percent figure for auto employment is from the 1947 Census of Manufactures, vol. 1, pp. 70–77.

42. U.S. Bureau of Labor Statistics, *Women in Factories*.

43. Robert C. Weaver, *Negro Labor: A National Problem* (New York: Harcourt, Brace, and World, 1946), 285; August Meier and Elliott Rudwick, *Black Detroit and the Rise of the UAW* (New York: Oxford University Press, 1979), 213.

44. Meier and Rudwick, *Black Detroit*, 215.

45. The figures on Chrysler for 1945–1946 are from Weaver, *Negro Labor*, 289. All the 1960 figures are from UAW documents submitted at the Hearings before the U.S. Commission on Civil Rights, held in Detroit on December 14–15, 1960, pp. 63–64.

46. See Meier and Rudwick, *Black Detroit*.

47. Ibid.; Weaver, *Negro Labor*.

48. The NAACP membership figure is from Meier and Rudwick, *Black Detroit*, 113. Their book is the best account of the development of the alliance between the UAW and Detroit black organizations in the 1940s. See also Karen Anderson, "Last Hired, First Fired: Black Women Workers during World War II," *Journal of American History* 69, no. 1 (June 1982): esp. 86–87, where she compares white male workers' attitudes toward women and blacks.

49. Both the employment figures and the quote are from Herbert R. Northrup, Richard L. Rowan, et al., *Negro Employment in Basic Industry* (Industrial Research Unit, Wharton School of Finance and Commerce, University of Pennsylvania, 1970), 65–75. The national employment figures are from the U.S. Census. Since they, unlike the figures for Detroit, include nonproduction as well as production workers, they overstate the difference between Detroit and the nation as a whole; the vast majority of nonproduction workers in this period were white. The quote is from the *Wall Street Journal*, October 24, 1957.

50. For an excellent analysis of some of these protests, see Nancy Gabin, "'They Have Placed a Penalty on Womanhood': The Protest Actions of Women Auto Workers in Detroit Area UAW Locals, 1945–1947," *Feminist Studies* 8, no. 2 (Summer 1982): 373–98.

51. See Milkman, *Gender at Work*.

52. I have uncovered no evidence of this for the auto industry specifically, but see Constance Green, "The Role of Women as Production Workers in War Plants in the Connecticut Valley," *Smith College Studies in History* 28 (1946): 64–65, who reports that "most companies frankly admitted that, given full freedom of choice after the war, if only out of deference to prevailing male opinion in the shops, management would revert to giving men's jobs, so called, only to men. And employers generally assumed that labor would permit no choice." Regarding management's concern about postwar unemployment, see Harris, *Right to Manage*, 95.

53. Patricia Sexton cites 1970 EEOC figures indicating that female employment in auto accounted for about 10 percent of the total—about the same level as twenty years earlier. See Patricia Cayo Sexton, "A Feminist Union Perspective," in *Auto Work and Its Discontents*, edited by B. J. Widick (Baltimore, Md.: Johns Hopkins University Press, 1976), 18–33.

Chapter 5

Women's History and the Sears Case

This chapter, like the preceding one, highlights the powerful role of employers and their hiring policies in shaping the sexual division of paid labor. In the 1980s, when Sears Roebuck was the world's largest retailer and the largest employer of women in the United States, a lawsuit launched by the U.S. Equal Employment Opportunity Commission (EEOC) shone a bright light on its hiring policies. The EEOC presented extensive evidence that those policies systematically excluded women from Sears's most highly paid sales jobs. The company's defense was that women themselves were not interested in taking commission sales jobs, due to their family commitments and other gender-specific characteristics. The Sears case was the last in a series of class-action sex-discrimination lawsuits filed against large companies by the EEOC in the 1970s, under Title VII of the 1964 Civil Rights Act, which prohibits sex discrimination in employment. There was no union presence at Sears; instead, the EEOC advocated on behalf of the firm's female workers. The trial featured two historians as expert witnesses, one testifying for Sears and the other for the EEOC, starkly revealing the ways in which scholarship can be implicated in the shaping of public policy.

Introduction

Are women's interests best served by public policies that treat women and men identically, ignoring the social and cultural differences between them? Or should we view those differences positively and seek greater recognition and status for traditionally female values and forms of behavior? This tension between equality and difference has divided feminists in a variety of contexts. It is central to the debates over "women's culture" in feminist historical scholarship, for example.[1] Scholars analyzing women's experience can hedge on the issue, aiming for a balanced perspective that incorporates the insights of both positions. But in more immediately political contexts, this luxury is seldom available. The issue has deeply split feminist activists working on pregnancy disability policy, with some advocating "special treatment" for pregnant women and others insisting on "equal treatment" (that is, that pregnancy-related disabilities must be treated exactly like any other disability).[2]

The scholarly and political dimensions of the question were joined together in a sex-discrimination case brought by the Equal Employment Opportunities Commission (EEOC) against Sears, Roebuck and Co. The case was tried in 1984 and 1985 in U.S. District Court in Chicago, and in early 1986 Judge John A. Nordberg decided in favor of Sears. (The EEOC later appealed the case unsuccessfully.)

Women's history and the issue of difference figured prominently in Sears's trial defense, based primarily on the claim that the underrepresentation of women in high-paying commission sales jobs was not due to discrimination, as the EEOC charged, but to women's own job preferences. Two well-known feminist historians, Rosalind Rosenberg and Alice Kessler-Harris, testified as expert witnesses in the case, presenting conflicting historical interpretations of women's relationship to work and the relative importance of workers' and employers' roles in shaping patterns of employment by sex.

Rosenberg, testifying for Sears, argued that the EEOC's case incorrectly assumed that women and men were alike in their values and job preferences and thus did not prove Sears had engaged in sex discrimination. "Men and women differ in their expectations concerning work, in their interests as to the types of jobs they prefer or the types of products they prefer to sell," Rosenberg's "Offer of Proof" stated. "It is naive to believe that the natural effect of these differences is evidence of discrimination by Sears."[3] This testimony was an important component of Sears's argument that the firm had not denied women opportunities for better-paid commission sales jobs, as the EEOC alleged, but that women simply "were less likely to prefer or have relevant experience in commission sales positions."[4]

Faced with Sears's invocation of the historical record, the EEOC presented its own expert witness, Alice Kessler-Harris, who argued that Rosenberg's testimony neglected the central issue of employers' willingness to hire on a nondiscriminatory, sex-blind basis. "What appear to be women's choices, and what are characterized as women's 'interests' are, in fact, heavily influenced by the opportunities for work made available to them," Kessler-Harris testified. "Where opportunity has existed, women have never failed to take the jobs offered. . . . Failure to find women in so-called non-traditional jobs can thus only be interpreted as a consequence of employers' unexamined attitudes or preferences, which phenomenon is the essence of discrimination."[5] This testimony bolstered the EEOC's claim that Sears had denied women opportunities to work in commission sales.

Historians, even feminist historians, frequently disagree with one another. But it is difficult to imagine a forum less tolerant of the nuanced, careful arguments in which historians delight than a courtroom. And rarely are the stakes so high in a scholarly debate. At the time, Sears was the world's largest retailer and the nation's largest private sector employer of women.[6] Sales work is highly sex-segregated, and no other major occupational group has a larger gender gap in pay.[7] The EEOC's case against Sears, had it been successful, could have made a real difference in the position of women salesworkers. Although the historical testimony of Rosenberg and Kessler-Harris was only one component of the lengthy and complex trial, which lasted ten months and generated more than nineteen thousand pages of transcripts, the case itself is very important. Not only does it offer valuable lessons about the uses of history in the courts, but it was also the last major antidiscrimination case brought by the government against a large corporation.

The Political Context of the EEOC's Case

The Sears trial took place against the background of the Reagan administration's reduced enforcement of antidiscrimination legislation and escalating political attacks on the concept of affirmative action.[8] The lawsuit against Sears was originally filed in 1979, and since then no new cases of comparable scope have been initiated by the EEOC.[9] Clarence Thomas, then the EEOC chair, publicly questioned the validity of the Sears suit, particularly its reliance on statistical evidence to demonstrate discrimination.[10] The *Washington Post* reported in 1985 that Thomas and other Reagan administration officials "privately make little secret of their desire to lose the [Sears] case, and lose it in a way that would explode any chance for future EEOC officials to bring class-action suits on the basis of statistics."[11]

The case originated in 1973, when an EEOC Commissioner's Charge against Sears was filed, alleging discrimination by race, sex, and national origin, in violation of Title VII of the Civil Rights Act of 1964. Over the next few years, the EEOC sought to resolve the charges through discussions with Sears, but no agreement was reached. In early 1977 the EEOC issued a Commission Decision that there was "reasonable cause" to believe Sears had discriminated against women and minorities in violation of Title VII. There followed renewed efforts to reach an out-of-court settlement, but in January 1979 the EEOC determined that conciliation efforts had failed, and the agency filed suit against Sears that October.[12]

The response of Sears to the EEOC's charges of discrimination was very different from that of other giant corporations in the 1970s. Unlike General Electric,

General Motors, and others faced with similar EEOC charges, Sears chose not to follow the lead of AT&T and the steel industry, both of which signed consent decrees in the early 1970s, providing millions of dollars in back pay to women and minorities and establishing elaborate affirmative action plans.[13] Sears did institute an affirmative action plan in 1974, the year after the original Commissioner's Charge was filed, requiring that in jobs where women and/or minorities were underutilized, one out of every two people hired be either female or a member of a minority group. However, the EEOC ultimately argued that in the period from 1973 to 1980, Sears continued to discriminate against women in hiring for commission sales jobs.[14]

On January 26, 1979, the day the EEOC notified Sears of its "failure to conciliate" but before the government had filed suit against the company, Sears went on the offensive with a lawsuit of its own—a class action directed against the EEOC and nine other government agencies. The suit charged that "the myriad Federal anti-discrimination statutes and regulations" conflicted with one another and were impossible to comply with, and that government policies themselves had created "an unbalanced workforce dominated by white males." Through the GI Bill and other pro-veteran measures, Sears argued, government policy had "deprived" employers of "a pool of qualified minority and female applicants"; yet now the government was accusing them of race and sex discrimination. "Society has been unable to resolve the dilemma between protecting the traditional husband-wife family unit and encouraging the independence of women apart from the family," Sears complained, and it asked the court to require the federal government to issue uniform guidelines.[15]

Sears's suit was thrown out of court a few months after it was filed. In the interim, however, it attracted a great deal of public attention. This was partly because of the suit's unprecedented line of argument. In addition, Sears was represented by Charles Morgan, a former civil rights lawyer and the former director of the Washington office of the American Civil Liberties Union (ACLU). Morgan left the ACLU in 1976 and went into private practice the following year. Sears was his first big client.[16] When asked by the *New York Times* about his views of discrimination and the law in 1979, when he filed Sears's suit against the government, Morgan said:

> I've always been against the Government. Where I come from [Birmingham, Alabama], Bull Connor was the government. What you've got to do is to make the Government use the law for the purposes for which it was intended. When you've got laws protecting women, minorities, the aged, the handicapped, including drug addicts and alcoholics and every kind of veteran, a company doesn't know what it should do because the Government is telling it too many confusing things. . . .

The Government has to get its priorities straight. There's just no equation between minorities and women.

At that point the *Times* asked him what his priorities would be, and Morgan replied, "Look, I know who the 13th, 14th, and 15th Amendments were intended for and that's still the priority."[17]

In fact, the EEOC's charges against Sears included race as well as sex discrimination. In October 1979, five months after Sears's preemptive suit was dismissed, the EEOC filed five suits against Sears—a nationwide suit alleging sex discrimination and four separate suits alleging race discrimination in hiring against blacks and Hispanics in specific Sears facilities.[18] Morgan represented Sears in all five cases.

Several reports appeared in the press in August 1979 (two months before the suits were filed) that EEOC staff lawyers were questioning whether the government could win its case against Sears in court. These reports cited "a series of confidential memos" from the office of Issie L. Jenkins, the EEOC's acting general counsel, suggesting a change in the Sears litigation strategy.[19] Instead of a single case against Sears, Jenkins's office recommended filing several separate suits: one nationwide sex-discrimination suit alleging bias in recruitment, hiring, promotion, pay, and other areas; a separate nationwide race-discrimination suit alleging discriminatory failure to promote minorities; as well as local race-bias suits alleging discrimination in hiring and layoffs at specific stores. The memos also suggested that the national sex-discrimination case was the strongest of the group.[20]

Because EEOC representatives are not permitted to comment on the leaked material, whether or how the agency's final litigation strategy was influenced by this advice is impossible to determine.[21] But the suits filed in October 1979 did separate the sex and race cases, a strategy generally consistent with what Jenkins's office had reportedly suggested.[22] A settlement was eventually reached in the race cases, while the nationwide sex-discrimination case gradually wended its way through the court system until it finally went to trial in 1984.[23]

The sex-discrimination case involved three basic charges. The EEOC accused Sears of failing to hire female job applicants for commission sales positions on the same basis as male applicants, failing to promote female noncommission salespersons to commission sales positions on the same basis as males, and paying women in certain management-level job categories less than similarly situated men.[24] The historical testimony of Rosenberg and Kessler-Harris concerned only the commission sales issues, and so the charge of sex discrimination in pay for management employees will not be explored in detail here.

The EEOC suit charged Sears with systematic discrimination against women; originally there were thirty-five individual charges of sex discrimination attached to it. But because most of these were not specifically relevant to the charges of hiring and promotion discrimination in commission sales or to the pay discrimination charge involving managers, the EEOC decided not to try the individual cases as part of its suit. One reason for this decision was that each individual case required detailed attention in its own right, which it would not get in this setting. Some of the cases were pursued separately by the individuals involved.[25]

The 1986 decision in the case emphasized the EEOC's failure to present any individual victims of discrimination as witnesses.[26] The EEOC, however, pointed out that testimony from a few individuals who believed they were victims of discrimination could do little to substantiate the charge of hiring discrimination because of the vast numbers of job applications Sears received, and also because in most cases an applicant who is not hired has no way of knowing the reason why.[27] The absence of testimony from individual victims may have also reflected the EEOC's limited resources, which were enormously taxed by the Sears case. The agency reportedly spent about $2.5 million on the protracted case, while Sears spent an estimated $20 million in legal fees.[28] In any event, the EEOC's case against Sears concentrated on statistical evidence of discrimination.

The EEOC presented extensive evidence of disparities between the female proportion of commission sales hires and the female proportion of sales applicants.[29] Between 1973 and 1980, nationwide, women made up 61 percent of full-time and 66 percent of part-time sales applicants at Sears. But women were only 27 percent of full-time commission sales hires in this period and only 35 percent of part-time commission sales hires—except in Sears's midwestern "territory," where women made up 52 percent of part-time commission sales hires in the 1973–80 period. Commission salespersons consistently earned more than noncommission salespersons and generally sold more expensive items, such as furniture, appliances, televisions, and home improvement materials. Between 1973 and 1980, *first-year* commission salespersons had median earnings about twice those of *all* noncommission salespersons.[30]

The EEOC conducted elaborate statistical analyses to determine whether "differences between male and female applicants in characteristics that might be associated with success" could explain the disparities between the proportion of women among sales applicants and the proportion hired in commission positions. The factors controlled for in the statistical analyses were job applied for, age, education, job type experience, product line experience, and commission product sales experience.[31] Those controls did reduce the disparities between expected and actual commission sales hires, but substantial and statistically significant disparities remained.[32] The EEOC also presented detailed statistical evidence regarding promotions, documenting statistically significant disparities between the expected and actual proportions of women among employees promoted from noncommission to commission sales positions in the 1973–80 period, for both part- and full-time workers.[33]

In support of its case that the statistical disparities were due to discrimination, the EEOC presented qualitative evidence of bias in Sears's hiring procedures along with the statistical data. In one of the EEOC memos leaked to the press in 1979, Acting General Counsel Issie L. Jenkins reportedly wrote that "in proving our case we intend to emphasize Sears's policy of allowing employment decisions to be dictated by the unguided subjective judgment of an essentially Anglo male supervisory workforce as the primary culpable aspect of the system."[34] In the trial itself five years later, the EEOC sought to do precisely this in presenting evidence about Sears's hiring procedures.

In describing Sears's hiring process, the EEOC noted that anyone who appeared at a Sears personnel office indicating an interest in employment was given an application to fill out and was interviewed. Later, the applicant might be interviewed a second time, depending on the first interviewer's impressions and on whether there were vacancies to be filled. Hiring decisions were ultimately made by the store manager or personnel manager. The only document in general circulation at Sears that offered managers guidance as to what sort of person to hire for a commission sales position was the "Retail Testing Manual," originally issued by Sears in 1953. The manual's profile of the commission salesperson (here called the "Big Ticket Salesman") was unmistakably masculine.

> Personality, supported by adequate mental ability, is important in Big Ticket Selling. This is illustrated by the fact that the Big Ticket Salesman is active and has a lot of drive. The high level of activity is backed by considerable physical vigor. He has a liking for tools, likes work which requires physical energy, and carries much of this energy and drive over into his selling activities. This information resulted from studying the Active and Vigor Scores for many Big Ticket Salesmen. These men also enjoy changing tasks frequently, and dislike work which requires them to remain at one task or activity for prolonged periods of time. They do not take chances unnecessarily but may, as their impulsive scores indicate, act somewhat impulsively.

Although the explicitly masculine pronouns were eliminated in the editions of the manual written from 1966 on, this description of commission sales jobs otherwise remained unchanged.[35]

The "Active" and "Vigor" Scores referred to here are from the Thurstone Temperament Schedule, a test that Sears policy required each applicant for a sales position to take before she or he could be hired. The test measured seven dimensions of temperament. On six of them, there were few differences between female and male scores, but on the seventh, the Vigor scale, there were dramatic differences.

The reason is evident from the twenty questions that made up the Vigor scale, which included the following:

"Do you have a low-pitched voice?"
"Do you swear often?"
"Have you ever done any hunting?"
"Have you participated in wrestling?"
"Have you participated in boxing?"
"Have you played on a football team?"

The EEOC presented evidence that Sears believed that "a woman who scored 9 on the Vigor scale would have the same behavior as a man who scored 14." But while the company's 1973 "Retail Testing Manual" set out different recommended Vigor scores for selecting women and men for many other jobs, it used the same standard for both sexes in its recommended scores for commission sales positions. According to the manual, a man scoring 14 would be considered to have a "best score," while a woman scoring 9 would be viewed as a poor risk—even though Sears believed their behavior would be the same.[36]

The manual and test materials bolstered the EEOC's case, but the argument that Sears had discriminated against women in commission sales jobs relied primarily on establishing the existence of, first, statistical disparities between the female proportion of hires and promotions and the female proportion of the relevant pools of available workers and, second, highly subjective employment processes. On both counts, the EEOC cited Title VII case law in support of its position.[37]

Sears did not dispute the EEOC's presentation of information about the hiring process itself, although it did contend that "tests were a minor consideration in commission sales selection."[38] The company also argued that the EEOC had to show that there was *intentional* discrimination against women ("disparate treatment") behind the statistical disparities.[39] Sears's "voluntarily-assumed affirmative action efforts" were cited as evidence of "the lack of an intention to discriminate." Management, Sears claimed, had made "stringent affirmative action efforts to recruit and encourage women to take commission sales jobs."[40] Sears also criticized the EEOC for not introducing testimony from victims of discrimination.[41] Lawyer Charles Morgan went so far as to suggest that "there was no victim here [in this trial] except one, and that one victim is Sears, Roebuck and Company."[42]

The bulk of Sears's defense, however, was devoted to challenging the validity of the EEOC's statistical analysis. The company argued that the EEOC's comparison of the representation of women among non-hired job applicants and among persons actually hired into commission sales jobs was improper—it was "comparing apples to oranges."[43] The proper comparison to make, Sears contended, was between the proportion of women among all sales applicants and the proportion among all (commission and non-commission) sales hires; or between the female proportion of applicants who specifically indicated a preference for commission sales and the female proportion of commission sales hires.[44] (However, Sears did not ask its job applicants if they specifically preferred commission sales positions.)

Sears's critique of the EEOC's statistical analysis primarily concerned the "assumption" that "male and female applicants were equally qualified for and interested in commission sales positions."[45] On the contrary, Sears argued, there were fundamental differences between women's and men's qualifications and preferences, and women were generally less suited to selling on commission. Commission salespeople, for one thing, must be willing to take risks.[46] And commission selling is highly skilled, specialized work, Sears contended.

> The commission salesperson must be able to determine customers' needs and match those needs with the product, trading up to better merchandise when possible. This requires intimate familiarity with, and ability to operate and demonstrate, several models in a product line, and frequently several product lines....
>
> The commission salesperson must be able to face and meet objections, and must be willing to risk rejection and failure by attempting to "close" the sale—asking for the order at the earliest possible time and repeatedly until the sale is closed....
>
> Although virtually all noncommission sales jobs can be filled by a sociable person with a pleasant, helpful personality and a reasonable ability to communicate and learn about relatively simple lines of merchandise, the combination of technical skills and specific personal characteristics found in effective commission salespersons distinguishes the latter as an elite among retail salespeople....
>
> One of the most important personal qualities a commission salesperson must possess may be variously described as aggressiveness, desire, "hunger," or more generally, motivation.[47]

Sears argued that the EEOC's "assumption" that women and men in the applicant pool had similar qualifications and preferences for this work was "incredible on its face." Actually, the EEOC's statistical analysis controlled for certain factors that might legitimately influence the distribution of jobs between men and women—such as age, experience, and education. But Sears claimed that even with these "adjustments," the EEOC had "grossly overestimated female availability for commission sales." In the end, Sears argued, "the reasonableness of the EEOC's a priori assumptions of male/female sameness with respect to preferences, interests, and qualifications is . . . the crux of the issue."[48]

Sears presented a series of witnesses from its own personnel operations who testified that "far more men than women ... were interested in and willing to accept commission sales jobs." Some Sears managers even testified "that they had interviewed every woman in the store and found not one who was willing to sell big ticket merchandise." Women were generally not interested in commission sales jobs, Sears sought to persuade the court, because of their

(1) fear or dislike of the competitive, "dog-eat-dog" atmosphere of most commission sales divisions; (2) discomfort or unfamiliarity with most product lines sold on commission ... ; (3) fear of being unable to compete, being unsuccessful and losing their jobs; (4) fear of nonacceptance by customers in such traditionally male-oriented divisions as hardware, automotive, installed home improvements, and tires; (5) distaste for the type of selling they believed was required in commission divisions; (6) preference for noncommission sales jobs; (7) preference for "keeping busy" and dislike of the relatively slower customer traffic in most commission divisions; (8) the overall belief that the increased earnings potential of commission selling was not worth the additional responsibilities, problems, pressure, and uncertainty.[49]

According to Sears, then, the underrepresentation of women among commission salespersons was due not to discrimination but to women's own preferences. In his summation, lawyer Charles Morgan ridiculed the very idea of sex discrimination. "Strange, isn't it," the former civil rights advocate suggested, "that we live in a world where there is supposed to be a monopsony of white men who somehow get up every morning trying to find a way to discriminate against their wives, their daughters, their mothers, their sisters."[50]

Historians in the Courtroom

To buttress its claim that most women are not interested in commission sales jobs, Sears introduced historical evidence into the case through the testimony of Rosalind Rosenberg. Sears asked other experts in women's history to testify on its behalf, but Rosenberg was the only one who accepted the invitation. Both Kathryn Kish Sklar and Carl Degler declined, and later both criticized Sears's use of historical evidence in the trial.[51] Rosenberg stated that she accepted the job because she thought that the EEOC's case against Sears was weak and the assumptions of the statisticians were untenable. In addition, she acknowledged that the fact that her ex-husband works for Morgan Associates, the law firm that represented Sears, may have played a role.[52]

Rosenberg's testimony marshaled evidence from the literature in U.S. women's history to challenge the "assumption that women and men have identical interests and aspirations regarding work." Citing the work of dozens of prominent scholars in the field (including Degler, Sklar, and Kessler-Harris herself), Rosenberg sought to persuade the court that "many workers, especially women, have goals and values other than realizing maximum economic gain."[53] Her sketch of the history of the sexual division of labor in the United States assigned great weight to women's distinctive values and interests. "Throughout American history," Rosenberg's "Offer of Proof" stated, "there has been a consensus, shared by women, that, for women, working outside the home is subordinate to family needs." As evidence for this, she cited hostility to married women's employment in the Depression, the reluctance of the government to provide childcare during World War II, and the unequal distribution of household labor between the sexes, concluding that "many women choose jobs that complement their family obligation over jobs that might increase and inhance [*sic*] their earnings potential."[54]

Although most of Rosenberg's testimony consisted of general statements about women and work, a few points related more directly to Sears's specific contentions in this case. "'Women tend to be more interested than men in the cooperative, social aspects of the work situation," her "Offer of Proof" asserts. "Men's more extensive experience in competitive sports," on the other hand, "prepares them for the competitiveness, aggressiveness, teamwork, and leadership required for many jobs."[55]

Rosenberg testified that the EEOC's statistician "assumes that given equal opportunity women will make the same choices that a man would make. And yet that assumption is based on a traditionally male model of how people behave in the universe, that is, the most important thing is economic maximization."[56] Women and men are in fact quite different, Rosenberg argued, and "difference does not always mean discrimination."[57]

After Sears introduced "history" into the case via Rosenberg, the EEOC responded in kind, recruiting Alice Kessler-Harris as a rebuttal witness.[58] She directly challenged Rosenberg's testimony and offered an alternative reading of the historical record. "History does not sustain the notion that women have, in the past, chosen not to take non-traditional jobs," Kessler-Harris testified. From women tavernkeepers in the nineteenth century to the women who entered heavy industry during World War II, she noted, "substantial numbers of women have been available for jobs at good pay in whatever field these jobs are offered." Rosenberg's (and Sears's) contention that women and men have different job interests ignores the social processes that generate such "interests," Kessler-Harris suggested: "The argument that women are only interested in certain kinds of work reflects women's perceptions of opportunities available to them which are themselves products of employers' assumptions and prejudices about women's roles."[59]

Kessler-Harris acknowledged that the issue of difference could not be entirely overlooked. "There is room for debate about how and to what extent women are different from men in terms of their culture and training and so on," she stated in her deposition.[60] And she later testified at trial that "surely interest in some abstract sense is one element that goes into the decisions that people make about jobs." But, she added, "that's complicated by the fact that the primary motive in job seeking is not to satisfy interest, but to satisfy need for income."[61] Kessler-Harris's overall objection to Rosenberg's testimony, then, was not that it had no validity, but that it was one-sided, over-generalized from limited information, and ignored the role of employers in shaping women's employment patterns. Kessler-Harris also accused Rosenberg of quoting out of context from Kessler-Harris's own writings as well as from other sources.[62] And she questioned Rosenberg's expertise in working women's history. "She's not an expert in the field of either wage earning women or working women; and . . . as a result, many of her statements and assumptions are incorrect."[63]

Rosenberg was given an opportunity to respond to Kessler-Harris's criticisms in court. She began her formal rebuttal by rejecting the EEOC's reliance on "statistical disparities" to prove that Sears had discriminated against women. "The overwhelming weight of modern scholarship in women's history and related fields supports the view that other Sears experts and I have put forward—namely that disparities in the sexual composition of an employer's workforce, as well as disparities in pay between men and women in many circumstances, are consistent with an absence of discrimination on the part of the employer."[64] Although Kessler-Harris had argued that *employers'* choices played the critical role in shaping women's employment patterns, Rosenberg implicitly accepted a different model of the labor market, one in which women's preferences and choices were more important than discrimination in explaining the statistical disparities.

Rosenberg's rebuttal also sought to discredit Kessler-Harris's testimony altogether, apparently in order to defend her own credibility. After all, Kessler-Harris was a scholar Rosenberg herself had identified as an expert in the field, and now Kessler-Harris was directly questioning not only Rosenberg's interpretation of working women's history but also the legitimacy of her claim to be an expert.

Rosenberg devoted most of her rebuttal to an effort to demonstrate that "Kessler-Harris the historian has written a great deal that is often at odds with her testimony in this case." Citing a series of examples, she claimed that Kessler-Harris was being dishonest in her role as a witness. "As Kessler-Harris well knows, it is simply not true that women have always taken advantage of opportunities to work in good jobs," Rosenberg wrote, quoting Kessler-Harris's reference to "ideological constraints" in the chapter on the Depression in her 1982 book *Out to Work*.[65] Rosenberg went on to state that Kessler-Harris's "testimony at trial regarding the experience of women during World War II is misleading ... and runs directly counter to her own published writing on this subject."[66] And in a twelve-page, single-spaced appendix to her rebuttal, Rosenberg juxtaposed "Kessler-Harris Statements in This Case" to "Kessler-Harris Contradictory Statements in Her Published Writing" on a series of six topics relevant to the case.

Although most of her rebuttal was devoted to enumerating these "contradictions," Rosenberg also sought to discredit Kessler-Harris's scholarship directly. The "assumption that all employers discriminate is prominent in [Kessler-Harris's] work," Rosenberg wrote. She then went on to suggest not only that Kessler-Harris had compromised her own scholarship in the service of the EEOC but also that her scholarship itself was of questionable validity and, indeed, written in the service of the larger cause of opposition to capitalism itself. "In a 1979 article," Rosenberg's rebuttal stated, Kessler-Harris "wrote *hopefully* that women harbor values, attitudes and behavior patterns potentially subversive to capitalism."[67]

The rebuttal also cited other scholarly writings characterized as inconsistent with Kessler-Harris's testimony and suggested that Kessler-Harris's perspective was overly simplistic, even "mono-causal." "My testimony has emphasized the complexity of the world in which women make decisions—choices—about their work," Rosenberg wrote, "and I reject the temptation to blame employers for everything I do not like about the condition of women." Elsewhere in the rebuttal she stated that "one of the most depressing aspects of Kessler-Harris's perspective is her view of woman as victim." Rosenberg concluded by commenting: "I myself might prefer a world in which as many women as men placed career ahead of family, in which as many women as men were ready, willing and able to sell furnaces or install plumbing, but that is not our world today. I have tried to show that nothing about our history, and nothing in the best recent scholarship about women in our history, would lead one to expect otherwise."[68]

Kessler-Harris did not have an opportunity to defend herself against Rosenberg's allegations in the course of the trial, but the EEOC's final cross-examination of Rosenberg did attempt to show that her rebuttal had misrepresented Kessler-Harris's and other scholars' views. For example, in support of her contention that Kessler-Harris gave more weight to cultural norms in her historical writings than in her trial testimony, Rosenberg had quoted the following passage from Kessler-Harris's *Out to Work*:

> In a broad sense, notions of propriety and role served as organizational principles for women's work force participation. They created a reciprocally confirming system in which successful job experiences for women were defined in terms of values appropriate to future home life: gentility, neatness, morality, cleanliness. . . . Although women typically chose jobs that reflected home-based

values, these choices, regulated as they were by social and cultural norms, could hardly be said to be free.[69]

EEOC attorney Karen Baker read into the court record the material that appeared in the ellipses:

> Male jobs, in contrast, encouraged such values as ambition, competition, aggression and increased income, all of which would add up to success. Such distinctions confirmed women's place in the home, even while they worked for wages. [A]nd they provided support for limiting women's access to jobs even where restrictions demonstrably left them in utter poverty.

Then Baker asked Rosenberg, "That statement about providing support for limiting women's access to jobs, even when those restrictions left women in poverty, that sentence refers to the way that cultural constraints were used by employers, doesn't it?"[70]

Similarly, Baker questioned Rosenberg's representation of economist Phyllis Wallace's work on AT&T, which Rosenberg cited in challenging Kessler-Harris's testimony that "women rapidly filled such non-traditional jobs as that of telephone company lineman in 1973 once AT&T was induced through legal action to allow them entry." Rosenberg's rebuttal characterized this statement as "false and misleading" and went on to state: "As Phyllis Wallace concluded, with some understatement, both the federal government and the company 'may have underestimated the effect of powerful social constraints' in limiting the availability of women interested in those positions."[71] In cross-examining Rosenberg, Baker read into the record the entire paragraph from Wallace's book containing the quotation Rosenberg had cited:

> Both the federal government and the company *may have underestimated the effect of powerful social constraints* on changing the characteristics of a fairly rigid internal labor market. A congressional report noted in September 1974 that the AT&T settlement had been difficult and expensive to monitor. The company may perceive its primary objective as providing telephone service, securing a fair return on its investment, protecting its markets from firms selling competitive equipment, and adjusting to lower levels of economic activity. John W. Kingsbury, AT&T Assistant Vice President, has noted that "our managers—and millions of others like them in business after business across the country—did not yet understand the need for some of the specific features required in new, formalized procedures which are necessary in order to speed the upward movement of women and minority group members. The threat of increased competition from individuals they perceive to be less qualified than themselves is part of the reason for this managerial reluctance. Basic prejudice may be another reason. And some managers may feel they are losing some

of their hard-earned management prerogatives. However, the main cause, I submit, is simply a resistance to change. Line managers at all levels of most organizations really don't understand the significance of new equal opportunity regulations, labor laws, OSHA [Occupational Safety and Health Administration], or a host of other external impingements on their primary responsibilities. And further, they tend not to view these external forces as their problem but as a personnel or legal matter."

"Now having read that, don't you agree, Dr. Rosenberg," Baker asked, "that the social constraints that Phyllis Wallace was talking about were those of management and its views of what it did and not the social constraints limiting the availability of women who are interested in these positions?" Ultimately, Rosenberg conceded that this was the case and requested that the Wallace quotation in her rebuttal be stricken from the record.[72]

On June 22, 1985, with Rosenberg's final testimony and cross-examination, the part of the trial involving historical evidence came to an end. The protracted trial itself ended the following week. Seven months later, the District Court in Chicago issued its decision in favor of Sears.[73] Shortly afterward, Sears filed a suit against the EEOC—and against the individual EEOC attorneys who handled the case—to recover its legal costs.[74]

Judge John A. Nordberg seemed to give the historical testimony considerable weight in justifying his acceptance of Sears's argument that women were uninterested in commission sales jobs and in rejecting the EEOC's statistical evidence of discrimination. Nordberg, a Reagan appointee who became a federal judge in 1982, characterized Rosenberg as a "well-informed witness who offered reasonable, well-supported opinions" and as "a highly credible witness." In contrast, his decision stated that Kessler-Harris's testimony "often focused on small segments of women, rather than the majority of women, in giving isolated examples of women who have seized opportunities for greater income in nontraditional jobs when they have arisen," and that it was "not supported by credible evidence." Nordberg contrasted Kessler-Harris's testimony to the "more convincing testimony . . . offered by Sears expert Dr. Rosalind Rosenberg." And in the very next paragraph, he concluded that the "EEOC's assumption of equal interest is unfounded and fatally undermines its entire statistical analysis."[75]

Aftermath of the Trial

After the trial itself ended, Rosenberg's role in the case was widely discussed and provoked much criticism in the scholarly community, especially among feminists. Few have agreed with Judge Nordberg's view that she was a more credible and convincing witness than Kessler-Harris. But most of the concern has focused on the political import of Rosenberg's testimony. Historian Ellen DuBois, for example, commented that

> the EEOC lawsuit is part of a political battle that has been altering the cultural configuration Rosenberg says she laments. She argues that history shows the situation is "too complicated" for an affirmative action program to remedy. This argument is the essence of conservatism and must be read as an attack on working women and sexual equality, an attack on the whole concept of affirmative action.[76]

In December 1985 the controversy was aired at a session of the Women and Society Seminar at Columbia University. Before an audience of at least 150 feminist scholars, Kessler-Harris and Rosenberg presented their views of the case and their respective roles in it. In the discussion that ensued, Rosenberg was criticized repeatedly, and although some comments were neutral, no one voiced support for her position.[77] One participant even proposed that the group issue a formal statement condemning Rosenberg's role in the case. Although no such action was taken at the seminar, later in the same month, at the American Historical Association's Annual Meeting in New York, a resolution was passed by the Coordinating Committee of Women in the Historical Profession (CCWHP) that read in part:

> We . . . are deeply concerned by certain circumstances and issues raised in the 1984–85 trial of a 1979 EEOC case against Sears Roebuck. In this trial . . . a respected scholar buttressed Sears's defense against charges of sex discrimination. . . . We urge attention to the following questions:
>
> (1) What responsibility do feminist scholars bear to the women's movement?
> (2) Would it be appropriate to seek to define a set of ethical principles for feminist scholarship and its use, similar to those accepted by other professional organizations?
> (3) What is the relationship of the ideology of domesticity to women's position in the work force? . . .
>
> We believe as feminist scholars we have a responsibility not to allow our scholarship to be used against the interests of women struggling for equity in our society.[78]

The resolution did not name Rosenberg directly, but it clearly expressed the concern of other feminist scholars about her role in the Sears case.

Rosenberg, however, steadfastly defended her actions, writing letters to various publications that covered the controversy and publishing an op-ed piece in the *New York Times*.[79] She told the Women and Society Seminar:

> I realize that many people disagree with my view of scholarly responsibility and believe that I showed poor political judgment in deciding to testify, that

I played into the hands of conservatives, and that my testimony, if successful, will leave large companies free to discriminate against women. I reject the view that scholarship should be subordinated to political goals. But even if I were to accept that view, I would still feel justified in having testified in this case, because I think that Sears has advanced women's interests, whereas the position taken by the EEOC *in this case* has *not*."[80]

Sears had advanced women's interests, Rosenberg believes, through its affirmative action plan which, starting in 1974, required that 50 percent of commission sales jobs go either to women or to minority males. "I believe the evidence shows not only that Sears was not discriminating against women but that it was successfully recruiting women into nontraditional jobs through a vigorous affirmative action program," she wrote.[81] Rosenberg was also influenced by the fact that the EEOC's case did not include direct testimony from women who were victims of Sears's discrimination. "I said in the beginning, 'If there's ever a complainant in this case, I'm not going to testify,'" Rosenberg recalled in an interview, "which strikes me in retrospect as a little bit crazy. . . . [But] for me, symbolically, the absence of complainants was critical."[82]

Another factor that induced Rosenberg to testify was that she genuinely believed that the EEOC's case was based on a faulty assumption, namely, "that men and women applying for sales positions at Sears were equally interested in commission sales."[83] She was not asked to testify as to Sears's "guilt or innocence," she insists. "I was simply asked to determine, from a historical point of view, whether the assumption on which the EEOC had built its case made sense."[84] This was part of Sears's broader effort to criticize the EEOC's statistical analysis. "What I conceived of myself as doing was challenging the assumptions of the statisticians," Rosenberg said. "Though I couldn't have done it if I didn't think that the evidence against Sears was very weak and unpersuasive."[85]

The fact that Charles Morgan's law firm was representing Sears also entered into her decision to testify, Rosenberg said. Not only did her ex-husband work for Morgan as a researcher, but also she "had known of Chuck Morgan going back twenty years, and had always respected him as an honest person." Finally, there was a moral aspect to her decision to testify. "Part of it too was my sense that people were reluctant to [testify for Sears] because they feared criticism," she said. "In the end I felt that if I said no it would be because I didn't have the nerve to say what I thought was right, or do what I thought was right. It was that Calvinistic burden I've carried from my childhood."[86]

Kessler-Harris also had to decide whether to testify. The EEOC asked her to do so, as a rebuttal witness, after the trial was already under way.[87] Told that Rosenberg, testifying on Sears's behalf, had cited her writings, Kessler-Harris later wrote, "I reacted viscerally to seeing my own work, badly distorted, put to the service of a politically destructive cause. I believed that the success of Sears's lawyers would undermine two decades of affirmative action efforts and exercise a chilling effect on women's history."[88] She strongly criticized Rosenberg's use of her work:

> With others in the field, I participated in developing the notion that an econo-
> mistic view of the labor market explained little about women's roles in it, and
> that a more complete picture could be obtained by examining the shaping role
> of ideology. . . . Rosenberg, apparently influenced by the political demands of
> the case, has distorted this interpretation into unrecognizability by arguing
> that the domestic ideology was itself responsible for the choices that women
> made. Her position negates the ways that employers are responsible for the
> structure of the labor market not least because they share in, and take advan-
> tage of, prevailing ideology.[89]

Ironically, Rosenberg does not see herself as an advocate of the concept of "women's culture" as it has developed in the literature on women's history. "I was and I continue to be skeptical of the utility of conceiving of men and women living in separate cultural worlds," she stated, and added that she thinks it is "wrong-headed" to view the Sears case through the prism of the broader controversy over questions of equality and difference.[90] Kessler-Harris, on the other hand, has been much more sympathetic to the notion of "women's culture," and her work has explored the ways in which difference influences the struggles of women in the workforce.[91] However, in her view, "the real issue in the Sears case was not whether women and men are different, but rather, whether the preferences of employers or those of women themselves best explain the underrepresentation of women in specific jobs."[92]

Both Kessler-Harris and Rosenberg testified under the peculiar constraints of the courtroom—constraints that demanded yes or no answers to complex questions and prohibited any expert witness from acknowledging disagreements or controversy within her field without losing her legitimacy as an expert. Under these conditions, Rosenberg argued from the perspective of difference, and Kessler-Harris emphasized the importance of opportunity in shaping the positions of women and men in the workforce. The broader controversy their testimonies tap into is one that cannot be easily resolved. But if feminist scholars can learn anything from the Sears case, it is that we ignore the political dimensions of the equality-versus-difference debate at our peril, especially in a period of conservative resurgence.

Important as the use of historical evidence was in this case, it seems likely that even without Rosenberg's testimony, Sears would have prevailed. The odds were heavily stacked in the giant retailer's favor. The EEOC's top official at the time,

Clarence Thomas, had publicly proclaimed his negative view of statistical evidence and his desire to lose the case. Sears spent eight times as much money as did the EEOC on legal work.[93] The judge was appointed by the Reagan administration, which had repeatedly proclaimed its opposition to affirmative action. In such a political context, feminist scholars must be aware of the real danger that arguments about "difference" or "women's culture" will be put to uses other than those for which they were originally developed. That does not mean we must abandon these arguments or the intellectual terrain they have opened up; it does mean that we should be self-conscious in our formulations, and aware that our work can be exploited politically.

Notes

This chapter was originally published in *Feminist Studies* 12, no. 2 (Summer 1986): 375–400.

1. See Ellen DuBois, Mari Jo Buhle, Temma Kaplan, Gerda Lerner, and Carroll Smith-Rosenberg, "Politics and Culture in Women's History: A Symposium," *Feminist Studies* 6 (Spring 1980): 26–64.

2. Compare, for example, Wendy Chavkin, "Walking a Tightrope: Pregnancy, Parenting, and Work," in *Double Exposure: Women's Health Hazards on the Job and at Home,* edited by Wendy Chavkin (New York: New Feminist Library of Monthly Review Press, 1984), 196–213; and Wendy W. Williams, "Equality's Riddle: Pregnancy and the Equal Treatment/Special Treatment Debate," *New York University Review of Law and Social Change* 13 (1984–85): 325–80. This controversy is a particular instance of the more general and much older debate over protective legislation. For discussion, see Ann Corinne Hill, "Protection of Women Workers and the Courts: A Legal Case History," *Feminist Studies* 5 (Summer 1979): 247–73; Alice Kessler-Harris, *Out to Work: A History of Wage-Earning Women in the United States* (New York: Oxford University Press, 1982), 180–214; and Patricia G. Zelman, *Women, Work, and National Policy: The Kennedy-Johnson Years* (Ann Arbor: UMI, 1982).

3. "Offer of Proof Concerning the Testimony of Dr. Rosalind Rosenberg," Defendant's Exhibit 3, Rosenberg version with notes, *EEOC v. Sears*, Civil Action No. 79-C-4373, U.S. District Court for the Northern District of Illinois, Eastern Division (hereafter cited as *EEOC v. Sears*), par. 24. Rosenberg told me that she did not write the "Offer of Proof" herself. "I wrote a series of memos and the lawyers extracted what they considered to be the most persuasive points that they wanted to see developed" (author's interview with Rosenberg, New York, N.Y., January 24, 1986). However, in her deposition and at the trial, Rosenberg stated that she agreed with all the statements in the "Offer of Proof." See "Deposition of Rosalind Rosenberg" (July 2, 1984), *EEOC v. Sears*, vol. 1, 10, and Trial Transcript, *EEOC v. Sears*, 10345 (March 11, 1985). These documents from the trial, and the others cited below, are in the Schlesinger Library, Radcliffe College, Cambridge, Massachusetts. Rosenberg's "Offer of Proof" and Kessler-Harris's "Written Testimony" (cited in note 5) were published in *Signs: Journal of Women in Culture and Society* 11 (Summer 1986).

4. "Trial Brief of Sears, Roebuck and Co." (September/October 1984), *EEOC v. Sears*, 27.

5. "Written Testimony of Alice Kessler-Harris" (June, 1985), *EEOC v. Sears*, pars. 2, 6, 13.

6. "U.S. Files Five Suits Charging Sears with Job Bias," *New York Times*, October 23, 1979, notes that Sears is the world's largest retailer. Allan Sloan and John J. Donovan, in "The Sears Case of Equal Job Opportunity," *New York Law Journal*, February 22, 1979, mention that Sears was (in 1979) the second-largest private employer of women, second only to AT&T. After the AT&T breakup, however, Sears moved into first place.

7. Year-round, full-time women salesworkers' median earnings were only 51.2 percent of men salesworkers' earnings in 1981. See U.S. Department of Labor, Women's Bureau, *Time of Change: 1983 Handbook on Women Workers*, Bulletin no. 298 (Washington, D.C.: GPO), 93. For general discussion of women and sales work, see Louise Kapp Howe, *Pink Collar Workers: Inside the World of Women's Work* (New York: Putnam's, 1977), 61–102; and Susan Porter Benson, "Women in Retail Sales Work: The Continuing Dilemma of Service," in *My Troubles Are Going to Have Trouble with Me: Everyday Trials and Triumphs of Women Workers*, edited by Karen Brodkin Sacks and Dorothy Remy (New Brunswick, N.J.: Rutgers University Press, 1984), 113–23.

8. See Clarice Stasz, "Room at the Bottom," *Working Papers* 9 (January–February 1982): 28–41; "Damage Report: The Decline of Equal Employment Opportunity Enforcement under Reagan," *Women Employed Advocates Bulletin* 3 (December 1982): 1–5; and "U.S. Plans to Ease Rules for Hiring Women and Blacks," *New York Times*, April 3, 1983.

9. However, litigation has by no means stopped completely. In November 1985, for example, the EEOC filed lawsuits charging three relatively small employers (the largest has 3,200 employees) with job discrimination. See "Agency Cites Statistical Evidence in Lawsuits on Job Discrimination," *New York Times*, November 13, 1985.

10. Clarence Thomas's criticisms of the use of statistical evidence closely parallel those used by Sears in its own defense (see below). "Every time there is a statistical disparity, it is presumed there is discrimination," Thomas told the *New York Times*. He added that such disparities could often be explained by other factors, such as culture, educational levels, "previous events," or commuting patterns. See "Changes Weighed in Federal Rules on Discrimination," *New York Times*, December 3, 1984.

11. "Despite Doubts, U.S. Presses to Resolve Sears Bias Case," *Washington Post*, July 9, 1985.

12. "Plaintiff's Pretrial Brief—Commission Sales Issues" (revised November 19, 1984), *EEOC v. Sears*, 2, 12, 17.

13. "Despite Doubts, U.S. Presses to Resolve Sears Bias Case." For details on the AT&T and steel consent decrees, see Phyllis A. Wallace, ed., *Equal Employment Opportunity and the AT&T Case* (Cambridge, Mass.: MIT Press, 1976); and Kay K. Deaux and Joseph C. Ullman, *Women of Steel: Female Blue-Collar Workers in the Basic Steel Industry* (New York: Praeger, 1983).

14. Sears's own account of its affirmative-action efforts may be found in "Trial Brief of Sears, Roebuck and Co.," 36–39. Sears claims to have begun its affirmative-action program in the late 1960s, but a plan that included women and had specific goals was not introduced until 1974. The EEOC's case is discussed in more detail below.

15. "Justice Dept. Seeks Dismissal of Sears Job-Rights Suit," *New York Times*, March 28, 1979; "Sears Suit Goes beyond Court," *New York Times*, April 6, 1979; Sloan and Donovan, "Sears Case."

16. "Sears Loses Its Suit over Job-Bias Rules," *New York Times*, May 16, 1979; George Kannar, "Sears Shall Overcome," *New Republic*, March 10, 1979, 18–21; "Sears Suit Stumbles," *Esquire*, April 24, 1979, 13–14.

17. Charles Morgan, quoted in "Sears Suit on U.S. Job-Bias Rules Puts Past Alliances to Strict Test," *New York Times*, January 29, 1979.

18. "U.S. Files Five Suits."

19. Rosalind Rosenberg has cited this in her own defense, in response to criticism of her role in the case. "I think that it is the responsibility of the scholar to see that public policy is based on sound premises, even if doing so means criticizing the EEOC," she said. "Back in 1979 Issie Jenkins, the black woman general counsel to the EEOC, warned that the enforcement image of the agency would be badly damaged if it pressed a case against Sears that was fundamentally flawed. Unfortunately, the agency did not heed her advice." (Written text of Rosenberg's statement at the Columbia University Women and Society Seminar, December 16, 1985, p. 8; hereafter referred to as the Rosenberg Seminar Statement.) It is not easy to determine whether Jenkins's advice was in fact heeded, as the discussion in the text below explains.

20. The first such report, upon which all of the others are based, was David B. Parker's "EEOC Discovers Its Investigation of Sears Is So Flawed, It Should Settle and Not Sue," *Employment Relations Report*, August 1, 1979. See also "EEOC Staff Recommends Dropping Suit against Sears," *Washington Post*, August 2, 1979; "U.S. Doubts It Can Win Sears Case," *Washington Star*, August 2, 1979; and "EEOC's Lawyers Question Plan to Sue Sears Over Job Bias," *Wall Street Journal*, August 3, 1979.

21. An EEOC representative told me this in a telephone interview on January 13, 1986. I learned also in this conversation that the reports of the leaked EEOC memos were ruled "inadmissible" as evidence during the 1985 trial.

22. As noted above, ultimately the EEOC filed a nationwide sex discrimination suit against Sears and four separate race discrimination suits involving specific facilities but no nationwide race discrimination suit. See "U.S. Files Five Suits."

23. "Despite Doubts."

24. "Plaintiff's Pretrial Brief-Commission Sales Issues," 1–2.

25. EEOC sources told me this in a telephone interview on January 29, 1986. I learned also that the 1977 Commission Decision also had consolidated numerous individual charges of sex and race discrimination received by the EEOC.

26. See Judge John A. Nordberg, "Memorandum Opinion and Order" (January 31, 1986), *EEOC v. Sears*, 102.

27. Closing Arguments, Trial Transcript, 18983–85, June 28, 1985.

28. "Despite Doubts." At press time, Sears had revealed only its "costs" in the case—not including attorneys' fees—which it is seeking to recover from the EEOC by court action. "Bill of Costs for Sears, Roebuck and Co." (March 3, 1986), *EEOC v. Sears*.

29. Applicants for commission and noncommission sales positions at Sears went through the same application process, and few specifically indicated an interest in commission sales positions in the 1973–80 period. See "Plaintiffs Pretrial Brief-Commission Sales Issues," 4, 28–30.

30. Ibid., 4, 39–41, 2–3, 27.

31. Ibid., 5, 48.

32. Two types of statistical analysis were performed: a logit analysis and a multivariate cross-classification analysis. The logit analysis of the six characteristics noted in the text reduced the expected female proportion of hires for full-time commission sales positions from 61 percent to 49 percent; the multivariate cross-classification analysis reduced it from 61 percent to 37 percent. The actual female proportion of hires was 27 percent, as noted above. See "Plaintiffs Final Argument" (June 26, 1985), *EEOC v. Sears*, 6–9. Similar results were obtained for part-time commission sales hires, discussed in "Plaintiff's Final Argument," 10–12. Detailed multivariate cross-classification analyses were also conducted for each of fourteen product lines, revealing disparities adverse to women in all but a few cases. For details, see "Plaintiff's Pretrial Brief-Commission Sales Issues," 53–55, 60–65. In addition, the EEOC analyzed "Sears Applicant Interview Guides" from 1978–80 for one region. The guides were forms that allowed job applicants to rate their own skills, interests, and experiences in various activities related to positions at Sears. Although analysis of the guides did show differences between women and men, the expected female proportion of full-time commission sales hires in four key product lines (major appliances, auto parts, home improvements, and hardware) was equal to or higher than the expected proportions yielded by the multivariate cross-classification analysis. See "Plaintiffs Final Argument," 12–14.

33. See "Plaintiff's Pretrial Brief—Commission Sales Issues," 42–48. Using two different methods, the analysis found disparities on a nationwide basis and in each territory and in each year (1973–80), except for the Eastern territory in 1980.

34. Parker, "EEOC Discovers."

35. "Plaintiffs Pretrial Brief—Commission Sales Issues," 7–9, 28–32, 36. The passage cited is on 32.

36. Ibid., 9–12, 33–37. The test questions appear on 34.

37. Ibid., 72–73.

38. See "Post-Trial Brief of Sears, Roebuck and Co." (June 26, 1985), *EEOC v. Sears*, 10n1.

39. "Trial Brief of Sears, Roebuck and Co.," 1–4; "Post-Trial Brief of Sears, Roebuck and Co.," 33–36. The EEOC contended that the outcome of the case would be the same whether it was treated as a "disparate treatment" case or as a "disparate impact" case, where intent to discriminate need not be demonstrated. See "Plaintiff's Pretrial Brief-Commission Sales Issues," 73; and "Plaintiffs Final Argument," 1–4.

40. "Trial Brief of Sears, Roebuck and Co.," 37, 39; "Post-Trial Brief of Sears, Roebuck and Co.," 7–10, 15–16.

41. "Trial Brief of Sears, Roebuck and Co.," 30–33; "Post-Trial Brief of Sears, Roebuck and Co.," 39–40.

42. Closing Arguments, Trial Transcript, 19059 (June 28, 1985).

43. "Trial Brief of Sears, Roebuck and Co.," 9, 25–26. Sears also criticized the EEOC's definition of "sales applicants" as all nonhired job applicants who did not specifically indicate a preference for a nonsales post on their application forms, and it also criticized the EEOC's assumption that the female percentage of these "sales applicants" was the female

percentage of "persons interested, qualified and available for commission sales positions" (ibid., 17). See also "Post-Trial Brief of Sears, Roebuck and Co.," 24–33.

44. "Trial Brief of Sears, Roebuck and Co.," 26. Sears also suggested (p. 8) another appropriate comparison would be between noncommission sales hires and commission sales hires—groups it insisted had very different characteristics.

45. Ibid., 18; "Post-Trial Brief of Sears, Roebuck and Co.," 21–24.

46. Sears asserted that "commission salespeople stand apart from the general run of retail sales personnel in that commission salespeople risk all or part of their income upon their ability to sell merchandise—usually more expensive, 'big ticket' merchandise...." See "Trial Brief of Sears, Roebuck and Co.," 10. However, even before 1977, when most commission salespersons were paid on a draw-versus-commission basis, these employees were guaranteed a minimum income each week, regardless of commissions. And beginning in January 1977, Sears's commission salespersons were paid on a salary-plus-commission basis. See "Plaintiffs Pretrial Brief—Commission Sales Issues," 26.

47. "Trial Brief of Sears, Roebuck and Co.," 10–13.

48. Ibid., 18, 20, 21. As mentioned above, the EEOC controlled for six factors: job applied for, age, education, job type experience, product line experience, and commission product sales experience.

49. "Post-Trial Brief of Sears, Roebuck and Co.," 9, 11–12.

50. Closing Arguments, Trial Transcript, 19064.

51. See Jon Wiener, "The Sears Case: Women's History on Trial," *The Nation* 241 (September 7, 1985): 161, 176–80. Degler, however, later stated that he regretted his decision not to testify, saying he was "too lazy and too cowardly to take the time to understand the methodological question." See Karen J. Winkler, "Two Scholars' Conflict in Sears' Sex-Bias Sets Off War in Women's History," *Chronicle of Higher Education* 31 (February 5, 1986): 1, 8.

52. Author's interview with Rosenberg.

53. "Offer of Proof," pars. 1 and 2. Kessler-Harris and Degler are cited in the first footnote of the "Offer of Proof." Sklar is not cited there but in the "Deposition of Rosalind Rosenberg," (July 3, 1984), vol. 2, 56–57. All three have objected to the use of their writings in this context, as has William Chafe. See Wiener.

54. "Offer of Proof," pars. 4, 8–11.

55. Ibid., par. 19.

56. Trial Transcript, 10357–58 (March 11, 1985).

57. "Deposition of Rosalind Rosenberg," (July 3, 1984), vol. 2, 98.

58. Rosenberg's deposition took place in July 1984; she testified at trial almost a year later, in March 1985. The EEOC contacted Kessler-Harris in September 1984, the month the trial began. In April 1985, Kessler-Harris was deposed, and she testified during the last month of the trial, in June 1985. Rosenberg then testified again, in rebuttal of Kessler-Harris, later in June 1985.

59. "Written Testimony of Alice Kessler-Harris." Emphasis added. The quotes are from pars. 2, 13, and 11, respectively.

60. "Deposition of Alice Kessler-Harris," (April 12, 1985), *EEOC v. Sears*, 241.

61. Trial Transcript, 16616 (June 7, 1985).

62. "Deposition of Alice Kessler-Harris."

63. Trial Transcript, 16498 (June 6, 1985).

64. "Written Rebuttal Testimony of Dr. Rosalind Rosenberg," June 1985, *EEOC v. Sears*, par. 1. Although Rosenberg, as noted above, had not written the earlier "Offer of Proof" herself, when asked if she had written the rebuttal testimony, she told the court "there's some editing but yes, I did." Trial Transcript, 18216 (June 22, 1985).

65. "Written Rebuttal Testimony of Dr. Rosalind Rosenberg," pars. 16a, 3, quoting Kessler-Harris, *Out to Work*, 259.

66. "Written Rebuttal Testimony of Dr. Rosalind Rosenberg," par. 4.

67. Ibid., par. 10, emphasis added. The citation is to Kessler-Harris, "American Women and the American Character: A Feminist Perspective," in *American Character and Culture*, edited by John Hague (Westport, Conn.: Greenwood, 1979), 228. In a similar vein, in a footnote to this paragraph (10) of her rebuttal, Rosenberg also characterizes Kessler-Harris as "herself an adherent of the dual labor market theory," and in the text she critically quotes Kessler-Harris's characterization of employers and government officials as "villains."

68. "Written Rebuttal Testimony of Dr. Rosalind Rosenberg," pars. 16, 11, 16.

69. Ibid., appendix, 1. The quote is from Kessler-Harris, *Out to Work*, 128.

70. Trial Transcript, 18278–79 (June 22, 1985).

71. "Written Rebuttal Testimony of Dr. Rosalind Rosenberg," par. 9. The Kessler-Harris statement cited here is from "Written Testimony of Alice Kessler-Harris," par. 5e. The Wallace quotation is from Wallace, *Equal Opportunity Employment*, 341–42.

72. Trial Transcript, 18268–70, 18285 (June 22, 1985). The italicized portion of the quotation from Wallace is the part Rosenberg had cited.

73. "Federal Judge Rules for Sears in Sex Bias Case," *New York Times*, February 4, 1986.

74. "Memorandum in Support of Petition of Sears, Roebuck and Co. for Attorneys' Fees and Expenses," February 11, 1986, *EEOC v. Sears*.

75. Prior to becoming a federal district judge, Nordberg was a state court judge in Illinois for several years. The information about his appointment was confirmed by Brenda Jones, his secretary. The quote is from Nordberg, "Memorandum Opinion and Order," 65, 79–81. See also Tamar Lewin, "Statistics Have Become Suspect in Sex Discrimination Cases," *New York Times*, February 9, 1986.

76. Wiener, 178–79. See also Winkler, 8.

77. An account of the seminar is provided in Phyllis H. Stock, "Update on the Sears Case," *CCWHP Newsletter* 17 (February 1986): 4–6. Although she had no supporters at the seminar, in other forums Rosenberg has been defended by scholars. Historian Thomas L. Haskell wrote a letter supporting her that appeared in *The Nation* 241 (October 26, 1985): 410. Another letter was circulated privately to several feminist historians by Catherine Clinton, expressing concern that the criticisms of Rosenberg were unprofessional and overly personalized. See Catherine Clinton to Dear Colleague, December 2, 1985 (copy in author's possession).

78. The resolution was passed at the business meeting of the CCWHP on December 30, 1985. The full text, along with a summary of the discussion at the meeting, appears in the *CCWHP Newsletter* 17 (February 1986): 6–8.

79. "A Feminist for Sears," letter from Rosalind Rosenberg to the Editor, *The Nation* 241 (October 26, 1985): 394, 410; "Sears Bias-Case Ruling: No 'Parade of Horribles,'" letter from Rosalind Rosenberg to the Editor, *Chronicle of Higher Education* 31 (March 12, 1986): 44; Rosalind Rosenberg, "What Harms Women in the Workplace," *New York Times*, February 27, 1986.

80. Rosenberg Seminar Statement, 9 (emphasis in the original). As mentioned above, this affirmative-action plan was instituted after the original EEOC commissioner's charge was filed in 1973.

81. "A Feminist for Sears," 394.

82. Author's interview with Rosenberg.

83. "A Feminist for Sears," 394.

84. Rosenberg Seminar Statement, 2.

85. Author's interview with Rosenberg.

86. Ibid.

87. In my interview with her, Rosenberg said she had agreed to testify at least a year before she gave her initial testimony in July 1984.

88. Alice Kessler-Harris, "*Equal Employment Opportunity Commission v. Sears, Roebuck and Company*: A Personal Account," *Radical History Review* 35 (April 1986): 75. This article sets out Kessler-Harris's retrospective view of the case in detail.

89. Alice Kessler-Harris, "Response to 'Written Rebuttal Testimony of Dr. Rosalind Rosenberg,'" November 27, 1985, circulated to members of the Women and Society Seminar, Columbia University.

90. Author's interview with Rosenberg.

91. Kessler-Harris, "*EEOC v. Sears*: A Personal Account."

92. Author's interview with Kessler-Harris, New York, N.Y., January 29, 1986.

93. "Despite Doubts."

Chapter 6

Gender and Trade Unionism
in Historical Perspective

This chapter provides a theoretically driven overview of a century of U.S. women's labor history, focusing on the variations among labor unions in policies and practices affecting women from the late nineteenth to the late twentieth century. Drawing on sociological theories that emphasize the critical importance of the formative stages of an organization's life for its long-term structure and behavior, the chapter compares unions that emerged from a series of labor upsurges: the craft unions created in the late nineteenth and early twentieth centuries, the industrial unions that took shape in the needle trades in the 1910s, the larger wave of industrial unions that emerged in the 1930s, and finally the public- and service-sector unions that formed in the 1960s and 1970s. Each had a distinct relationship to women workers, both because of structural variations in the types of unions that predominated in each period and because of changes in the wider society that influenced unionists' views of gender. The chapter applies this analytic framework to explain inter-union variations in women's membership and leadership.

Labor unions have been the primary organizational vehicle available to represent the interests of American working women and to struggle on their behalf against the twin inequalities of gender and class. Organized labor's record in relation to women is, to be sure, rather mixed. On the one hand, unions have frequently fought to improve the wages and working conditions of employed women and have often challenged sex discrimination as well. Unionized women have always earned more and had better protection against management abuses than their unorganized sisters. They have also enjoyed greater access to meaningful representation in the workplace (or "voice") than their nonunionized counterparts.[1] On the other hand, women have always been underrepresented in the ranks of organized labor relative to their numbers in the workforce as a whole. Moreover, like other formal organizations, unions have frequently excluded women from positions of leadership and power and, in some historical settings, even from membership. And all too often, unions have failed to represent the interests of women workers adequately or to do battle against gender inequality at work; in some cases they have even fought to maintain male privileges at the expense of women workers.

This chapter critically evaluates the emerging literature on the relationship between women and unions and poses a question buried in that literature but rarely addressed explicitly within it—namely, under what conditions have unions been effective political vehicles for women workers? "Political" here is meant not in the narrow sense of formal, electoral politics but in the broader sense of collective action and potential empowerment. While the evidence available is still too fragmentary to attempt to resolve this question definitively, it can be addressed in a partial way by examining the conditions that foster women's union membership, on the one hand, and women's participation and leadership in unions, on the other. The variations among individual labor organizations in regard to women's union membership, participation, and leadership, I will argue, reflect the diverse historical conditions under which particular unions were first established and their varying degrees of "maturity" as organizations.

The Debate about Women and Unions

Most of the research on women and unions is a product of the feminist scholarship in history and social science that began to proliferate in the 1970s. The first wave of literature was largely descriptive and compensatory in nature, and its primary aim was to refute the conventional wisdom on the subject: that women workers were less militant, less easily unionized, and less active in unions than similarly situated men. Leonard Sayles and George Strauss exemplified that traditional view in their claim that "women present a major problem to the union. Not only are they hard to organize but, once organized, they are less likely to participate."[2] By reconstructing the historical record of women's efforts to unionize and their many struggles at the workplace to improve their lot, feminist scholars sought to falsify this view of women as passive, "problem" workers and demonstrated that throughout the long history of conflict between workers and employers, "We Were There," as the title of one popular survey of the subject put it.[3]

This research also revealed the failure of unions to deliver their potential benefits to women workers. For example, historians documented the exclusionary practices of craft unions in the early part of the century, when many labor organizations barred women from membership or actively discouraged them from organizing, and argued that unions themselves were the "problem," not women—in effect transposing the terms of the traditional view. As Alice Kessler-Harris suggested in one of the most sophisticated treatments of this issue, "When we stop asking why women have not organized themselves, we are led to ask how women were, and are, kept out of unions." Kessler-Harris acknowledged that there were genuine obstacles to organizing women but argued that, even in the first years of the twentieth century, these "were clearly not insurmountable barriers. Given a chance, women were devoted and successful union members, convinced that unionism would serve them as it seemed to be serving their brothers."[4] Similarly, Meredith Tax concluded that one of the main reasons women were unorganized in this early period was that "no one would organize them. And when anyone tried, women often showed that, despite all these barriers, they were raring to go."[5]

In addition to the question of why women were less often unionized than men, feminist scholars reexamined the issue of women's participation and leadership within those unions that did not exclude them from membership. Here, too, they documented a pattern of hostility toward women's participation on the part of male union officials, as well as a host of broader social and cultural factors discouraging women from becoming activists or leaders.[6] This feminist perspective on unionism emerged simultaneously with and drew directly upon the critique of institutional labor history by social historians and the revisionist labor history and radical social science that constructed unions as essentially conservative institutions.

If unions have been, as the literature suggests, indifferent or even hostile to the plight of women workers, some explanation of this phenomenon is required. Although there have been few explicitly theoretical efforts to account for the apparent failure of labor unions to provide women workers with the agency to improve their lot, two dominant approaches to this problem can be distinguished, one emphasizing structural factors and the other cultural ones. The structural perspective explains male-dominated trade unionism in terms of gender inequality in the larger society. In this view, women's exclusion from and subordinate role within labor unions is critical for preserving the patriarchal order that restricts women to the home or to poorly paid jobs. Women's economic subordination, in turn, makes it difficult for them to organize or to participate actively in trade unions. Perhaps the most influential contribution here has been that of Heidi Hartmann, who argues that "men's ability to organize in labor unions . . . appears to be key in their ability to maintain job segregation and the domestic division of labor."[7] In this view, as Cynthia Cockburn put it in her study of London printers, trade unions are "male power bases" that struggle "to assure patriarchal advantage."[8]

The second approach focuses attention not on the material interests of male workers but rather on their cultural domination of trade union institutions. This perspective draws on the concept of "women's culture" in feminist historiography and also on historical and ethnographic accounts of women's activity in the workplace. In this view, male and female workers define their relationship to work in distinct ways, owing to their contrasting roles in society and their sex-segregated experience in the workplace.[9] Unions, the argument goes, have typically been part of male culture and are not the proper place to look for expressions of women workers' interests and struggles. Thus Susan Porter Benson's analysis of women salesworkers documents a rich female work culture that is sharply opposed to management—and yet has no relationship to unionism.[10] Even where women are union members, in this view, the union is often culturally alien to them. Not only are union meetings typically held in bars, and at night, so that women must compromise their respectability if they are to attend, but the entire discourse of unionism is built on images of masculinity. Thus Beatrix Campbell concludes that the labor movement is essentially a "men's movement," and Sallie Westwood's ethnography of a British garment shop observes that "the union seemed as far away as management, locked into an alien world of meetings and men which somehow never seemed to relate to the world of women in the department."[11]

The structural and cultural explanations of women's subordinate position within unions are by no means mutually exclusive. Indeed, while most commentators emphasize one or the other, some (especially in the British literature) have merged the two. Separately or in combination, what is most appealing about these theoretical perspectives is their apparent comprehensiveness: they explain not only women's underrepresentation in the ranks of union members and activists but also their general exclusion from positions of power in labor organizations and the relatively scant attention paid to women's special concerns by most unions. Yet despite their valuable insights into the global problem of male-dominated trade unionism, these theories are far less useful for explaining the wide range of historical *variation* in union behavior toward women that is so richly documented in the historical and sociological literature.

The concept of patriarchy, which is at the core of the structural perspective, is essentially ahistorical, as others have noted.[12] The argument that women's subordination within organized labor is an aspect of patriarchy makes it difficult to explain historical changes in the nature and extent of male domination of the labor movement. Moreover, while this perspective explains many specific cases where unions do operate as a vehicle for male workers' interests, it fails to take account of the conflicting nature of those interests in relation to women workers. As I have argued elsewhere, this view presumes that men's *gender* interest in maintaining male domination will inevitably take precedence over their *class* interest in gender equality, whereas historically there are instances of the opposite as well.[13]

Similarly, the conception of the asymmetric relationship of unions to gender-specific cultures, while usefully illuminating many specific instances of female marginality in labor unions, comes dangerously close to reifying the historically specific differences between male and female workers. It mirrors the ideology that justifies women's subordination within the labor market by reference to the assumption that women are less committed, more family-oriented workers than their male counterparts. And, ironically, like the pre-feminist literature on women and trade unions, this perspective fails to acknowledge the many historical and contemporary examples of female labor militancy that rely on conventional forms of union behavior.

Seemingly paradoxically, another stream of feminist scholarship also draws on the concept of women's culture but focuses on female mobilization into and within unions rather than on male domination of organized labor. For example, Temma Kaplan and Ardis Cameron have shown how women's culture and "female consciousness," rooted in traditional domestic concerns, can propel women into broad, community-based labor struggles alongside their male neighbors and kin.[14] Other scholarship has linked women's work culture to a distinctively female form of leadership in union organizing and to the mobilization of women workers within established union structures, suggesting that women's culture and unionism may not be incompatible after all.[15]

This work is critically important, for it begins to address the central question that is obscured by the more deterministic structural and cultural accounts of male-dominated unionism: *Under what conditions* have unions been effective vehicles for women workers' collective action? With the dramatic rise in women's labor force participation over the course of the twentieth century, and especially since World War II, the possibilities for female collective action and empowerment through unionism have become increasingly important. Drawing on the historical scholarship on women's labor struggles, we can begin to specify the conditions under which those possibilities are realizable. But this requires loosening the deterministic grip of the prevailing structural and cultural perspectives on male-dominated unionism in favor of a genuinely historicized analysis. Rather than presuming that men will always act to protect their gender interest, we must ask: Under what circumstances have they done so, and when have they instead pursued their class interest in gender equality? Similarly, rather than presuming that women's culture and unionism are inherently incompatible, we should explore the conditions under which they have and have not proved to be so.

An Organizational Perspective

Another limitation of the literature on women and unions is that, despite (or perhaps because of) the fact that it has called attention to the ways in which unions are gendered organizations, it has tended to ignore the implications of the gender-neutral organizational characteristics and dynamics of unionism for women. Although this was an understandable and necessary reaction to the long tradition of gender-blind analysis of union behavior, it may have inadvertently sacrificed valuable insights. In rescuing those insights, the literature on women and organizations (which, however, includes virtually no direct discussion of unions) can serve as a model. Indeed, many of the organizational factors operating to marginalize women from leadership positions in the corporations they face across the bargaining table also operate within unions, and with similar results. An obvious example is the premium on trust and loyalty that, as Rosabeth Moss Kanter has shown, leads corporate executives to be wary of recruiting women or other individuals with backgrounds different from their own (whose actions are therefore less predictable) for top positions.[16] A parallel dynamic operates within unions, where trust and loyalty are at least as important. (Unions, of course, differ from corporations in that they are not simply institutions but are also part of a social movement that mobilizes on a variety of fronts on behalf of workers' interests, including those of the unorganized. The labor movement, moreover, has a strong democratic and egalitarian tradition that is explicitly opposed to the hierarchical structure of the business world—which, after all, makes no pretense of being democratically run. Given this tradition, should the labor movement not be held to a higher standard of democracy in general, and responsiveness to the needs of women and other socially oppressed groups in particular, than corporate organizations? Perhaps it should. But there has always been a tension between the goals of unionism as part of a social movement and the tasks it is engaged in as an ongoing institution: the classic tension between union democracy and union bureaucracy.[17] And in their bureaucratic aspect, at least, unions seem to operate very much like other formal organizations—and not only in regard to women.)

Another organizational factor that fosters union leaders' distrust of women is that the very existence of labor organizations is defined by a relationship of continual conflict with a more powerful adversary: the employer on whom union members depend for their livelihoods. The unions' structurally weaker position tends to generate a siege mentality among their leaders, which in turn encourages suspicion and hostility toward any group that is perceived as making "special" demands. Union hostility toward women is often rooted in this fundamentally gender-neutral organizational dynamic (which nevertheless can and frequently does have a gender-specific outcome) rather than simply in "patriarchy" or male culture.

Organizational analysis can provide insight not only into such general dynamics, which tend to marginalize women within all labor movement institutions, but also into the factors producing variations among unions in their degree of openness or hostility toward women. To begin with, consider the implications for this problem of Arthur L. Stinchcombe's classic discussion of social structure and organizations, which emphasizes the persistence of organizational forms, once established, over time. Following Stinchcombe's argument that "organizational forms and types have a history, and . . . this history determines some aspects of the present structure of organizations of that type," we can hypothesize that unions that arose in different historical periods would vary systematically in their treatment of women in the present as well as the past.[18]

In the United States, at least, the growth of unionization has occurred in readily distinguishable waves, and in each period of growth over the past century both the dominant form of unionism and the social position of women varied markedly. If, as Stinchcombe suggested, the basic goals, structures, values, and ideologies of individual unions are shaped early in their institutional life and tend to persist intact thereafter, it follows that the prevailing type of union structure (craft, industrial, and so on), the position of women in the industrial setting, and the state of gender relations more broadly in the historical period in which a particular union originates will be significant in explaining that union's behavior. Although Stinchcombe himself was not particularly concerned with gender issues, his theory of organizational inertia provides a tool with which to historicize the structural and cultural theories of women's relationship to unionism. It can incorporate into a broader framework the historical shifts in the material interests of men and women and their respective cultures, which have not remained static but have been significantly affected by such factors as the long-term rise in female labor force participation and the strength of feminist consciousness in particular periods.

While his overall argument emphasized the persistence and stability of organizational structures, Stinchcombe also discussed what he called the "liabilities of newness," arguing that in the earliest period of their existence, organizations are relatively fragile and unstable entities.[19] Other commentators have developed a similar notion and applied it to union organizations in particular. Richard A. Lester, for example, has suggested that as unions "mature," their organizational behavior changes significantly. When a labor organization first comes into existence, it is by definition on the offensive (albeit in an uphill battle); later, once it has won nominal acceptance from the employer, management increasingly takes the initiative, while the union typically settles into a reactive and often defensive role. In addition, openness to alternative ideologies and modes of organizing is generally greater in the early period of a labor union's life than in its more mature phases, when it has settled into a routine existence and has an officialdom with a stake in maintaining its established traditions.[20] This life-cycle view of organizations complicates Stinchcombe's theory and has a different emphasis, but it is not necessarily inconsistent with the view that organizations once established (or "mature") tend toward structural inertia.

Extending this idea to the problem of women and trade unions, we can hypothesize that, in general, unions would be more open to demands from women and feminist approaches to organizing in their youth than in their maturity. Moreover, both bureaucratization and the development of a siege mentality among trade union leaders—which, as was already noted, tend to marginalize women within union organizations—are typically minimal in the early stages of a union's history, and both intensify as it matures. Once again, then, the gender-blind organizational logic described by theories of union maturity can help explain differences among unions that are at different life stages at a given point in time.

Four Cohorts of American Unions

In American labor history, at least four major waves of unionization that have produced four distinct cohorts of labor organizations can be identified. The problem is simplified by the fact that each of these cohorts coincides with particular structural forms of union organization (craft, industrial, and so on), each of which recruited in specific types of occupations or industries. Each of the four union cohorts had a different historical relationship to women workers, and to a large extent the differences have persisted into the present day. Thus a historical perspective, informed by Stinchcombe's analysis of organizational inertia as well as union maturity theories, offers a potential basis for explaining variations in women's position in unions.

The oldest group of unions, some of them with roots going back deep into the nineteenth century, are the old-line craft unions, such as the building trades "brotherhoods" or the printers. These unions tend to be the most hostile to women not only because of their maturity but also because of the nature of the relationship they established to women when they were formed. Initially, their constituency of craftsmen saw women's labor as a threat to established skill and wage levels, and they therefore typically excluded women from union membership (until as late as the 1940s in some cases) and generally viewed them with suspicion. Indeed, the entire logic of craft unionism was predicated on the importance of skill, and employers' reliance on it, as the primary source of workers' power. This generated exclusionary practices directed not only against women but against all unskilled workers. It is perhaps not accidental that craft unions have been the main focus of analysis for those scholars who argue that labor organizations serve as an instrument of patriarchy.[21] But these unions are only one component of the labor movement, and far from typical.

A second cohort of unions emerged in the 1910s, primarily in the clothing industry. The "new unionism" of this period was at once an outgrowth of the craft union tradition and a departure from it, in both respects anticipating the industrial unionism of the 1930s. Craft exclusionism was effectively abandoned by the International Ladies' Garment Workers' Union (ILGWU) and the Amalgamated Clothing Workers (ACW) in this period, even though originally it was the skilled male cutters alone who were organized. In the wake of the militancy of women workers, most notably in the New York garment workers' strike of 1909–10, vast numbers of unskilled and semiskilled women were incorporated into these unions' ranks. The "new unionism" recognized women workers' need for organization and also broadened the definition of unionism to encompass not only economic but also social functions, pioneering in such areas as union-sponsored healthcare and educational programs. Yet the leaders of these unions still viewed women as an entirely different species of worker than men. For in this period women were still typically employed for a relatively brief part of their lives, particularly in the clothing industry. Male union leaders as well as working women themselves viewed women's needs as different from those of men in the 1910s. Women's militant organizing efforts were centered not on economic demands for gender equality but rather on moral appeals for better protection against management abuses. These appeals implicitly or explicitly invoked their special vulnerability as women.[22] Under these conditions, it was hardly surprising that the leaders of the "new unions" viewed women paternalistically and not as equal partners, or that these unions' officialdoms remained overwhelmingly male despite the dramatic feminization of their memberships. Like the old-line craft unions, these unions have remained deeply marked by the legacy of their historical origins; their predominantly male leaderships continued to view their majoritarian female (and by the late twentieth century, immigrant female) memberships paternalistically, as weak workers in need of protection.

A third cohort of unions took shape in the massive industrial organizing drives of the 1930s. The mass-production industries in which the Congress of Industrial Organizations (CIO) unions emerged were overwhelmingly male—steel, auto, rubber, electrical manufacturing. But insofar as women were part of the production workforce in these industries, the CIO organized them alongside men from the outset. And the attitude of this generation of unionists toward women workers was quite different from that of either the old craft unionists or the "new unionists" of the 1910s. In the 1920s and 1930s, in the aftermath of the suffrage victory and with growing labor force participation among married women, the claim of women to equal treatment in the public sphere gained ground.[23] The CIO opposed discrimination on the basis of sex, color, or creed in a deliberate departure from craft union traditions and practices. While older views of "woman's place" still persisted within the CIO unions, the inclusionary logic of industrial unionism and its formal commitment to the ideal of equality opened up new possibilities for women in organized labor.[24] This became particularly explicit during World War II, when women poured into the basic industries that had been organized by the CIO immediately before the war, and women's issues (such as equal pay for equal work, nondiscriminatory seniority, and female representation in labor leadership) gained a prominent position on union agendas.[25] After the war, while women once again became a minority within the workforce of the basic industries, this cohort of unions retained a formal commitment to equality and antidiscrimination efforts. The United Auto Workers' Union (UAW), for example, was an early advocate of national legislation against sex discrimination and later became the first labor union in the nation to endorse the Equal Rights Amendment.[26]

Finally, a fourth group of unions emerged in the post–World War II period in the expanding service and clerical occupations, predominantly in the public sector but also in some private sector institutions (for example, hospitals). Initially, in the 1950s and 1960s these unions organized mainly blue-collar male workers, such as garbage collectors and highway workers. Subsequently, however, the majority of their recruits were pink- and white-collar workers (including many professionals) in occupations where women are highly concentrated. Women were not unionized "as women" but as teachers, as hospital workers, as government clerks, and so on. However, their massive recruitment during a period of feminist resurgence and growing acceptance of the goal of gender equality ultimately led this cohort of unions to reformulate traditional labor issues in innovative ways that were especially relevant to women. For example, the American Federation of State, County and Municipal Employees (AFSCME) and the Service Employees International Union (SEIU), the two largest unions in this cohort, led campaigns for pay equity or "comparable worth" in the 1980s.[27] More generally, both because of their relative youth and because they emerged in a period of feminist resurgence, these unions have been especially receptive to women's leadership and to efforts to mobilize around women's issues.

The striking differences among these four cohorts of labor organizations in regard to their relationship to women workers are traceable, at least in part, to the different historical periods in which each was ascendant. Each period was characterized by a different configuration of gender relations in the larger society, and each wave of unionism had different structural characteristics (craft, craft/industrial, industrial, service sector) and a different organizational logic. Of course, this is only a first approximation: many other factors—among them, economic shifts and dislocations, political and legal influences—can affect the relationship of unions to women workers. Examining the problem through a comparison of cohorts, moreover, makes it difficult to distinguish clearly between the effects of what are in fact separate variables: the organization's age, the historical period in which it originated, the type of industry, and the type of union involved. The difficulty is that all of these tend to coincide historically within each of the four cohorts. A fuller analysis might come from detailed comparative case studies of individual unions within the same cohort, which would facilitate finer distinctions. This should be an important part of the agenda for future research in this area. But in the interim, a framework that is sensitive to cohort differences among unions and to the internal process of "maturation" within labor organizations may begin to explain some of the variations in women's involvement in trade unions and in unions' effectiveness for women that remain unaccounted for in the existing literature.

Women's Union Membership

Consider the issue of women's union membership. Although nonmembers often benefit indirectly from the activities of unions, members benefit a great deal more. They also have direct access to political resources vis-à-vis their employers that nonmembers typically lack. The degree to which women are recruited into the ranks of organized labor, then, is one major determinant of the degree to which unions effectively represent their interests. The density of female unionization has fluctuated considerably over time, but at no point have a majority of U.S. working women been union members, and, perhaps more significant, the male unionization rate has always been greater than the female rate. Why is this the case, and what explains the variations over time and across industries and sectors?

To address these questions, we must first note that, at least since 1935, becoming a union member in the United States was and is associated primarily with employment in a firm or industry that has been targeted by union organizers. Under the American legal and industrial-relations system, whether or not an individual joins a labor union is rarely a matter of individual choice. Indeed, one can infer nothing about gender-specific preferences from the observation that a greater proportion of male workers (the figure was 23 percent in 1984) than of female workers (14 percent in that year) are union members.[28] Rather, the best predictor of union membership is one's industry or occupation, which in turn determines the likelihood that a union is present in a given workplace.

Since jobs are highly sex-segregated, women and men are not evenly distributed through industries or occupations, and in general the gender distribution of unionism is an artifact of the sexual division of labor. On the whole, throughout the century "men's jobs" have more often been unionized than women's. Yet there are also vast differences in unionization rates within both the male and female labor markets. In 1984 only 2.5 percent of the women (and 3.5 percent of the men) employed in finance, insurance, and real estate were union members, for example, while in the public sector 33 percent of the women (and 39 percent of the men) were unionized at that time. Moreover, both survey data and analyses of union election results suggest that unorganized women are more interested in becoming union members than their male counterparts, although this probably was not true in the early twentieth century.[29]

As theories of union maturation emphasize, unions (or their subdivisions) historically have tended to recruit new members for a period of time and then to stabilize in size, concentrating on serving their established members rather than on continuing to expand. For this reason, a union's gender composition at any given point in time reflects the past and present composition of the occupation, industry, or sector it targeted for unionization in earlier years. While efforts to preserve the organization over time frequently lead existing unions to undertake recruitment efforts (targeting workers employed in the same industries and occupations as their established membership), few have successfully expanded their jurisdictions to take in wholly new constituencies. (An important exception here is the Teamsters Union, which has recruited vast numbers of female members and which has diversified over a long period, far beyond its traditional base in the trucking industry.) Similarly, some industrial unions, facing severe membership losses because of reduced employment levels in their traditional jurisdictions, have launched efforts to recruit service-sector workers, but these efforts have had limited effectiveness.

Each of the four union cohorts described above focused its original recruitment efforts on specific types of workers, and their membership composition remained broadly similar for many decades. Each cohort of unions was guided by a distinctive and essentially gender-neutral organizational strategy, which, however, had highly gender-specific results. The early twentieth century craft unions took in primarily skilled workers. Their strategy of limiting access to skills with high market value functioned to exclude women from both craft employment and union membership in many industries—not only because of their gender but also because of their unskilled status. Whereas from one perspective this exclusionism reflected the interest of male workers in maintaining the system of patriarchy, an equally plausible account might simply stress that exclusionism—which was directed not only against women but also against immigrants, blacks, and other unskilled workers—was an organizational feature inherent in craft unionism.

Although craft unionism was the predominant form of unionism in the United States at the turn of the century, it soon gave way to new forms that lacked its structural bias toward exclusionism, first with the "new unionism" of the 1910s and later with the industrial unionism of the 1930s. Here the organizational strategy was simply to recruit everyone the employer hired within a given industrial jurisdiction. In the clothing industries that were the focus of the "new unionism," this meant organizing unprecedented numbers of women. By 1920 nearly half (43 percent) of the nation's unionized women were clothing workers.[30] The CIO, too, while recruiting many more men than women, greatly increased women's unionization level. But because the CIO's strategy centered on organizing blue-collar workers in durable-goods manufacturing where relatively few women were employed, the results for women were less dramatic than in the 1910s, when organization centered on the heavily female clothing trade. In both cases, though, what determined the extent of female unionization was not the union's strategy but the pre-existing gender composition of the workforce in the targeted industry. Where women were numerous among production workers, as in clothing in the 1910s and electrical manufacturing in the 1930s, they were recruited into unions in large numbers; where they were few, as was the case during the 1930s in auto and steel (the two largest industries organized by the CIO), their numbers in the union ranks were correspondingly small. And in the 1930s there was little interest in organizing the already considerable numbers of women employed in clerical and service jobs in the tertiary sector.

While the organizational logic of craft unionism had excluded women not so much "as women" but rather because they were unskilled workers, now the inclusionary logic of industrial unionism reversed the situation—but still without any particular effort to recruit women as women. There is some fragmentary evidence that occupations and industries where women predominated in the workforce were slighted because of their gender composition by CIO unions, as Sharon Strom has suggested for the case of clerical workers.[31] But in general, the targets of CIO organizing drives were selected on the basis of considerations that involved not gender but rather the strategic importance of organizing mass-production industries to build the overall strength of the labor movement.

The same was true of the organizing drives that brought hospital workers, teachers, and a wide variety of clerical and service employees into the labor movement in the postwar period. The growth of this fourth cohort of unions (together with the decline of the second and third cohorts due to deindustrialization) resulted in a substantial feminization of union membership in the 1970s and 1980s: by 1984, 34 percent of all unionized workers were women, a record high.[32] However, this came about not because union organizers sought to recruit women specifically but instead as a by-product of their recruitment of particular categories of workers who seemed ripe for unionization. Feminization was essentially an unintended consequence of this process.[33]

On the whole, then, although throughout the twentieth century women's overall unionization level was lower than men's, much of the gender gap was the result of gender-neutral strategic and organizational factors and the pre-existing segregation of women into jobs which were less likely to be unionized than those held by men. While it is reasonable to criticize the labor movement for its general failure to challenge job segregation by sex or to target more "women's jobs" in its recruiting drives, a major part of the explanation for the general sex differential in unionization rates, and for the wide variations among unions' sex composition as well, lies in gender-neutral organizational factors operating within a sex-segregated labor market.

Participation and Leadership

Another crucial dimension of unions' political effectiveness for women is the extent of female participation and leadership in labor organizations. There is considerable variation among unions in this area as well, and while obviously the extent of women's union membership is one relevant factor, by itself it is not a satisfactory predictor of women's participation or leadership. In the 1980s the ILGWU, for example, was notorious for the lack of significant female representation in its leadership, despite an 85 percent female membership.[34] More generally, even in industries or occupations where women are highly unionized, their participation in labor-union activities is typically less extensive than men's, although the extent to which this is the case varies considerably. Positions of union leadership, to an even greater degree than voluntary participation, tend to be male-dominated, especially at the upper levels, although again this is more true of some unions than of others. What accounts for women's underrepresentation among labor activists and leaders? Under what conditions can the "barriers to entry" for women be overcome? And what explains the variations among unions in the extent of women's representation among participants and leaders?

Research addressing these questions has focused primarily on identifying the specific personal attributes associated with union participation and leadership and those that function as obstacles to activism. Divorced and single women, for example, are more likely than married women to be union participants and leaders, and extensive domestic responsibilities are an obstacle to activism for many women.[35] These findings help account for gender differences in union participation and leadership and also explain why some women are more likely to participate or lead than others. However, this approach provides, at best, a partial explanation. It is necessary to examine not only the attributes of women themselves but also those of the labor organizations in which their participation and leadership is at issue.

In younger unions, which are involved primarily in recruitment of new members and organization building, women's participation and leadership is often more extensive than in more mature unions. Most of the celebrated examples of women's militancy and leadership come from these early stages in union development, especially organizational strikes, such as the garment workers' "uprising" of 1909–10 or the 1984 strike of Yale clerical workers.[36] But the level of women's participation and leadership tends to decline as unions become more formally organized (and bureaucratized) institutions that concentrate on collective bargaining and other means to protect and win benefits for an already established membership. Male rank-and-file union participation also tends to decline as union organizations mature, but the shift between union democracy and bureaucracy that accompanies maturation is especially complex for women.

In mature unions the problem of women's underrepresentation among activists and leaders is a specific case of the more general phenomenon of women's exclusion from leadership roles in virtually all mixed-sex formal organizations. Indeed, the record of unions in this respect is no worse than that of the corporations with which they negotiate. In both unions and corporations, married women and those with heavy domestic responsibilities are less likely to become leaders than other women. And, as noted above, Rosabeth Moss Kanter's organizational analysis of women's exclusion from top corporate positions is relevant to unions as well. In both cases, and perhaps even more so in the case of unions, with their siege mentality, tremendous value is placed on trust and loyalty among officeholders, especially at the top levels of the organizational hierarchy. This premium on loyalty encourages the process of "homosexual reproduction," whereby males in top positions "reproduce themselves in their own image," which Kanter has described so well for corporate organizations.[37]

Conventional organizational analysis also helps explain why, when special positions are created for women within the union's organizational structure, the (presumably unintended) effect is usually to marginalize female leaders and exclude them from the centers of union power. A good example is the UAW Women's Bureau, created during World War II to cope with the sudden influx of women workers into the union's ranks. The bureau, while doing valuable work, was organizationally isolated and marginal to the union. In contrast, those few (by definition "exceptional") women who rise through the union hierarchy on the same terms as men, and without being defined as specialists in women's concerns, seem to be taken more seriously.[38] But this route to power within the union is often blocked by the emphasis on loyalty and its attendant mechanism of "homosexual reproduction."

Another factor limiting women's access to leadership posts in mature unions is the lack of available positions. The number of vacancies narrows as membership (and with it the size of the organization) stabilizes. This reduction in the number of opportunities for advancement in the leadership structure is even more severe in unions than in other "mature" organizations, because union officialdoms are one of the few avenues of upward mobility open to workers. In a corporate or governmental organization, officeholders' careers might carry them from one organization to another. But in the case of unions, positions of leadership, once obtained, are rarely relinquished, especially at the upper levels. Despite the formally democratic electoral machinery within unions, in practice paid officials seldom depart from their posts unless they win promotion to a higher one, retire, or die.[39] Thus, in a mature labor organization, unless membership, and with it leadership, is expanding rapidly, the possibilities (for both sexes) of gaining a leadership post are relatively restricted compared with those in a young union that is still actively recruiting new members and thus expanding its leadership structure.

Other critical influences on the opportunities for women to become union leaders, and especially paid officials, include the position of women in the employment structure of the jurisdiction within which the union operates, and, more broadly, the state of gender relations in the larger society during the period when the organization first develops. The more extensive women's participation in the public sphere generally, and in positions of power or importance in particular, the better their prospects for movement into union leadership posts at a given point in time. Moreover, women's prospects will be correspondingly brighter in organizations that are relatively young or experiencing rapid growth at the time. Indeed, over the twentieth century, and particularly in the postwar period, as women's exclusion from the public sphere has diminished, female representation in the leadership of successive cohorts of unions has increased.

In the late nineteenth and early twentieth centuries, when the craft unions first emerged as a powerful force, women were still largely excluded from positions of leadership in public life. They were barred from membership in most of the craft unions, and so the question of their participation and leadership in these unions seldom arose. And while all the craft unions were forced to remove their formal bans on women's membership by the mid-twentieth century, most continued long afterward to view women as interlopers, making it almost unimaginable that they would ascend to positions of power within these unions. As late as 1985 such unions as the International Brotherhood of Electrical Workers (IBEW), the International Association of Machinists (IAM), and even the giant Teamsters Union had no female representation whatsoever among their officers or on their governing boards—despite the fact that more than one-fourth of the members of both the Teamsters Union and the IBEW were female.[40]

The "new unions" created in the 1910s, despite their majoritarian female memberships, also developed as male-led organizations and retained overwhelmingly male leaderships, with only a token female presence. Early on, these unions established a pattern of paternalistic (and male) leadership over an unstable (and largely female) membership, a pattern that has been preserved intact ever since. It was further reinforced by the peculiar structure of the clothing industry, in which the two major unions are relatively large, impersonal institutions representing a workforce scattered among a multitude of small and often unstable firms. The membership of these unions has always been mostly female and foreign-born. The special vulnerability of these workers, in turn, encouraged paternalistic leadership made up largely of men drawn from earlier immigrant generations who were already well assimilated in the larger society.

The third cohort, the CIO unions, emerged in a period when women's position in public life was quite different than it had been in the 1910s. Not only had women won the vote, but by the 1930s a generation of middle-class professional women had become well entrenched in American society, especially in the public sector.[41] While the older notion of "woman's place" remained more resilient in the working class than in the middle class, the CIO unions embraced the ideology of formal equality between the sexes. The main difficulty was that in most cases the membership of these unions was overwhelmingly male. Thus the population of potential female leaders was quite limited in the crucial, formative years. The CIO unions continued to have limited, token female representation at the upper levels of leadership—far more than in the case of the craft unions but still below the level of female representation among their members.

In the case of the fourth cohort of unions, the service- and public-sector organizations that emerged in the 1970s and 1980s, the pattern is quite different. These unions developed not only in a period of resurgent feminism, but also at a time when the concept of "affirmative action" had legitimacy in the liberal political culture. In addition, unions such as AFSCME, the SEIU, and the teachers' and nurses' unions and associations had a large pool of educated female members to draw from when recruiting their leadership. While even in these unions the extent of female leadership at the top levels remained smaller than their majoritarian representation among the membership, as a group these unions have a much better record than their predecessors. They not only exhibit a substantial female presence at the upper levels of leadership, but they also have accumulated a large cadre of women leaders at the local, regional, and district levels. In 1985, for example, 319 of the SEIU's 820 local officers were female, as were 9 of its 61 joint council officers. Similarly, 45 percent of AFSCME's local executive board members and 33 percent of its local presidents were women in 1985.[42]

Conclusion

Far from being monolithic, then, the labor movement's relationship to women workers varies significantly, both among unions and over time. Historical perspectives on the organizational logic and the particular orientation toward women of the four cohorts of labor unions help explain some of these variations, which the prevailing structural and cultural perspectives on women and unions cannot account for. As a first approximation, the political effectiveness of unions for women workers can be understood as a product of the historical conditions under which each wave of unions first developed, and of their age and maturity as organizations. In general, the older unions, both because of their advanced age and because of the specific historical circumstances in which they originated, have been less effective than their younger counterparts in regard to women's recruitment into leadership, even in cases where they have large numbers of women workers among their members. The youngest cohort of service- and public-sector unions has been much more receptive to feminist concerns than the older unions. While the legacy of tradition seems to be a serious obstacle to women's advancement in many of the older unions, the experience of the newest cohort, with its large female membership and growing representation of women in leadership, offers a basis for optimism.

Notes

Originally published in *Women, Politics, and Change*, edited by Louise A. Tilly and Patricia Gurin, 87–107. © 1990 Russell Sage Foundation, 112 East 64th Street, New York, N.Y. 10065. Reprinted with permission.

1. Richard B. Freeman and James L. Medoff, *What Do Unions Do?* (New York: Basic, 1984).

2. Leonard R. Sayles and George Strauss, *The Local Union* (New York: Harcourt, Brace, and Word, 1967), 124.

3. Barbara Meyer Wertheimer, *We Were There: The Story of Working Women in America* (New York: Pantheon, 1977).

4. Alice Kessler-Harris, "Where Are the Organized Women Workers?" *Feminist Studies* 3 (1975): 93, 94.

5. Meredith Tax, *The Rising of the Women: Feminist Solidarity and Class Conflict, 1880–1917* (New York: Monthly Review, 1980), 32.

6. Barbara Meyer Wertheimer and Anne Nelson, *Trade Union Women: A Study of Their Participation in New York City Locals* (New York: Praeger, 1975); Mary Margaret Fonow, "Women in Steel: A Case Study of the Participation of Women in a Trade Union" (PhD diss., Ohio State University, 1977).

7. Heidi Hartmann, "Capitalism, Patriarchy, and Job Segregation by Sex," in *Women and the Work-Place: The Implications of Occupational Segregation*, edited by Martha Blaxall and Barbara Reagan (Chicago: University of Chicago Press, 1976), 159.

8. Cynthia Cockburn, *Brothers: Male Dominance and Technological Change* (London: Pluto, 1983), 33, 35.

9. Leslie Woodcock Tentler, *Wage-Earning Women: Industrial Work and Family Life in the United States, 1900–1930* (New York: Oxford University Press, 1979).

10. Susan Porter Benson, *Counter Cultures: Saleswomen, Managers, and Customers in American Department Stores, 1890–1940* (Urbana: University of Illinois Press, 1986).

11. Beatrix Campbell, *Wigan Pier Revisited: Poverty and Politics in the Eighties* (London: Virago, 1984), 129; Sallie Westwood, *All Day, Every Day: Factory and Family in the Making of Women's Lives* (Urbana: University of Illinois, 1984), 69–70.

12. Veronica Beechey, "Reproduction, Production and the Sexual Division of Labor," *Cambridge Journal of Economics* 3 (1979): 203–25; Sheila Rowbotham, "The Trouble with 'Patriarchy,'" in *The Woman Question: Readings on the Subordination of Women*, edited by Mary Evans (Oxford: Fontana, 1982); Iris Young, "Socialist Feminism and the Limits of Dual Systems Theory," *Socialist Review* 10 (1980): 169–88.

13. Ruth Milkman, *Gender at Work: The Dynamics of Job Segregation by Sex during World War II* (Urbana: University of Illinois Press, 1987).

14. Temma Kaplan, "Female Consciousness and Collective Action: The Case of Barcelona, 1910–1918," *Signs: Journal of Women in Culture and Society* 7 (1982): 545–66; Ardis Cameron, "Bread and Roses Revisited: Women's Culture and Working-Class Activism in the Lawrence Strike of 1912," in *Women, Work, and Protest: A Century of Women's Labor History*, edited by Ruth Milkman (Boston: Routledge and Kegan Paul, 1985).

15. Karen Sacks, *Caring by the Hour: Women, Work, and Organizing at Duke Medical Center* (Urbana: University of Illinois Press, 1987); Cynthia B. Costello, "'WEA're Worth It!' Work Culture and Conflict at the Wisconsin Education Association Insurance Trust," *Feminist Studies* 11 (1985): 497–518.

16. Rosabeth Moss Kanter, *Men and Women of the Corporation* (New York: Basic, 1977), chap. 3.

17. See Robert Michels, *Political Parties: A Sociological Study of the Oligarchical Tendencies of Modern Democracy* (Glencoe, IL: Free Press, 1949 [1915]); Seymour Martin Lipset, *Political Man: The Social Bases of Politics* (Garden City, NY: Doubleday, 1960), chap. 12.

18. Arthur L. Stinchcombe, "Social Structure and Organizations," in *Handbook of Organizations*, edited by James G. March (Chicago: Rand McNally, 1965), 153.

19. Ibid., 148–50.

20. Richard A. Lester, *As Unions Mature* (Princeton, N.J.: Princeton University Press, 1958).

21. For example, Hartmann, "Capitalism, Patriarchy, and Job Segregation by Sex."

22. Alice Kessler-Harris, "The Debate of Equality for Women in the Work Place: Recognizing Differences," in *Women and Work: An Annual Review*, edited by Laurie Larwood, Ann H. Stromberg, and Barbara A. Gutek (Beverly Hills, Calif.: Sage, 1985).

23. See the discussion in Nancy F. Cott, "Across the Great Divide: Women in Politics Before and After 1920," in *Women, Politics, and Change*, edited by Louise A. Tilly and Patricia Gurin (New York: Russell Sage Foundation, 1990).

24. Sharon Hartman Strom, "Challenging 'Women's Place': Feminism, the Left, and Industrial Unionism in the 1930s," *Feminist Studies* 9 (1983): 359–86.

25. Milkman, *Gender at Work*, chap. 6.

26. Nancy Gabin, "Women and the United Automobile Workers' Union in the 1950s," in Milkman, *Women, Work, and Protest*.

27. Deborah E. Bell, "Unionized Women in State and Local Government," in Milkman, *Women, Work, and Protest*.

28. Larry T. Adams, "Changing Employment Patterns of Organized Workers," *Monthly Labor Review* 108 (1985): 25–31.

29. Ibid.; Thomas A. Kochan, "How American Workers View Labor Unions," *Monthly Labor Review* 102 (1979): 22–31; "Labor Letter," *Wall Street Journal*, March 25, 1986.

30. Leo Wolman, *Growth of American Trade Unions, 1880–1923* (New York: National Bureau of Economic Research, 1924).

31. Strom, "Challenging 'Women's Place,'" 372.

32. Adams, "Changing Employment Patterns."

33. Bell, "Unionized Women."

34. Naomi Baden, "Developing an Agenda: Expanding the Role of Women in Unions," *Labor Studies Journal* 10 (1986): 229–49.

35. Wertheimer and Nelson, *Trade Union Women*, 91, 115.

36. See Tax, *Rising of the Women*; Molly Ladd-Taylor, "Women Workers and the Yale Strike," *Feminist Studies* 11 (1985): 465–89.

37. Kanter, *Men and Women*, 48.

38. Milkman, *Gender at Work,* chap. 6.

39. Lipset, *Political Man*, chap. 12, attributes this to the "one-party system" of union government.

40. Baden, "Developing an Agenda."

41. Susan Ware, *Beyond Suffrage: Women in the New Deal* (Cambridge, Mass.: Harvard University Press, 1981).

42. Baden, "Developing an Agenda," 239. Unfortunately, comparable data for earlier years are not available.

Chapter 7

Union Responses to Workforce Feminization in the United States

This chapter focuses on the ways in which unions in the United States responded to the rapid feminization of the labor force that began in the 1970s. It starts off by analyzing data on the wide range of variation in the extent of women's representation in union membership and union leadership in the late twentieth century. Those data provide strong empirical support for the theoretical framework elaborated in chapter 6, which explained inter-union variations through analysis of the distinct historical eras in which individual unions first formed. The data also show that although strong female representation among union members is a necessary condition for women moving into positions of union leadership, it is not a sufficient condition. In addition, through a detailed analysis of data on union organizing drives, this chapter explores the relationship between the gender composition of the workforce and the likelihood of organizing success. The key finding is that unions are most likely to win organizing drives in workplaces that are predominantly female. More surprising, however, is that unions are more likely to win in settings that are predominantly male than in those with gender-mixed workforces. The chapter concludes with an overview of the ways in which the public- and service-sector unions that took shape in the 1960s and 1970s began to seriously engage "women's issues" in the 1980s.

The rapid feminization of the U.S. labor force that took off in the 1970s and 1980s, against the background of a popular feminist resurgence, generated unprecedented changes in the relationship of women workers to the organized labor movement. Union membership became increasingly feminized, and issues of special concern to women workers gained new prominence on many unions' collective-bargaining and political agendas.

Yet rapid private-sector deunionization and related processes of economic restructuring, which occurred in precisely the same period that the social effects of workforce feminization first became manifest, set limits on union responsiveness to the growth of the female workforce. The resilient historical traditions of male-centered unionism further constrained the capacities of many labor organizations to address the needs of their newly enlarged female constituencies. Indeed, the process of change has been uneven, with some unions responding lethargically and others more creatively to feminization. In general, the unions that have most effectively met the challenge posed by the gender transformation of the labor market have been those few that have gained rather than lost members in recent years (typically, relatively young organizations recruiting primarily in the public sector). In these unions, a new kind of gender politics has emerged, combining demands for gender equality with a recognition of the special burdens imposed by socially constructed gender differences on women workers.

This chapter explores the factors shaping recent union responses to work-force feminization in the United States, with particular attention to inter-union variations and to changing labor movement approaches to women workers. I argue that although women's advancement in the labor movement has been less extensive than gender transformations in the workforce and in the larger society might lead one to expect, the innovative gender politics that has emerged in those unions least constrained by the forces of deunionization or patriarchal traditions suggests some basis for optimism. In the event of a future revival of organized labor, when the conditions favoring change that now exist in only a few unions could become more widespread, women workers and gender politics may have a central place in the union movement.

The feminization of the labor force in the United States in the late twentieth century is widely recognized as the single most important transformation in the workplace, if not in the larger society, to occur during the postwar period. While the process of incorporating women workers into the waged labor force began in the early nineteenth century, only after World War II did a sustained attachment to paid work become typical for adult women. The overall female labor-force participation rate rose from 34 percent in 1950 to 43 percent in 1970, and then to 58 percent in 1990. The male participation rate, in comparison, was 77 percent in 1990, down from 86 percent in 1950. Women made up nearly half (45 percent) of the labor force in 1990, compared with 29 percent in 1950.[1]

The proportion of women among the country's union members has also grown dramatically in the postwar period, from only 24 percent in 1970 to 38 percent twenty years later.[2] This feminization of union membership, however, occurred in the context of an equally dramatic process of deunionization of the workforce as a whole. Among nonagricultural workers, union density was twice as high in 1956 as in 1986, falling from 36 percent to 18 percent in those three decades. The only major area of union growth has been in the public sector; private-sector union density has declined steadily since its peak in the mid-1950s.[3] The feminization of union membership is due largely to the extensive recruitment of women into public-sector unions, combined with large losses of male union membership in the private sector.

The general erosion of union density is one major constraint on labor-movement responses to workforce feminization. Another is the legacy of patriarchal union traditions. As many feminist commentators have noted, unions as institutions often have been indifferent or even hostile to women workers and have developed as male-dominated institutions that represent the sectional interests and cultural orientations of male workers.[4] Yet these accounts tend to overlook the fact that unions vary considerably in the degree to which they recruit women members, as well as in the extent to which women gain leadership roles within them, and in their level of engagement with issues of special concern to women workers. Indeed, union responses to the process of workforce feminization have been far from uniform.

Public-sector unionism, the site of the most extensive change in the relationship of women to the labor movement, is the most recent in a series of waves of worker organization that shaped the labor movement in the twentieth century. As chapter 6 elaborates, organized labor today is the product of four such waves of unionization, each of which recruited in a distinct sector of the economy and had a different relationship to women workers: the craft unionism of the late nineteenth century, the "new unionism" of the 1910s, the industrial unionism of the 1930s and 1940s, and finally the public-sector unionism of the 1960s and 1970s.

The particular historical contexts in which each type of unionism arose shaped their varied approaches to women workers—approaches that later crystallized into institutional traditions that have persisted intact ever since. Thus, to understand the relationship of labor unions to the growing population of women workers requires an appreciation of the diverse historical processes from which each of them originated.

Women and Unions in Historical Perspective

Throughout the twentieth century, as table 7.1 shows, the feminization of the U.S. labor force was accompanied by a parallel feminization of union membership, although with a definite lag. The table reveals the extent to which women workers were recruited into unions during each historical wave of labor organization. It is

Table 7.1. Feminization of the U.S. Labor Force and of Union Membership, 1920–1988

Year	Number of Women in the Workforce	% of All Workers	Number of Women Union Members	% of All Union Members
1910[a]	7,789,000	20.9	76,750	3.6
1920[a]	8,430,000	20.4	397,000	7.9
1930[a]	10,679,000	22.0	260,000	7.7
1940[a]	13,015,000	24.4	800,000	9.4
1944[a]	19,110,000	34.7	3,000,000	21.8
1954[a]	19,678,000	31.1	2,950,000	16.6
1956[a]	21,495,000	32.2	3,400,000	18.6
1960[a]	23,240,000	33.4	3,304,000	18.3
1964[a]	25,412,000	34.8	3,413,000	19.1
1968[b]	29,204,000	37.1	3,940,000	19.5
1970[b]	31,543,000	38.1	5,398,000	23.9
1974[b]	36,211,000	39.4	6,038,000	25.0
1978[b]	42,631,000	41.6	6,857,000	28.1
1980[c]	45,487,000	42.5	7,191,000	31.9
1985[c]	51,050,000	44.2	6,910,000	35.6
1990[c]	56,554,000	45.3	7,327,000	38.4

[a] Unions

[b] Unions and employee associations

[c] Represented by unions and employee associations (including nonmembers covered by contracts)

Sources: 1910–1944 data: Gladys Dickason, "Women in Labor Unions," *Annals of the American Academy of Political and Social Science* 251 (May 1947): 70–71. 1956–1980 data: U.S. Department of Labor, Bureau of Labor Statistics, *Directory of National Unions and Employee Associations, 1979,* Bulletin 2079 (1980), 62; U.S. Department of Labor, Women's Bureau, *Time of Change: 1983 Handbook on Women Workers,* Bulletin 298 (1983), 4–9. 1985–1990 data: U.S. Department of Labor, Bureau of Labor Statistics, *Employment and Earnings* 33, no. 1 (1986); U.S. Department of Labor, Bureau of Labor Statistics, *Employment and Earnings* 34, no. 1 (1987), 219; U.S. Department of Labor, Bureau of Labor Statistics, *Employment and Earnings* 38, no. 1 (1991), 163, 228.

evident that the craft unionism of the late nineteenth century and the first decade of the twentieth produced only minimal organization among women. Historically these unions, which banded together in the American Federation of Labor (AFL) in the 1880s, viewed women's labor as a threat to skill and wage levels, and most of them therefore excluded women (as well as blacks and many immigrant groups) from membership outright—until as late as the 1940s in some cases.[5] This was male-centered unionism in its most extreme form, the source of deeply patriarchal labor-movement traditions. Indeed, the craft unions that originated in this period—such as the construction-trades "brotherhoods" and the machinists' union—have long been among those least receptive to women workers and their specific concerns, faithful to the legacy of their own past.

A second wave of unionism appeared in the 1910s, centered in the garment industry. This "new unionism," at once an outgrowth of craft unionism and a forerunner of the industrial unions of the 1930s, generated a fivefold increase in the number of women union members, as table 7.1 shows. The clothing-trades unions abandoned craft exclusionism in this period and recruited huge numbers of unskilled and semiskilled workers into their ranks, the vast majority of them young women. By 1920 almost half (43 percent) of all female union members were employed in the clothing trades.[6] Despite the feminization of their memberships, however, the leaders of these unions remained overwhelmingly male, and they developed an enduring tradition of viewing their women members paternalistically—as weak workers in need of special protection, not as equal partners in the labor struggle.

The 1920s and early 1930s was an era of deunionization, much like the late twentieth century, when the absolute number of both female and male union members fell. But as early as 1940, the massive industrial organizing drives of the late 1930s brought the number of women union members to twice the 1920 level, as table 7.1 shows. By 1944, the peak of the wartime economic mobilization, there were three million women union members—nearly eight times the 1920 figure. But since these gains were paralleled by equally dramatic increases in union density among male workers, women's representation among union members lagged far behind their increased presence in the workforce.

While most of the Congress of Industrial Organizations (CIO) unions targeted predominantly male-employing industries and had an almost exclusively male leadership, their attitude toward women was different from that of their predecessors. Against the background of the suffrage victory and the growth of women's employment in the 1920s and 1930s, there was a shift in the larger political culture away from the traditional emphasis on the differences between women and men workers (implicit in both craft-union exclusionism and the paternalism of the "new unions") and toward a new, modern vision of gender equality. The CIO captured this new political thrust, explicitly opposing discrimination on the basis of sex, color, and creed, in a deliberate departure from craft-union tradition. Although this was a limited notion of gender equality, rooted in principles of class solidarity and in opposition to employer efforts to divide the workforce through discriminatory policies, some of the unions that emerged in this period became leading supporters of legislation against sex discrimination in the 1960s.[7] With the exception of the World War II years, however, women remained peripheral to most of these unions, which were based in the heavily male basic manufacturing sector.

Finally, starting in the 1960s (precisely when overall union density in the United States began to fall) a fourth group of unions assumed prominence, mainly in the public sector but also in some private-sector service industries, such as healthcare. Only in this period, as table 7.1 shows, did the gap between women's representation among union members and in the larger workforce begin to narrow significantly. Despite the fact that women were a rapidly expanding component of the overall workforce during these years, union density among them remained relatively stable, while for men it fell, at first gradually and later more sharply. In 1956, 31 percent of men and 16 percent of women workers were unionized; by 1990, the figure was 21 percent for men, while among the rapidly expanding pool of women workers, it held nearly steady at 15 percent.[8] In this period, recruitment of women accounted for most of the growth in total union membership.

The unions most active in this recent wave of worker organization rarely set out to organize women "as women"; rather, the feminization of their memberships was an unintended consequence of recruiting heavily in fields where women workers are particularly well represented: first teaching, then healthcare, and later public-sector clerical and service work. Ultimately, because this organizing occurred in a period of feminist resurgence and of broad changes in gender relations in the larger society, these unions not only recruited women as members but also (albeit to a much lesser extent) as leaders.

The unions that came of age in this period also became particularly active in reformulating traditional labor issues in order to better address the concerns of women workers. For example, the American Federation of State, County and Municipal Employees (AFSCME) and the Service Employees International Union (SEIU), the two largest unions in this category, led major campaigns for pay equity or "comparable worth" in the 1980s.[9] Indeed, partly as a result of these efforts, unionization has significantly narrowed the gender gap in earnings in the public sector.[10]

The diverse responses of unions to workforce feminization, then, reflect their varying historical roots, with the youngest and most dynamic unions tending to be most responsive to women workers and their special concerns. This pattern has been reinforced by the characteristically greater openness of younger organizations to new ideas and modes of operation and by the relative inflexibility of more "mature" unions with a more routinized existence and an entrenched bureaucracy that is loyal to established traditions. The youngest unions are also those least hobbled by deunionization. In governmental agencies, especially at the state and local level, management opposition to unionism is far less formidable than in comparable private-sector workplaces, and unionization is thus considerably easier to achieve. Political pressure as well can often be exerted to advance unionism in the public sector.[11] While organization remains minimal among the millions of women workers in such deeply anti-union private industries as banking and insurance, some inroads were made among clericals employed by manufacturing firms with unionized blue-collar workforces in the postwar period.[12] Many clerical workers employed by private-sector universities (similar to public-sector institutions in that they are nonprofit operations with above-average vulnerability to political pressures) also successfully unionized in the 1980s.[13]

Pattern of Women's Union Membership and Leadership

As a result of the rapid growth of unionism among pink- and white-collar women workers, the composition of the organized female labor force began to look quite different from the traditional image of the labor movement. As table 7.2 shows, in 1991 nearly half (45 percent) of all women union members were employed either in education or public administration, even though these sectors account for only 17 percent of all women in the workforce. Another 28 percent of the unionized female workforce were employed in either sales or service jobs, reflecting (although still lagging behind) the enormous growth in employment in these sectors in the postwar decades. Only 14 percent of unionized women worked for manufacturing firms, labor's traditional stronghold. While manufacturing-based unions declined with deindustrialization, unionism expanded in the public and service sectors, and this growth was based on extensive recruitment of women.

While the industrial breakdown shown in table 7.2 does not fully correspond to the historical waves of unionization identified above, these data make it obvious that the public-sector unions have come to dwarf all of their predecessors in female membership recruitment. The same basic pattern is also apparent in table 7.3, which shows female membership (and leadership) in the eleven individual unions that had two hundred thousand or more women members in 1985. Many of these organizations are based wholly or partly in the public sector; in some cases their traditional jurisdictions (as suggested by their names) bear at best a

Table 7.2. Women Members of Labor Organizations, Selected Industry Groups, 1991

Industry Group	Number of Women Union Members (thousands)	Women Members as a Percentage of		Distribution of All Women Workers (%)
		Organized Women in All Industries	All Women Employed in This Industry	
Public administration	594	9.7	24.9	4.9
Education	2,141	34.9	35.1	12.5
Services	1,150	18.7	7.1	33.1
Wholesale and retail trade	574	9.4	5.6	20.9
Transportation, communication, and public utilities	679	11.1	30.0	4.6
Finance, insurance, and real estate	92	1.5	2.1	8.9
Manufacturing	867	14.1	13.4	13.3
Mining and construction	35	0.6	6.1	1.2
Agriculture, forestry, and fishing	6	0.1	1.7	0.7
All industries	6,138	100.0	12.6	100.0

Source: U.S. Current Population Survey.

Table 7.3. Female Membership and Leadership in Selected Labor Organizations, 1978–1990

Organization	Year	Women Members (in thousands)	Women as % of All Members	Women Officers and Board Members	Women as % of Officers and Board Members
National Education Association	1978	1,240	75	5	55
	1985	1,000	60	3	33
	1990	n/a	n/a	6	67
International Brotherhood of Teamsters	1978	481	25	0	0
	1985	485	26	0	0
	1990	400	25	0	0
United Food and Commercial Workers	1978	480	39	2	3
	1990	983	51	3	8
American Federation of State, County, and Municipal Employees	1978	408	40	1	3
	1985	450	45	4	14
	1990	600	50	5	17
Service Employees International Union	1978	312	50	7	15
	1985	435	50	9	18
	1990	420	45	13	34
American Federation of Teachers	1978	300	60	8	25
	1985	366	60	11	32
	1990	455	65	11	32
Communication Workers of America	1978	259	51	0	0
	1985	338	52	1	6
	1990	338	52	1	6
International Brotherhood of Electrical Workers	1978	304	30	0	0
	1985	330	30	0	0
	1990	240	30	0	0
Amalgamated Clothing and Textile Workers Union	1978	331	66	6	15
	1985	226	65	3	9
	1990	160	61	5	20
International Ladies Garment Workers Union	1978	279	80	2	7
	1983	219	85	3	13
	1990	145	83	4	22
Hotel and Restaurant Employees	1978	181	42	1	4
	1985	200	50	2	8
	1990	143	48	1	4

Sources: 1978 data are from Coalition of Labor Union Women, Center for Education and Research, *Absent from the Agenda: A Report on the Role of Women in American Unions* (New York: mimeo, 1980), tables 3 and 5; 1983–85 data are from Naomi Baden, "Developing an Agenda: Expanding the Role of Women in Unions," *Labor Studies Journal* 10, no. 3 (1986): 236, 238; 1990 data are from Dorothy Sue Cobble, "Introduction," in *Women and Unions: Forging a Partnership,* edited by Dorothy Sue Cobble (Ithaca, N.Y.: Cornell University Press, 1993).

remote relationship to the sectors in which their members are actually employed. The extreme case of this is the Teamsters' union, which by 1990 had half a million female members scattered through a wide range of occupations and industries. The Communication Workers of America (CWA) also has recruited extensively outside its traditional jurisdiction, in both the public and private sectors. And virtually all of the unions listed have undertaken some efforts to recruit white-collar workers—often female—outside their traditional base. For example, the Hotel and Restaurant Employees organized clerical workers at Yale University in the 1980s, and even the International Ladies' Garment Workers (ILGWU) set up a Professional and Clerical Employees division.

Recruitment of female members is only one aspect of the impact of work-force feminization on organized labor. As the case of the clothing unions in the 1910s illustrates, a large percentage of women in a union's membership may be a necessary precondition for a transformation in the gender composition of union leadership and for union attention to "women's issues," but it is by no means a sufficient condition for such a transformation. The influx of female members into a range of different labor organizations has had a limited effect on the overall character of these unions or their institutional functioning, especially at the national level. Women's representation in top leadership posts, as table 7.3 shows, has consistently lagged far behind their representation in union membership.

Although the data are much too fragmentary to warrant any definite conclusions on this point, it is suggestive that the two unions in this group with no women at all among their national officers and board members (the Electrical Workers and the Teamsters) are both old-line AFL craft unions. In contrast, those organizations with the most extensive representation of women (the two teachers' unions, AFSCME and SEIU) are public-sector (or in the case of SEIU, public- and service-sector) unions that grew rapidly starting in the 1960s and 1970s. Female leadership has also grown at the local and regional levels of the public-sector unions. For example, 33 percent of AFSCME's local presidents and 45 percent of its local union officers were female in 1982.[14] Similarly, in 1985, 319 of SEIU's 820 local officers were female, as were 9 of its 61 joint council officers.[15]

As for the private-sector unions, it is difficult to see how women's leadership could grow significantly without a revival of membership recruitment, and even then the tradition of male leadership would be a formidable obstacle to progress. At the same time, the feminization of union membership that has taken place already in the public sector might also be a likely outcome in the private sector if unions were able to overcome the conditions generating deunionization and begin organizing successfully there.

The effects of radical economic restructuring in the 1970s and 1980s have made such recruitment difficult. Yet the effects of restructuring on women and men have been quite different. Factory closings and industrial decline generally have affected male workers more severely than their female counterparts, since men have long been far more concentrated in the manufacturing sector.[16] Another type of restructuring, however, has had a far greater impact on women, namely the erosion of traditional patterns of full-time, permanent employment. Women are the vast majority of part-time workers, temporary workers, and homeworkers, and the growth of such forms of "contingent work," loosening the traditional bond between the firm and the worker, present special problems for unions.[17] It is remarkable that despite this additional obstacle, organizing efforts since the 1970s have been more successful in recruiting women workers than men into unions, even in the private sector.

Gender and Union Organizing in the 1980s

Accumulating evidence suggests that unorganized women, far from being an obstacle to union growth or a factor contributing to the decline of unionism (as is sometimes alleged), and contrary to the once-conventional maxim that women are less "organizable" than men, have a greater propensity to unionize than unorganized men. In a 1977 survey, for example, 41 percent of female nonunion workers but only 27 percent of male nonunion workers responded "for" when asked, "If an election were held with secret ballots, would you vote for or against having a union or employees' association represent you?"[18] Other survey research has yielded similar findings.[19]

Women workers not only tend to express pro-union attitudes more often than men but are also more inclined to support unionization in actual practice, on those rare occasions when they have the opportunity to do so, as voting data from National Labor Relations Board (NLRB) elections (which cover only private-sector workers) indicate. An analysis of 226 union organizing campaigns that culminated in NLRB elections held in 1982–83 found that unions won half of the campaigns where women made up 75 percent or more of the workforce (mostly in healthcare) but only 39 percent of those where less than half the workers were women (mostly in manufacturing).[20]

A similar analysis of 189 election campaigns from 1986–87 found an even more pronounced gender differential: unions won 57 percent of the elections in units where women were 75 percent or more of the workforce but only 33 percent of those where the workforce was less than half female. This was the case despite the fact that nearly all the organizers leading the election campaigns in the sample (over 90 percent) were male. Interestingly, the win rate was higher (61 percent) for those few campaigns led by female organizers than for those led by males (41 percent).[21]

My analysis of the data from the 1986–87 campaigns reveals a more complex relationship between the gender composition of the labor force and the likelihood of winning an election.[22] As figures 7.1 and 7.2 show, in this sample, unions were most likely to win elections in units with overwhelmingly (95 percent or more) female workforces. For these units the win rate was a spectacular 90 percent (although the number of cases is small), double the rate for the sample as a whole (43 percent). Win rates consistently declined as the female percentage of the workforce fell, except for the units with an overwhelmingly male workforce, where the win rate was higher than for those with gender-mixed workforces (but still much lower than for the overwhelmingly female units).

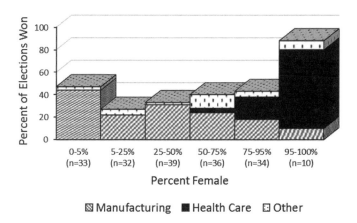

FIGURE 7.1. Election Wins by Percent Female and by Industry. (Industry breakdown is for wins only.)

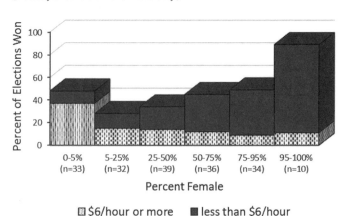

FIGURE 7.2. Election Wins by Percent Female and by Average Wage Rates. (Wage rate breakdown is for wins only.)

The units with high percentages of women tended to be healthcare workplaces, and most had low average wages (under $6 per hour); those with high percentages of men were typically manufacturing units, and most had relatively high average wages ($6 or more). Independent of their gender composition, units in the sample with low average wages had significantly higher win rates (51 percent) than those with higher wages (35 percent). Units with a high proportion (over 75 percent) of minority workers (black, Hispanic, or Asian) also had significantly higher win rates (65 percent) than those with less than 75 percent minority workers (35 percent).[23] Manufacturing units had lower win rates (40 percent) than healthcare units (55 percent), while units in other industries were in between (45 percent), although these differences are not statistically significant.

As figures 7.1 and 7.2 also show, some of these variables are highly correlated: units with a high percentage of women tended to have low average wages and to be in nonmanufacturing industries.[24] Thus a multivariate analysis is needed to determine whether each variable has independent significance in affecting win rates when the others are taken into account. I conducted logistic regression analysis to estimate the simultaneous effects of four characteristics of the work unit (percent female, percent minority, average wage, and industrial sector—with the latter dummy coded as manufacturing vs. nonmanufacturing) on election outcomes (win vs. lose).

The results indicate that (as in the univariate analysis) percent female, percent minority, and average wage had significant effects on the probability of winning.[25] Percent female still had an independent and significant effect on winning, but once the other variables were controlled, what started as a J-curve became a more symmetrical U-curve. The main reason for this is that most of the work units with a very high percentage of women were also low-wage units, so that controlling for wages depresses the extreme right end of the curve.

Figure 7.3 shows the estimated effects of percent female on winning an election, holding percent minority, average wage, and industry constant at their means. Like figures 7.1 and 7.2, this U-shaped curve indicates that unions were most likely to win elections in work units that are gender homogeneous and least likely to win where the workforce is evenly mixed between men and women. For example, the odds of winning an election were more than twice as high (2.1 times greater) when the workforce was 95 percent female than when 45 percent of the workforce was female, holding other factors constant. The odds of winning were nearly twice as high (1.9 times greater) when the workforce was 95 percent male than when it was 55 percent male, again holding other factors constant.

Figure 7.4 shows the combined effects of percent female, holding constant the average wage and industry, on the probability of winning, disaggregating the data between manufacturing and nonmanufacturing and between cases where average wages are less than $6 per hour and those where average wages are $6 per

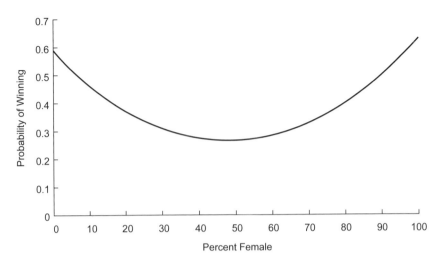

FIGURE 7.3. Estimated Probability of Winning by Percent Female (evaluated at the means of average wage, manufacturing, and percent minority).

hour or more. This graph reveals that, regardless of average wage and regardless of industry, the probability of winning is greatest at extreme values of percent female. In addition, regardless of percent female or industry, the probability of winning is greatest when average wages are low; and regardless of wages and percent female, the probability of winning is greater in nonmanufacturing than in manufacturing units.

Furthermore, figure 7.4 suggests that wages were more salient than industry in differentiating the win rates of various work units across all possible levels of percentage female. More specifically, units where workers averaged less than $6 an hour were more than twice (2.2 times) as likely to vote to unionize as units where average wages were $6 an hour or more, holding other factors constant. By contrast, nonmanufacturing units were only slightly (1.2 times) more likely than manufacturing units to vote in favor of unionization. This pattern is not especially surprising, of course, since the effects of industry on winning were not statistically significant.

Overall, the probability of winning unionization was greatest in work units with a low average wage and either a very high or very low percentage of women; conversely, the probability of winning was smallest in units with high wages and a gender-mixed workforce. Specifically, units with a high percentage of females (95 percent) in nonmanufacturing workplaces with low average wages (the typical features of an overwhelmingly female unit) were almost five (4.8) times more

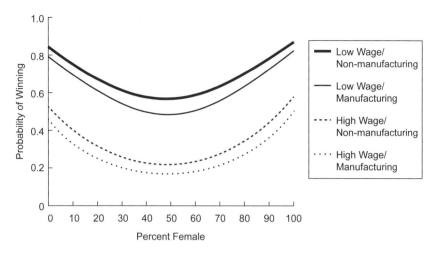

FIGURE 7.4. Probability of Winning by Percent Female, Wage Rates, and Industry

likely to unionize than manufacturing units with a 45 percent female workforce and high average wages (the low point of the curve). In contrast, units with a high percentage of males (95 percent) in manufacturing workplaces and with high average wages (the typical characteristics of predominantly male units) were only about twice as likely to unionize as manufacturing units with high average wages and a 55 percent male workforce (the low point of the curve).

It is not especially surprising that low wages would, all else being equal, give workers a greater propensity to unionize than higher wages. But it is less obvious why, independent of their low wages, women would have a greater propensity to unionize than men, and why gender-homogenous work units would be more easily organized. One possible explanation is that gender-specific work cultures, the salience of which has been documented extensively in qualitative research by ethnographers and historians, facilitate the building of solidarity among workers, whereas it is more difficult to forge unity in a workforce that is divided along gender lines.[26] The standard idiom of unionism, rooted in the craft- and industrial-union traditions, relies on a "macho," hardhat imagery of militancy that has long been problematic for women workers and has increasingly become so for white-collar men, to whom adversarial, "cigar-chomping" unionism is often anathema.[27]

Traditional calls to militancy may be more effective in building solidarity in all-male blue-collar work units than in gender-mixed settings. Similarly, while in organizing predominantly female work groups the labor movement has often relied on appeals to gender-specific concerns and sometimes even on "pre-union" associations that exist entirely outside the established union structure,[28] such tactics may be less effective in galvanizing support for unionism in gender-mixed workforces.

Although this dilemma may be difficult to overcome, it is noteworthy that unions, especially in the public and service sectors, were in the forefront of a new mode of advocacy on gender issues in the 1980s, best exemplified by the demand for government and business support for parental leave and childcare, and by campaigns for pay equity. In earlier years, organized labor was generally unreceptive to "women's issues" unless they were formulated in the class-based language of traditional unionism (as were, for example, protective legislation and equal pay for equal work, which were both defined as policies that would prevent employers from taking advantage of women's special vulnerability and thus protect male wage standards). But starting in the 1980s, partly in response to the growth of female labor leadership, many unions came to recognize that they ignore the special interests of women at their peril, and emerged as key allies of the feminist movement.

Toward a New Gender Politics

The issues that cemented this new alliance are rooted in important shifts in the composition of the female workforce that took place in the 1970s and 1980s. The most spectacular change was the increased workforce involvement of married women and mothers. Whereas before World War II the typical female wage worker was unmarried and few mothers of young children were employed outside the home, by the 1980s wives and mothers were more likely to be in the labor force than not. In 1950 only 24 percent of married women (husband present) were in the labor force, and as recently as 1970 only 30 percent of married women with children under six years old were employed or seeking employment. By contrast, in 1987 married women (husband present) had a labor-force participation rate of 56 percent—equal to the rate for the overall female population in that year—and for married women with children under age six the rate was 57 percent.[29]

This historic shift dramatically heightened the long-standing tension between women's family and work commitments. For most women, this conflict was still resolved at the individual level, perhaps most commonly through the "choice" of part-time work. In 1990, more than one-fourth of women workers (26 percent, compared with only 11 percent of men) worked part time, and others, in increasing numbers, had "temporary jobs" or worked at home.[30] The issue of family-work conflict has become increasingly politicized, galvanizing demands for both governmental and corporate policies on such matters as parental leave and childcare.

While pressing for legislation guaranteeing parental leave to working parents, unions have also won childcare and parental leave benefits for some of their members at the bargaining table. For example, the ILGWU established a childcare center in New York's Chinatown in 1983 and won parental leave for 135,000 of its members in 1988. The following year the CWA and the IBEW (International Brotherhood of Electrical Workers) negotiated a contract with AT&T that provided $5 million for support of community child- and dependent-care services, as well as unpaid parental leave for up to a year, with guaranteed reinstatement. Many other unions have also successfully pursued family-work issues at the bargaining table.[31]

Another equally explosive issue is that, despite the dramatic growth of female labor-force participation, stark inequalities between female and male workers persist. While elite women have made substantial advances in professional and managerial occupations formerly monopolized by men, the vast majority of working-class women remain concentrated in poorly paid, low-status, sex-segregated jobs.[32] In 1990, women's weekly earnings for full-time work averaged 72 percent of full-time male weekly earnings.[33] Employers have continued to treat women as a source of cheap labor, different from and not interchangeable with men, despite growing pressure for equality and government policies that nominally endorse that goal. The growth of predominantly female part-time, temporary, and at-home employment has further reinforced gender inequalities, creating a new female ghetto of insecure, poorly paid, low-status, and highly sex-stereotyped work.

The most effective response to the persistence of the gender gap in pay in the 1980s was the campaign for "comparable worth" or pay equity, which centered on the claim that jobs traditionally performed by women have been systematically undervalued in terms of wages and that equity requires a new, gender-neutral evaluation of the skills, responsibilities, and effort involved in various jobs, on which basis pay adjustments can be made.[34] Unions were the critical actors in this effort, bringing all of the major lawsuits, directly negotiating comparable-worth adjustments at the bargaining table and in some cases even making pay equity a strike issue.[35] Particularly prominent in this area were AFSCME, SEIU, and the National Union of Hospital and Health Care Employees, District 1199.[36]

Drawing on the escalating tension between family and work, on the one hand, and the unmet demand for an end to sex discrimination at work, on the other, a new form of gender politics took shape in the 1980s in which unions played a central role. Whereas historically advocates of equal treatment for women and men, irrespective of any socially or culturally constructed gender differences, often came into conflict with those who took gender differences as given and sought to protect traditionally female values and types of behavior, the new gender politics in the labor movement synthesized the apparently contradictory strategic impulses of equality and difference. This approach embraced the goal of equality for women but at the same time took a positive view of gender differences and on this basis elaborated a critique, rooted in traditionally female values, of the basic structure of the world of work, with its highly individualistic and competitive male culture.

The pay equity issue is a good illustration. While in practice comparable-worth reforms can be criticized for their limited, technocratic nature, they were rooted in an innovative and deeply radical critique of the gender ideology structuring the workplace.[37] Supporters of parental and pregnancy leaves, while sometimes divided on the legal details of special versus equal treatment,[38] also launched a critique, from a different angle, of the values that shape workplace policies. Implicit in all of these reform efforts is, as Alice Kessler-Harris puts it, "a belief that gender equality will be achieved only when the values of the home (which have previously been assumed to keep women out of the workplace or to assign them to inferior places within it) are brought to the workplace where they can transform work itself."[39] Thus the new gender politics accepted difference as a strategic basis for making demands that ultimately move toward equality. It also became the basis for a new mode of unionism that moved women workers and their concerns from the margin to the center.

These developments suggest a basis for optimism about the future for women in organized labor. Women have a greater propensity to unionize than men (especially in predominantly female work groups), and unions have paid far more attention to gender issues than in previous historical eras. The increased representation of women in positions of leadership and the emergence of gender issues as a central concern in the younger, most dynamic unions could even presage a broader transformation in the labor movement, if it were to grow in size and influence once again.

Notes

This chapter was originally published in *The Challenge of Restructuring: North American Labor Movements Respond,* edited by Jane Jenson and Rianne Mahon (Philadelphia: Temple University Press, 1993), 226–50.

1. U.S. Department of Labor, Women's Bureau, *Time of Change: 1983 Handbook on Women Workers,* Bulletin 298 (1983), 9, 11; U.S. Department of Labor, Bureau of Labor Statistics, *Employment and Earnings* 38, no. 1 (1991), 16.

2. U.S. Department of Labor, Bureau of Labor Statistics, *Directory of National Unions and Employee Associations, 1979,* Bulletin 2079 (1980), 62; U.S. Department of Labor, *Employment and Earnings* 38, p. 228.

3. See Richard B. Freeman, "Contraction and Expansion: The Divergence of Private Sector and Public Sector Unionism in the United States," *Journal of Economic Perspectives* 2, no. 2 (1988): 63–65.

4. Heidi Hartmann, "Capitalism, Patriarchy, and Job Segregation by Sex," in *Women and the Work-Place: The Implications of Occupational Segregation*, edited by Martha Blaxall and Barbara Reagan (Chicago: University of Chicago Press, 1976); Cynthia Cockburn, *Brothers: Male Dominance and Technological Change* (London: Pluto, 1983).

5. Alice Kessler-Harris, "Where Are the Organized Women Workers?" *Feminist Studies* 3 (1975).

6. Leo Wolman, *Growth of American Trade Unions, 1880–1923* (New York: National Bureau of Economic Research, 1924).

7. Cynthia Harrison, *On Account of Sex: The Politics of Women's Issues, 1945–1968* (Berkeley: University of California Press, 1988).

8. Linda H. LeGrande, "Women in Labor Organizations: Their Ranks Are Increasing," *Monthly Labor Review* 101, no. 8 (1978): 9; U.S. Department of Labor, *Employment and Earnings* 38, 228. The data for these years are not strictly comparable, due to changes in government enumeration methods, but the overall trend toward feminization of union membership in the context of general deunionization is unmistakable.

9. Deborah E. Bell, "Unionized Women in State and Local Government," in *Women, Work, and Protest: A Century of U.S. Women's Labor History*, edited by Ruth Milkman (Boston: Routledge and Kegan Paul, 1985), 280–99.

10. Richard B. Freeman and Jonathan S. Leonard, "Union Maids: Unions and the Female Workforce," in *Gender in the Workplace,* edited by Clair Brown and Joseph A. Pechman (Washington, D.C.: Brookings Institution, 1987), 189–216.

11. Freeman, "Contraction and Expansion."

12. David Wagner, "Clerical Workers: How 'Unorganizable' Are They?" *Labor Center Review* (Amherst, Mass.) 2, no. 1 (1979): 20–50.

13. Molly Ladd-Taylor, "Women Workers and the Yale Strike," *Feminist Studies* 11, no. 3 (1985): 465–89; Allan R. Gold, "Union's Victory at Harvard Seen as Spur to Labor Drive," *New York Times*, May 19, 1988; James Green, "Union Victory: An Interview with Kristine Rondeau," *Democratic Left*, September–October (1988): 4–6; Richard W. Hurd, "Learning from Clerical Unions: Two Cases of Organizing Success," *Labor Studies Journal* 14, no. 1 (1989): 30–51.

14. Bell, "Unionized Women," 288.

15. See Naomi Baden, "Developing an Agenda: Expanding the Role of Women in Unions," *Labor Studies Journal* 10, no. 3 (1986): 239.

16. Ruth Milkman, *Gender at Work: The Dynamics of Job Segregation by Sex during World War II* (Urbana: University of Illinois Press, 1987).

17. Eileen Appelbaum, "Restructuring Work: Temporary, Part-time, and At-home Employment," in *Computer Chips and Paper Clips: Technology and Women's Employment*, edited by Heidi I. Hartmann, vol. 2 (Washington, D.C: National Academy Press, 1987), 268–310.

18. Richard B. Freeman and James L. Medoff, *What Do Unions Do?* (New York: Basic, 1984), 29.

19. See Thomas A. Kochan, "How American Workers View Labor Unions," *Monthly Labor Review* 102, no. 4 (1979): 25; Michael Goldfield, *The Decline of Organized Labor in the United States* (Chicago: University of Chicago Press, 1987), 137.

20. AFL-CIO Department of Organization and Field Services, *AFL-CIO Organizing Survey* (Washington, D.C: mimeo, 1984), appendix, 18.

21. This difference is of marginal statistical significance ($p < .10$) using either a two-tailed t-test or a Fisher's exact test (two-tailed); this may be due to the very small number of cases ($n = 18$) where the organizers were female. AFL-CIO Department of Organization and Field Services, *AFL-CIO Organizing Survey: 1986–87 NLRB Elections* (Washington, D.C.: mimeo, 1989), 6.

22. The AFL-CIO collected data (via retrospective interviews with lead organizers) on 189 single-union organizing campaigns in units of more than fifty workers that took place during the period from July 1986 to April 1987. A total population of 981 NLRB single-union elections involving AFL-CIO affiliates with units of more than fifty workers were held in the United States in this period. The sample was not random but shaped by differential access to various unions and their organizers, and in some respects the sample is not representative. Most important for present purposes, it underrepresents campaigns by unions that most often recruit women and minority workers. The Teamsters are not included in the sample at all, yet they petitioned for one-third of the elections in this period. Also underrepresented in the sample are the Service Employees International Union, the Amalgamated Clothing and Textile Workers Union, and the Retail, Wholesale, and Department Store Workers' Union, all of which (like the Teamsters) organize women and minority low-wage workers to a greater than average degree.

The mean workplace in the sample had a nearly even mix of men and women (45 percent female), identical to the mix in the nation's workforce. Minorities (blacks, Hispanics, and Asians) made up 26 percent of the workforce, higher than in the national workforce. Wages averaged $6.55 per hour (the median wage, however, was $6.00 per hour) in the sample, lower than in the nation as a whole. Another way in which the sample is quite different from the national workforce is that more than two-thirds (68 percent) of the units were in the manufacturing sector.

Kate Bronfenbrenner conducted additional interviews to correct for these sampling problems. Her own analysis using the improved data confirms the basic findings presented here on the relationship of gender to organizing success. This suggests that the sampling problems, while noteworthy, are not fatal for present purposes. See Kate Bronfenbrenner, "Seeds of Resurgence: Successful Union Strategies for Winning Certification Elections and First Contract Campaigns" (Ph.D. diss., New York State School of Industrial and Labor Relations, Cornell University, 1993).

23. One-tailed t-tests reveal that election outcomes differ significantly ($p < .05$) for percent female, percent minority, and average wage.

24. Pearson correlation coefficients are $-.48$ for percent female with average wage and $-.46$ for sector (manufacturing vs. nonmanufacturing) with average wage.

25. The following table shows the beta coefficients for each variable in the model. The model specifies a curvilinear function for percent female, as represented by the variables PFEM (percent female) and PFEM^2 (the square of percent female), because inspection of the data (as seen in Figures 7.1 and 7.2) revealed that a U- or J-shaped function best describes the association between win rates and the proportion of women in the workforce. The model specifies a logarithmic function for average wage (AVGWAGE and LOGWAGE) because inspection of the data (not shown here) revealed that while increases in wages were associated with a decrease in win rates, the effects of wages were not linear but were greatest at low

wage levels and flatter at higher wage rates. Models that included interaction effects among the independent variables were also tested, but the coefficients for the interaction effects were not significant.

Variable	Beta	Partial R
INTERCEPT	6.55***	
PFEM	−.057***	−.162
PFEM^2	.001***	.159
AVGWAGE	.427	.021
LOGWAGE	−4.98**	.112
PMIN	.010*	.076
MFG	−.314	.000

*Significant at .10 level, two-tailed.
**Significant at .05 level, two-tailed.
***Significant at .01 level, two-tailed.

26. On women's work culture, see Sallie Westwood, *All Day, Every Day: Factory and Family in the Making of Women's Lives* (Urbana: University of Illinois Press, 1984); Cynthia Costello, "'WEA're Worth It!' Work Culture and Conflict at the Wisconsin Education Association Insurance Trust." *Feminist Studies* 11, no. 3 (1985): 497–518; Karen Sacks, *Caring by the Hour: Women, Work, and Organizing at Duke Medical Center* (Urbana: University of Illinois Press, 1988); Susan Porter Benson, *Counter Cultures: Saleswomen, Managers, and Customers in American Department Stores, 1890–1940* (Urbana: University of Illinois Press, 1986); and Dorothy Sue Cobble, "'Practical Women': Waitress Unionists and the Controversies over Gender Roles in the Food Service Industry, 1900–1980," *Labor History* 29, no. 1 (1988): 5–31. On men's work culture, see David Montgomery, *The Fall of the House of Labor* (New York: Cambridge University Press, 1987); and Cynthia Cockburn, *Brothers*. On both women's and men's work cultures, see Patricia Cooper, *Once a Cigar Maker: Men, Women, and Work Culture in American Cigar Factories, 1900–1919* (Urbana: University of Illinois Press, 1987).

27. Charles C. Heckscher, *The New Unionism: Employee Involvement in the Changing Corporation* (New York: Basic, 1988), 62–70.

28. Nancy Seifer and Barbara Wertheimer, "New Approaches to Collective Power: Four Working Women's Organizations," in *Women's Organizing: An Anthology,* edited by Bernice Cummings and Victoria Schuck (Metuchen, N.J.: Scarecrow, 1979), 152–83.

29. U.S. Department of Labor, Bureau of Labor Statistics, *Labor Force Statistics Derived from the Current Population Survey, 1948–87,* Bulletin 2307 (1988), 791, 805.

30. U.S. Dept. of Labor, *Employment and Earnings* 38, no. 1 (1991), p. 26; Appelbaum, "Restructuring Work."

31. Chinatown Day Center, "A Haven for 80, but 500 Must Wait," *New York Times*, March 10, 1988; Labor Letter, *Wall Street Journal*, July 19, 1988; Amanda Bennett and Cathy Trost, "Benefit Package Set by AT&T, Unions Shows Power of Families in Workplace," *Wall Street Journal*, May 31, 1989.

32. Andrea H. Beller, "Trends in Occupational Segregation by Sex and Race, 1960–1981," in *Sex Segregation in the Workplace: Trends, Explanations, Remedies*, edited by Barbara F. Reskin (Washington, D.C.: National Academy Press, 1984), 11–26.

33. U.S. Dept. of Labor, *Employment and Earnings* 38, no. 1 (1991), 230.

34. Donald J. Treiman and Heidi I. Hartmann, eds., *Women, Work, and Wages: Equal Pay for Jobs of Equal Value* (Washington D.C.: National Academy Press, 1981).

35. Lisa Portman, Joy Ann Grune, and Eve Johnson, "The Role of Labor," in *Comparable Worth and Wage Discrimination: Technical Possibilities and Political Realities*, edited by Helen Remick (Philadelphia: Temple University Press, 1984), 219–37.

36. Alice Cook, *Comparable Worth: The Problem and States' Approaches to Wage Equity* (Manoa: University of Hawaii, Industrial Relations Center, 1983), 16.

37. Sara Evans and Barbara Nelson, "Comparable Worth: The Paradox of Technocratic Reform," *Feminist Studies* 15, no. 1 (1989): 171–90.

38. Lise Vogel, "Debating Difference: Feminism, Pregnancy, and the Workplace," *Feminist Studies* 16, no. 1 (1990): 9–32.

39. Alice Kessler-Harris, "The Debate of Equality for Women in the Work Place: Recognizing Differences," in *Women and Work: An Annual Review*, edited by Laurie Larwood, Ann H. Stromberg, and Barbara A. Gutek (Beverly Hills, Calif.: Sage, 1985), 157.

Chapter 8

Two Worlds of Unionism

Women and the Twenty-First Century Labor Movement

Just as the labor market itself is highly segregated by sex, so too the labor movement is organizationally divided along gender lines. The gender composition of a given labor union tends to reflect the composition of the occupational or industrial jurisdiction in which that union operates. For example, the private-sector building trades unions are predominantly male, since the construction industry itself employs very few women. The situation is similar, although less extreme, in the industrial unions in basic manufacturing. In contrast, women make up the majority of public sector and healthcare union members, because they predominate among workers employed in those labor market sectors. This chapter adds another dimension to the analysis of gender and unionism in chapters 6 and 7, documenting early twenty-first-century patterns of union membership by gender, occupation, and industry, along with analysis of racial and ethnic patterns. The analysis also includes a comparison of the composition of union membership to that of the U.S. labor force as a whole. Finally, the chapter considers the implications of the fact that the labor movement is highly segmented along gender lines for understanding the dynamics of the relationship of women workers to unions in an era of labor movement decline.

Economic inequalities among women have grown since the 1970s, even as women's earnings have become an increasingly important source of support for poor and working-class families.[1] And although gender inequalities in the labor market have been diminished somewhat, the persistence of job segregation by sex and the concentration of women workers in low-wage jobs remain formidable problems.[2] Thus the potential benefits of union membership for women workers in the United States have become increasingly salient.

Yet the influence of organized labor has been radically diminished in precisely the same period in which female employment and its contribution to the welfare of working families has expanded so dramatically. Unionization rates have plummeted, employers have become increasingly adept at "union avoidance," and the legally protected right to organize has come to be honored more in the breach than in the observance. Only 12.5 percent of all U.S. wage and salary workers were unionized in 2004, compared to a peak of about 35 percent in the mid-1950s. Moreover, in the private sector, the unionization rate in 2004 was less than 8 percent.[3] The political influence of organized labor has also suffered substantial erosion, although less than the union membership figures themselves would suggest.[4]

For the minority of workers who are unionized, however, organized labor remains a powerful source of economic empowerment. This is especially the case for women workers. Women who are union members earn considerably more than their nonunion counterparts. In 2004, female union members earned, on average, $19.18 per hour, which was 127 percent of the average earnings of nonunion female workers ($15.05 per hour). The wage premium for men was considerably smaller: male union members in 2004 earned, on average, $21.24 per hour, or 109 percent of the average earnings of nonunion male workers ($19.46). Nevertheless, the average for nonunion men was higher than the average for unionized women workers.[5]

The "union premium" is not limited to wages. Both female and male union members are far more likely than their nonunion counterparts to have employer-paid fringe benefits, from health insurance to pensions to paid time off. In 2003, unionized workers were about 28 percent more likely to be covered by employer-provided health insurance than their nonunion counterparts, and the health insurance unionized workers receive covers a greater share of medical costs. The union advantage is even greater in regard to pensions: union members were 54 percent more likely to have pension coverage than their nonunion counterparts in 2004, and the types of pensions union members have are generally superior to those provided by nonunion employers. Similarly, union workers had more paid vacation and paid holidays than nonunion workers—about 14 percent more, on average, in 2004.[6]

Unions often secure improved conditions of employment not only for their own members but also for the workforce as a whole, mainly through their legislative efforts. One important example is minimum wage legislation, a long-standing labor movement priority at both the federal and state levels. Although almost all female union members earn more than the minimum wage, nonunion women have always been overrepresented among low-wage workers. Thus women workers are the main beneficiaries of increases in state and federal minimum wages, for which organized labor has long been the primary advocate.

Labor's legislative accomplishments since the 1980s also include pay equity, job protection for pregnant workers, and family leave—all of which benefit women workers generally, not only the minority who are union members. The main proponents of the federal Family and Medical Leave Act of 1993, for example, were unions with large female memberships;[7] a decade later, unions were also the prime movers behind the 2002 passage of California's paid family leave program.[8]

Even in its weakened state, then, the U.S labor movement today is a leading advocate for the interests of women workers. Unions directly represented over 6.5 million women workers in 2004, and they have indirectly improved the situation of millions of nonmembers as well. Kate Bronfenbrenner goes so far as to claim that "labor unions are the only major U.S. institution equipped to help women overcome [discriminatory] barriers in the workplace."[9] Organized labor's role in this arena has expanded as struggles for gender equality have gained support throughout the wider society.

Yet, like other organizations and institutions, unions inevitably reflect the wider social arrangements in which they are embedded. Just as gender inequality has been a persistent feature of American society, so too has it been a problem within the House of Labor. Throughout most of U.S. history, not only were women a minority of union members, but they were almost never able to gain positions of union leadership. Many male unionists believed that women were "unorganizable," a view that often became a self-fulfilling prophecy. Union leaders tended to see "women's issues" as divisive, and the majority of union agendas neglected to include such concerns as gender inequality in pay, discrimination based on marital status or pregnancy, flexible working hours, childcare, and the like.

At the discursive level, too, at least until the late twentieth century, unions were overtly male-dominated institutions. Labor iconography was laden with images of traditional masculinity—from hard hats to bulging muscles to cigars. This not only mirrored the material reality of male domination within the organized labor movement, but it also diminished the likelihood that women workers would turn to unionism as a potential vehicle for their own empowerment.

The cultural construction of unionism as quintessentially male was never entirely accurate—women have always worked (both inside and outside the household), and from the earliest period they organized themselves into unions even when male labor leaders were indifferent to their concerns, as the scholarly literature in women's labor history has taken great pains to document. Yet women remained at the margins of organized labor.

All this began to change in the World War II years, and even more so during the 1960s and 1970s, as women's presence in the U.S. workforce expanded and paid employment became increasingly central to their economic well-being. As not only the workforce but also union membership has become increasingly feminized, the gender gap has narrowed substantially—although women's unionization rate still lags behind men's. Unprecedented numbers of women have moved into union leadership, even if they remain underrepresented relative to the female share of union membership. More and more labor leaders have come to recognize that women workers, far from being unorganizable, are more receptive than men (on the average) to unionization efforts.[10] Attention to "women's issues" has also increased within labor's ranks, both in collective bargaining and in the legislative arena.

Progress has been especially rapid since the leadership of the AFL-CIO took a progressive turn with the ascent of John Sweeney to the federation's presidency in 1995. Sweeney established a Working Women's Department within the AFL-CIO for the first time and reconfigured its Executive Council in a deliberate effort to increase the number of women (as well as people of color) in leadership. And when a group of six unions left the AFL-CIO to form the Change to Win (CTW) Federation in 2005, a woman was elected as its top officer (Anna Burger of the SEIU). Apart from these changes at the national level, the number of women leaders in individual unions has also grown since the 1970s.[11]

A closer look, however, reveals that the pace of change has been markedly uneven, in part because the U.S. labor movement has a highly decentralized structure. Some of the nation's largest unions are affiliated with neither the AFL-CIO nor CTW, and even affiliates tend to jealously guard their autonomy. Thus the Sweeney administration's call for improving women's status in the labor movement has had limited effectiveness, and in both federations there is wide variation among unions in regard to gender matters.

Just as job segregation by sex continues to bifurcate the labor market, so, too, male and female workers have sharply differentiated relationships to the U.S. labor movement. Many individual unions are still extremely male dominated in both membership and leadership, maintaining their traditional stance toward women and gender issues. At the other end of the spectrum, among the unions that have a substantial female membership, some have begun to seriously promote gender equality. In that sense it is somewhat misleading even to speak of women and "the" labor movement.

Several factors shape the variations among unions in relation to women and gender. One, as I have argued elsewhere,[12] involves the legacy of the past, and especially the historical period in which particular unions first took shape. In general, newer unions, whose historical formation occurred when women were a more substantial part of the workforce and when notions of gender equality were more widely accepted, tend to be more woman-friendly.

However, this perspective is incomplete. A wave of union mergers in the late twentieth and early twenty-first centuries have disrupted the historical continuity that once made the period of formation of many individual unions such a strong predictor of their relationship to women. And whereas some unions have undergone serious membership erosion, others have achieved significant expansion—typically not only leading to growth in the numbers of female members in their ranks but also opening up greater opportunities for leadership than exist in unions that are stagnating or shrinking in size.

Perhaps the single most-often-cited factor shaping the distinct gender regimes of individual unions is the gender composition of the membership, which is itself highly variable. Occupational segregation by sex, despite some diminution over recent decades, persists as a key axis of division within the labor market.[13]

Sex segregation in the labor market also has had a large impact on the gender composition of many unions, especially those that are occupationally based. Some such unions represent overwhelmingly male constituencies—notably the building trades, the pilots, and the firefighters, which have correspondingly limited interest in "women's issues." Other occupational unions have largely female constituencies—for example, the teachers' and nurses' unions—and these tend to be far more engaged in issues of special interest to women and supportive of gender equality.

Unions that are organized along industrial or sectoral rather than occupational lines also vary in their relationship to gender questions. The cohort of industrial unions that took shape in the 1910s in the textile and garment industries had a largely female membership but a paternalistic male leadership. By contrast, those that emerged in the late 1930s and 1940s in industries like auto and steel, even though they had a more male-dominated workforce, embraced an antidiscrimination ideology from the start—an ideology that was primarily focused on racial divisions but that union women often seized upon to promote gender equality.[14] Both these cohorts of industrial unions have been dramatically reduced in size since the 1970s due to deindustrialization and outsourcing. This, in turn, has limited their ability to respond to changing gender arrangements in the wider society.

By contrast, public sector unions, which are among the few labor organizations that have grown substantially since the 1970s, along with those representing healthcare and service workers, have vast female memberships. These unions have emerged as strong advocates of gender equality and other specific concerns of women workers. During the 1980s, for example, public sector unions took the lead in the struggle for pay equity. And because this is the main growth sector within organized labor, leadership positions open up relatively frequently. As a result, these are the unions where women have made the greatest gains in the top ranks of union leadership.

Union Membership Trends:
Feminization and Segregation

With the dramatic influx of women into the workforce since the 1970s, as well as changes in the distribution of unionization across occupations, industries, and economic sectors, the long-standing gender gap in union membership has narrowed substantially. As figure 8.1 shows, by 2004, 11.1 percent of all employed women were unionized, only slightly below the 13.8 percent figure for employed men.[15]

Looking at the same data from another angle, the unmistakable trend is one of union feminization. As figure 8.2 shows, even as the nation's overall unionization rate has declined, the female share of union membership has expanded rapidly. In 2004, 43 percent of all the nation's union members were women—a record high, up from 34 percent only twenty years earlier, and just slightly below the 48 percent female share of the nation's wage and salary workforce.

Yet the feminization phenomenon masks another critical feature of the unionized workforce, namely that women union members are far more highly concentrated than their male counterparts in particular sectors, industries, and occupations. Thus in 2004, 60.8 percent of all unionized women were employed in the public sector (local, state, or federal government), compared with only

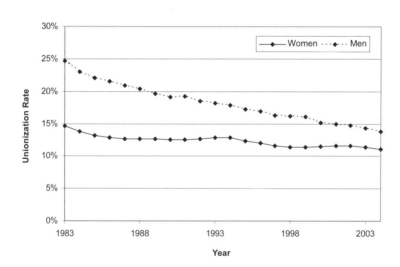

FIGURE 8.1. The Declining Gender Gap in Unionization Rates, United States, 1983–2004.
Source: U.S. Department of Labor, Bureau of Labor Statistics, *Women in the Labor Force: A Databook,* Report 985 (May 2005): 81–82.

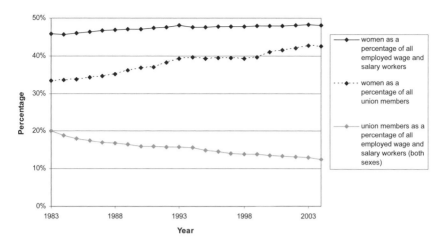

FIGURE 8.2. Feminization of the Workforce and of Union Membership, and Declining Unionization, United States, 1983–2004.
Source: U.S. Department of Labor, Bureau of Labor Statistics, *Women in the Labor Force: A Databook,* Report 985 (May 2005): 81–82.

36.7 percent of unionized men. Women are also more likely than men to be employed in the public sector (regardless of their union status): 19.1 percent of all female workers in the United States (compared with 13.5 percent of male workers) were employed in the public sector in 2004.

Only 5.4 percent of women employed in the private sector are unionized, compared with 10.1 percent of private-sector men; the disparity is similar in manufacturing—historically a union stronghold—where 8.3 percent of women are unionized, compared with 15.0 percent of men. By contrast, the gender gap in the public sector is much smaller (35.3 percent of women and 37.8 percent of men are unionized). Indeed, the growth of public sector unionism is the key underlying trend driving the recent feminization of union membership.

Figure 8.3 shows the concentration of female union members across major industry groups in 2004. More than two-thirds of them (70.9 percent) are accounted for by only three industry groups—education, healthcare, and public administration.[16] By contrast, those three industry groups accounted for only 39.2 percent of the female wage and salary workforce. These are important and heavily female-employing industries, but as a comparison of the top and bottom pie charts in the figure reveals, the importance of education and public administration in the world of female union membership is far greater than in the overall female workforce. (Healthcare services, by contrast, actually accounted for a

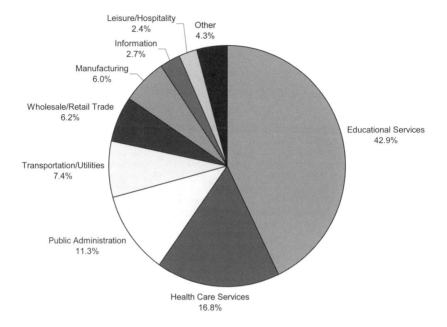

Female Union Members

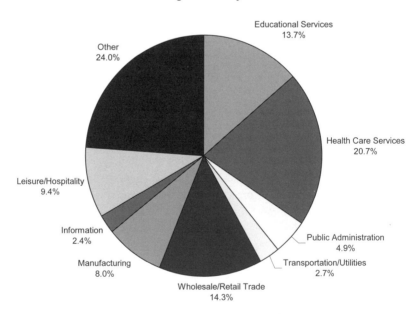

Female Wage and Salary Workers

FIGURE 8.3. Female Union Members and Female Wage and Salary Workers, by Major Industry Group, United States, 2004.
Source: Current Population Survey, Outgoing Rotation Group Earnings Files, 2004.

greater share of the female workforce than of female union members, as is also the case for other private-sector industries.)[17]

As figure 8.4 shows, the distribution of male union members across industry groups is far less concentrated, with 70.2 percent spread across five industry groups in 2004: manufacturing, transportation/utilities, public administration, construction, and education. These five industry groups accounted for only 30.9 percent of the male wage and salary workforce, again a far less concentrated distribution than that among female workers. Public administration actually accounted for a somewhat larger share of male than female union members (14.5 versus 11.3 percent). But whereas more than four out of every ten women union members were employed in education, that industry accounted for a relatively small share (12.4 percent) of male union members. By contrast, slightly more than half (50.4 percent) of all male union members were in manufacturing, construction, and transportation/utilities—all predominantly private-sector industries that were the traditional strongholds of organized labor.[18]

Just as the world of work is highly sex segregated, so too the world of unionism is sharply bifurcated into male and female segments. In the twenty-first century, the typical male union member is a private-sector blue-collar "hardhat," whereas the typical female union member is a public-sector white-collar or professional worker employed in education, healthcare, or public administration. In some cases, male and female unionization overlap—thus, as figure 8.3 shows, in 2004 transportation/utilities and manufacturing accounted for 7.4 and 6.0 percent of female union members, respectively (in contrast to construction, which accounted for less than 1 percent); similarly, as figure 8.4 shows, both public administration and education accounted for substantial shares of male union membership. But on the whole, U.S. union membership is strongly gender differentiated.

The industrial distribution of women union members also varies with race, ethnicity, and nativity, as figure 8.5 shows. In 2004 nearly half (49.2 percent) of white women union members were employed in education, a far higher proportion than for any nonwhite group. While a relatively modest 25.7 percent of black women union members were found in education, another 50.8 percent were in healthcare, public administration, and transportation/utilities, while these three industry groups accounted for less than one-third of all unionized white women. Asian women union members also had a distinctive profile, with a relatively high concentration in healthcare, which accounted for nearly one-third (31.6 percent) of them. Unionized Hispanic women were more evenly distributed across industries than the other groups shown; in their case, manufacturing accounted for a relatively large share of the total. Foreign-born women union members also had a distinctive profile.[19]

Male Union Members

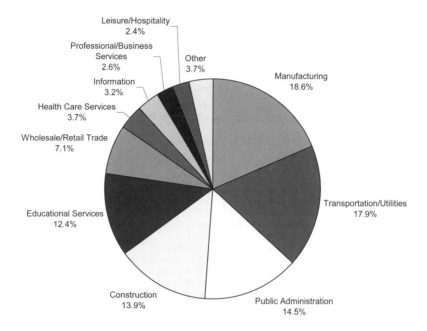

Male Wage and Salary Workers

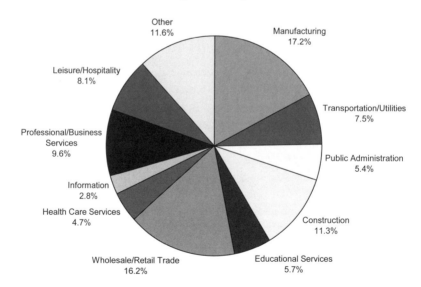

FIGURE 8.4. Male Union Members and Male Wage and Salary Workers, by Major Industry Group, United States, 2004.
Source: Current Population Survey, Outgoing Rotation Group Earnings Files, 2004.

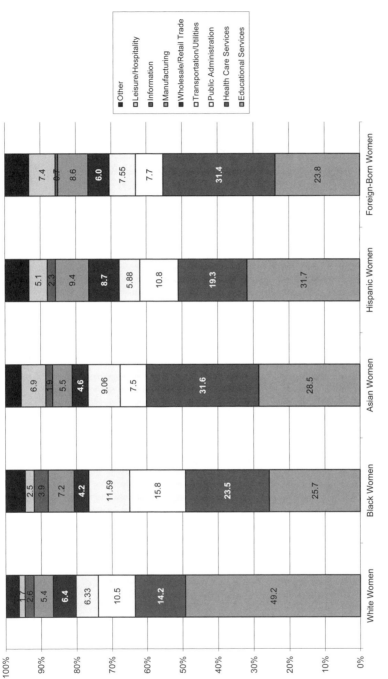

FIGURE 8.5. Women Union Members by Race/Ethnicity, Nativity, and Major Industry Group, United States, 2004. Note: "White Women," "Black Women," and "Asian Women" do not include "Hispanics."

Source: Current Population Survey, Outgoing Rotation Group, Earnings Files, 2004.

As one might expect, there are also differences in unionization rates for women of different races and ethnic groups, and between foreign- and native-born women, but these variations are relatively modest. In 2004, 10.9 percent of white women were unionized, compared with 13.6 percent of black women, 11.1 percent of Asian women, and 9.9 percent of Hispanic women; in that year, 9.7 percent of foreign-born women and 11.3 percent of native-born women were union members.

National data are not available on the distribution of women and men across individual unions, but such data do exist for California, the nation's most populous state, for 2001–02. These are shown in figure 8.6. They once again expose the high degree of gender differentiation among union members. Women are concentrated in a relatively small number of public sector unions: CSEA, CTA/NEA, AFSCME, and AFT alone accounted for about half of all unionized women in the state, and this does not include the substantial public-sector membership of SEIU, CNA, CWA and others.[20] Overall, 61.9 percent of the state's female union members were found in public-sector unions in 2001–02, and another 13.8 percent were in "mixed" unions that included both public- and private-sector workers. By contrast, 36.5 percent of California's male union members were in public sector unions, and another 20.9 percent in mixed unions.[21]

As figure 8.6 also shows, the unions now affiliated with CTW accounted for about one-fifth of California's female union members in 2001–02, and an even larger share—more than one-third—were in independent unions, which remain unaffiliated with either of the nation's large labor federations. CTW unions accounted at that time for nearly a third of the state's male union members, of whom just under one-fifth were in independents. California's male members were dispersed over a far larger number of unions than were their female counterparts in California in 2001–02. Some large unions—the CTA/NEA, SEIU, IBT and UFCW—accounted for large shares of both male and female union members, but apart from that the distributions were highly gendered. It is striking that among the six unions that accounted for the largest share of the state's male union members, three are building trades unions (IUOE, UBC, and LIUNA), whereas a tiny proportion of the state's women union members were in those unions (1.1 percent, 0.6 percent, and 1.1 percent, respectively) in 2001–02. Nearly one-third (30.1 percent) of all male union members in California at that time were in the building trades, compared with only 2.9 percent of women union members. And if one considers only the private sector, the building trades' share of male union membership was nearly half (46.7 percent) of the state's male union members.[22]

Gender and "Organizability"

Demographic variations in unionization rates are sometimes read as a gauge of the degree to which various categories of workers are interested in becoming part

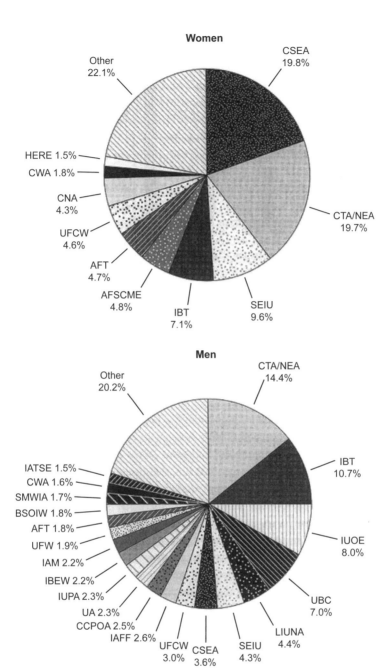

FIGURE 8.6. Union Members, by Gender and International Union, California, 2001–2002. (See abbreviations in front of book for the full names of unions.) Source: California Union Census. See Ruth Milkman and Daisy Rooks, "California Union Membership: A Turn-of-the-Century Portrait," *The State of California Labor 2003* (University of California Press, 2003), 19.

of the organized labor movement. However, this is often highly misleading. In the United States, where the workforce remains highly segmented by gender as well as race, ethnicity, and nativity, the main determinant of unionization rates for any given population group is the extent to which a given sector, industry, or occupation in which they are concentrated has been successfully organized at some point in the past. As the disparities between the top and bottom portions of figures 8.3 and 8.4 suggest, the development of unionism has been extremely uneven. That unevenness is itself an artifact of the U.S. industrial relations system, which since 1935 has been based not on individual decisions about union affiliation but instead on a winner-take-all electoral process that leads to the unionization (or not) of entire workplaces. Given the limited amount of recent organizing, in most cases the main determinant of whether a given individual is a union member is where she or he happens to be employed and whether that workplace became (and remained) unionized at some previous time—regardless of that individual's pro- or anti-union sympathies.[23] Similarly, unionization rates by gender, race, nativity, and so on reveal little about the preferences of any particular category of workers.

Figure 8.7, which shows unionization rates and employment distribution separately for the highly unionized public sector and the largely nonunion private sector for a variety of demographic groups, suggests the underlying dynamic. The U.S. public sector is far more highly unionized than the private sector, not because public sector workers are more pro-union (although they may be, since the experience of unionization itself tends to foster more positive attitudes toward unionism, all else being equal) but because there is generally less resistance to union activity when the employer is the federal, state, or local government than when it is a private-sector company.

As figure 8.7 shows, regardless of gender, race, ethnicity or nativity, public-sector workers are far more extensively unionized than their private-sector counterparts. For example, although few Hispanic immigrants (of either sex) are employed in the public sector, among the few who are, the unionization rate is similar to the public-sector rates of other demographic groups.

Male unionization rates are higher than those of women in both the public and private sectors, as figure 8.7 shows, but that is not because men are more pro-union than women. Indeed, the available evidence (albeit fragmentary) suggests that precisely the opposite is true. Survey after survey finds that women have more positive attitudes toward unionism in particular, and toward collective approaches to workplace problem solving generally, than do men. Women are also more likely than men to state that they would vote for union representation in their own workplace, given the opportunity.[24] The attitudinal data, in short, indicate that, at least in the late twentieth and early twenty-first centuries (comparable

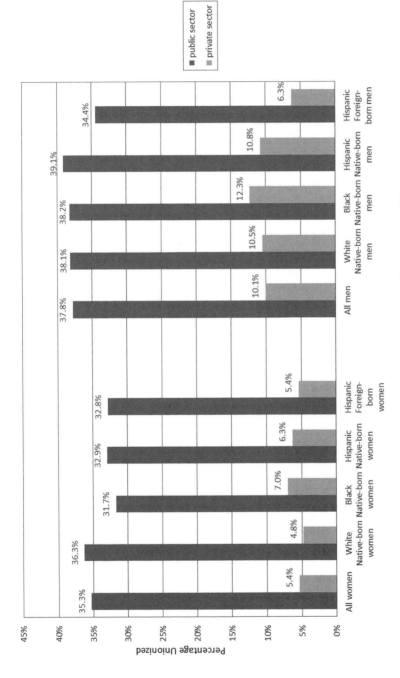

FIGURE 8.7. Unionization Rates, by Sector, for Selected Demographic Groups, United States, 2004.

Source: Current Population Survey, Outgoing Rotation Group Earnings Files, 2004.

data are not available for earlier periods), women are in fact more "organizable" than their male counterparts, contrary to the traditional stereotypes.

Further evidence regarding women's greater receptivity to unionism emerges from data on actual organizing campaigns. Women have accounted for the majority of new workers organized each year in the United States since at least the mid-1980s, as Kate Bronfenbrenner has shown. In addition, her research demonstrates that unions are significantly more likely to win representation elections in private-sector workplace units where women make up the majority of the workforce than in gender-mixed or male-dominated units; the probability of winning is even higher in units where women of color are the predominant group.[25] There are no systematic data of this kind available on public-sector organizing outcomes, but women make up the majority of such high-profile hotbeds of organizing as homecare and childcare workers. Yet the focus of such recruitment drives typically is not on gender issues so much as on low-wage work (and, in some cases, ethnic minority and/or immigration status); it is because of women's persistent concentration in low-wage work that they have disproportionately benefited from these organizing successes.

Women and Union Leadership

One important factor that contributes to success in organizing women is having a female presence on union organizing staffs. Bronfenbrenner's research shows that the proportion of women among lead union organizers has increased over time, from about 12 percent of all sampled representation election campaigns in the late 1980s to 21 percent sampled at the end of the twentieth century. Significantly, in the latter sample, among campaigns where the workplaces involved had a predominantly female workforce, 42 percent were led by female organizers. As this research also shows, having women as lead organizers is associated with a higher union win rate in representation elections.[26]

Organizers are on the front lines of labor's efforts to survive and grow, but they are among the least powerful members of union staffs and elected leaderships. Men continue to dominate top union leadership posts throughout the labor movement. In those unions whose memberships are overwhelmingly male, women leaders are few and far between. But in unions where females make up the bulk of the membership, there has been considerable growth in the number of women among high-level union leaders.

Table 8.1 shows the relevant data for 1978 and 2000 for a selection of labor unions with the largest numbers of female members. In almost every case the ratio of the female proportion of top leaders to the female proportion of members grew over this period—in several cases from a single-digit base or from zero! Although

Table 8.1. Female Membership and Leadership in Selected U.S. Labor Unions, 1978 and 2000

Labor Union	Data Year	Female Members	Female % of Members	Female % of Top Leaders[a]	Female % of Top Leaders / Female % of Members (ratio)
American Federation of State, County, and Municipal Employees (AFSCME)	1978	408,000	40	3	8
	2000	728,000	52	38	73
American Federation of Teachers (AFT)	1978	300,000	60	25	42
	2000	600,000	60	39	65
Service Employees International Union (SEIU)	1978	312,000	50	15	30
	2000	650,000	50	32	64
National Education Association (NEA)	1978	1,240,000	75	55	73
	2000	1,500,000	61	33	54
Union of Needletrades, Industrial and Textile Employees (UNITE)[b]	1978	610,000	72	11	15
	2000	330,000	66	30	45
Hotel Employees and Restaurant Employees (HERE)	1978	181,000	42	4	10
	2000	185,000	48	18	38
Communication Workers of America (CWA)	1978	259,000	51	0	0
	2000	320,000	51	12	24
United Food and Commercial Workers (UFCW)	1978	480,000	39	3	8
	2000	700,000	50	11	22
International Brotherhood of Teamsters (IBT)	1978	481,000	25	0	0
	2000	450,000	30	4	13

[a] "Top leaders" refers to Union Officers and Executive Board Members.
[b] In 1978, this union was made up of two separate entities: the International Ladies' Garment Workers Union (ILGWU) and the Amalgamated Clothing, Textile and Garment Workers Union (ACTWU); they merged in 1995 to form UNITE. The 1978 data shown in the table merge (and in the rightmost three columns) are a weighted average of the figures for the ILGWU and ACTWU.
Source: Cobble, "On the Edge of Equality?" and author's computations.

the individual unions vary greatly, and in no case does the female proportion of leaders equal the female proportion of union members, the representation of women among top leaders (union officers and executive board members) has increased dramatically over time in all these unions. Even in cases where membership has declined, there have been steady advances in the representation of women at the top level of these unions, all of which have large female memberships. Although there is no systematic source of data on this topic for the unions with predominantly male memberships, women are seldom found among the top

221

leaders in those organizations. Thus in leadership as in membership, the labor movement is bifurcated along gender lines, into two worlds of unionism.

Among the unions shown in table 8.1, only three remain affiliated with the AFL-CIO. The nation's largest union, with a majority female membership, the NEA, has long been an independent union, and in the summer of 2005 SEIU, UNITE HERE (the product of a merger between UNITE and HERE that took place in 2004), the UFCW, and the IBT disaffiliated and became part of the new Change to Win Federation (along with the UFW and the much more male-dominated Carpenters and Laborers unions). Some heavily female public sector unions—notably AFSCME and AFT—however, remain within the AFL-CIO. As noted above, CTW is headed by Anna Burger, the first woman to lead a major labor federation in U.S. history.

Conclusion

Women's share of union membership and leadership has increased over time, although not as rapidly as their share of the workforce has grown. Women are disproportionately employed in the public sector and in healthcare, which are among the few growth sectors for U.S. unions. There is evidence that women are more positive than men in their view of organized labor and more receptive to unionization opportunities as well. Moreover, the language and iconography of labor is far less male dominated than it was in the past, at least in the unions with substantial female membership. And women have a particularly visible presence in the few growing sectors of the organized labor movement. These changes are all the more impressive in the context of the broader challenges facing organized labor as it struggles to survive in an extremely hostile political environment and facing employers who are intransigently opposed to unionism.

Yet organized labor in the United States continues to be made up of a highly segmented set of institutions. The long tradition of granting autonomy to individual unions, combined with the continuing reality of occupational segregation by sex in the labor market, has meant that the world of women's unionism is largely institutionally separated from that of men. As labor struggles to reorient and remake itself in the twenty-first century, this is among the many challenges it will face.

Notes

Originally published as Ruth Milkman, "Two Worlds of Unionism: Women and the New Labor Movement," from *The Sex of Class: Women Transforming American Labor*, edited by Dorothy Sue Cobble. Copyright © 2007 by Cornell University Press. Used by permission of the publisher.

1. Leslie McCall, "Increasing Class Disparities among Women and the Politics of Gender Equity," in *The Sex of Class: Women Transforming American Labor*, edited by Dorothy Sue Cobble (Ithaca, N.Y.: Cornell University Press, 2007), 15–34.

2. See Vicky Lovell, Heidi Hartmann, and Misha Werschkul, "More than Raising the Floor: The Persistence of Gender Inequalities in the Low-Wage Labor Market," in Cobble, *Sex of Class*, 35–58.

3. Barry T. Hirsch and David A. Macpherson, *Union Membership and Earnings Data Book: Compilations from the Current Population Survey* (Washington, D.C.: Bureau of National Affairs, 2005), 27.

4. Taylor E. Dark, *The Unions and the Democrats: An Enduring Alliance* (Ithaca, N.Y.: Cornell University Press, 1999).

5. Hirsch and Macpherson, *Union Membership*, 21.

6. Lawrence Mishel, Jared Bernstein, and Sylvia Allegretto, *The State of Working America 2004/2005* (Ithaca, N.Y.: Cornell University Press, 2005), 192–93.

7. Dark, *Unions and the Democrats*, 166.

8. Netsy Firestein and Nicola Dones, "Unions Fight for Work and Family Policies—Not for Women Only," in Cobble, *Sex of Class*, 140–54. See also chap. 10, this volume.

9. Kate Bronfenbrenner, "Organizing Women: The Nature and Process of Union-Organizing Efforts Among U.S. Women Workers since the Mid-1990s," *Work and Occupations* 32, no. 4 (2005): 441–63.

10. See chap. 7, this volume.

11. Dorothy Sue Cobble, "On the Edge of Equality? Working Women and the U.S. Labour Movement," in *Gender, Diversity and Trade Unions: International Perspectives*, edited by Fiona Colgan and Sue Ledwith (New York: Routledge, 2002), 235–37.

12. See chap. 6, this volume.

13. Lovell, Hartmann, and Werschkul, "More than Raising the Floor."

14. Milkman, "Gender and Trade Unionism"; Dorothy Sue Cobble, *The Other Women's Movement: Workplace Justice and Social Rights in Modern America* (Princeton, N.J.: Princeton University Press, 2004).

15. The text and figures that follow, unless otherwise indicated, are based on an analysis of Current Population Survey data for 2004. The dataset was created by merging the basic monthly CPS Outgoing Rotation Group files for January through December 2004. The sample includes civilian wage and salary workers age sixteen or older. The sample definition and weighting procedures are identical to those described in the introduction to Hirsch and Macpherson, *Union Membership*.

16. There is extensive overlap between female union membership in these three industry groups and in the public sector as a whole, where (as noted above) nearly two-thirds of unionized women are employed: 89.6 percent of female union members in education, 30.0 percent of those in healthcare, and 100 percent of those in public administration are public-sector employees.

17. The industry groups aggregated as "other" in the bottom half of figure 8.3 are mainly composed of poorly unionized but heavily female-employing fields such as financial services, which accounted for 8.7 percent of all female wage and salary workers in 2004; professional

and business services, which accounted for another 8.5 percent; and "other services," which accounted for another 5.1 percent. "Other" also includes agriculture, mining, and construction, but these industry groups employed minuscule numbers of women.

18. In the bottom half of figure 8.4, "other" is primarily comprised of financial services, which accounted for 5.5 percent of male wage and salary workers in 2004, "other services," which accounted for another 4.0 percent; as well as the far smaller agriculture and mining industry groups.

19. The industrial distribution of male union members also varies with race, ethnicity, and nativity, although those variations are not documented here.

20. See list of abbreviations in the frontmatter of this volume for the full names of these unions and those shown in figure 8.6.

21. Ruth Milkman and Daisy Rooks, "California Union Membership: A Turn-of-the-Century Portrait," in *The State of California Labor 2003* (Berkeley: University of California Press, 2003), 18.

22. Ibid.

23. Of course, at the time of initial organization, the relative proclivities of particular groups toward unionism—along with many other factors—do matter.

24. See Richard B. Freeman and Joel Rogers, *What Workers Want* (Ithaca, N.Y.: Cornell University Press, 1999); Peter D. Hart Research Associates, "Working Women's View of the Economy, Unions, and Public Policy," in *Not Your Father's Labor Movement*, edited by Jo-Ann Mort (New York: Verso, 1998), 69–85.

25. Bronfenbrenner, "Organizing Women"; see also chap. 7, this volume.

26. Bronfenbrenner, "Organizing Women."

Chapter 9

The Macrosociology
of Paid Domestic Labor

RUTH MILKMAN, ELLEN REESE, AND BENITA ROTH

This chapter poses the question: what explains variation in the proportion of the labor force employed in paid domestic labor over time and space? In contrast to an older, modernization-theory-based literature that argued that paid domestic labor declines and ultimately disappears in the course of economic development, the analysis points to the occupation's expansion in the 1980s in southern California and the wide variations among the world's rich countries in the proportion of the female workforce employed in paid domestic labor. The chapter argues that a crucial, neglected factor in explaining such geographic variation is the extent of economic inequality. This factor is overlooked not only in the modernization-theory-based literature but also in later microsociological studies of paid domestic labor in the United States. The latter studies highlight the ways in which race, ethnicity, and citizenship status are implicated in interactions between employers of domestics and the workers themselves, but largely ignore the enduring significance of class in the employer/domestic relationship. By analyzing 1990 census data for the one hundred largest metropolitan areas in the United States, the chapter shows that income inequality (as well as, but independent of, the proportion of the female labor force made up of African Americans and Latinas, the proportion of the female labor force that is foreign born, and maternal labor force participation) is a significant predictor of the proportion of the female labor force employed in domestic labor.

Domestic labor performed for a wage, or what the U.S. Census Bureau calls "private household service," is among the oldest forms of wage labor. Once the single most common female occupation in the United States, it declined dramatically in economic importance over the first three-quarters of the twentieth century, and by the early 1970s, sociologists were writing obituaries for it.[1] Nevertheless, interest in this type of employment was reawakened in the 1980s and 1990s, most notably among gender scholars. As Rollins has pointed out, domestic service is of particular interest from a feminist perspective because both employer and employee (in the contemporary United States) are typically female.[2] Following Rollins's lead, several important studies have excavated the microsociology of the relationships between women who employ maids and nannies and those who labor in such jobs, analyzing in particular the ways in which interaction between employer and employee are mediated by racial, ethnic, and citizenship-based inequalities among women.[3]

This inquiry draws on—and at the same time points to a crucial gap in—this late-twentieth-century feminist literature in the social sciences. Our point of departure is the observation that, despite the frequently invoked rubric of "race, class, and gender," the empirical focus of most feminist research on inequalities among women has been limited to racial and ethnic divisions and to some extent divisions between native-born and immigrant women. Although this scholarship has added a great deal to sociological understandings of gender and quite properly challenged earlier notions of a universal female (and male) social experience, it has largely ignored the issue of *class* divisions among women. This is especially problematic given the increasing salience of class in the late twentieth century, as income inequalities widen among households and individuals of all racial and ethnic groups, and among citizens and noncitizens alike. Without questioning the importance of race, ethnicity, or immigration status, we want to bring class back into the discussion.

At the same time, our analysis highlights the importance of gender in the dynamic of widening economic inequality in the contemporary United States. There is now extensive documentation of the rapid growth in inequality in income and wealth in this country (and indeed worldwide) since the 1970s. Yet this literature focuses almost entirely on growing inequality among households and among male workers; when women are considered at all, the primary focus is the narrowing of the gender gap in earnings. Much attention has been devoted to the precipitous decline in real wages among men, especially less educated men, and indeed this is one major component of the post-1970s reduction in gender inequality in earnings. Few commentators have focused on the fact that inequalities in earnings among women also have grown dramatically: between 1969 and 1989, the Gini coefficient, a standard summary measure of economic inequality, rose from .344 to .386 for women workers ages twenty-five to fifty-four (it rose even more for men in this age group, from .316 to .414).[4]

In fact, the broader increase in economic inequality has occurred in an age of vastly expanded economic opportunities for educated, upper-middle-class women (largely a white group, but now also including significant numbers of women of color)—precisely the population most likely to demand and have the means to purchase paid domestic labor. Meanwhile, the real earnings of less educated, poorer women have been stagnant and, for some subgroups, have declined significantly from what were always relatively low levels. Consider the data for the years between 1979 and 1989 on the real earnings of full-time, year-round, women workers aged twenty-five to thirty-four—the age group most affected by economic restructuring. The real earnings of those with four or more years of postsecondary education rose 17 percent (much more than the 5 percent increase that males with the same characteristics enjoyed); by contrast, for those with twelve or fewer years of education, real earnings fell by 2 percent (compared with a 13 percent drop for their male counterparts).[5]

If we turn from individuals to households, the effects of this economic polarization are magnified even further, given the increasing number of professional dual-earner households, on one hand, and the long-standing pattern of class endogamy on the other. Today, many married (or cohabiting) professional-managerial men and women pool their incomes; at the other pole of the income distribution, it is increasingly common for households to be supported solely by a poorly paid female single parent—the much discussed "feminization of poverty."[6] Thus, gender is deeply implicated in the story of growing income inequality in late-twentieth-century America.

Paid domestic labor is in many respects a microcosm of the growing class inequality among women. The elite corps of professional and managerial women, whose ranks have expanded so dramatically, can now purchase on the market much of the labor of social reproduction traditionally relegated to them as wives and mothers. By contrast, the workers who perform this labor are typically women on the lower rungs of the economic ladder, often women of color and/or immigrants. It is precisely the interactions between these two groups of women that have stimulated the burgeoning scholarship on the microsociology of domestic labor. This literature has produced many valuable insights, yet it has neglected analysis of the *macro*sociology of paid domestic labor, which is our focus here.[7]

Specifically, we pose the following question: What explains variation in the proportion of the labor force employed in paid domestic labor? Even a casual survey reveals enormous variation over time and space in the extent of employment in this occupation. For example, in contemporary Kuwait, domestic servants are ubiquitous; in Scandinavia, although once numerous, they are relatively rare. And as we shall show, even within the late-twentieth-century United States, paid domestic labor was far more widespread in some metropolitan areas than in others.[8] The explanation for such inter- and intranational variations is far from obvious. The conventional wisdom among an older generation of commentators who explored this issue was that the occupation's long-term decline in the advanced capitalist world was a product of "modernization"; yet the occupation's importance varies substantially even among the rich, developed nations of Europe and North America. Moreover, in some parts of the United States, employment in paid domestic labor has actually increased (as a proportion of the female labor force) since the 1990s.

We argue here that a crucial determinant of the extent of employment in paid domestic labor in a given location is the degree of economic inequality there. This largely overlooked factor helps account for variations in the size of the occupation among developed countries, as well as the growth of employment in domestic labor in some locations. With the exception of one obscure treatise published in 1946 by economist George Stigler, the relationship between inequality and the dynamics of employment in paid domestic labor has not been explored at all in the literature. Here we make the case for its importance, building on Stigler's previously untested hypothesis from many years ago. We explore theoretically the mechanism by which greater economic inequality generates greater employment in this occupation, and then we present an empirical test of this hypothesis. Although our empirical analysis is limited to the United States (specifically to the nation's one hundred largest metropolitan areas in 1990), we believe that our argument has broader applicability.

To be sure, the extent of economic inequality is not the only important factor influencing the size of the occupation. Literature on the U.S. case highlights the concentration of women of color and immigrant women in paid domestic work, and our analysis confirms the importance of race and immigration, as well as the rate of labor force participation among mothers of young children (a crucial source of demand for the services of paid domestic laborers). But our goal here is to highlight the key factor that most other commentators have ignored by demonstrating that the extent of employment in paid domestic labor (as a proportion of the female labor force) varies directly with the level of class inequality (operationalized here using a standard measure of household income inequality)—independent of race, immigration, and maternal labor force participation rates. All else being equal, in locations where income inequality is great, the occupation is relatively large, whereas locations with minimal income inequality are also those where the occupation is of trivial importance or even absent. Before developing this argument in detail, however, we briefly review previous scholarship on the occupation, both to highlight the gaps it contains and to situate our contribution here. We begin with the microsociological work that has dominated the literature since the 1970s and then turn to the earlier, macrosociological literature.

The Microsociology of Paid Domestic Labor

Several detailed studies have analyzed paid domestic labor from the perspective of the women who actually perform it, highlighting how employee/employer interactions reflect the social hierarchies of race, citizenship, and class. Rollins's pioneering study, for example, focused on the relationships between African American women who cleaned homes in Boston and the white women who employed them.[9] Using participant observation as well as extensive interviewing with both employers and workers, Rollins reported that "all domestics concurred that employers appreciated some forms of deference and outward signs of subservience" and argued that "this formed the essence of the employer/domestic relationship."[10] She analyzed these interactional dynamics in detail, documenting what she calls "maternalism" on the part of the employers and deference and *ressentiment* on the part of the domestic workers. For Rollins, the racial/ethnic dimension of the relationship is particularly salient:

> While any employer-employee relationship is by definition unequal, the mistress-servant relationship—with its centuries of conventions of behavior, its historical association with slavery throughout the world, its unusual retention of feudal characteristics, and the tradition of the servant being not only of a lower class but also female, rural, and of a despised ethnic group—provides an extreme and "pure" example of a relationship of domination in close quarters.[11]

Similarly, Romero, in a valuable study of Chicana domestics, emphasized the stigma attached to domestic work.[12] She made an important contribution to the discussion by exposing the ways in which domestic workers themselves have sought "to transform and improve the occupation by eliminating the vestiges of servitude." Examples of this include shift from live-in to day work, from hourly pay to pay by the job, and other efforts to increase workers' autonomy and to resist "personalized and asymmetrical relationships with employers and . . . to establish a businesslike environment."[13] Romero also highlighted the importance of race and immigration, commenting that "as domestic service becomes increasingly dominated by women of color, particularly immigrant women, the occupation . . . is now bringing race relations into the middle-class homemaker's home."[14]

Whereas Rollins and Romero focused their research on domestic workers whose main responsibilities involved cleaning and housekeeping, others have documented the experiences of nannies in the United States, pursuing similar themes. For example, Colen's research on West Indian domestics (both cleaners and nannies) in New York City emphasized the ways that "the ideology of family is used to manipulate the worker. . . . It is used to encourage people who are *not* family members to perform tasks or to tolerate treatment that may be exploitative."[15] Colen also highlighted the special vulnerability of undocumented immigrant domestics whose employers agree to sponsor them for legal status as permanent residents, a multiyear process rife with opportunities for superexploitation. And Wrigley's study of nannies in Los Angeles and New York emphasized the enormous cultural differences between black or brown immigrant nannies and their white, native-born, wealthy employers.[16] In one of the few microsociological studies that has explicitly considered class divisions, Wrigley exposed the contrast between nannies' experience of the job—with its long hours, social isolation, and extreme demands—and their employers' expectations of subservience on one hand and stimulation for the children on the other. Comparing middle-class European au pairs to working-class immigrant nannies, Wrigley shows as well that the greater the class gap between parents and caregivers, the greater the prevalence of extreme forms of exploitation.

Much of this literature roundly condemns female employers of domestic workers as exploiters of their less fortunate sisters. Indeed, some authors argue that private household workers are more exploited than other kinds of workers. Rollins, for example, states,

> What makes domestic service as an occupation more profoundly exploitive than other comparable occupations grows out of the precise element that makes it unique: the personal relationship between employer and employee. What might appear to be the basis of a more humane, less alienating work arrangement allows for a level of psychological exploitation unknown in other occupations.[17]

Similarly, Romero claims that domestic employment is more exploitative than other occupations accessible to immigrant women and women of color.

> Even though Chicanas and Mexican immigrants are usually hired for low-level and unskilled factory jobs, employers outside domestic service do not demand the same level of deference and servility. Even low-paid service positions do not carry the stigma found in domestic service.[18]

Domestic employment does have some unusual features that allow latitude for superexploitation: social isolation, the unity of workplace and residence for employers (and for live-in domestics, for employees as well) and the intimacy that this implies, as well as an abject lack of state or social regulation. Yet compared with working in a garment sweatshop, in agriculture, or even as a minimum-wage fast-food server, this occupation may be relatively attractive to workers, the above claims to the contrary notwithstanding. Indeed, Romero herself reported that domestics often prefer the occupation to the available alternatives, mostly because of the flexibility with which the work can be scheduled. "On the one hand," she noted, "cleaning houses is degrading and embarrassing; on the other, domestic service can be higher paying, more autonomous, and less dehumanizing than other low-status, low-skilled occupations."[19] This observation belies the frequent claims in the microsociological literature on domestic service that this occupation is uniquely exploitative. Indeed, many other types of work are also sites of exploitation, as any sociologist should be well aware.

Another feature of this literature, which is at once a strength and a weakness, is that it calls attention to the salience of race, ethnicity, and immigration status as a marker of difference between employers and employees in the domestic labor relationship. In many parts of the world, including North America, this is indeed a critical part of the story, and its prominence in this interview-based body of microsociological research is hardly surprising. However, all too often the focus on race, ethnicity, and immigration obscures the enduring significance of social class in the employer/domestic relationship. Romero explicitly argues that whereas social class divisions were important in shaping relations between domestics and their employers in the past, today "we find the proliferation of master-servant relationships in which race, ethnicity, and gender replace class as immutable social structures dictating a person's place in the hierarchy."[20] We question the validity of this view and argue that (as Wrigley also emphasizes)[21] social class persists as a crucial factor shaping the situation of private-household workers. Before developing that argument, we briefly review the macrosociological literature on domestic service.

The Modernization Paradigm and the Macrosociology of Domestic Labor

Whereas the feminist sociological literature on domestic service is overwhelmingly micro in focus, an earlier generation of commentators did engage the issue we pursue here—namely, what explains variation in the proportion of the labor force employed in paid domestic labor? That earlier work was conducted mostly within a modernization-theory paradigm. Its general thrust was to note the historical decline of the occupation in Western Europe and the United States and, by the 1970s, to predict its global demise. For example, Collver and Langlois suggested on the basis of a wide-ranging cross-national analysis of female labor force participation patterns that "in the process of development, employment in private domestic service diminishes with respect to that in other sectors of the female labor force."[22] Similarly, Chaplin, reviewing evidence about the decline of the occupation in several countries, concluded that "the incidence of domestic service is a prime social indicator of the level and quality of industrialization and modernization."[23] And Coser, in a classic article on the occupation published in

1973, argued that domestic service was already "obsolescent" in the highly developed, modern United States.[24] "Domestic employment has lost the shreds of genteel respectability it may once have possessed," declared Coser. "'The status is now so stigmatized that it can hardly attract potential recruits among ordinary citizens. . . . When conditions have reached such an impasse, the status and role become obsolescent."[25]

Coser's article did the vitally important work of excavating the historical links between class inequality and domestic servitude. As he noted, in the past "the master-servant relationship . . . was the prototypical relationship between superior and inferior."[26] Similarly, the Norwegian sociologist Vilhelm Aubert argued that the status of servant was "ascribed" and, in an explicitly Parsonsian analysis, attributed its decline (a phenomenon that occurred far sooner and more dramatically in post–World War II Scandinavia than elsewhere) to the triumph of universalism over particularism.[27] The difficulty with these perspectives, however, is that they mistakenly assumed that highly unequal social relationships are incompatible with "modern" social conditions. Coser made a great deal of the argument that once servants enter into impersonal contractual (in other words, "modern") relationships with their employers, their role, with its inherent intimacy and lack of specificity ("diffuseness"), is ineluctably undermined. Yet the microsociological literature reviewed above documents the survival into the late twentieth century of precisely the features of domestic service—intimacy, loyalty, as well as stigma and *ressentiment* (a term used by both Rollins and Coser)—that Coser viewed as incompatible with modern society.

As these commentators would have expected, in the case of the United States, census data suggest that the long-term decline of "private household service" occupations continued through 1990. In that year, the U.S. Census Bureau found just under half a million women, or 1 percent of all employed females (along with 26,234 men) in such occupations. This includes all employed persons enumerated in the census who indicated that employment in a private household was

Table 9.1. Women Employed in Private Household Service in the United States, 1940–1990

Year	Number of Women	% of All Employed Women
1990	494,920	0.94
1980	562,888	1.4
1970	1,109,855	3.8
1960	1,664,763	7.9
1950	1,337,785	8.5
1940	1,976,078	17.7

Source: U.S. Census Bureau, Census of Population, various years.

their primary occupation. They could be working full time or part time, living in or outside the employer's household, working as launderers and ironers, cooks, housekeepers and butlers, childcare workers, or cleaners and servants, though the vast majority were in the latter two occupational categories.[28] As table 9.1 shows, the level of employment in these occupations as a share of all female employment in 1990 represents a dramatic decline even relative to the preceding half-century. However, *contra* Coser, there is evidence that a partial reversal of this trend may be emerging. In contrast to the national trend, as table 9.2 shows, in the three largest metropolitan areas of southern California, both the absolute number of women employed in private household occupations and the relative size of this group (measured here as the percentage of all employed women in this occupational category) *increased* between 1980 and 1990. Although this does not seem to be the case elsewhere in the nation, this development in and around Los Angeles, "the American city the world watches for signs and portents,"[29] directly contradicts Coser's prediction.

The modernization-theory-based explanation for international variation in the size of the domestic labor force is also problematic because it cannot account for differences among nations at comparable levels of economic development. This approach might appear to offer a satisfactory explanation for the fact that paid domestic labor still employs vast numbers of people in the third world, even though it has declined dramatically in the first. For example, in Mexico, the 1990 census found 11 percent of all economically active women employed as domestic servants,[30] compared with only 1 percent in the United States. But this theoretical perspective cannot explain the contrasts apparent today among countries that, by any standard, are highly developed economically. For example, Sweden, with a far more egalitarian income distribution than the United States and many other highly developed nations, had minuscule numbers of domestic workers in 1990. In Sweden in 1987 the share of income received by the richest one-tenth of the

Table 9.2. Women Employed in Household Service in Southern California, 1980–1990

Metropolitan Area	1980		1990	
	Number of Women	Proportion of All Employed Women	Number of Women	Proportion of All Employed Women
Los Angeles–Long Beach	24,788	1.66	41,988	2.30
San Diego	4,357	1.32	7,193	1.39
Anaheim–Santa Ana[a]	3,543	0.86	7,307	1.30

[a] Also includes Garden Grove in 1980.

Source: U.S. Census Bureau, *1980 Census of Population, General Social and Economic Characteristics,* California, table 121, pp. 6–258; U.S. Census Bureau, *1990 Census of Population and Housing, Social and Economic Characteristics,* Metropolitan Areas, table 34, pp. 1665, 1705.

population was 2.7 times that of the poorest one-tenth, whereas in the United States in 1986 the richest one-tenth's share was 5.9 times that of the poorest one-tenth.[31] Although, as we have seen, only about 1 percent of all women workers were employed as paid domestic servants in the United States in 1990, this was many times the level in Sweden, where the 1990 figure was so tiny that it was not even published in the Swedish census.[32] Of course, there are other differences between Sweden and the United States that are relevant here—most obviously the fact that in Sweden, universal childcare and other social services are provided by the state, whereas in the United States such state provision is minimal. By comparing metropolitan areas within the United States, however, as we do below, we can hold such factors as state provision constant.

Economic Inequality and Paid Domestic Labor

What accounts for the 1980s expansion in domestic service employment in southern California? Is this a harbinger that the long-term historical decline of employment in domestic labor could soon be reversed for the nation as a whole? More generally, what explains the geographic variation in the proportion of the female labor force employed in this occupational category? As table 9.3 shows, although in 1990 the Los Angeles–Long Beach metropolitan area had the nation's highest level of employment in domestic labor, and although the proportion of

Table 9.3. Women Employed in Private Household Service in Selected United States Metropolitan Areas, 1990

Metropolitan Area	Number of Women	Proportion of All Employed Women
Honolulu, HI	611	.32
Milwaukee, WI	1,259	.38
Minneapolis, St. Paul, MN–WI	2,921	.46
Boston, MA	4,076	.56
Detroit, MI	5,105	.57
Chicago, IL	8,025	.59
Philadelphia, PA	6,368	.59
Phoenix, AZ	3,421	.75
Atlanta, GA	5,686	.81
Tulsa, OK	1,626	1.07
Washington, DC–MD–VA	14,439	1.37
New Orleans, LA	3,411	1.41
New York, NY	27,395	1.49
Houston, TX	11,264	1.61
Miami-Hialeah, FL	8,312	2.00
Los Angeles–Long Beach, CA	41,998	2.30

Source: U.S. Census Bureau, 1990 Census of Population and Housing, Social and Economic Characteristics, Metropolitan Areas, table 34, pp. 1596–727.

all employed women in this occupational group is modest everywhere, there is substantial variation among metropolitan areas. In Honolulu, Milwaukee, and Minneapolis, for example, less than one-half of 1 percent of all employed women are in this occupation; at the other extreme, in Miami and Los Angeles–Long Beach, more than 2 percent of all employed women did this type of work in 1990.[33]

Here, we attempt to explain these variations. Although Coser's modernization hypothesis is already invalidated by the very fact of extensive variation within a highly developed and modern economy (as well as the partial reversal of the occupation's decline), we can test other hypotheses that are implicit in the literature reviewed above. We begin with some key factors that might be expected to affect the supply and demand of paid domestic labor. Historically in the United States, immigrants and women of color have long been important sources of labor supply for this occupation.[34] Similarly, today, the massive surge of immigration since the 1960s is an obvious source of labor supply—most notably in southern California (the most popular immigrant destination in this period) but also for Miami, Houston, and New York. Another factor is the presence of a large population of native-born women of color, who constituted the bulk of the labor force in this occupation for most of the twentieth century. As the microsociological literature emphasizes,[35] employers often prefer to hire women from a different race or ethnicity as domestic workers because the status differential helps them negotiate the employment relationship in the intimate setting of the household. Thus, we would expect the proportion of foreign-born women in the labor force in a given metropolitan area, as well as the proportion of African American and Latina women, to influence the size of the occupation. In some of the cities shown in table 9.3, like New Orleans and Washington, D.C., domestic workers are numerous and disproportionately African American. However, in other cities (for example, Boston, Detroit, and Philadelphia), where African Americans are the main source of paid domestic labor, employment in this occupation is much smaller. As table 9.4 shows, African Americans, Latinas, and the foreign born (who made up 12.2 percent, 7.3 percent, and 9.3 percent of the female labor

Table 9.4. Female Private Household Workers in the United States, 1990, by Detailed Occupation, Race, Hispanic Origin, and Nativity

	Total Females	% Black	% Hispanic	% Foreign-Born
Launderers and ironers	1,634	16.0	15.0	11.8
Cooks	8,088	30.2	13.8	25.4
Housekeepers and butlers	30,780	33.6	32.5	41.6
Childcare workers	144,422	9.8	13.6	18.4
Cleaners and servants	312,884	32.8	26.6	31.2
Total	497,808	26.1	23.0	27.9

Source: Unpublished U.S. Census Data (Public Use Microdata Sample, 1990).

force in the United States in 1990, respectively) are all overrepresented in this occupation, although African Americans are actually slightly underrepresented among those domestics classified as childcare workers.[36]

Immigrant women and women of color alike have fewer opportunities in the labor market than do their native-born, white counterparts, due to race discrimination and their low ranking on job queues for more desirable jobs.[37] In the case of immigrants, lack of full citizenship rights and limited English proficiency may further limit employment opportunities. Given these disadvantages, immigrants and women of color may be more likely than other women to seek employment as domestics, particularly because their other occupational options are generally inferior to paid domestic labor. Although pay rates and working conditions vary widely within the broad category of paid domestic labor, many maids and nannies earn far more than their counterparts in agriculture, unskilled factory, and service jobs, and working conditions are often far superior as well.[38] Typically domestic work is compensated on an all-cash, informal basis, so that actual pay rates are effectively far higher than the nominal wages paid; this further enhances the desirability of this type of employment relative to the available alternatives.

On the demand side, one might expect maternal labor force participation to be an important factor. As many commentators have noted,[39] female labor force participation generally has contributed to the rapid growth of the personal-services sector, of which paid domestic labor is one important component. We expect demand for such services to be especially extensive in households with young children where the mother is in the labor force, and indeed, the labor force participation rates of mothers of preschool children have risen dramatically since the 1970s. Although the availability of group childcare has increased, high-quality childcare remains scarce and is often available for limited hours. As the 1993 "Nannygate" case illustrated, wealthy households (especially those where the mothers are elite professionals) today often employ nannies to care for their young children.[40] More generally, the persistence of the traditional gender division of household labor, as well as the increased number of households headed by females, suggests that men have not increased their contributions to domestic labor significantly.[41] For these reasons, we expect that metropolitan areas with higher maternal labor force participation rates will have greater demand for domestic servants than other metropolitan areas.

The analysis we present here includes these variables and also highlights a somewhat less obvious factor that, we argue, is critical for explaining variation in the extent of employment in domestic labor—namely, the extent of economic inequality. As is now well documented, starting in the late 1970s there was a sharp increase in inequality in the distribution of both income and wealth in the United States.[42] Although this is a national trend, the extent of income inequality varies substantially among metropolitan areas. For example, in 1989 (as reported in the 1990 census) the ratio of the income received by the richest 5 percent of households to that received by the poorest 20 percent was 3.5 percent in Honolulu and 3.8 percent in Minneapolis, compared with 8.4 percent in New Orleans and 8.6 percent in New York. Los Angeles was in the middle, with a ratio of 5.6 percent.

All else being equal, it is logical to expect that the greater the extent of economic inequality in a community—in other words, the greater the disparity in resources between rich and poor households—the more easily rich households can afford to employ less-fortunate persons as domestic servants. Demand for assistance with domestic tasks is always present, especially in households with young children.[43] There is a vast amount of labor required to maintain households, especially in the United States, where quality childcare is often difficult to obtain; the desire for domestic help is virtually universal in households with young children where both parents are employed outside the home. In many settings, too, employing domestic help enhances the social status of the employer's family, further contributing to latent demand for such labor. Latent demand becomes effective demand when domestic assistance is easily affordable; this is where the mechanism of economic inequality comes into play. When the gap in incomes between rich and poor is large, the relative cost to the rich of domestic help is correspondingly small. A wide disparity between rich and poor also helps produce a ready supply of domestic laborers, since the greater the extent of inequality in a local labor market, the fewer the opportunities for disadvantaged workers like immigrants and women of color to find desirable jobs. Thus, the greater the level of inequality between classes, the greater the extent of employment in paid domestic labor.

This dynamic is completely ignored in the literature. As we noted earlier, commentators like Romero explicitly dismiss the notion that class might be a factor shaping the dynamics of employment for domestics. Our claim is that in addition to the racial and ethnic factors stressed by Rollins, economic inequality along class lines (independent of race) is an important predictor of the size of the occupation. That is, in metropolitan areas where income inequality levels are high, we would expect high levels of employment in paid domestic labor. We arrived at the hypothesis independently, but we subsequently learned that economist George S. Stigler proposed it in a long-forgotten treatise on domestic labor published in 1946. Surveying the cross-national data available at the time, Stigler noted:

The wealth of a nation has no obvious effect upon the number of servants. . . . A possible explanation of these wide differences among nations is associated with Thorstein Veblen: "The need of vicarious leisure, or conspicuous consumption of service, is a dominant incentive to the keeping of servants." That is, the equality of the distribution of income, rather than the amount, may be a factor of considerable importance. A society with relatively many families at both ends of the income scale would provide both a large supply of servants and a large demand. Unfortunately this conjecture cannot be tested either internationally or nationally, because of lack of data on income distributions.[44]

Although, in our analysis, demand for domestic labor is far more complex than Veblen's construction of it as a form of conspicuous consumption (see also endnote 43 on Stigler's own differences with Veblen), we agree that income inequality is a critical consideration. To our knowledge, besides Stigler's, there is no other published work on paid domestic labor that has pointed this out.

One would think, given the explosion of statistical data collection in the post–World War II period, that lack of data would no longer be an impediment to testing this idea. However, reliable cross-national data on income distribution remain difficult to obtain, and comparable data on employment in domestic service in various nations are also extremely elusive.[45] Still, there is scattered evidence of the relationship between the size of the domestic labor force and the extent of economic inequality in the available cross-national data. It is striking that in relatively egalitarian societies (recall the Swedish example cited earlier), paid domestic labor is a rarity. By contrast, in the third world, the fact that income disparities between rich and poor are so extreme (rather than simply the level of "modernization") may be a crucial reason that extensive use of paid domestic labor remains the norm among the privileged classes.

Here we shift the focus from international to intranational variations, for which comparable data on both income distribution and employment in domestic service do exist (although they are not entirely unproblematic, as we shall see). Below, we test the hypothesis that greater income inequality is associated with greater prevalence of paid domestic labor, independent of supply-and-demand factors. We do this by using a cross-sectional analysis of 1990 census data for the one hundred largest United States metropolitan areas. We focus on urban areas because paid domestic labor is concentrated in cities; moreover, by analyzing the one hundred largest metropolitan areas, we have a sufficiently large sample to generate statistically significant results. Below, we present a regression model that confirms the independent significance of income inequality (along with other key variables) in predicting the proportion of the labor force employed in private household occupations.

Data and Analysis

Most of our data are derived from the published 1990 U.S. Census of Population and Housing. Our data on income inequality and on the proportion of the female labor force that is foreign born (two variables for which published data are not

238

available) draw on the 1990 Census Public Use Microdata Sample (PUMS). Our units of analysis are metropolitan areas; our sample includes the nation's one hundred largest metropolitan areas.[46] Although census data are well known to suffer from undercounting problems (particularly for immigrants and racial minorities, both of which are overrepresented among domestic workers), they are the most comprehensive data available. Moreover, the likelihood that domestic workers are undercounted makes the analysis below a very strong test of our hypothesis, as more accurate data would increase the range of many of the variables.[47]

Table 9.5 shows the variables used in our analysis and the mean, median, range, and standard deviation for each. Our dependent variable is the extent of domestic service employment, measured as the percentage of the female labor force employed in private household service occupations.[48] The independent variables include two proxies for the two most common sources of supply of paid domestic labor: the percentage of the female labor force that is made up of African Americans and Latinas, and the percentage of the female labor force that is foreign born. We include also a proxy for demand, namely, the labor force participation rate for mothers whose youngest child is age six or younger. Finally, and most important, we include a measure of household income inequality, namely, the ratio of the household income reported by the top 5 percent of the income distribution to the household income reported by the bottom 20 percent. Although many other measures of inequality could have been used here, we chose this one because, in our view, it captures the two most relevant parts of the population: the richest households, who are the most likely to employ domestic labor, and the poorest

Table 9.5. Descriptive Statistics for Variables Used in the Analysis (for the 100 largest metropolitan areas in the United States in 1990)

	Mean	Median	Range	Standard Deviation
Domestic service employment (as a percentage of the female labor force)	0.78	0.70	(0.30, 2.13)	0.35
Percentage African Americans and Latinas in the female labor force	20.77	19.41	(1.34, 70.23)	12.57
Percentage foreign-born in the female labor force	9.44	5.49	(1.56, 52.27)	9.09
Mothers' labor force participation rate (youngest child age six or younger)	60.24	60.92	(47.59, 71.53)	5.36
Household income inequality ratio (for 5% divided by bottom 20%)	4.60	4.50	(3.08, 8.55)	0.98

households, from which the bulk of the supply of workers in this occupation presumably are drawn.[49]Although individual income inequality has grown as well (among both men and women, as discussed above), for our purposes the inequality among households remains the most important form of inequality. Not only does the increasing prevalence of dual-income households among the upper reaches of the income distribution magnify the effect of growing inequality in individual incomes, but also it is this stratum of the population where we expect the greatest effective demand for domestic labor. These households can easily afford to employ domestic workers, and, in addition, the very presence of husbands in them contributes to demand, both because many men remain reluctant to perform domestic tasks themselves and because they add to the volume of such work that must be done.

Table 9.6 shows the results of ordinary least squares regression of domestic service employment on the independent variables. We present a series of models, first to establish inequality as a strong predictor of domestic service employment (model 1) and then to show that it remains significant when the supply-and-demand variables described above are included in the model. In all the models shown (except model 2, which omits the inequality variable), our hypothesis that household income inequality is positively related to domestic service employment

Table 9.6. Unstandardized Coefficients for Ordinary Least Squares Regressions of Domestic Service Employment on Independent Variables, 100 Largest United States Metropolitan Areas in 1990 (standard errors in parentheses)

Independent Variable	Model 1	Model 2	Model 3	Model 4	Model 5
Household income inequality	0.1826*** (0.0304)	—	0.0545** (0.0306)	0.1524*** (0.0265)	0.0742*** (0.0298)
African Americans and Latinas as percentage of female labor force	—	0.0164*** (0.0023)	0.0175*** (0.0024)	—	0.0124*** (0.0028)
Foreign-born as percentage of female labor force	—	0.0089*** (0.0033)	—	0.0190*** (0.0030)	0.0106*** (0.0033)
Maternal labor force participation[a]	—	0.0074* (0.0047)	0.0045 (0.0046)	0.0116** (0.0050)	0.0091** (0.0046)
Intercept	−0.0577 (0.1429)	−0.0879 (0.2910)	−0.1045 (0.3152)	−0.7972** (0.3421)	−0.4631 (0.3211)
Multiple R^2	0.2693	0.5504	0.5322	0.4883	0.5779

[a] Expressed in 1% units; for example, in model 3, for each 1% change in the percentage of the female labor force made up of African Americans or Latinas (PFAL), there was a change of 0.0873% in domestic service employment.

*$p \leq .10$ (one-tailed tests). **$p \leq .05$ (one-tailed tests). ***$p \leq .01$ (one-tailed tests).

is verified, and in each model this result is statistically significant. Model 5 offers the fullest explanation for the dependent variable and includes all four independent variables discussed above.[50]

As table 9.6 indicates, the difference in the multiple R^2 between model 2 and model 5 is slight. However, an F test shows that the difference is statistically significant. In any case, model 5 is the best model for predicting the extent of domestic service employment, because it alone contains all of the important causal variables.[51] Also note that adding household income inequality (in model 5) changes all the coefficients shown in model 2. Most notably, the coefficient for the percentage of the female labor force that is African American or Latina is much lower in model 5. This suggests that part of the effect of this variable on domestic service employment shown in model 2 is spurious, due to the high correlation between this variable and household income inequality (the correlation coefficient is 0.591).[52]

One finding from this analysis is that maternal labor force participation is not statistically significant in model 3 and barely significant in model 2. We believe that this is because maternal labor force participation is negatively correlated with the other variables, and especially because of the strong negative correlation between it and the percentage of the female labor force that is foreign born. The effect of maternal labor force participation on the dependent variable is thus obscured by the omission of other relevant variables from the model.

The results show also, as expected, that a large supply of women of color[53] is positively related to domestic service employment. Because this variable, as well as the percentage of the female labor force that is foreign born, provides both partial proxies for labor supply, we ran regressions with each of these variables separately (models 3 and 4) in addition to model 5, which includes both.[54] The supply variables are statistically significant in all the models.[55]

Discussion

Our analysis of the United States' one hundred largest metropolitan areas was designed to test a series of hypotheses about the factors explaining variability in the extent of employment in paid domestic labor. We criticized the earlier literature on this issue, grounded in modernization theory, which claimed that the level of economic development in a given society is the key to predicting the proportion of the female workforce engaged in this occupation.[56] Although we could not directly test the development hypothesis with our data, the very fact of extensive variability across metropolitan areas within a single, highly developed nation reveals the inadequacy of that approach. Instead, we have focused on household income inequality as one critical influence on the size of this occupation. The greater the disparity in resources between rich and poor households, the more easily the former can employ members of the latter as domestic laborers.

We do not claim that household income inequality is the only important predictor of the size of the domestic labor occupation; on the contrary, the availability of a labor supply composed of women disadvantaged by race and/or citizenship status—itself an index of a different type of social inequality—is also important in the U.S. case. Indeed, we draw on the microsociological scholarship on domestic servants reviewed above,[57] much of it preoccupied with precisely these forms of social inequality as they are played out in interactional settings involving domestics and their employers, to generate hypotheses about race and immigration. As our regression analysis showed, the proportion of the female labor force made up of African Americans and Latinas is a significant predictor of the extent of employment in paid domestic labor. Similarly, the proportion of the female labor force that is foreign born is also a significant factor. Both women of color and foreign-born women workers have relatively few labor market options compared with their white, native-born counterparts and thus offer a ready labor supply in this occupation. However, in contrast to Romero's claim that class is no longer an important factor in the dynamics of paid domestic labor, we have shown that income inequality is a significant predictor independent of factors like race and citizenship.

We have argued also that *demand* for domestic services is especially present in households where mothers are gainfully employed outside the home. The regression analysis presented above supports our contention that maternal labor force participation is positively related to the size of the occupation; however, this variable is significant only when the supply and inequality variables are included in the model. While this is somewhat speculative and not shown by the regression analysis, we believe that although households with young children and mothers in the labor force may wish to have help with domestic tasks, it would be more difficult for them to find or afford such help in the absence of these other conditions. Most important for our argument, they are much more likely to be able to employ domestic servants if there is a wide gap between their own household income and that of the persons potentially available to perform such work.

Conclusion

It follows that if the growth of income inequality continues, leading to a more polarized class structure, the paid domestic service occupation will also increase in size, as was the case in the 1980s in southern California. We would expect similar developments in the United States as a whole and in the many other countries where household income inequality levels are increasing. We hope that future researchers will explore these issues in other national (and regional) settings. Another area ripe for more investigation is the extent to which our argument here would also apply to the wide range of personal service occupations (from catering to personal shopping to home healthcare), which, like paid domestic work, are primarily marketed to individuals and households with high incomes and which grew significantly in the late twentieth century.

As inequality grows, as the most affluent households become relatively richer and as real wages for the rest of the population decline, it becomes easier for the wealthy to afford the personal services provided in private homes by maids and nannies. As journalist Nicholas Lemann prognosticated in 1996, it is possible to envision a future America where "the work force evolved to the point where about a quarter of it was made up of domestic servants—closer to what the situation in America had been before World War II."[58] In short, thanks to the growth of economic inequality in the United States generally—and inequality among women in particular—Coser's report of the death of this ancient occupation appears to have been grossly exaggerated.

Notes

This chapter was originally published in *Work and Occupations* 25, no. 4 (1998): 483–510.

1. David Chaplin, "Domestic Service and Industrialization," *Comparative Studies in Sociology* 1 (1978): 97–127; Lewis A. Coser, "Servants: The Obsolescence of an Occupational Role," *Social Forces* 52, no. 1 (1973): 31–40.

2. Judith Rollins, *Between Women: Domestics and Their Employers* (Philadelphia: Temple University Press, 1985). Historically, and in some countries in Africa and Asia today, males have also been extensively employed in this occupation. See Karen Tranberg Hansen, *Distant Companions: Servants and Employers in Zambia, 1900–1985* (Ithaca, N.Y.: Cornell University Press, 1989).

3. For example, see Abigail B. Bakan and Daiva K. Stasiulis, "Making the Match: Domestic Placement Agencies and the Commercialization of Women's Household Work," *Signs* 20, no. 2 (1995): 303–35; Evelyn Nakano Glenn, *Issei, Nisei, War Bride: Three Generations of Japanese American Women in Domestic Service* (Philadelphia: Temple University Press, 1986); Mary Romero, *Maid in the U.S.A.* (New York: Routledge, 1992); Julia Wrigley, *Other People's Children* (New York: Basic, 1995).

4. See Frank Levy, "Incomes and Income Inequality," in *State of the Union: America in the 1990s*, vol. 1, edited by Reynolds Farley (New York: Russell Sage Foundation, 1995), especially 13–18.

5. See Suzanne Bianchi, "Changing Economic Roles of Women and Men," in Farley, *State of the Union*, vol. 1, especially 133; Leslie McCall, "Spatial Routes to Gender Wage (In)equality: Regional Restructuring and Wage Differentials by Gender and Education," *Economic Geography* 74, no. 4 (1998): 379–404.

6. See Frank Levy, "Incomes and Income Inequality," 20–21.

7. Exceptions include parts of Hansen, *Distant Companions*, and Nicky Gregson and Michelle Lowe, *Servicing the Middle Classes: Class, Gender, and Waged Domestic Labour in Contemporary Britain* (New York: Routledge, 1994). Neither, however, deals with the case of the United States. Among the few U.S.-focused studies to touch on these issues are: Leslie Salzinger, "A Maid by Any Other Name: The Transformation of 'Dirty Work' by Central American Immigrants," in *Ethnography Unbound*, edited by Michael Burawoy (Berkeley: University of California Press, 1991), 139–77; and Terry A. Repak, "Labor Recruitment and the Lure of the Capital: Central America Migrants in Washington, D.C.," *Gender and Society* 8, no. 4 (1994): 507–24.

8. However, such geographical variation apparently does not exist in England, as geographers Nicky Gregson and Michelle Lowe were surprised to find in one of the few place-sensitive studies of paid domestic work. See Gregson and Lowe, *Servicing the Middle Classes*, 42–43.

9. Rollins, *Between Women*.

10. Ibid., 147.

11. Ibid., 8–9.

12. Romero, *Maid in the U.S.A.*

13. Ibid., 143.

14. Ibid., 69.

15. Shellee Colen, "'With Respect and Feelings': Voices of West Indian Child Care and Domestic Workers in New York City," in *All American Women: Lines That Divide, Ties That Bind*, edited by Johnnetta B. Cole (New York: Free Press, 1986), 60. See also Shellee Colen, "'Just a Little Respect': West Indian Domestic Workers in New York City," in *Muchachas No More: Household Workers in Latin America and the Caribbean*, edited by Elsa Chaney and Mary Garcia Castro (Philadelphia: Temple University Press, 1989), 171–97; Shellee Colen, "'Like a Mother to Them': Stratified Reproduction and West Indian Childcare Workers and Employers in New York," in *Conceiving the New World Order: The Global Politics of Reproduction*, edited by Faye D. Ginsburg and Rayna Rapp (Berkeley: University of California Press, 1995), 78–102; Cameron Lynne Macdonald, "Shadow Mothers: Nannies, Au pairs, and Invisible Work," in *Working in the Service Society*, edited by Cameron Lynne Macdonald and Carmen Sirianni (Philadelphia: Temple University Press, 1996), 244–63.

16. Wrigley, *Other People's Children*.

17. Rollins, *Between Women*, 156.

18. Romero, *Maid in the U.S.A.*, 90.

19. Ibid., 12; see also Ida Susser, "The Separation of Mothers and Children," in *Dual City: Restructuring New York*, edited by John H. Mollenkopf and Manuel Castells, 207–24 (New York: Russell Sage Foundation, 1991), especially 217–18.

20. Romero, *Maid in the U.S.A.*, 75 (emphasis added).

21. Wrigley, *Other People's Children*.

22. Andrew Collver and Eleanor Langlois, "The Female Labor Force in Metropolitan Areas: An International Comparison," *Economic Development and Cultural Change* 10, no. 4 (1962): 380.

23. David Chaplin, "Domestic Service," 123.

24. Coser, "Servants."

25. Ibid., 39.

26. Ibid., 31.

27. Vilhelm Aubert, "The Housemaid: An Occupational Role in Crisis," *Acta Sociologica* 1, no. 3 (1956): 149–58.

28. This does not include employees of organized firms that offer cleaning services; such workers would be classified as service workers rather than in private household service. The extent to which private household workers caring for elderly or sick people were included in this category is unclear. The 1990 census did not have a separate occupational category for home-health workers. There was a category for homecare aides in the occupational group "welfare service aides," but this probably only included those paid from public funds. The occupational codes for private household cleaners and servants did include the category "companion," and some privately paid home health workers may have been enumerated into this classification, whereas others might have been classified as health or nursing workers despite the fact that their work takes place in private households (U.S. Census Bureau, Housing and Household Economic Statistics Division, private communication). After 1990, the U.S. Census Bureau made extensive changes in its system of occupational categories.

29. David Reid, ed., *Sex, Death, and God in L.A.* (Berkeley: University of California Press, 1992), xxxi.

30. Instituto National de Estadistica Geografia e Informatica (INEGI), *XI Censo General de Poblacion y Vivienda, 1990, Estados Unidos Mexicanos,* CD-ROM.

31. Anthony B. Atkinson, Lee Rainwater, and Timothy M. Smeeding, "Income Distribution in OECD Countries: The Evidence from the Luxembourg Income Study (LIS)" Social Policy Studies No. 18 (1995) Paris: Organization for Economic Cooperation and Development, table 2; see also Keith Bradsher, "Widest Gap in Incomes? Research points to U.S.," *New York Times,* October 27, 1995.

32. We made some efforts to obtain data on the Swedish case through correspondence with the government agency Statistics Sweden. That agency provided us with unpublished data on the number of domestic servants employed in private homes from 1960 to 1990, reporting that the number fell from 68,800 in 1960 to 1,364 in 1980 and to only 2 in 1990. In 1990, about 4.5 million people were economically active in Sweden, including about 2.2 million women. When we wrote back to Statistics Sweden, questioning whether the 1990 data it had provided could possibly be accurate, our correspondent agreed that there were probably more than two servants in the country, but added:

> It is very seldom that a family have domestic servants [in Sweden] because it is very expensive to pay them a fair salary. . . . It is just a few families in the very high upper class that have such help these days. I know for instance, no family in my neighborhood or of my relatives or of my colleagues who have or have had any domestic servants in the last ten years. That was much more common in the 1960s and 1970s.

33. The actual range may be greater than these data indicate, and the extent of employment in this occupation generally may be higher than they suggest due to census undercounting, a problem we explore more fully below. Indeed, undocumented immigrants are a large part

of the workforce in this occupation in many areas. Live-in domestics are particularly likely to be undercounted. See note 55 for more discussion of the undercount issue.

34. See Claudia Goldin, *Understanding the Gender Gap: An Economic History of American Women* (New York: Oxford University Press, 1990); David M. Katzman, *Seven Days a Week: Women and Domestic Service in Industrializing America* (Urbana: University of Illinois Press, 1978).

35. Especially Rollins, *Between Women.*

36. The occupational categories shown in table 9.4 are archaic ones, more suitable to analysis of domestic labor in the early twentieth century. We suspect that many of those classified here as cleaners and servants perform childcare duties as well.

37. See Barbara F. Reskin and Patricia A. Roos, eds., *Job Queues, Gender Queues: Explaining Women's Inroads into Male Occupations* (Philadelphia: Temple University Press, 1990).

38. See Romero, *Maid in the U.S.A.,* 12.

39. For example, see Heidi Hartmann, "Changes in Women's Economic and Family Roles in Post-World War II United States," in *Women, Households, and the Economy,* edited by Lourdes Benería and Catherine R. Stimpson (New Brunswick, NJ: Rutgers University Press, 1987), 33–64; and for a more global view, Tom Elfring, "New Evidence on the Expansion of Service Employment in Advanced Economies," *Review of Income and Wealth,* series 35, no. 4 (1989): 409–40.

40. See Rosanna Hertz, *More Equal Than Others: Women and Men in Dual Career Marriages* (Berkeley: University of California Press, 1986); Macdonald, "Shadow Mothers"; Susser, "Separation of Mothers and Children."

41. Arlie Hochschild, *The Second Shift* (New York: Viking, 1989).

42. Frank Levy and Richard J. Murnane, "U.S. Earnings Levels and Earnings Inequality: A Review of Recent Trends and Proposed Explanations," *Journal of Economic Literature* 30 (1992): 1333–81; Edward Wolff, *Top Heavy: A Study of Increasing Inequality of Wealth in America* (New York: Twentieth Century Fund, 1995).

43. George Stigler noted this too in commenting on Veblen's suggestion (cited in the excerpt from Stigler reproduced later in the main text of this chapter) that domestic service was mainly a case of "conspicuous consumption." Stigler comments in a footnote of *Domestic Servants in the United States, 1900–1940,* Occasional Paper 24 (New York: National Bureau of Economic Research, 1946), on p. 6:

> Only the childless Veblen would write: "In the modern [1899] industrial communities the mechanical contrivances available for the comfort and convenience of everyday life are highly developed. So much so that body servants, or indeed, domestic servants of any kind, would now scarcely be employed by anybody except on the ground of a canon or reputability carried over by tradition from earlier usage."
>
> A century later, despite the invention of disposable diapers and other such conveniences, the notion that households with young children have minimal labor requirements remains absurd.

44. Ibid., 6.

45. Stigler, ibid., 3, noted that "a large scale survey of the number of domestic servants in other countries is not feasible because of the baffling differences in classifications of

occupations between both countries and censuses." This problem has actually been aggravated by the occupation's decline in the decades since.

46. We used the one hundred largest metropolitan statistical areas (MSAs) or primary metropolitan statistical areas (PMSAs) for analysis; in other words, we broke down all consolidated metropolitan statistical areas (CMSAs) into their subcomponents and then selected the one hundred most populated MSAs or PMSAs for use in our analysis.

47. Virtually all available estimates of the number of private household workers in the United States indicate that the 1990 census figures substantially understate the actual extent of employment in paid domestic labor. The widely respected Current Population Survey, for example, found 753,066 women (and 28,934 men) employed as private household workers in 1990 (these figures are the annual averages), more than 1½ times the number enumerated by the 1990 census. See U.S. Department of Labor, Bureau of Labor Statistics, *Employment and Earnings* 38, no. 1 (January 1991), 187. And, the U.S. Internal Revenue Service (IRS) received tax forms for approximately 435,500 household employees in 1990—accounting for about 80 percent of the employed private household workers counted by the U.S. Census, according to unpublished data we obtained from the IRS. In 1990, the agency received a total of 1,524,481 Forms 942, *Employer's Quarterly Tax Return for Household Employees*. We were advised by IRS Statistics Office Section Chief Russell Geiman to divide this figure by 3.5 to estimate the number of domestic workers reported to the IRS. His rationale for this procedure was that whereas, on one hand, a household reporting employment of more than one domestic worker in a quarter files only one form (thus the numerator may underestimate the true number of workers), some households do not file the forms in all four quarters of the year (thus the denominator should be less than 4).

The IRS figures are widely acknowledged to represent only a fraction (though no one knows how small a fraction) of actual employment of private household workers, due to widespread noncompliance with the law. See David J. Morrow, "Nanny-Tax Tally of '95: Who Paid, Who Lied?" *New York Times*, April 21, 1996. Indeed, in 1990, before the 1993 Nannygate episode drew so much public attention to the existence of the legal requirements, noncompliance was presumably even higher than it is today.

Additional indications that the 1990 census figures fail to capture the full extent of employment in private household occupations come from estimates of the number of persons employed as nannies. Whereas the 1990 census counted 144,000 in-home childcare workers among the larger population of private household workers (see table 9.4), other estimates are considerably larger. On the high end, the International Nanny Association claims that there are between one million and three million full-time nannies in the United States. See Kirk Johnson, "The Nanny Track: A Once-Simple World Grown Complicated," *New York Times*, September 29, 1996. We contacted Wendy Sachs, president of the International Nanny Association, who indicated that this figure is an estimate based on an unscientific poll of about two hundred people affiliated with the organization, including many owners of employment agencies that place nannies in private households.

A more conservative estimate is derived from the 1993 Survey of Income and Program Participation, which found about 385,000 in-home babysitters (nonrelatives who provide care within the child's home), nearly triple the figure in the 1990 census. This survey, reported in Lynne M. Casper, "What Does It Cost to Mind Our Preschoolers?" *Current Population*

Reports: Household Economic Studies, P70-52 (U.S. Department of Commerce, Economics and Statistics Administration, Census Bureau, September 1995), focuses on childcare arrangements for preschoolers. Because children are the unit of analysis, not caregivers, some adjustments were necessary to the published data, which indicated that 621,000 preschool children were cared for in their own homes by nonrelative babysitters in fall 1993. Of these, 246,000 were found to be making separate payments to the caregivers. An additional 278,000 were found to be making shared payments, indicating that the caregiver was caring for more than one family's children. On the advice of Lynne Casper of the U.S. Census Bureau, who supervised the study (private communication), we arrived at our estimate of 385,000 in-home babysitters by adding 246,000 to half the 278,000 shared in-home babysitters. We ignored the additional 97,000 in-home babysitters (nonrelatives) to whom, according to the survey, no payments were made. Casper was unable to explain this anomaly but believes that our estimate of 385,000 is conservative.

48. Note that this is slightly different from the data shown in tables 9.1, 9.2, and 9.3, where the denominator is employed women rather than all women in the labor force. The latter category also includes those who are unemployed and actively seeking employment.

49. The top 5 percent of households may seem too small a portion of the population for the employer group in cities like Los Angeles and Miami, where domestic service is more extensive; but for the nation as a whole this appears to be the relevant employer group—though there are no reliable data available on the employer population. We did test some other measures of household income inequality, as well as income inequality among women, as discussed in note 50.

50. We tested a number of other models, not shown here. Regression results for the full model using a different measure of household income inequality—the ratio of the household income reported by the top 20 percent to the household income reported by the bottom 20 percent—yielded similar results to those shown in the text. Using this measure, household income inequality had a positive (unstandardized coefficient = 0.0280) and statistically significant relationship to domestic service employment. However, a third measure of household income inequality, the ratio of the top 10 percent to the bottom 20 percent, although positively related to domestic service employment, did not have a statistically significant relationship to domestic service employment in model 5 but did in model 4. Regression results for full models using a variety of measures of personal income inequality among women (as opposed to the household income inequality measures discussed above and in the text) indicated that this type of inequality had no relationship to our dependent variable, whether the measure was inequality in personal income among all women or among all women older than age twenty-nine. Here, the coefficients were negligible and not statistically significant. In addition, regression results for models including the average welfare payment per person in each metropolitan area, those including 1990 unemployment rates for each metropolitan area, and those including median household income for each metropolitan area yielded no statistically significant results for any of these variables. In addition, we ran the regressions omitting Los Angeles and New York, to test the possibility that these were extreme outliers, but found that the results were still in the expected direction and still statistically significant.

Finally, we ran the analysis adding interaction terms, to rule out the possibility that it was an interaction between race or immigration and inequality that was the key to the story here. We ran the full model including (a) the interaction of household income inequality and percentage of the female labor force that is African American or Latina; (b) the interaction of household income inequality and the percentage of the female labor force that is foreign born; and (c) the full model with both the interactions listed in a and b above. In all three of these models, the interaction terms were not statistically significant at the 0.05 level, and in all of them, household income inequality remained statistically significant.

51. Our methodological premise here is that obtaining unbiased parameter estimates through a correctly specified model is the most important task for social scientists, and performing well on goodness-of-fit tests, such as those based on the amount of variance explained, is secondary. Omitting relevant variables from a causal model leads to biased estimates and/or a misrepresentation of the causal relations between variables. There are at least two reasons not to reject a fuller model because of a small incremental change in multiple R^2. First, the variance explained by any one independent variable depends in part on the range and variance of the other variables in the model and so may not provide an accurate indication of the causal importance of that variable. Second, multiple R^2 measures the fit of the entire model, and cannot be divided up into unique causal components. The multiple R^2 of a nested model can be affected by the covariance between an included variable and an omitted variable (for example, the percentage of the female labor force that is African American or Latina, and household income inequality, respectively, in model 2), and therefore many do not vary much from the fuller model. See Richard A. Berk, "Causal Inference for Sociological Data," in *Handbook of Sociology,* edited by N. J. Smelser (Newbury Park, Calif.: Sage, 1988), especially 161–70; Otis Dudley Duncan, *Introduction to Structural Equation Models* (New York: Academic, 1975), 55–66; Stanley Lieberson, *Making It Count: The Improvement of Social Research and Theory* (Berkeley: University of California Press, 1985), 117.

52. Although this correlation is relatively high, it is not high enough to preclude including both variables in the same model. By contrast, the correlation coefficient between household income inequality and the percentage of the female labor force that is foreign born is a much lower .228. Below is the full correlation matrix for the variables used in the analysis:

	HII	ALFLF	FBFLF	MLFP
HII	1.000	0.591	0.228	−0.159
ALFLF		1.000	0.576	−0.147
FBFLF			1.000	−0.316
MLFP				1.000

53. This variable includes only African American and Latina women, because Asian Americans are much less often employed in paid domestic labor.

54. We also ran all the models using percentage population foreign born (instead of percentage of employed females who are foreign born) as a proxy for this component of supply. Although the coefficients (not shown) change slightly, the results are virtually identical to

those in table 9.6 in terms of which variables prove significant. Because domestic laborers are overwhelmingly female, and the foreign-born population includes large numbers of children (as well as men) who are not part of the labor supply we are interested in here, we feel that the variable we use in the analysis is the best available for this purpose.

55. In an effort to adjust for the probable undercounting of domestic workers, we re-ran our regression analysis after making some adjustments based on the U.S. Census Bureau's Post-Enumeration Survey (PES), part of a settlement agreement of a lawsuit filed by several major city governments. The bureau surveyed 165,000 housing units, matching their answers to the original census records to see if they were either uncounted or erroneously enumerated and based on this, issued the corrected PES data. (For details about the undercount debates and a useful assessment of the validity of the census data and of the PES, see Harvey M. Choldin, *Looking for the Last Percent: The Controversy over Census Undercounts* (New Brunswick, N.J.: Rutgers University Press, 1994), especially 206–26. See also California Legislature, Joint Interim Hearing, Senate Committee on Elections and Reapportionment, Assembly Elections, Reapportionment, and Constitutional Amendments Committee, "1990 Census and the Undercount," December 13, 1989; U.S. Department of Commerce, "Census Bureau Releases Refined Estimates from Post-Numeration Survey of 1990 Census Coverage," press release, June 13, 1991, Bureau of the Census, Economics and Statistics Administration, mimeo.; U.S. Congress, *House Committee on Post Office and Civil Service, Subcommittee on Census and Population: Problem of Undercount in the 1990 Census*, 100th Congress, First Session (July 14, 1987).

Unfortunately, for the variables of interest to us, the PES-adjusted data are only slightly better than those originally reported. When we re-ran our regression analysis after making some adjustments based on the PES, we got virtually identical results. But the PES allowed us to make adjustments for only two of the variables used in our analysis. We were able to adjust our dependent variable, domestic service employment, and one of our independent variables, the percentage of the female labor force made up of African Americans and Latinas. The mean, median, range, and standard deviation for the adjusted variable "domestic service employment" are unchanged from those shown in table 9.5, although some of the data do change slightly. However, the adjustment does change the descriptive statistics for the percentage of the female labor force that is African American or Latina, as shown below. The changes are marginal but in the expected direction: they result in a greater range and standard deviation and higher means and medians.

	Mean	Median	Range	Standard Deviation
Unadjusted	20.77	19.41	(1.34, 70.23)	12.57
Adjusted	21.29	19.99	(1.38, 72.48)	12.96

We adjusted our data by applying the undercount rate reported in the PES for Hispanic females, Black females, and all females to the dependent variable (domestic service employment) and one of our independent variables (percentage of the female labor force made up of African Americans and Latinas), using unpublished undercount rates for all females, black females, and Hispanic females, obtained directly from Greg Robinson at the U.S. Census

Bureau (following his advice, we used the July 1992 "357 PES," the last in a series of three PES estimates), we computed the adjustments as follows:

$$\text{Adjusted Count} = \frac{\text{Unadjusted Count}}{1 - \text{Undercount Rate}}$$

For example, the original census count for the number of Hispanic females in the United States was 10,966,000. The "357 PES" revised estimate for this population is 11,468,942, and the undercount rate for Hispanic females was .00438525. This can be expressed as follows:

$$11,468,942 = \frac{10,966,000}{1 - .00438525}$$

By applying this formula to the data for each of the 100 metropolitan areas in our sample, we were able to derive revised estimates for domestic service employment. We applied the formula to each ethnic component of the numerator (female domestic servants [divided into Hispanic, black, and non-black female domestic servants]) and to the denominator (the female labor force [again adding the revised estimates for each ethnic group]). Similarly, we applied the formula to the Hispanic and black female labor force in each metropolitan area, summing the two to derive the adjusted counts for our variable, percentage of the female labor force that is African American or Latina. (Because the PES unfortunately did not attempt to estimate the degree to which the foreign born were undercounted, we were unable to adjust our variable, percentage of the female labor force that is foreign born.)

Regression results using the PES-adjusted data (not shown) were similar to those in table 9.6, which is not surprising given the minimal adjustments made possible by the PES. But if, as most experts contend, the undercount is disproportionately high for African Americans, Latinas, the foreign born, and the poor, then accurate data would spread out the range of all our variables except maternal labor force participation. This might yield stronger results. Metropolitan areas with populations that include large numbers of uncounted poor persons would have higher household income inequality ratios; those with large undercounts of African Americans and Latinas would have a higher proportion of the female labor force from these groups; and those with large undercounts of the foreign born would also have a higher proportion of the female labor force that is foreign born than enumerated in the 1990 census and even than shown in our adjusted data. The dependent variable, similarly, would show a greater range among metropolitan areas. Thus the 1990 census data, and even the PES-adjusted data, offer a very strong test of our hypothesis. More accurate data—unfortunately not available—might offer stronger results.

56. Chaplin, "Domestic Service"; Collver and Langlois, *Female Labor Force*; Coser, "Servants."

57. Colen, "'With Respect and Feelings,'" "'Just a Little Respect,'" "'Like a Mother to Them'"; Rollins, *Between Women*; Romero, *Maid in the U.S.A.*; Wrigley, *Other People's Children*.

58. Nicholas Lemann, "The Haves Have Less," *New York Times Magazine*, September 29, 1996, 102. This is drawn from a brilliant dystopian essay, purportedly written by the daughter of Michael Young, author of the 1958 sociological classic *The Rise of the Meritocracy* at age

one hundred in the year 2096. It is worth citing the passage from which the sentence quoted in the text is extracted in full:

During the period in the late 20th century when the American welfare system was being abolished, there was a lot of talk (from both sides of the political debate, paradoxically) about how the society was moving toward masses of hungry children roaming the streets while the rich took refuge inside walled compounds. In the event, there was relatively little of that sort of thing. Instead, the work force evolved to the point where about a quarter of it was made up of domestic servants—closer to what the situation in American had been before World War II. They lived in the attics and basements of other people's houses or in clusters of huts at the edges of towns, and did not send their children to school, to spare everyone embarrassment. People had a sense that the servants, while pleasant and deferential enough face to face, were only barely under control, and that unspeakable things went on in the huts. All of the "troubled" schools that had once occasioned so much hand-wringing were shut down.

Chapter 10

Class Disparities, Market Fundamentalism, and Work–Family Policy

Lessons from California

This chapter explores the political economy of U.S. work–family policies in the context of market fundamentalism—the idea that public policy should not interfere with market forces, so that regulation of labor markets should be minimal or nonexistent—which has been increasingly influential since the 1970s. Both the 1993 federal Family and Medical Leave Act and the 2002 California law that created the nation's first paid family leave program faced strong resistance from organized business interests, who denounced such laws as "job killers." However, because family-leave policies have strong public support across the political spectrum, advocates were able to isolate business interests politically by building broad coalitions in support of these laws. Moreover, these family-leave programs turned out to have minimal impact on business—and in some respects a positive impact. The chapter also highlights the importance of class differences among women in relation to paid family leave. While many employers provide paid time off to professionals and managers who need to care for a newborn or for an ill family member, low-wage workers typically have little or no access to such wage replacement. The latter benefit most from laws like California's, which offers paid family leave to all private-sector workers. Yet due to limited awareness of the existence of the California program, and the fact that awareness is lowest among low-wage workers, preexisting class inequalities among women persist in regard to access to paid leave.

The problem of reconciling work and family commitments is not new; indeed, it has been a central concern for feminists since the birth of industrial capitalism. The issue increasingly has entered the mainstream of public debate, as maternal labor force participation rates have climbed to unprecedented levels and the "male-breadwinner/female-homemaker" family has declined throughout the global North. In wealthy nations on both sides of the Atlantic, despite the fact that the vast majority of wives and mothers today are employed outside the home, gendered expectations (and behavior!) regarding housework and family care have been altered relatively little. What Gornick and Meyers call "partial gender specialization," with women continuing to shoulder the vast bulk of caregiving labor alongside their paid work,[1] is now the norm. The resulting time pressures on mothers and other women with significant care and work commitments, as well as on those men with such commitments, have sparked growing concern about work–family "balance."

The United States has long been on the leading edge of these transformations. Second-wave American feminists succeeded in opening up professional opportunities for women as early as the 1960s and early 1970s, even as ongoing economic restructuring (especially the growth of the tertiary sector) increased demand for women workers in the labor market as a whole. On the supply side, meanwhile, sharply declining real incomes among non-college-educated men since the 1970s led growing numbers of married women and mothers to join the labor force to keep their families afloat.

Over the years since, although outright gender discrimination in the labor market and job segregation by gender have by no means disappeared, young women's career aspirations have risen substantially, and gender-based wage disparities in entry-level jobs have narrowed. The resulting pattern is one of accumulating disadvantage for women, in which the gender gap in pay widens over the life course, particularly for mothers.[2] Mothers' greater labor-market disadvantage partly reflects the persistently asymmetric gender division of housework and family care, but there is also evidence of an employer-driven "motherhood penalty" in the managerial and professional ranks, while fathers in these occupational categories enjoy a wage premium.[3]

By the twentieth century's end, as working hours grew longer and time demands intensified in the "new economy," both genders expressed the desire for relief with ever-growing urgency. The "time bind," as Arlie Hochschild memorably labeled it a decade ago,[4] is especially acute in the United States. Survey after survey has found work–family balance to be high on the wish list for working Americans (even as feminism itself remains, for many, anathema). And public support has burgeoned for policy measures to ease the burden on employed parents. In a 2003 survey of adult Californians, for example, 85 percent of respondents expressed support for paid family leave, with extensive majorities in every demographic category and across the political spectrum.[5] In a rare exception to the ongoing rollback of state regulation of the labor market, political momentum for positive governmental intervention on this front had grown rapidly. Yet most employed women in the United States must still find private, individual "solutions" to "their" problems with work–family balance. Feminists and labor activists have long promoted more collective approaches, but with limited success.

Indeed, the nation's famously minimalist welfare state, along with an exceptionally strong tilt toward gender neutrality in those laws and policies that do exist, has produced what is incontestably the industrialized world's most meager public provision for work–family support. In this respect, the United States could hardly be more different from Europe, where a long and deeply entrenched family policy tradition, historically rooted in demographic concerns as well as in social-democratic efforts to use the state as a social leveler, has generated a vast state-sponsored apparatus of support for women (and sometimes men) who are actively involved in both caregiving and paid work. On the other hand, feminist influence on this policy arena developed later in Europe than in the United States and was (at least initially) weaker.

This chapter focuses on two distinctive dimensions of the U.S. case, both of which are far less salient in the European context: first, class disparities in existing access to work–family support; and second, the influence of market fundamentalism, which is the key political impediment to legislative proposals in this area. After briefly discussing each of these phenomena as they are manifested in the nation as a whole, I turn to the case of California, the state that has led U.S. work–family policy in the twenty-first century. California's paid family leave program, established by a law passed in 2002 and implemented in 2004, offers a model of what might be possible in other "blue" states and perhaps eventually at the federal level.[6] However, California's experience also presents a cautionary tale in regard to the ongoing challenges facing advocates of change in the work–family arena, at least in the absence of a broader macropolitical and cultural shift that legitimizes state intervention in the workplace.

Class Disparities

Social class profoundly affects both patterns of time use and access to employer-provided benefits that facilitate work–family reconciliation.[7] Along both dimensions, professionals and managers (regardless of gender) are sharply differentiated from the rest of the workforce. Even pumping breast milk at work is an option available mainly to well-paid professional women, while for lower-income mothers it is "close to impossible."[8] Such class disparities are hardly new, but they have intensified in the past few decades as economic inequalities have grown— both within the employed female population and among men.[9] The pattern is stark, with access to paid time off for caregiving purposes widely available to professionals and managers (albeit on a modest scale by European standards) and largely inaccessible to the rest of the workforce.[10]

The limited wage replacement currently available for family-related absences from work in the United States primarily takes the form of employer-provided benefits—ranging from paid sick leave and paid vacation or "paid time off" (which combines sick leave and vacation) to disability insurance (commonly used for pregnancy-related leaves). Some employers—often as a result of collective bargaining agreements—also provide paid maternity or parental leave benefits. Eligible workers typically draw on a patchwork of employer-provided benefits (in a few states supplemented by state-sponsored disability insurance programs)[11] for income support when the arrival of a new child or a serious family illness necessitates an absence from work for any significant amount of time. But for many, especially those outside the managerial and professional occupations, wage replacement for caregiving purposes is not available at all, since in the United States even paid sick leave, paid vacation, and similar employer-provided benefits are far from universal. Indeed, between 1996 and 2000, only 42 percent of U.S. women who were employed during their first pregnancy received *any* type of paid leave when the child was born.[12]

Prior to the early 1990s the United States lacked any formal policy provision for parental leave, apart from the 1978 Pregnancy Discrimination Act (PDA), which requires employers to offer wage replacement for pregnancy-related "disabilities" to the same extent as they do for other disabilities. This law did not mandate any disability coverage, however, and to this day many employers (especially smaller ones) provide none. The legal framework guiding the PDA was explicitly gender neutral, reflecting concern among feminists at the time that sex discrimination might increase if leaves were provided only to mothers.[13] Indeed, this longstanding concern has been borne out by evidence that mothers who take advantage of employer-provided "work–family benefits" suffer substantial wage penalties.[14]

In the 1980s and early 1990s several states passed laws providing job-protected (but unpaid) family leaves, and the federal government followed suit in 1993 with the Family and Medical Leave Act (FMLA). That law guarantees job-protected, unpaid leaves of up to twelve weeks to eligible workers who need time off to care for a new baby or for a seriously ill family member.[15] Yet FMLA is limited in several critical ways. First, not everyone is aware of its provisions. Survey data suggest that, as late as 2000, seven years after it became law, only about 60 percent of U.S. workers knew that FMLA existed.[16] Second, fewer than half of all private-sector workers meet the FMLA's eligibility requirements: to be covered, workers must be employed in establishments with at least fifty employees within a seventy-five-mile radius and must have worked at least 1,250 hours during the previous year. Fewer than one-fifth of new mothers are covered by the FMLA.[17] Third, because the FMLA provides only unpaid leaves, even those who are covered often cannot afford to take advantage of the law.

Both the frequency and length of family leaves taken by new mothers in the United States increased significantly following the passage of the FMLA (although this was not the case for new fathers, despite the gender-neutral character of the legislation). Leaves to care for seriously ill family members (especially parents) also increased.[18] The number of mothers who quit their jobs or were fired as a result of a first pregnancy declined after the FMLA's passage, from about 39 percent in the 1980s to 28 percent in the late 1990s, according to U.S. government data. However, the same data also show that more than half of maternity leaves remain entirely unpaid.[19]

The data on the distribution of paid and unpaid leaves vividly illustrate the salience of class disparities: between 1996 and 2000, 59 percent of college-educated women who were employed during pregnancy received some sort of paid leave after the birth of their first child, but only 18 percent of those with less than a high school education did so.[20] All else equal, workers employed by large firms had greater access to paid leave benefits than did those working in small and medium-sized businesses. With the important exception of unionized workers (a steadily declining group), professionals, managers, and other highly educated, highly paid workers are far more likely than nonsupervisory, low-wage, less-educated workers to have access to any employer-provided paid leave benefits. Ironically, despite their limited participation in caregiving activities, male workers are also more likely to have formal access to such benefits than their female counterparts.[21]

Despite the passage of the FMLA, many U.S. workers had no access to family leave whatsoever. Even among those who are covered by the FMLA, in the absence of adequate provision for wage replacement, a large proportion cannot afford to take a leave from work for more than a brief period when caregiving needs arise. A survey of employees conducted for the U.S. Department of Labor in 2000 found that among FMLA-eligible respondents who indicated that they had recently needed family leaves but could not take them, the vast majority reported that the reason was financial. The same survey found that, among those who did take FMLA-covered leaves, economic worries remained salient, with more than half of respondents (54 percent) expressing concern about not having enough money to pay their bills. More than one-third of the female leave-takers surveyed (38 percent) and 30 percent of male leave-takers received no pay whatsoever during their FMLA-covered leaves.[22]

Similarly, in a 2004 screening survey of California employees who either had recently experienced or expected soon to experience the triggering events that would qualify them for benefits under the state's new paid family leave program, 18 percent of respondents indicated that they had needed but not taken a leave to care for a new child or a seriously ill family member in the preceding two years. Once again, the most frequently cited reason for not taking the needed leave was financial. Within the group that needed leave but did not take it, 61 percent of respondents reported that they "definitely" would have gone on leave if they "could have received some income to make up for lost pay," and another 25 percent reported that they "probably" would have done so. Among female respondents earning $9 per hour or less within the group who needed but did not take leave, fully 100 percent indicated that they "definitely" would have gone on leave if they could have received wage replacement.[23]

Not only is access to employer-provided benefits concentrated in the upper echelons of the labor force, but public discussion of work–family issues in the United States also focuses primarily on the needs and dilemmas of the affluent. This phenomenon dates back at least to 1963, when Betty Friedan's bestseller, *The Feminine Mystique*, highlighted the anomie of college-educated homemakers in the post–World War II years and urged them to embrace careers to solve "the problem that has no name."[24] Millions of women have since followed Friedan's advice, and indeed today unprecedented numbers are employed in managerial and professional jobs.

Public attention to the work–family reconciliation dilemmas facing this elite group of women is extensive and growing.[25] But the far more difficult plight of the majority of the female workforce, toiling away in low-wage, gender-stereotyped "pink collar" jobs, remains largely invisible. Even Arlie Hochschild's insightful 1997 book, *The Time Bind*, fell into the trap of generalizing from the experience of women in managerial jobs to that of Everywoman.[26]

In fact, the character of work–family issues varies greatly by social class. As Jerry Jacobs and Kathleen Gerson have shown,[27] managers and professionals (of both genders) in the United States typically work far longer hours than lower-level employees. Although many nonsupervisory workers would prefer to work *more* hours than are readily available to them,[28] those who aspire to successful careers in elite occupations are expected to work extremely long hours. This contrasts starkly with the European pattern and is directly tied to the far higher level of inequality in the U.S. earnings distribution, perhaps because the most elite workers receive such disproportionately large returns for working extra hours.[29]

That the norm of extensive work hours is so deeply embedded in managerial and professional culture presents a poignant dilemma for mothers in elite occupations, particularly in view of the late-twentieth-century ideology of "intensive mothering."[30] That ideology has been disproportionately adopted by the nation's most affluent families, eager to reproduce their class position; by contrast, working-class parenting takes a very different form.[31] Ironically, the escalating time demands on the nation's upper-tier workers emerged just when large numbers of highly educated women first gained access to elite professional and managerial jobs. Mary Blair-Loy has starkly exposed the hegemony of the "male model" at the highest levels of the contemporary corporate world, where family involvement for women (as well as men) is effectively precluded by a deeply entrenched culture that demands total "24/7" commitment to the firm.[32] The same problem, if in a less extreme form, is pervasive throughout the managerial ranks. Indeed, even when firms are putatively "family-friendly," available benefits often go underutilized for this reason.[33] As Blair-Loy observes, some top women managers respond by "opting out," abandoning their fledgling careers, or in some cases forgoing motherhood entirely.[34] Others use their abundant financial resources to hire substitute caregivers.[35]

In contrast, low-income workers in the United States are regularly forced to choose between economic security and providing vital care for family members. Parents who have access to paid sick leave or paid vacation are five times more likely to stay home with a sick child than are those who lack such benefits, and ill children recover more quickly when parents are present.[36] Yet paid leave is disproportionately available to those with the greatest economic resources. One survey found that two-thirds of low-income mothers (compared to slightly over one-third of middle- and upper-income mothers) lose pay when they miss work because a child is sick.[37] Apart from lost income, missing work under such conditions often has other negative employment consequences.

At the other extreme, public welfare provisions for the indigent have been radically restructured so as to require workforce participation from poor single mothers who formerly had access to state assistance while caring for their children at home.[38] And the nation's large and growing disenfranchised population of unauthorized immigrants is often unable or unwilling to access even the meager public provisions that do exist (from FMLA, to state-sponsored disability programs, to what remains of "welfare").

Class disparities, then, are a key feature of the U.S. work–family landscape. Although there are some exceptions (most notably, unionized workers who gain access to employer-provided family leave and related benefits through collective bargaining), on the whole professionals and managers enjoy far more extensive work–family options—including paid leave, flexible hours, and so on—than their counterparts in clerical, service, sales, and other low-wage jobs. Such highly paid professionals and managers are also better able to afford the wide array of commodified services—from prepared meals to paid domestic labor and private childcare—available on the open market, on which affluent families increasingly rely to reconcile the demands of work and family.

Elsewhere in the industrialized world, governments have long since established universal social benefits that support children and families, which were from the start intended to moderate class disparities. The growing popular concern about work–family balance and the groundswell of public support for paid family leave suggest the prospect that such policies might eventually take root in the United States. But for that to occur, a key obstacle must be overcome—namely, the anti-statist market fundamentalism that is hegemonic among employers and that also influences the wider political culture.

Market Fundamentalism

Popular support for national family leave legislation has been on the rise in the United States since at least the 1980s. But even the comparatively minimalist FMLA became law in the face of sustained opposition from organized business interests, which effectively blocked its passage for many years. Earlier, the business lobby had also strenuously opposed the PDA;[39] but they lost this battle in 1978. Passing such legislation became still more difficult in the period of conservative ascendancy that followed. Congress approved family and medical leave bills twice under President George H. W. Bush, who vetoed the legislation both times. The issue was then debated in the 1992 election campaign, and a revised version of the legislation was passed by the new Congress in January 1993. A month later, the FMLA was signed into law by President Clinton—the very first bill he signed after taking office.[40]

In the post-Clinton years, political momentum shifted to the state level. California passed the nation's first paid family leave law in 2002, and the program it established came into effect in mid-2004. In 2005 paid leave bills were introduced in twenty-six states.[41] Despite business opposition, in Washington State a paid family leave law was passed and signed in 2007, although funds have not been appropriated to launch the program. New Jersey (which, like California, has a longstanding state disability insurance program) also created a paid family leave program through a law passed and signed in 2008, and Rhode Island followed in 2013. Federal legislation creating a national paid family leave program has been proposed as well.

The best-documented and indeed prototypical case in the history of political contestation over work–family policy in the United States is the seven-year campaign against the FMLA, led by the national Chamber of Commerce and small business groups. Cathie Jo Martin succinctly summarizes the arguments that business made against the bill at the time:

> Small business predicted dire economic impacts to companies from the high costs of hiring replacement workers . . . [and] also argued that the new benefit would constrict the creation of jobs and hurt female workers by motivating

employers to discriminate against women in hiring . . . and reduce the flexibility with which managers and workers could negotiate compensation packages.[42]

It was perfectly acceptable for companies to offer such benefits voluntarily (as indeed many already did), but organized business passionately opposed any employer "mandate" in this (or any other) area. As Martin rendered the dominant business view: "Although parental and disability leaves are excellent employee benefits, Congress should not dictate benefits. Doing so is contrary to the voluntary, flexible and comprehensive benefits system that the private sector has developed."[43] Similar arguments were advanced by business interests at the state level in response to proposals for paid family leave legislation.[44]

The specific claims of negative effects on business from employer mandates are largely unsustainable (as discussed below); but this practical reality has yet to undercut the ideological framework that continues to dominate the business side of the policy debates. Indeed, market fundamentalism, or "the idea that society as a whole should be subordinated to a system of self-regulated markets,"[45] is the most salient political obstacle to the development of work–family policy in the twenty-first-century United States. It has been the central trope of organized business opposition to the FMLA and subsequent legislative efforts to address work–family issues and has increasingly penetrated the wider political culture as well. As Margaret Somers and Fred Block argue, Anglo-American societies, with their Lockean legacy and longstanding distrust of the state, have been particularly influenced by this ideology since the 1970s, and among these societies the United States is the most extreme case.[46]

Business opposition to family leave legislation is part of a broader animus against "employer mandates," which are routinely denounced as "job-killers." This is a logical corollary of the broader ideology of market fundamentalism. With rare exceptions, employers consistently oppose—often on explicitly ideological grounds—virtually all labor and social legislation that would move the United States toward European-style family policies, including minimum- and living-wage laws. The New Deal order—let alone the corporate liberalism of a century ago—has lost any legitimacy it once enjoyed among employers. In my fieldwork I have even encountered managers who, blissfully ignorant of practices in the rest of the world, assert that the introduction of paid family leave in the United States would endanger the nation's global competitiveness. For example, one California manager, aghast at the state's 2002 law, exclaimed, "That's why we moved our call center to Ireland!"—apparently unaware that paid family leave had existed in Ireland for half a century.

Although this ideological consensus has virtually no defectors at the public, political level, many employers' practical experience with FMLA and other work–family balance policies nevertheless appears to have been quite positive. More than a decade after the FMLA's passage, there is little evidence to support earlier concerns of business that its enactment would be highly burdensome. On the contrary, managers on the ground report little difficulty in adhering to the law's provisions. A 2000 U.S. Department of Labor employer survey found that nearly two-thirds (64 percent) of respondents found it "very easy" or "somewhat easy" to comply with the FMLA, with even larger majorities (84 percent and 90 percent, respectively) reporting that the law had "no noticeable effect" or a "positive effect" on their productivity and profitability.[47] Indeed, many employers expanded their own provision of family and medical leave benefits in the aftermath of the law's passage.[48] Administering such leaves rapidly became a routine feature of the human resource management repertoire of many large U.S. companies.

Field interviews with managers—to be sure, mostly in large, family-friendly firms—echo the 2000 Department of Labor survey data in confirming that FMLA compliance has been unproblematic for most covered employers.[49] "Back when we didn't have [FMLA], if you told me this is what I had to do, I think I would have shot myself," one said. "But now that we do it on a day-to-day basis, it's no big deal." Many of these informants indicated that FMLA leaves related to pregnancy were especially easy to handle, since they could plan ahead to cover the work involved during an absence of predictable duration. In contrast, leaves tied to family medical crises took all concerned by surprise, but most interviewees viewed such events as an unavoidable part of doing business and effectively manageable under the FMLA.

Most of those interviewed felt that the positive benefits of FMLA outweighed its drawbacks, and some were positively enthusiastic. "You always have perfunctory whining," one human resource manager at a nonprofit research firm told us. "But everyone has problems from time to time and we understand that employees need time off occasionally." And a manager at a computer-chip design company defended the decade-old federal law against ongoing criticism from colleagues in the business world, asserting that, as far as productivity and profitability were concerned, FMLA was a "non-event." "When we're talking about bottom-line issues, I've never heard anyone say, 'The real problem is FMLA.' No one has ever said, 'The share price of our stock stinks, and if we could only repeal this leave law we'd be doing better.'"

Several managers suggested that the availability of FMLA leaves had improved organizational morale, as well as facilitating retention of valued employees. "The people who get the leaves appreciate it," a manager at a large food-processing firm asserted. "In the long term, we get better productivity, because employees feel they are supported by the company," a computing engineering firm manager reported. "Overall, it helps with the morale." Similarly, a manager at a large retailer (which offered paid time off only to the minority of its employees who were full-timers) noted, "Yes, people have the burden of picking up the slack for someone else on leave, but they also know that someone will do this for them if they need it." Still another manager at an entertainment firm commented, "Turnover would be much higher in the absence of FMLA leaves."

In keeping with the pragmatic approach of these on-the-ground managers in family-friendly firms who recognize the positive features of the FMLA and related policies, some work–family advocates have devoted a great deal of energy to advancing the "business case" for paid family leave and, more generally, for a family-friendly workplace. They point to the considerable costs associated with (a) employee turnover—in other words, the cost of recruiting and training new workers to replace those who quit for family-related reasons; (b) absenteeism; and (c) lost productivity associated with employees who remain at work while preoccupied with the unmet needs of their families or while trying to juggle caregiving with paid work.[50]

Although systematic evidence on these matters is difficult to obtain, some companies have done their own calculations and have concluded that generous work–family benefits can indeed offer large cost savings. Merck, for example, estimated that its own six-month parental leave policy saved $12,000 per employee in turnover-related costs; similarly, Aetna reported saving $2 million in hiring and training costs, because 91 percent of its employees returned after taking family leave.[51]

In some cases, employer recognition of such costs has led them to improve their own benefit packages—especially in cases where this could improve retention of female professionals and managers with firm-specific training and/or for whom recruitment costs are especially high (for example, in professions like law and accounting or in skilled occupational fields facing labor shortages, such as nursing). It may well be the case, as Joan Williams has so eloquently argued,[52] that even employers in low-wage, female-dominated sectors like the retail or service industries—which rarely provide even health insurance or paid sick leave to their workers, much less paid family leave—would be economically better off if they devoted some degree of attention to work–family needs. But such low-road employers often appear to view high turnover positively, since it keeps the bulk of their payroll clustered at entry level and makes it easy to adjust to market fluctuations.[53] Even in the case of managers and professionals in whom firms have sunk extensive training investments, and thus have a real interest in retaining, as Mary Blair-Loy has eloquently argued, ideology often trumps economic rationality.[54]

Many employers who offer generous work–family benefits to their own employees nevertheless adamantly oppose legislative proposals that would require such provisions, standing in firm solidarity with the rest of the business community in opposing all legislative "mandates." It follows that, as long as the ideology of market fundamentalism remains dominant, efforts to appease business interests are not likely to be effective. The only hope of overcoming business opposition to paid family leave and other legislative proposals is to advance a competing, morally compelling narrative that can prevail over the anti-statist narrative of the fundamentalists. Such a narrative must emphasize the human needs left unmet in the absence of comprehensive policies for work–family support. Only on that basis will it be possible to mobilize enough political support to secure the passage of state-sponsored paid family leave and related work–family legislation in the face of business objections.

Indeed, that is how advocates finally won passage of both the FMLA[55] and the California law.[56] Both achievements, to be sure, were ultimately subject to political compromises and included major concessions to the demands of organized business—although the business lobby nevertheless opposed them to the bitter end. In both cases, organized labor (also anathema to most U.S. employers and to market fundamentalists generally) did much of the political strategizing and lobbying to win passage of the legislation, in coalition with women's rights groups and advocates for children, the elderly, and the disabled.

An effective coalition of this sort is possible, in part, because of the widespread public perception that work–family pressures are at a crisis point. Polls show overwhelming popular support for such measures as paid sick days and paid family leave laws, the hegemony of market fundamentalism notwithstanding. In a 2003 survey of California adults, for example, 89 percent of non-college-educated respondents supported paid family leave, compared with 82 percent of respondents with some college or higher levels of education.[57] That difference is statistically significant, but more surprising than the strong support among those who are least likely to have any access to employer-provided benefits is the high level of support among the more educated group, many of whom presumably have employer-provided benefits to draw on. This may reflect the fact that, in the absence of job security, even at the most family-friendly firms, managers and professionals often hesitate to take advantage of work–family benefits, fearing (with good reason) that if they do, they will be seen as lacking in career commitment.[58] Universal state-supported paid family leave programs would level the playing field in this respect, so that more privileged workers would benefit too, even if the bulk of the material benefits went to those who lack any paid leave options at all.

Some advocates feared that the 2003 California recall election removing Gray Davis from office and catapulting the pro-business Arnold Schwarzenegger into the governor's seat might lead to a rollback or modification of the California paid family leave program, which took effect just before the recall. But this did not occur, perhaps because paid leave enjoys such broad popular support—both across the political spectrum and across class boundaries. As both this example and the widespread managerial complacency that set in shortly after the FMLA became law well illustrate, once business opposition to legislation of this type is successfully overcome, employers tend to accept defeat pragmatically, make the necessary adjustments in their day-to-day practices, and move on. All the more reason for advocates to concentrate on struggling for state intervention rather than seeking to persuade or placate organized business.

California's Paid Family Leave Program

The history of California's paid family leave program—a key legislative success in the work–family area—is worth examining in more detail. Although its provisions are minimal by European standards, it nonetheless represented a breakthrough in the U.S. context. When the California law was proposed in 2002, it faced intense opposition from the state's business lobby, just as the PDA and FMLA had on the federal level in earlier years. The California Chamber of Commerce and other business groups vigorously opposed the proposed bill. Ignoring the accumulated evidence from the previous decade's experience with the FMLA, they argued that a paid family leave program would impose excessive burdens on employers, especially small businesses.[59]

Although organized business ultimately failed to block the bill's passage, it did win modifications to the initial version of the legislation.[60] Nevertheless, on September 23, 2002, the nation's first comprehensive paid family leave program was signed into law by California's then-governor Gray Davis, and benefits became available to most employed Californians starting on July 1, 2004. The program provides up to six weeks of partial pay for eligible employees who need time off work to bond with a new child or to care for a seriously ill family member. It builds on California's long-standing state disability insurance (SDI) system, which for decades has provided income support for medical and pregnancy-related leaves. Like SDI, the paid family leave program is nearly universal in coverage: apart from some self-employed people, virtually all private-sector employees are included. (Public-sector workers are included only if they opt in through the collective-bargaining process, but many of them already had access to paid leave benefits more extensive than those provided by the new law.)

Unlike the FMLA, then, California's paid family leave program covers all private-sector employees, regardless of the size of the organization they work for, including most part-time workers. (To be eligible, employees must have earned $300 or more during any quarter in the "base period" five to seventeen months before filing a claim). The program is thus especially valuable for low-wage workers, many of them female, who have limited or no access to employer-sponsored benefits providing any type of paid time off.

Even before the passage of this new law in 2002, California provided more income support for family leave than most other states. Under SDI, nearly all pregnant women employed in the private sector, as well as some in the public sector, could already receive partial wage replacement for four weeks before delivery and for an additional six to eight weeks afterward.[61] California's paid family leave builds on the SDI model. As with SDI, there are no direct costs to employers: the benefit is funded entirely by an employee payroll tax (0.6 percent of wages). Eligible workers can receive, after a one-week waiting period, up to 55 percent of their normal weekly earnings, with a maximum of $959 per week in 2009 (the maximum is indexed to the state's average weekly wage) for up to six weeks a year.[62]

Eligible leaves include those for bonding with a new biological, adopted, or foster child; this benefit is available to fathers as well as mothers. For biological mothers, the new benefit supplements the pregnancy disability benefits previously available under SDI. Although it does not increase the amount of job-protected leave available to women who have given birth, paid family leave does provide six additional weeks of partial wage replacement. Also eligible are leaves to care for specified seriously ill family members (parents, children, spouses, or domestic partners). The law does not provide job protection, however, nor does it guarantee the continuation of health and/or pension benefits (although in many cases leave-takers have these additional protections under the FMLA or other laws). Employers may require workers to take up to two weeks of unused vacation leave before collecting paid family leave benefits.

Among the specific concerns business lobbyists cited in explaining their opposition to California's paid family leave legislation was that employers would incur significant costs in covering the work of absent employees, in the form of increased overtime payouts, payments for temporary replacements, additional training costs, and so on.[63] Thus, the ways in which employers covered the work of those on leave in the period prior to the California law's implementation are of some interest. A 2004 employer survey found that the work of employees who went on family-related leaves for a week or more was typically covered by "assigning the work temporarily to other employees." Fully 90 percent of employer respondents reported that this was the primary method they used to cover the work of nonexempt employees during family leaves, and the figure was only slightly lower (83 percent) for exempt employees.

While this suggests a homogeneity in approaches to the problem, field interviews revealed a rich variety of arrangements for covering the work of employees during both brief and extended absences. Most employers had developed systematic, often ingenious methods for handling such situations. Making provision for covering the work of absent employees is a business necessity, entirely apart from family leave. Managers constantly face the possibility that an employee may quit precipitously, become seriously ill and unable to work, enter the military, take an extended vacation or unpaid leave, and so on. Similarly, several informants mentioned that it was common for immigrant workers (who make up a substantial part of California's workforce) to make extended visits to their home countries—sometimes to care for an ill family member, but in other instances simply for a long visit. Under all these circumstances, many of which occur frequently but unpredictably, the work of absent employees needs to be covered. Thus, virtually all employers have long since developed mechanisms for ensuring that work will be covered during employee absences. In many cases they are able to do so with little difficulty, although sometimes the costs (in overtime pay, or fees to temporary employment agencies) can be significant. Still, these costs are modest relative to those associated with employee turnover, which is both more frequent than leave-taking or absenteeism and generally more expensive for employers to address.

The California program, despite its limitations, did manage to institutionalize paid family leave in the inhospitable political setting of the United States. Its practical impact has been constrained by two interrelated factors, however: a lack of awareness of its existence on the part of large segments of the state's population, and a low take-up rate. A survey conducted in fall 2003, about a year after the law was passed, found that only 22 percent of adult Californians were aware of the paid family leave program's existence.[64] In a follow-up survey in the summer of 2005, the figure was a somewhat higher 30 percent but still well below the same respondents' awareness of the FMLA, which was 59 percent in the initial 2003 survey and 57 percent in the 2005 follow-up. In a 2007 follow-up survey, the awareness level had actually fallen slightly. Moreover, those most in need of paid leave—low-income workers, those with limited education, and the foreign born—were the least likely to be aware of the state program. In 2007 only 14 percent of respondents with household incomes of $25,000 or less were aware of the program, while 36 percent of those with household incomes over $75,000 knew of it. The program's potential as a social leveler cannot be realized if those who stand to benefit most remain unaware of its existence.

The business groups that opposed the California paid leave law warned that the costs of implementation might be higher than those the state had projected. Instead, however, the opposite has been the case, partly because the take-up rate for the new program has been so modest. In the program's first year (July 1, 2004, to June 30, 2005), a total of 176,000 claims were received by the state, representing slightly more than 1 percent of the thirteen million eligible workers. The following year the number of claims actually fell slightly, to 137,000. Most of the claims (just under 90 percent) were for bonding with a new child, more than 80 percent of which were submitted by women.[65] The limited data available on the take-up rate by income suggest that the profile of claimants by income largely mirrors the income distribution of the eligible workforce, except for the fact that workers earning $12,000 or less a year (about 20 percent of those eligible) are underrepresented among claimants, making up about 16 percent, perhaps because they are least likely to be aware of the paid leave program.[66]

Because the events that precipitate eligibility for leave are spread over the life course, a relatively small proportion of the workforce will go on leave from work to care for new children or ill family members at any one time. Indeed, California employers surveyed in 2004 (just before the new law took effect) reported that, in the previous year, an average of only 1.1 percent of their workers had taken a leave of more than one week due to childbirth or adoption, while just 1.8 percent had taken a leave of more than a week in order to stay home with a seriously ill child, parent, spouse, or domestic partner.

Moreover, insofar as employers are able to coordinate their own benefits with the new state program, the more family-friendly firms actually enjoy cost savings. As one manager predicted in an interview conducted shortly before the program went into effect, "Paid family leave in California was intended to help people who don't have any pay during maternity leave or medical leaves. But in fact the main beneficiaries will be higher-paid workers who already have paid sick leave and vacation and who will use the state program to top off their current benefits." This is confirmed by the fact that, among the minority of adult Californians surveyed in 2007 who were already aware of the state program, 45 percent had learned about it from their employers; no other source of information was more frequently cited (though an equal proportion had learned about it from the mass media). Until awareness of the program expands well beyond those workers whose employers are coordinating it with their own benefits, the California law will do little to ameliorate the disparity between workers who already had access to paid leaves (via employer-sponsored benefits) and those who lacked such access.

In short, the reality of California's paid family leave program is far less problematic for employers than the business lobbyists initially claimed. Not only are excellent systems already in place for covering the work of employees who are absent for extended periods, but the costs of those systems are modest and counterbalanced by the savings associated with reduced turnover and absenteeism. Moreover, those employers whose workers use the state benefits instead of—or in tandem with—long-standing employer-financed benefits are enjoying additional savings.

Conclusion

In the United States, where market fundamentalism is a deeply entrenched feature of the political culture, organized business opposition to paid family leave and other legislative work–family "mandates" is unrelenting. This resistance is rooted in a broader agenda of opposition to state regulation of all sorts, so that appeals to economic rationality—even if they are demonstrably correct—are unlikely to have much impact.

Rather than arguing within the terms set by business advocates, which are embedded in the larger market-fundamentalist narrative, those who favor public-policy interventions to create paid leave programs and other work–family supports would do well to focus on two interrelated tasks. The first is to develop a strategy to surmount the organized lobbying efforts of business in the political arena, and the second is to advance an alternative narrative that reframes work–family issues in terms of human needs.

The strategic challenge is to build a coalition between labor unions, women's rights groups, senior organizations, those representing the disabled, and children's advocates—which collectively have the potential to exercise more political clout than the Chambers of Commerce and the rest of the business lobby. The legislative history of the FMLA and the California paid family leave program both suggest that this is a viable path. Organized labor, which despite sharp declines in union density still has considerable political influence,[67] was crucial in both these cases. More generally, both the FMLA and the California program became law because broad political coalitions were able to mobilize enough support to overcome the intransigent opposition of organized business.

As part of such an effort, claims that the proposed legislative initiatives for paid family leave and the like will have dire economic consequences can be countered by the arguments developed by advocates of the "business case." Similarly, it is helpful to point out that decades of experience elsewhere show that government-mandated paid leave benefits far more generous than the ones now on offer in California are neither utopian nor incompatible with sustainable economic growth. But business is unlikely to relent in its opposition in response to such rational appeals. For an advocacy campaign to succeed, the defensive counterclaims must be coupled with an offensive strategy that frames the issue within an alternative narrative.

That narrative should be focused on a straightforward insistence that paid family leave and other state-sponsored work–family policies deserve public support not only on economic grounds but primarily because such policies meet urgent human needs. Those needs exist across class lines, even if they are especially pressing among the most disadvantaged populations. As noted above, polling data show overwhelming popular support for paid family leave programs, paid sick days legislation, and other work–family interventions, even among putatively conservative segments of the population. This popular support is rooted in the recognition that working families urgently need access to paid leave and other types of family support and that employers are not providing such access—especially not to those with the least ability to purchase substitute care in the marketplace.

The challenge, in short, is to outmaneuver the formidable business lobby politically. This is best accomplished not by engaging business on its own market-fundamentalist ideological terrain but instead by appealing directly to the hearts and minds of the public with a narrative that focuses on the family-centered human needs of children, the seriously ill, and the elderly. Coupling such a narrative with strategic coalition building, as the California case suggests, can be an extremely effective organizing approach, even in the face of the nation's long-standing anti-statist tradition. Among other positive benefits, such efforts can help to move the United States in the direction of greater gender and class egalitarianism.

Notes

This chapter was originally published in *Gender Equality: Transforming Family Divisions of Labor*, edited by Janet C. Gornick and Marcia K. Meyers (New York: Verso, 2009).

1. Janet Gornick and Marcia Meyers, *Families That Work: Policies for Reconciling Parenthood and Employment* (New York: Russell Sage Foundation, 2003).

2. Virginia Valian, *Why So Slow? The Advancement of Women* (Cambridge: MIT Press, 1998); Jennifer Glass, "Blessing or Curse? Work-Family Policies and Mothers' Wage Growth over Time," *Work and Occupations* 31 (2004): 367–94.

3. Shelley J. Correll, Stephen Benard, and In Paik, "Getting a Job: Is There a Motherhood Penalty?" *American Journal of Sociology* 112 (2007): 1297–338.

4. Arlie Hochschild, *The Time Bind: When Work Becomes Home and Home Becomes Work* (New York: Metropolitan, 1997).

5. Ruth Milkman and Eileen Appelbaum, "Paid Family Leave in California: New Research Findings," *The State of California Labor* 4 (2004): 45–67.

6. In 2007, Washington State passed a paid family leave bill into law (although funding for it has not yet been appropriated). New Jersey passed a paid family leave bill into law in 2008, and Rhode Island followed five years later.

7. The racial and ethnic disparities that are highly correlated with class are also salient, although I do not discuss them here, partly because of a paucity of data and partly because professionals and managers of color are treated quite similarly to their white counterparts in this arena.

8. Jodi Kantor, "On the Job, Nursing Mothers Find a 2-Class System," *New York Times*, September 1, 2006.

9. Suzanne Bianchi, "Changing Economic Roles of Women and Men," in *State of the Union: America in the 1990s*, vol. 1, edited by Reynolds Farley (New York: Russell Sage Foundation,

1995), 107–54; Leslie McCall, *Complex Inequality: Gender, Race and Class in the New Economy* (New York: Routledge, 2001).

10. Jody Heymann, *The Widening Gap: Why America's Working Families Are in Jeopardy— and What Can Be Done about It* (New York: Basic, 2000).

11. State disability insurance programs, which can be used to support pregnancy-related leaves, have existed in California, Hawaii, New York, New Jersey, Rhode Island, and Puerto Rico for many years but are absent in the rest of the United States.

12. Julia Overturf Johnson and Barbara Downs, *Maternity Leave and Employment Patterns of First-Time Mothers: 1961–2000*, Current Population Reports P70–103 (October 2005), 9.

13. Some states did enact legislation creating benefits exclusively for pregnant women in this period, later challenged in the courts by employers who argued that the PDA pre-empted such "special treatment." The Supreme Court ruled otherwise, however, in 1987. For an excellent analysis of this history, see Lise Vogel, *Mothers on the Job: Maternity Policy in the U.S. Workplace* (New Brunswick, N.J.: Rutgers University Press, 1993).

14. Glass, "Blessing or Curse?"

15. The FMLA also mandates unpaid, job-protected leaves for an eligible employee's own illness, including pregnancy-related "disability."

16. Jane Waldfogel, "Family and Medical Leave: Evidence from the 2000 Surveys," *Monthly Labor Review* 124, no. 9 (2001): 17–23.

17. Christopher Ruhm, "Policy Watch: The Family and Medical Leave Act," *Journal of Economic Perspectives* 11 (1997): 175–86.

18. Wen-Jui Han and Jane Waldfogel, "Parental Leave: The Impact of Recent Legislation on Parents' Leave Taking," *Demography* 40, no. 1 (2003): 191–200; Waldfogel, "Family and Medical Leave."

19. Johnson and Downs, *Maternity Leave*, 9.

20. Ibid., 12.

21. Heymann, *Widening Gap*; Milkman and Appelbaum, "Paid Family Leave."

22. Waldfogel, "Family and Medical Leave."

23. These data are from a screening survey conducted in 2004 by the author and Eileen Appelbaum of employed Californians who either had recently experienced, or expected to experience in the near future, a life event such as the birth of a new child, or a serious family illness, triggering the need for family leave.

24. Betty Friedan, *The Feminine Mystique* (New York: Norton, 1963).

25. Among many examples, see Mary Blair-Loy, *Competing Devotions: Career and Family among Women Executives* (Cambridge, Mass.: Harvard University Press, 2003); Mary Ann Mason and Eve Mason Ekman, *Mothers on the Fast Track: How a New Generation Can Balance Family and Careers* (New York: Oxford University Press, 2007); Correll, Benard, and Paik, "Getting a Job"; Pamela Stone, *Opting Out: Why Women Really Quit Careers and Head Home* (Berkeley: University of California Press, 2007).

26. Hochschild's key finding was the counterintuitive and intriguing one that many women actually *preferred* to spend time at work rather than with their families and thus often did not take advantage of the "family-friendly" policies provided by the firm that was the focus of her case study. However, the media spin on the book mainly focused on the ill effects for children and families of this preference, and of maternal employment more generally. See

Ruth Milkman, "A Dream Come True [review of Hochschild, *The Time Bind*]," *Women's Review of Books* 15, no. 1 (October 1997).

27. Jerry Jacobs and Kathleen Gerson, *The Time Divide: Work, Family, and Gender Inequality* (Cambridge, Mass.: Harvard University Press, 2004).

28. For an extreme example, see Susan Lambert, "Making a Difference for Hourly Employees," in *Work-Life Policies*, edited by Ann C. Crouter and Alan Booth (Washington, D.C.: Urban Institute, 2009), 169–195.

29. See Richard B. Freeman, *America Works: Critical Thoughts on the Exceptional U.S. Labor Market* (New York: Russell Sage Foundation, 2007), chap. 4.

30. Sharon Hays, *The Cultural Contradictions of Motherhood* (New Haven, Conn.: Yale University Press, 1996).

31. Annette Lareau, *Unequal Childhoods: Class, Race, and Family Life* (Berkeley: University of California Press, 2003).

32. Blair-Loy, *Competing Devotions*.

33. See Hochschild, *Time Bind*; Mindy Fried, *Taking Time: Parental Leave Policy and Corporate Culture* (Philadelphia: Temple University Press, 1998); Glass, "Blessing or Curse?"

34. See also Stone, *Opting Out*.

35. Rosanna Hertz, *More Equal than Others: Women and Men in Dual-Career Marriages* (Berkeley: University of California Press, 1986).

36. American Academy of Pediatrics, Committee on Hospital Care, "Family-Centered Care and the Pediatrician's Role," *Pediatrics* 112 (2003): 691–96; Christopher Ruhm, "Parental Leave and Child Health," *Journal of Health Economics* 19 (2000): 931–60; Heymann, *Widening Gap*, 57–59.

37. Kaiser Family Foundation, *Women, Work, and Family Health: A Balancing Act* (Menlo Park, Calif.: Kaiser Family Foundation, 2003), available online at http://kff.org/uninsured/issue-brief/women-work-and-family-health-a-balancing.

38. Ellen Reese, *Backlash Against Welfare Mothers: Past and Present* (Berkeley: University of California Press, 2005); Margaret R. Somers and Fred Block, "From Poverty to Perversity: Ideas, Markets, and Institutions over 200 Years of Welfare Debate," *American Sociological Review* 70 (2005): 260–87.

39. Vogel, *Mothers on the Job*, 71.

40. Cathie Jo Martin, *Stuck in Neutral: Business and the Politics of Human Capital Investment Policy* (Princeton, N.J.: Princeton University Press, 2000); Anya Bernstein, *The Moderation Dilemma: Legislative Coalitions and the Politics of Family and Medical Leave* (Pittsburgh: University of Pittsburgh Press, 2001).

41. National Partnership for Women and Families, *Where Families Matter: State Progress Toward Valuing America's Families: A Summary of 2005 Initiatives* (2006), available at http://paidfamilyleave.org/pdf/state_roundup05_summary.pdf.

42. Martin, *Stuck in Neutral*, 221–22.

43. Ibid., 221.

44. Natalie Koss documents this for the case of California in "The California Temporary Disability Insurance Program," *Journal of Gender, Social Policy and Law* 11 (2003): 1079–87.

45. Somers and Block, "From Poverty to Perversity," 261.

46. Ibid., 282.

47. U.S. Department of Labor, *Balancing the Needs of Families and Employers: Family and Medical Leave Surveys, 2000 Update* (Rockville, Md.: Westat, 2001).

48. Ruhm, "Policy Watch"; Jane Waldfogel, "Family Leave Coverage in the 1990s," *Monthly Labor Review* 122, no. 10 (1999): 13–21; Waldfogel, "Family and Medical Leave"; Han and Waldfogel, "Parental Leave."

49. Eileen Appelbaum and I conducted management interviews and site visits to a convenience sample of nineteen establishments in California in 2003–04, and an additional thirteen in New Jersey in 2005, on which I draw here. The samples included firms in a variety of industries, but most were medium-to-large companies; indeed, all but four of the thirty-two were large enough to be covered by the FMLA. For more details on the New Jersey cases, see Eileen Appelbaum and Ruth Milkman, *Achieving a Workable Balance: New Jersey Employers' Experiences Managing Employee Leaves and Turnover* (New Brunswick, N.J.: Center for Women and Work, Rutgers University, 2006).

50. See Jodie Levin-Epstein, *Getting Punched: The Job and Family Clock* (Washington, D.C.: Center for Law and Social Policy, 2006); Joan C. Williams, *One Sick Child Away from Being Fired: When "Opting Out" Is Not an Option* (San Francisco, Calif.: Work Life Law, UC Hastings College of the Law, 2006), available online at http://www.worklifelaw.org/pubs/onesickchild.pdf.

51. Martin, *Stuck in Neutral*, 157.

52. Williams, *One Sick Child*, 25–34.

53. See Lambert, "Making a Difference."

54. Blair-Loy, *Competing Devotions*.

55. See Taylor Dark, *The Unions and The Democrats: An Enduring Alliance* (Ithaca, N.Y.: Cornell University Press, 1999), 166; Martin, *Stuck in Neutral*; Bernstein, *The Moderation Dilemma*, 125–26.

56. Labor Project for Working Families, *Putting Families First: How California Won the Fight for Paid Family Leave* (Berkeley: Labor Project for Working Families, 2003), available online at http://www.working-families.org/publications/paidleavewon.pdf.

57. Milkman and Appelbaum, "Paid Family Leave," 53.

58. Fried, *Taking Time*; Hochschild, *Time Bind*; Glass, "Blessing or Curse?"

59. Koss, "California Temporary Disability Insurance Program."

60. Whereas the original bill had provided twelve weeks of paid leave, with costs evenly split between a tax on employers and one on employees, business won elimination of the employer tax. Ultimately, employees alone were saddled with the full cost of the program, and the benefit was cut back to six weeks. Business pressure also led to an amendment providing that employers could require employees to use up to two weeks of paid vacation time before receiving the state-paid family-leave benefit. With these modifications, the California bill was passed in August 2002 by a legislature with a strong Democratic majority and was signed into law by then-governor Davis the following month. See Labor Project for Working Families, *Putting Families First.*

61. In addition, since the late 1970s, the California Fair Employment and Housing Act (FEHA) has guaranteed women who are disabled because of pregnancy, childbirth, or

related conditions, the right to up to four months of job-protected leave. The California Family Rights Act (CFRA), passed in 1991 (two years before the FMLA), provided additional rights; it was amended in 1993 to conform to the federal FMLA. Used together, FEHA and CFRA permit a pregnant woman disabled by pregnancy to take up to four months' leave, as well as an additional (unpaid but job-protected) leave for bonding with a new child extending beyond what the federal law provides, up to a total of four months. A 1999 amendment to the state's FEHA requires employers with five or more workers to provide reasonable accommodations to pregnant women. And a 1999 "kin care" law requires California employers who provide paid sick leave to allow workers to use up to half of it each year to care for sick family members. For more details see Milkman and Appelbaum, "Paid Family Leave."

62. These family leave benefit payments (unlike SDI benefits) have been deemed taxable by the U.S. Internal Revenue Service—a development that was not anticipated by those who crafted the legislation.

63. Koss, "California Temporary Disability Insurance Program."

64. Milkman and Appelbaum, "Paid Family Leave."

65. Employment Development Department, State of California, unpublished data in author's possession.

66. Rona Levine Sherriff, *Balancing Work and Family* (Sacramento: California Senate Office of Research, 2007), 7.

67. See Dark, *Unions and the Democrats*.

Chapter 11

Women's Work and
Economic Crisis Revisited

Comparing the Great Recession
and the Great Depression

This chapter returns to the topic of chapter 1, namely, the impact of economic crisis on women—this time comparing the Great Depression of the 1930s to the Great Recession and the 2008 financial crisis. Despite the many changes in gender relations that unfolded in the intervening decades, the structural effects of these two economic downturns were similar. In both, male unemployment rose more, and sooner, than that of women, reflecting the concentration of male workers in key industries like construction and manufacturing where employment declines were especially severe. In both the Great Depression and the Great Recession, birth, marriage, and divorce rates declined as well. Nevertheless, because women's employment was widely accepted as legitimate by the twenty-first century, the backlash was far more muted than in the 1930s. Another striking difference between the two periods was that whereas in the 1930s there were major efforts to reduce class inequalities in response to the economic collapse, in the aftermath of the Great Recession class inequalities—including class inequalities among women—continued to widen.

The 2008 financial crash gave rise not only to profound economic distress but also to a surge in popular anxieties about shifting gender arrangements. Among the more sophisticated of those anxieties was Hanna Rosin's 2012 book, *The End of Men*—excerpts of which also appeared as cover stories in the *Atlantic* and the *New York Times Magazine*.[1] Rosin pointed out that in 2009, for the first time ever, women constituted a majority of U.S. workers, and that even earlier their average educational level had exceeded that of men. She also highlighted the growing number of households in which women were the main breadwinners while men were under- or unemployed. These "gender role reversals" and related developments, she declared, signaled "the emergence of an American matriarchy, where the younger men especially are unmoored, and closer than at any other time in history to being obsolete."[2]

Rosin claimed to be "unhampered by ideology," neither approving nor disapproving of what she termed "the rise of women." In contrast, Kay S. Hymowitz, of the conservative Manhattan Institute, sounded the alarm about the same set of trends in her 2011 book *Manning Up: How the Rise of Women Has Turned Men into Boys*.[3] Similarly, in 2013 *New York Times* columnist David Brooks portrayed the plight of American men as "tragic," a "catastrophe." Without any hint of irony Brooks waxed nostalgic for traditional masculine values like "reticence, ruggedness, invulnerability and the competitive virtues," going so far as to invoke the memory of John Wayne and the bygone Wild West.[4]

These writers all saw "the rise of women" as a long-term trend rather than one caused by the 2008 economic crisis, but it is no coincidence that their commentaries appeared in the immediate aftermath of the Great Recession. As the U.S. labor market rapidly contracted starting in 2007, hitting industries like construction and manufacturing especially hard, the male unemployment rate rose sharply, and by early 2008 it exceeded the female rate. That led pundits to dub the downturn "the Man-cession" or the "he-cession." They presumed that the gender disparity in unemployment was a novel phenomenon, but in fact the jobless rate among men also had exceeded that of women during the Great Depression of the 1930s. That historical fact had long since been obliterated from public memory, however, and not only was conspicuously absent from the post-2008 narrative about "the end of men" but also was ignored in broader comparisons between the two deepest economic crises of the past century.

Echoes of the 1930s are salient not only in the gendered pattern of unemployment that emerged in 2008 but also in the downturn's demographic impact and its repercussions for families and households. For example, birth rates fell precipitously during both the Great Depression and the Great Recession, and marriage and divorce rates fell as well. In both periods, many families facing unemployment, home foreclosure, and/or bankruptcy survived by "doubling up" into multigenerational households. Women's unpaid household work also expanded in both crises, as they substituted their own labor for goods and services—from restaurant meals to housecleaning and childcare—previously purchased in the marketplace. In both periods, moreover, there were gender "role reversals" in households where women remained employed while their male partners, husbands, or fathers suffered job loss. Although such role reversals were less widespread in the 1930s, when married women's labor force participation was relatively low, they attracted more attention and concern than in the 2000s, when married women's employment was accepted as normal.

Indeed, as I will argue, despite the vast improvement in women's status, the huge increases in female labor force participation rates, and the substantial reduction of gender inequality between the 1930s and the period after 2008, in structural terms the Great Recession's gender dynamics largely recapitulated those of the Great Depression. Yet in other respects there were enormous differences between the two periods. Most important, women's work outside the home—especially that of married women—had not yet become legitimate in the 1930s. Thus the cultural backlash against women workers during the Depression was far more vitriolic and was accompanied by critical shifts in employer practices and public policy—for example, measures that explicitly barred married women from many types of employment.[5] Marriage bars were unthinkable by the twenty-first century, even as angst over the accumulated improvements in women's economic status like that expressed by Rosin, Hymowitz, and Brooks was widely felt in the aftermath of the 2008 financial crash. Such concerns had been growing for some time but now found a broader audience. In the end, however, the backlash failed to gain much traction, in striking contrast to the experience of the 1930s.

Moreover, the broader political response to the Great Recession had little in common with the Great Depression. Whereas the 1930s crisis set the stage for the New Deal and its explicit efforts to reduce inequality, along with a historic upsurge in unionization, such developments were conspicuously absent after 2008. The 2009 American Recovery and Reinvestment Act did provide a modest economic stimulus, but its scale and scope were minimal relative to the Works Progress Administration and other New Deal measures (even considering the fact that the depth of the economic crisis was far greater in the 1930s). The 2011 Occupy Wall Street uprising did galvanize public concern about surging economic inequality—concern that endured long after the uprising itself had dissipated. But it utterly failed to alter the disparities in income and wealth that had been widening since the 1970s or to reverse the sharp decline in unionization over the same period. Indeed, far from unleashing a new New Deal, the twenty-first-century United States instead has given rise to a new Gilded Age, with economic inequality soaring to levels not seen since before World War I.

Surprisingly little attention has been devoted to the gender dimension of the renewed growth of inequality since the 1970s. Yet the growing polarization of income *among* women that emerged alongside—and is in many respects obscured by—the unprecedented progress toward gender equality over that period has greatly amplified the broader rise in inequality, as I will show. Before elaborating that point, however, I compare and contrast the gender dynamics of the Great Depression and the Great Recession. After documenting the structural parallels in patterns of unemployment by gender in the two downturns and their impact on households and families, I discuss the cultural and political backlash against women that the 1930s crisis generated. Finally, I turn to the implications of the sharp contrast between the compression in income and wealth inequality that followed the Great Depression and the relentless growth in inequality that began in the 1970s and continued during and after the Great Recession, with a particular focus on widening class disparities among women in the twenty-first century.

Gender and Unemployment

From the earliest period, job segregation by gender has been a deeply embedded feature of the U.S. labor market, and it remains so to the present day (despite a significant decline in the *extent* of segregation in the late twentieth century, detailed below). That simple fact is central to understanding the gendered pattern of unemployment in economic downturns—both ordinary recessions and the two more serious crises under consideration here. Economic contractions are uneven; they do not affect all sectors of the labor market equally. More specifically, because employment in "cyclically sensitive" industries like construction and durable-goods manufacturing is extremely male dominated, men's unemployment tends to increase more than women's during economic slumps, all else being equal. In protracted crises like the Great Depression and the Great Recession, women's unemployment also tends to rise substantially, but to a lesser extent and later than men's.[6]

I documented this dynamic for the 1930s in an earlier study, drawing primarily on contemporary U.S. Census data.[7] The 1930 census recorded an official unemployment rate of 4.7 percent for women and 7.1 percent for men.[8] This reflected the fact that in the industries and sectors most impacted by the post-1929 crisis, employment had long been male dominated. Nearly one-third (32.1 percent) of all male workers reported to the 1930 census-takers that they had been employed in "manufacturing and mechanical industries," compared with only 17.5 percent of all female workers; overall unemployment in that category—in which the Census Bureau included building construction at the time—stood at 12.8 percent in 1930.[9]

The 1940 census, similarly, found that women's unemployment was lower than men's, but that since 1930 the gender gap had narrowed substantially: 15.4 percent of the experienced male labor force was unemployed, while for females the figure was 13.6 percent.[10] Data for the intervening years of the Depression decade are nonexistent or flawed, but the rudimentary figures for 1930 and 1940 expose the basic pattern. The crucial point is that even in the 1930s, when U.S. capitalism faced its deepest and most prolonged crisis, job segregation by gender remained intact. The vast majority of employers continued to treat male and female labor as non-interchangeable, despite skyrocketing male unemployment and widespread popular disapproval of women's employment—especially married women's employment—during the Great Depression.

A similar dynamic unfolded seven decades later. As unemployment spiked sharply upward in 2008, peaking at double the pre-crisis level in late 2009, once again its gender distribution reflected the interaction of enduring job segregation in the labor market, on the one hand, and the differential impact of the economic contraction on specific industries and sectors, on the other. Manufacturing comprised a much smaller part of the U.S. workforce in the twenty-first century than it had in the 1930s, but because the 2008 crisis was centered in the construction sector, which is even more male dominated than manufacturing, male unemployment rose particularly sharply, especially in the initial phase of the downturn, as figure 11.1 shows.

Government data collection has improved greatly since the 1930s, recording changes in the official unemployment rate on a monthly basis.[11] As figure 11.1 shows, male unemployment (seasonally adjusted) peaked at 10.4 percent in October 2009, when female unemployment was 8.0 percent. Women's unemployment peaked about a year later, at 8.4 percent (in November 2010). While for men, unemployment began to subside in the final months of 2009, the female unemployment rate remained flat through late 2011, as job losses spread across the economy, gradually spreading to the heavily female-employing public-sector and private-sector service jobs. During 2012 men's unemployment fell faster than women's, and by that year's end, the male rate was just below that for females, as figure 11.2 shows. 2013 and 2014 (not shown) brought further

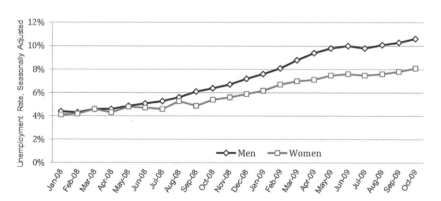

FIGURE 11.1. U.S. Unemployment by Gender, Workers 20 Years Old or Older, January 2008–October 2009.
Source: U.S. Bureau of Labor Statistics, available at http://data.bls.gov/cgi-bin/surveymost.

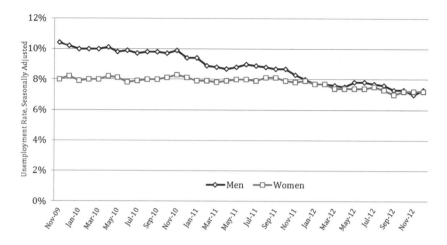

FIGURE 11.2. U.S. Unemployment by Gender, Workers 20 Years Old or Older, November 2009–December 2012.
Source: U.S. Bureau of Labor Statistics, available at http://data.bls.gov/cgi-bin/surveymost.

fluctuations, with the male unemployment rate again exceeding the female rate at some points.

To be sure, gender is only one dimension of variation here. During both the Great Depression and the Great Recession, unemployment rates varied far more by race and educational attainment than by gender. Although unemployment data by race for the 1930s are limited,[12] it is indisputable that African Americans and other "non-whites" disproportionately suffered job losses during the Depression. White women's labor force participation continued its long-term rise, growing from 23.7 percent in 1930 to 24.5 percent in 1940, but the participation rate for nonwhite women—which had exceeded that of white women in earlier decades—fell precipitously, from 43.3 percent in 1930 to 37.6 percent in 1940.[13] In addition, unemployment rates were disproportionately high for workers with limited education and skill in the 1930s.[14]

The Great Recession echoed the Great Depression in this regard as well: as figure 11.3 shows, in 2010 there were far wider disparities in unemployment rates by education and race than by gender. Class differences among women are especially stark: college graduates were much less likely to be unemployed than those with less education, especially among white women but also among women of color.

Across class lines, both during the 1930s and after 2007, young people faced with a bleak labor market often chose to continue their schooling rather than to seek paid employment. But the gender patterns were starkly different in the

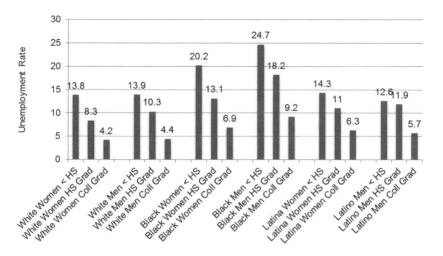

FIGURE 11.3. Unemployment Rates by Gender, Race, and Education, Workers 25 Years Old or Older, annual averages, 2010.
Source: U.S. Bureau of Labor Statistics. http://www.bls.gov/cps/cpsrace2010.pdf.

two periods. In the 1930s, male high school enrollment rose faster than female enrollment did, reversing an earlier trend and perhaps reflecting the fact that unemployment rates were higher for men than for women.[15] Yet even during the Depression decade women were more likely than men to actually complete high school: 26.3 percent of women age twenty-five or older were high school graduates in 1940, compared with 22.6 percent of men in that age group. The female edge did not extend to postsecondary education in this period, however: in 1940, only 3.8 percent of women and 5.5 percent of men age twenty-five or older had graduated from college. Four years later, with the passage of the 1944 GI Bill, the gender gap in college graduation rates would begin to widen further. However, women maintained their lead in high school graduation rates until the early 1970s.[16]

In the late twentieth century, however, young women began to overtake young men at all levels of educational attainment. By 2007 nearly one-third (33.0 percent) of women ages twenty-five to twenty-nine had completed at least four years of college, compared with slightly more than one-fourth (26.3 percent) of men in that age group. Similarly, 89.1 percent of women ages twenty-five to twenty-nine had completed high school by 2007, compared with 84.9 percent of men in that category.[17] That same year film critic David Denby remarked on a new cultural phenomenon that mirrored this change, which he dubbed the "slacker-striver romance," a genre that featured "the slovenly hipster and the female straight arrow," casting the "self-dramatizing [male] underachiever as hero" while making "jokes and romance out of the struggle between male infantilism and female

ambition."[18] Soon after, during the Great Recession, school and college enrollment rates increased for both women and men, but this time—in contrast to the
1930s—the rate of increase was greater for women than for men. In 2009 and 2010,
the number of women aged eighteen to twenty-four enrolled in school rose by
130,000, more than twice the increase (53,000) for men in the same age group.
On the other hand, young women were more likely than young men to drop out
of the labor force entirely during this period.[19]

In summary, both in the early 1930s and in 2008–09, thanks to continuing job
segregation by gender and specifically women's underrepresentation in the sectors
that were hardest hit by the economic downturns, the upsurge in unemployment
disproportionately affected men. In both periods, women's unemployment rose
less, and later, than men's did. This parallel between the Great Depression and
the Great Recession is all the more remarkable in light of the enormous shifts in
gender relations that occurred in the intervening decades. Not only did female
labor force participation increase dramatically, from 24.8 percent in 1930[20] to
59.5 percent in 2008,[21] but the postwar decades also saw major improvements in
women's legal, political, and social status, a resurgence of feminism, and sweeping
changes in popular attitudes about gender. Full gender equality remains elusive,
to be sure, but by any standard great progress has been made since the 1930s.

Nevertheless, the gendered pattern of unemployment during the Great Recession essentially echoed that of the Great Depression, primarily because job segregation, the key lynchpin of gender inequality in the labor market, remains so
extensive. Segregation was reduced somewhat beginning in the 1970s, to be sure,
particularly in the upper reaches of the labor market (a point to which I will
return). But it remains the case that key sectors like construction and durable-
goods manufacturing, which are particularly vulnerable in economic slumps,
are overwhelmingly male-dominated, and that is precisely what triggered the
"Man-cession."

Gender and Family Dynamics in Economic Crises

Both the economic downturn of the 1930s and the one that began in 2007–08
had strikingly similar effects on family dynamics. In both, birth rates, and to a
lesser degree marriage and divorce rates, fell. In both, multigenerational households became more prevalent, and many women substituted their own unpaid
labor for goods and services that their households had previously purchased in
the marketplace. And in both eras there were "role reversals" within many families, with married women working outside the home while their husbands were
unemployed or underemployed. All these changes disproportionately affected
working-class families, which had fewer resources to draw upon when the crisis
hit than their more affluent counterparts did.

The Great Depression was the only twentieth-century economic downturn that reduced the *lifetime* fertility rates of those who were young adults at the time. Subsequent, milder recessions led to short-term declines in births, but typically these involved women postponing having children rather than forgoing them entirely.[22] It is too early to assess the long-term effects of the Great Recession in this regard, but the number of births per one thousand women of childbearing age (fifteen to forty-four years old) did fall sharply between 2007 and 2011, from 69.5 to 63.2 (the 2011 rate is the lowest ever recorded), and the declines were greatest in states hardest hit by the recession. The post-2007 fall in birth rates was not evenly distributed across the population, however: younger women, low-income women, and foreign-born Latinas were affected disproportionately.[23]

The impact of economic downturns on marriage and divorce rates tends to be more modest. Even the Great Depression had a short-term rather than permanent effect on marriage rates, although marriages did fall sharply after 1929. The average age of marriage increased as well for those who came of age during the 1930s, but the vast majority of that generation (more than 93 percent) did eventually marry. Similarly, while the number of divorces fell by 24 percent between 1929 and 1932, reflecting the challenge of the immediate costs of arranging a divorce as well as that of financing two separate households under Depression conditions, the lifetime probability of marriages ending in divorce did not change.[24]

Marriage rates fell after 2007 as well, but they already had been declining for many years prior to that; similarly, cohabitation rates rose with the downturn, continuing the longstanding pre-2007 trend.[25] But the Great Recession did have a short-term effect: the median age of first marriage rose to a record high in 2010, and the number of new marriages declined by 5 percent between 2009 and 2010—a far more rapid decline than in earlier years, and one that was especially large for non-college-educated adults.[26] Divorce rates also fell noticeably after 2007, in another echo of the 1930s, but it remains to be seen whether this will turn out to be a short- or long-term trend.[27]

The impact of these two deep economic downturns on families had additional dimensions as well. In both the Great Depression and the Great Recession vast numbers of people lost their homes due to unemployment or foreclosure (or both), and many of those affected moved into their parents' or children's households—"doubling up," as it was called in the 1930s. In both periods, many young people who had struck out on their own returned to their parents' households as well. But whereas in the 1930s, these survival strategies marked a reversal of the long-term trend from extended- to nuclear-family households, the situation was very different in the twenty-first century. Rising housing costs had already generated substantial growth in multigenerational households beginning in the early 1980s; after the 2008 crash and the massive wave of foreclosures it unleashed, this trend accelerated sharply.[28] The share of the population living in multigenerational households increased from 15.5 percent in 2009 to 18.1 percent in 2012, a far more rapid rise than before. Not only were unemployed and underemployed young adults especially likely to move in with their parents, but "doubling up" also involved entire families moving in with parents or children. But this phenomenon, not surprisingly, was much less widespread among the college-educated than among those with less education.[29]

Even in mild recessions, as household incomes decline with rising unemployment, consumption of basic goods and services tends to fall, especially for working-class families who spend the bulk of their incomes on necessities. Thus in the 1930s, not only durable goods like automobiles and appliances but also clothing and prepared meals suffered severe slumps in sales; domestic service employment also fell. In households facing severe income loss, women often substituted their own labor for goods and services they had previously purchased. Home canning and sewing thus surged in popularity during the Depression, and many more women did their own cleaning and cooking rather than hiring day workers or domestic servants.[30]

Once again the Great Recession echoed the 1930s in this respect. It was the first postwar recession in which consumption fell sharply, not only for durable goods but also for nondurable goods and services.[31] Restaurant sales fell sharply, and there were reports of women devoting more time and effort to "strategic shopping," that is, buying household necessities in less expensive stores and shifting to cheaper brands.[32] As in the 1930s, then, although probably not to the same extent, women substituted their own unpaid labor for commodified goods and services they had purchased before the downturn.

At the outset of the Great Depression, married women were much less likely to be employed outside the home than they were in 2007, yet many families experienced "role reversals" in the wake of the economic crisis. Since jobs often were more available to women than men, when husbands were unemployed or underemployed, their wives often became the sole or primary breadwinners—in some cases as new labor force entrants. Reliable statistics on how prevalent this phenomenon was in the 1930s do not exist, but it fascinated sociologists at the time and was extensively documented in books like Mirra Komarovsky's *The Unemployed Man and His Family*.[33] The following case is representative of those described in this literature:

> Until 1930, Mr. Fetter was able to support his family. After that date his earnings from irregular work were supplemented by his wife's earnings of $9.00 per week in a restaurant. *Both husband and wife disliked to have the wife work, but there seemed no other solution of the economic problem.*[34]

As this example suggests, "role reversals" increased women's economic responsibilities but did not necessarily improve their status. Because the change was so tightly associated with severe economic deprivation, many of those affected strongly preferred the pre-Depression gender arrangement and looked back on it fondly. Thus crisis-engendered role reversals tended to reproduce rather than undermine long-standing patriarchal norms. Indeed, many children born in the 1930s would later become the progenitors of the postwar baby boom, against the cultural backdrop of the 1950s "feminine mystique." As Glen Elder observed in his classic longitudinal study of that generation, *Children of the Great Depression*, "receptivity to traditional [gender] roles is concentrated among women who grew up in deprived households that depended heavily upon the involvement of female members [during the 1930s]."[35]

The postwar growth in demand for women's labor, however, would later propel massive numbers of married women and mothers into paid work. In 1955 only 28.5 percent of married women with a spouse present in the household were in the labor force—a much higher rate than in the 1930s but also well below the 35.7 percent labor force participation rate for all women at that time. Over the next forty years, married women's participation more than doubled, reaching 61.0 percent in 1995, exceeding that year's overall female labor force participation rate of 58.9 percent.[36] Mothers of young children also entered the labor force in vast numbers in the late twentieth century. As late as 1975, only 34.3 percent of those with children under age three were in the labor force; by 2000, that figure had climbed to 61.0 percent.[37] Wives and mothers continued to shoulder the bulk of responsibility for housework and childcare, yet by the turn of the century the vast majority of them were employed outside the home.

This transformation, along with the broader cultural shift toward more gender-egalitarian norms that began in the 1960s and 1970s, slowly but surely undermined the formerly hegemonic idea that men were entitled to earn a "family wage" sufficient to support a stay-at-home wife and children. By the twenty-first century, that notion—once deeply entrenched, although in practice unattainable for many of those who aspired to it—had become an anachronism. Whereas in 1977, 63 percent of women and 69 percent of men in the United States agreed with the statement "It is much better for everyone involved if the man is the achiever outside the home and the woman takes care of the home and family," by 2011, only 26 percent of women and 38 percent of men endorsed this view.[38] Reflecting the stagnation in male real earnings since the mid-1970s, the "new normal" for married-couple households was for both adults to be in the labor force with minimal interruptions. As Elizabeth Warren, who later was elected as a U.S. Senator, and Amelia Warren Tyagi presciently observed in 2003, the unintended consequence was "the two-income trap"—rendering families economically vulnerable in the case of job loss for either partner.[39]

During the Great Recession, although unemployment rates never even came close to the level of the 1930s, "role reversals" were probably more frequent, simply because a much higher proportion of married women were employed both before and during the crisis. From 2008 to 2011, married men's unemployment rate exceeded that of married women (married women were also far less likely to lose their jobs than unmarried women).[40] As in the 1930s, those individuals who experienced gender role reversals often expressed nostalgia for the pre-Recession situation. For example:

> Three days before Christmas, and two months after the birth of their youngest child, Kevin was laid off. . . . He and Cheryl decided he should go back to school. . . . [Cheryl] took the only job she could find: a $7-an-hour position at a gas station. . . . Kevin has started taking over more child-care duties . . . and doing more housework, and Cheryl says that *while it's nice to have her husband better appreciate all she did as a stay-at-home mom, she'd trade that for her old life—instantly.*[41]

> When [her husband] lost his job, her boss allowed her to go to fifty-five hours a week from forty. . . . Rhonda's long working days—she leaves at around 5 am and is gone until early evening—have altered her role in the family, not to mention his. *She still views him—and he views himself—as the chief provider, if not today then in the long run, when her income, they hope, will once again become secondary.*[42]

The incidence of such role reversals was limited—the share of all two-parent families with children less than eighteen years old in which the mother was the only jobholder rose from 4.9 percent in 2007 to 7.4 percent in 2009.[43] But this situation nevertheless helped fuel the gender anxiety that emerged with the 2008 crash, discussed at the beginning of this chapter.

At the same time, the recession years saw modest growth in the population of "stay-at-home mothers," which rose from 26 percent of all mothers with children under 18 in 2008 to 29 percent in 2012 (including single, cohabiting, and married mothers). About two-thirds of those staying home were married, and 85 percent of the latter group reported that they were staying at home in order to provide direct care for their families. Another 5 percent of the married stay-at-home mothers were sufficiently affluent (with a median household income of about $132,000) that the family could easily survive on one income. However, the growth in stay-at-home mothers may not have been a result of the recession, as a trend in that direction was already emerging a few years earlier. The proportion of mothers who were not employed outside the home had declined steadily over the last three decades of the twentieth century and hit a record low of 23 percent in 1999. However, soon after that, the long-term decline began to reverse itself; the recession may well have accelerated that process.[44] The 2012 figure (29 percent) was roughly similar to the level in the late 1980s.[45]

In any case, this shift toward "traditional" family arrangements does not appear to have been the product of changing public opinion. In 2012 only 18 percent of adults surveyed by the Pew Research Center believed that "women should return to their traditional role in society," and 58 percent "completely disagreed" with that view, up from 29 percent in 1987.[46] By contrast, a virulent backlash against married women's employment emerged during the 1930s, a backlash that had serious effects on public policy and employer practices.

The Family Wage and Married Women's Employment in the 1930s

The economic crisis breathed new life into the "family wage" ideal, which already had begun to erode in the 1910s and 1920s as more and more married women began to enter the labor force. As unemployment surged after 1929, married women, especially those with employed husbands, were scapegoated as interlopers who were taking "men's jobs." In 1931, New York State Assemblyman Arthur Swartz denounced married women workers as "undeserving parasites,"[47] and that same year the American Federation of Labor's executive committee declared that "married women whose husbands have permanent positions . . . should be discriminated against in the hiring of employees."[48] By 1936, 82 percent of respondents to a Gallup Poll agreed that married women with employed husbands should not be working; that figure rose to 90 percent by 1939.[49] George Gallup himself stated that he had never seen respondents "as solidly united in opposition as on any subject imaginable, including sin and hay fever."[50]

Letters to President Franklin Roosevelt expressed similar sentiments. "Could not something be done to prohibit employers from hiring any woman that does not of necessity have to work?" Norman Best wrote from Greenville, Ohio, in May 1933. "If possible I am sure millions more heads of families would be put back to work at better wages than are paid women and many homes saved as well as many made happier."[51] Nor were such views held exclusively by men. In 1938, for example, Mrs. Agnes Drufke of Chicago implored in a letter to the president:

> . . . if every man financialy [sic] independent and holding a job some other man could fill (probably just as good) would give this said job up, and if every woman employed that really does not have to work, would stay home and raise a family or take up some hobby (she would be much happier too) Im [sic] positive there would be plenty of work to go around and hence end the depression.[52]

Such pleas presumed that the jobs married women held would otherwise employ men, ignoring the realities of job segregation by sex. Moreover, this was not mere talk. Many employers introduced or strengthened policies prohibiting the hiring of married women as well as policies mandating that female employees who were hired when they were single be immediately dismissed once they married. Such policies, known as "marriage bars," were especially common in public schools, and often predated the Depression. In 1928, 61 percent of U.S. public school districts barred the hiring of married women, and 52 percent had policies against retaining women who married while on the job. But marriage bars became even more widespread after the 1929 stock market crash: by 1940, 87 percent of school districts would not hire married women, and 70 percent would not retain them after marriage.

The 1932 federal Economy Act included a "married persons" clause stipulating that whenever layoffs took place in the executive branch, married persons whose spouses were federal government employees should be the first to go.[53] Despite the gender-neutral language, in practice this nearly always meant firing married women. By 1940 nine states had established similar policies; many local governments also introduced them during the 1930s.[54]

Although marriage bars were less prevalent in the private sector, they did exist, especially in larger firms, and similarly to what took place in the public sector, they were expanded in the 1930s. Precise figures are difficult to locate, but a 1931 survey of large firms employing white-collar workers in seven major cities found that 25 percent of female employees in the sample were subject to marriage bars. No strictly comparable figures for other years exist, but the available evidence suggests that private-sector marriage bars became more widespread as the Depression wore on.[55]

Despite the widespread popular hostility to married women's employment, in practice economic necessity often trumped ideological backlash. Married women's labor force participation continued its long-term growth during the 1930s, rising from 11.7 percent in 1930 to 13.8 percent in 1940. That increase was only a little slower than in the previous decade, when the rate grew from 9.0 percent to 11.7 percent.[56] Marriage bars were also sometimes evaded successfully, and many married women with unemployed husbands sought work out of sheer economic desperation, despite the cultural sanctions.

In keeping with the egalitarian culture of the New Deal era, there was also some popular support for married women's employment in cases where their husbands' earnings were limited. A 1939 Gallup poll asked respondents whether they were in favor of a law prohibiting employment for married women if their husbands earned more than $1,000 a year, and 56 percent responded affirmatively. That figure rose to 67 percent when a similar question was asked with husbands' hypothetical earnings set at $1,600 a year.[57]

Marriage bars, and the public disapprobation that married women's employment evoked, exacted a heavy toll. Although in many other respects the economic impact of the Depression disproportionately affected working-class women, the backlash against women's employment had a powerful impact on college-educated, professional women as well. This was particularly true in relation to marriage bars because many professional women were interested in continuing to work outside the home after marriage. In the 1930s, professionals of both sexes were less likely to lose their jobs than most other occupational groups, and in absolute terms the number of female professionals—with the notable exception of teachers—increased slightly during the 1930s.[58] But at the same time, in absolute terms, growth in female professional employment slowed dramatically relative to the pre-Depression years and lagged behind the growth of the overall female labor force. As a share of all employed women, professionals declined from 14.2 percent in 1930 to 12.3 percent in 1940, due largely to the measures affecting married teachers; in contrast, the share of professionals among employed men increased slightly (from 4.0 percent to 4.7 percent) over that decade.

The vast majority of female professionals in this period were in the "semi-professions" of nursing, teaching elementary and secondary school, social work, and librarianship, although that had begun to change in the 1910s and 1920s. The female percentage of physicians, lawyers, and college faculty members grew during those two decades, and for physicians and lawyers, growth continued through the Depression as well, although by twenty-first-century standards the numbers were minuscule. In 1930 women made up 4.0 percent of all physicians, and the figure rose to 4.6 percent in 1940; similarly, the female share of lawyers grew from 2.1 percent to 2.4 percent over the Depression decade. Women's share of college faculty was much higher—32.0 percent in 1930—but it then fell to 27.0 percent over the next decade, paralleling the employment decline among female elementary and secondary schoolteachers. In this particular field the decline would continue for many years after the Depression: the female share of college faculty stood at only 19.0 percent in 1960.[59] Shortly after that, however, the elite professions opened their doors to women; indeed, few occupations were more affected by the resurgence of feminism. In part because the gateway to entry was through educational institutions, which tend to be more meritocratic and less gender segregated than employment settings, the proportion of women in law, medicine, and academe alike grew dramatically in the half-century after 1960.

Inequality among Women and the Great Recession

One of the most striking differences between the situation of women in the 1930s and in the twenty-first century is the growth in inequality *among* women. A key driver of that inequality, ironically, was the entrance of women into prestigious fields with relatively high salaries, including the elite professions as well as high-level management jobs, during the closing decades of the twentieth century. Moreover, such jobs tended to be less affected by the Great Recession than those at lower levels of the labor market. As table 11.1 shows, women's representation in the elite fields of law, medicine, and academe continued to increase between 2007 and 2013, despite the economic downturn. The female share of employment in management occupations also rose in the aftermath of the recession, although only slightly: from 37.5 percent in 2007 to 38.2 percent in 2013. In larger organizations, most female managers were located at the middle and lower levels, but by 2007, 25.6 percent of all chief executives were female (for organizations of all sizes); that figure rose to 26.8 percent in 2013.[60]

To be sure, after 2007 the long-term deterioration of job quality in high-level managerial and professional occupations, which was also associated with the feminization of these fields during the preceding decades, continued and perhaps even accelerated. But there was no echo of the fall-off in female professional employment that took place in the 1930s. Instead, the overall percentage of women in professional fields rose slightly during and after the Great Recession, as table 11.1 shows. This is all the more remarkable in view of the fact that after 2007, women's share of employment fell modestly in the traditionally female professions of secondary school teaching, nursing, and social work. That trend, however, predated the recession in the two largest female professions, namely, teaching and nursing.[61]

Married women's labor force participation also grew slightly during the Great Recession. It had increased steadily in the 1970s and 1980s and then leveled off in the 1990s. By 2000, 61.1 percent of married women (with a spouse present in the household) were in the labor force, and the figure hovered around that level over the next decade, with only slight year-to-year fluctuations. Recall that even during the 1930s, despite the fierce ideological attacks on married women workers,

Table 11.1. Percent Female of Employed Persons in Selected Professions, 1995, 2007 and 2013

	1995	2007	2013
All Professional and Related Occupations	52.9	56.2	57.1
Physicians and Surgeons	24.4	30.0	35.5
Lawyers	26.4	32.6	33.1
Postsecondary Teachers	45.2	46.2	50.2
Secondary School Teachers	57.0	56.9	56.7
Registered Nurses	93.1	91.7	90.1
Social Workers	67.9	82.0	80.3

Note: Data collection methods changed between 1995 and 2007; changes shown over that period should be interpreted cautiously.
Source: U.S. Bureau of Labor Statistics, Current Population Survey, available at http://www.bls.gov/cps/cps_aa1995_1999.htm

their labor force participation rate grew. That was also the case after 2007, but the increase was small and short-lived: married women's labor force participation rose from 61.0 percent in 2007 to 61.4 percent in 2008; the figure in 2009 was also 61.4, followed by a slight dip to 59.5 percent in 2012.[62]

Overall, the gender anxiety that surfaced during the Great Recession was far milder and had far more limited effects on women's daily lives than the backlash against women that had gripped the nation in the 1930s. By 2008 the formerly hegemonic family-wage ideology had long since faded into obsolescence, and the legitimacy of paid employment for women, regardless of marital status, was firmly established as well. Moreover, the ideals (if not the realities) of equal opportunity and equal treatment for women in the workplace were deeply entrenched, not only legally but also culturally. To be sure, there was less progress on the home front, as wives and mothers were still burdened with the vast majority of unpaid housework and caregiving, and in other arenas double standards on the basis of gender proved difficult to dislodge. But on the whole, the long historical arc of incremental progress toward eroding gender inequality continued its trajectory in the twenty-first century, barely interrupted by the Great Recession.

Against this background, the widely circulated concerns about "the rise of women" I described at the beginning of this chapter ultimately failed to gain much traction. Instead, and in sharp contrast, Sheryl Sandberg's 2013 book *Lean In*, which celebrated the achievements of elite women and encouraged ambition among the entire female population, became a runaway best seller.[63] Women continued their economic advances in the workplace and continued as well to surpass men in educational attainment. Even job segregation by sex had been reduced relative to the mid-twentieth century, and as a result the gender gap in earnings also narrowed. These trends were further reinforced by the "Man-cession," since men bore the brunt of rising unemployment.

Thus one point of contrast between the two economic crises involves the backlash against women's employment, which was far less effective after the 2008 crash than it had been seven decades earlier. An even more striking difference between the two periods lies in their contrasting approaches to the problem of growing economic inequality. The Great Depression generated a political response, in the shape of the New Deal, as well as a historic upsurge of labor union organizing. Their combined impact led to what economic historians Claudia Goldin and Robert A. Margo famously called the "Great Compression"—a major reduction in income inequality that began in the 1930s and would endure for another four decades.[64] In sharp contrast, in the aftermath of the Great Recession, which followed a three-decade period of widening disparities in income and wealth, no such political response took hold. The strong popular critiques of growing inequality and of the power of "the one percent" articulated during and after the Occupy Wall Street uprisings notwithstanding, inequality has continued to grow in the years since the 2008 crash, reaching levels comparable to that of the Gilded Age a century earlier.[65]

What has attracted far less attention, however, is the sharp increase in economic inequality among women, which began to emerge before the Great Recession and has continued to expand since. Obscured by the simultaneous decline in the extent of gender inequality, class inequalities among women have expanded to an historically unprecedented degree.

One dimension of this problem involves the recent emergence of class dispari-ties in regard to the long-standing phenomenon of occupational segregation by gender, an enduring linchpin of gender inequality and also the most important driver of gender disparities in earnings. (That is so because unequal pay for equal work, although still all too often present, is a smaller component of the overall gender gap in earnings than the fact that female-dominated jobs typically pay less than male-dominated jobs with comparable skill requirements.) Whereas between 1900 and 1960 the extent of occupational segregation by sex was noto-riously impervious to change,[66] it began to decline substantially in the United States after 1960. The standard measure of segregation, "the index of dissimilar-ity," which specifies the proportion of men or women who would have to change jobs to have both genders evenly distributed through the occupational structure, declined sharply between 1960 and 1990, and in later years continued to fall at a less rapid pace, as figure 11.4 shows.[67] This led in turn to a steady decline in

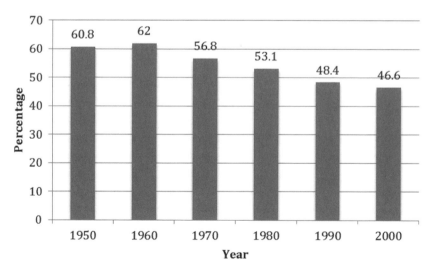

FIGURE 11.4. Occupational Segregation by Gender, United States, 1950–2000.
Source: Index of dissimilarity computed from U.S. decennial census data (IPUMS),
http://www.bsos.umd.edu/socy/vanneman/endofgr/ipumsoccseg.html.

the gender gap in earnings. Among full-time workers, women's annual earnings were, on average, 59.94 percent of men's in 1970; by 2010 the ratio had grown to 77.4 percent.[68]

The narrowing of the gender gap in earnings and the associated reduction in the extent of occupational segregation reflect real progress toward gender equality. However, that progress has been limited and sharply skewed by the rapid growth in class inequality over the late twentieth century. More specifically, occupational segregation by sex has declined sharply in professional and managerial jobs but has hardly declined at all in lower-level occupations, as figure 11.5 shows.[69] High-wage "male" jobs in industries like construction and durable-goods manufacturing remain extremely sex-segregated, as do low-wage "female" jobs like childcare, domestic service, and clerical work. College-educated women have disproportionately benefited from occupational integration, while less-educated women are much more likely to be in traditionally sex-stereotyped jobs with low pay and low status.[70]

As one would expect, college-educated and professional-managerial women tend to earn substantially higher salaries than those women who remain ghettoized in poorly paid, highly segregated jobs at lower levels of the labor market. This is one of the reasons income inequality among women has grown, even as

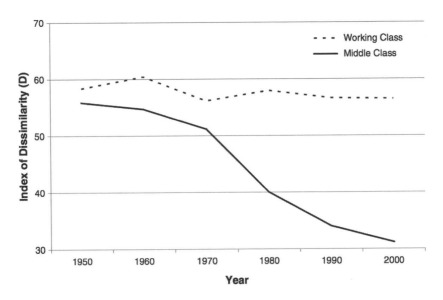

FIGURE 11.5. Class Differences in Occupational Segregation by Gender, 1950–2000. Source: David A. Cotter, Joan M. Hermsen, and Reeve Vanneman, "Gender Inequality at Work," *The American People: Census 2000* (New York: Russell Sage Foundation; and Washington, D.C.: Population Reference Bureau, 2004), 14.

the overall gender gap in pay has declined. A similar pattern of inequality applies to benefits: women in professional and managerial positions are far more likely to have access to employer-provided health insurance, as well as paid sick days and paid parental leave, than women in lower-level jobs.[71] And women in elite fields are also disproportionately likely to be able to purchase paid domestic help and other services to replace their own unpaid labor inside the home.

But the class pattern of gender disparities in earnings in the late twentieth century is complicated: although in *absolute* terms highly educated women in elite occupations have been able to advance economically to a much greater extent than women in lower-level jobs, the *relative* decline in earnings inequality by gender was actually smaller for women at the upper levels—simply because the earnings of men in elite jobs rose far more rapidly than the earnings of any other group. Indeed non-college-educated men have experienced a steady and steep decline in real earnings since the 1970s, a key factor contributing to the narrowing of the overall gender gap in pay.[72] Further complicating the picture is that women in high-level managerial and professional jobs are required to work longer hours than women in most lower-level jobs; and if they are parents, women also face the time demands of "intensive mothering," aimed at ensuring that their children obtain elite educational credentials and reproduce their class status.[73]

The surge in economic inequality since the 1970s has been greatly amplified by endogamous marriage and "assortative mating"—that is, the long-standing tendency for people to choose partners and spouses from class (and racial) backgrounds similar to their own. This pattern disproportionately benefits highly educated women in elite occupations who share a household with a male spouse or partner at a similar occupational level. Those women, even if they earn substantially less than their spouses or partners, indirectly benefit from the soaring incomes of those men—as well as from their wealth, which is distributed far more unequally than income. Indeed, income homogamy has increased for married couples since the 1970s, alongside the growth in overall income inequality.

Further intensifying this effect among affluent professional-managerial women who choose to marry or cohabit with a partner (not all such women do so, of course, but a large majority do) is the fact that such unions typically have lower separation and divorce rates than those of less privileged women. The result is a stark class contrast, even in an age of soaring inequality: while highly educated married or cohabiting employed women benefit from their spouses' or partners' high incomes, supplementing their own high (relative to those of less educated women) earnings, the poorest households are disproportionately headed by single mothers subsisting on extremely low wages.[74]

Class inequality is hardly a new phenomenon, and at the outset of the Great Depression in particular (prior to the "Great Compression" mentioned earlier) it was also at a peak level. But in the 1930s, when married women's labor force participation rate was a fraction of what it is today, the multiplicative effects of homogamy were relatively small. Considered in that light, class inequality among women in the United States has never been greater than it is in the twenty-first century. That seems unlikely to change in the absence of any significant policy interventions to address the problem of soaring inequality, whose victims include millions of women struggling to survive in the low-wage labor market.

Notes

1. See Hannah Rosin, *The End of Men and the Rise of Women* (New York: Riverhead, 2012); "The End of Men," *The Atlantic*, July–August 2010; "Who Wears the Pants in This Economy?"; *New York Times Magazine*, September 2, 2012, 22–29, 38.

2. Rosin, *End of Men*, 82.

3. Kay S. Hymowitz, *Manning Up: How the Rise of Women Has Turned Men into Boys* (New York: Basic Books, 2011).

4. David Brooks, "Men on the Threshold," *New York Times*, July 16, 2013.

5. For an excellent discussion of this issue, see chapter 3 of Alice Kessler-Harris, *A Woman's Wage: Historical Meanings and Social Consequences* (Lexington: University Press of Kentucky, 1990), 53–74.

6. Women's unemployment rate consistently rose less than men's during the many recessions that took place between the Great Depression and the Great Recession, but before 1980 the female rate rarely rose enough to exceed the male one in absolute terms. Starting in the 1980s, however, men's unemployment typically surpassed that of women during recessions and later rebounded during the recovery (the female rate is typically higher than the male rate in nonrecessionary periods) narrowed but did not close, with some exceptions starting in the 1980s. See Randy Albelda, "Gender Impacts of the 'Great Recession' in the United States," in *Women and Austerity: The Economic Crisis and the Future for Gender Equality*, edited by Maria Karamessini and Jill Rubery (New York: Routledge, 2014), 86–87.

7. Ruth Milkman, "Women's Work and Economic Crisis: Some Lessons of the Great Depression," *Review of Radical Political Economics* 8, no. 1 (1976): 73–97, reprinted in slightly abridged form in this volume (chapter 1).

8. In "The Labor Market during the Great Depression and the Current Recession" (Washington, D.C.: Congressional Research Service, June 19, 2009), Linda Levine reports revised unemployment rates of 4.2 percent for women and 5.4 percent for men for 1930, adjusted to conform to the labor force definitions used in the 1940 census.

9. In the 1930 census, the "building industry," or what is now called "construction," was treated as a subcategory of "manufacturing and mechanical industries." At that time, 38.8 percent of all men (but less than one percent of all women) ordinarily employed in "manufacturing and mechanical industries" were in the building industry. Building industry workers were 99.6 percent male and had an unemployment rate of 19.0 percent, higher than any other sector. See U.S. Census Bureau, *15th Census of the United States 1930*, vol. 1 (1930), table 22, pp. 53–54.

10. Levine, "Labor Market."

11. U.S. unemployment data remain problematic in some respects, particularly for "discouraged workers" who have given up searching for work (although the government does attempt to enumerate them), and also in regard to part-time workers who would prefer full-time work. For this reason, many twenty-first-century commentators refer to employment-to-population ratios rather than unemployment data, which measure unemployment as a share of the labor force (defined as those working or actively seeking work). Labor force participation rates declined by more than two percentage points since the start of the Great Recession, for both men and women. See Heidi Schierholz, "Labor Force Participation: Cyclical versus Structural Changes since the Start of the Great Recession," Issue Brief #333 (Washington, D.C.: Economic Policy Institute, May 24, 2012). To facilitate comparison with the 1930s, however, I focus primarily on unemployment data here.

12. Levine, "Labor Market."

13. Claudia Goldin, *Understanding the Gender Gap: An Economic History of American Women* (New York: Oxford University Press, 1990), 17.

14. Claudia Goldin and Robert A. Margo, "The Great Compression: The Wage Structure in the United States at Mid-Century," *Quarterly Journal of Economics* 107, no. 1 (1992): 22.

15. U.S. Census Bureau, "Educational Attainment of the Population 25 Years and Over in the United States, 1940," news release, 16th Census of the United States, 1940, series 10, no. 8 (April 23, 1942), http://www.census.gov/hhes/socdemo/education/data/cps/1946/p10-8/p10-8.pdf.

16. U.S. Census Bureau, "CPS Historical Times Series Tables: Table A-1, Years of School Completed by People 25 Years and Over, by Age and Sex: Selected Years 1940 to 2013" (2014), http://www.census.gov/hhes/socdemo/education/data/cps/historical.

17. Ibid.

18. David Denby, "A Fine Romance: The New Comedy of the Sexes," *New Yorker*, July 23, 2007, 59–65.

19. Catherine Rampell, "Instead of Work, Younger Women Head to School," *New York Times*, December 29, 2011. That drop may have contributed marginally to the gender disparity in unemployment rates, since individuals who are not in the labor force are not officially counted as unemployed.

20. Goldin, *Understanding the Gender Gap*, 17.

21. U.S. Bureau of Labor Statistics, *Women in the Labor Force: A Databook*, Report 1034 (December 2011), http://www.bls.gov/cps/wlf-databook-2011.pdf, p. 8.

22. Andrew Cherlin, Erin Cumberworth, S. Philip Morgan, and Christopher Wimer, "The Effects of the Great Recession on Family Structure and Fertility," *Annals of the American Academy of Political and Social Sciences* 650 (2013): 216; Glen H. Elder Jr., *Children of the Great Depression: Social Change in Life Experience* (Chicago: University of Chicago Press, 1974).

23. See Cherlin et al., "Effects of the Great Recession," 218–20; and S. Philip Morgan, Erin Cumberworth, and Christopher Wimer, "The Great Recession's Influence on Fertility, Marriage, Divorce and Cohabitation," in *The Great Recession*, edited by David B. Grusky, Bruce Western, and Christopher Wimer (New York: Russell Sage Foundation), especially 221–33. As Cherlin et al. show (see p. 222), the sudden drop in Mexican immigration after 2008 was a key driver of the decline in birth rates among foreign-born Latinas; in previous

years, birth rates were consistently higher for recent immigrants than for those who had lived in the United States longer.

24. Cherlin et al., "Effects of the Great Recession," 216.

25. Ibid., 223–24; Morgan, Cumberworth, and Wimer, "Great Recession's Influence," 233–35.

26. D'Vera Cohn, Jeffrey S. Passel, Wendy Wang, and Gretchen Livingston, "Barely Half of U.S. Adults Are Married—A Record Low" (Washington, D.C.: Pew Research Center, Social and Demographic Trends Project, December 2011).

27. Cherlin et al., "Effects of the Great Recession," 224; Morgan, Cumberworth, and Wimer, "Great Recession's Influence," 234–35.

28. Katherine S. Newman, *The Accordion Family: Boomerang Kids, Anxious Parents, and the Private Toll of Global Competition* (Boston: Beacon, 2012), 42–43; Cherlin et al., "Effects of the Great Recession," 225–28. Another factor that contributed to the growth of multi-generational households after 1980 was immigration, especially from Mexico and Central America, since immigrants are more likely to live in such households than people born in the United States. That makes the post-2008 increase in "doubling up" even more significant, since new immigration dropped to a trickle with the economic downturn.

29. Richard Fry and Jeffrey S. Passell, "In Post-Recession Era, Young Adults Drive Continuing Rise in Multi-generational Living" (Washington, D.C.: Pew Research Center's Social and Demographic Trends, July 2014), 8; Cherlin et al., "Effects of the Great Recession," 228.

30. Cecile Tipton LaFollette, *A Study of the Problems of 653 Gainfully Employed Married Women Homemakers*, Contributions to Education No. 619 (New York: Teachers College, Columbia University, 1934), 95–102.

31. Ivaylo D. Petev, Luigi Pistaferri, and Itay Saporta-Eksten, "An Analysis of Trends, Perceptions and Distributional Effects in Consumption," in Grusky, Western, and Wimer, *Great Recession*, 162.

32. Louis Uchitelle, "From Two Breadwinners to One," *The Nation*, May 4, 2011; Michael Luo, "Still Working, But Forced to Make Do with Less," *New York Times*, May 29, 2009; Paul Taylor, Rich Morin, Rakesh Kochhar, Kim Parker, D'Vera Cohn, Mark Hugo Lopez, Richard Fry, Wendy Wang, Gabriel Valasco, Daniel Dockterman, Rebecca Hinze-Pifer, and Soledad Espinoza, "A Balance Sheet at 30 Months: How the Great Recession Has Changed Life in America" (Washington, D.C.: Pew Research Center, Social and Demographic Trends Project, June 2010), 53–54.

33. Mirra Komarovsky, *The Unemployed Man and His Family: The Effect of Unemployment upon the Status of the Man in Fifty-Nine Families* (New York: Dryden, 1940).

34. R. S. Cavan and K. H. Ranck, *The Family and the Depression: A Study of One Hundred Chicago Families* (Chicago: University of Chicago Press, 1938), 57, emphasis added.

35. Elder, *Children of the Great Depression*, 239.

36. Susan B. Carter, "Labor Force," in chapter Ba of *Historical Statistics of the United States, Earliest Times to the Present: Millennial Edition*, edited by Susan B. Carter, Scott Sigmund Gartner, Michael R. Haines, Alan L. Olmstead, Richard Sutch, and Gavin Wright (New York: Cambridge University Press, 2006), http://dx.doi.org/10.1017/ISBN-9780511132971.Ba.ESS.02, table Ba571-578.

37. Bureau of Labor Statistics, *Women in the Labor Force*, 19.

38. Andrew J. Cherlin, *Labor's Love Lost: The Rise and Fall of the Working-Class Family in America* (New York: Russell Sage Foundation, 2014), 15.

39. Elizabeth Warren and Amelia Warren Tyagi, *The Two-Income Trap: Why Middle-Class Parents Are Going Broke* (New York: Basic, 2003).

40. Albelda, "Gender Impacts," 91.

41. Stephanie Hanes, "How the Recession is Reshaping the American Family," *Christian Science Monitor*, June 14, 2009, emphasis added.

42. Uchitelle, "From Two Breadwinners to One," emphasis added.

43. U.S. Congress Joint Economic Committee, "Understanding the Economy: Working Mothers in the Great Recession" (2010), 3.

44. Among all stay-at-home mothers in 2012 (including single, cohabiting and married mothers), 6 percent reported that they were staying at home because they could not find work, but this does not account for much of the decline. For more details, see D'Vera Cohn, Gretchen Livingston, and Wendy Wang, "After Decades of Decline, A Rise in Stay at Home Mothers" (Washington, D.C.: Pew Research Center, Social and Demographic Trends Project, April, 2014).

45. Ibid.

46. Ibid.

47. Lois Scharf, *To Work and to Wed: Female Employment, Feminism and the Great Depression* (Westport, Conn.: Greenwood, 1980), 45.

48. William H. Chafe, *The American Woman: Her Changing Social, Economic and Political Role, 1920–1970* (New York: Oxford University Press, 1972), 108.

49. Stephanie Coontz, *A Strange Stirring: The Feminine Mystique and American Women at the Dawn of the 1960s* (New York: Basic, 2011), 44.

50. Susan Ware, *Holding Their Own: American Women in the 1930s* (Boston: Twayne, 1982), 27.

51. Lawrence W. Levine and Cornelia R. Levine, *The Fireside Conversations: America Responds to FDR during the Great Depression* (Berkeley: University of California Press, 2010), 71.

52. Ibid., 233. See also Kessler-Harris, *A Woman's Wage*, 53–54, 63–74.

53. Scharf, *To Work and to Wed*, 46.

54. Goldin, *Understanding the Gender Gap*, 165–66.

55. Ibid., 161–65.

56. Ibid., 17. Among nonwhite married women, however, labor force participation did fall, from 33.2 percent in 1930 to 27.3 percent ten years later. Nevertheless, as in previous years this rate greatly exceeded that for white married women, which was only 12.5 percent in 1940. For these statistics, see also ibid., 17.

57. Hazel Erskine, "The Polls: Women's Role," *Public Opinion Quarterly* 35, no. 2 (1971): 283–84.

58. Scharf, *To Work and to Wed*, 86.

59. Cynthia Fuchs Epstein, *Woman's Place: Options and Limits in Professional Careers* (Berkeley: University of California Press, 1971), 7.

60. Comparable figures are not available for earlier years, due to changes in the U.S. government's data collection methodology. See http://www.bls.gov/cps/cps_aa1995_1999 .htm.

61. Shaila Dewan and Robert Gebeloff, "More Men Enter Fields Dominated by Women," *New York Times*, May 21, 2012.

62. For the data from 1970 to 2010, see Table 598 of the *U.S. Statistical Abstract* (2012 edition), available at: http://www.census.gov/compendia/statab/cats/labor_force_employment _earnings.html. The 2012 figure is from U.S. Department of Labor, 2014.

63. See Sheryl Sandberg, *Lean In: Women, Work and the Will to Lead* (New York: Knopf, 2013).

64. Goldin and Margo, "The Great Compression."

65. Thomas Piketty, *Capital in the Twenty-First Century* (Cambridge, Mass.: Harvard University Press, 2014).

66. Edward Gross, "Plus Ca Change . . . The Sexual Structure of Occupations over Time," *Social Problems* 16, no. 2 (1968): 198–208; Ruth Milkman, *Gender at Work: The Dynamics of Job Segregation by Sex during World War II* (Urbana: University of Illinois Press, 1987).

67. The data for 1990 to 2000 are not strictly comparable to one another due to changes in the methodology used by the U.S. Census, but all available data suggest that the decline in segregation gradually leveled off and was essentially flat after 2000. See Francine D. Blau, Peter Brummund, and Albert Yung-Hsu Liu, "Trends in Occupational Segregation by Gender 1970–2009: Adjusting for the Impact of Changes in the Occupational Coding System," *Demography* 50, no. 2 (2013): 471–92.

68. Institute for Women's Policy Research, "The Gender Wage Gap: 2013," Fact Sheet C413 (Washington, D.C.: Institute for Women's Policy Research, March 2014).

69. The data shown in figure 11.5 are decennial U.S. Census data (IPUMS) for workers ages twenty-five to fifty-four. "Middle-class occupations" are defined as professional and managerial (including nonretail sales) occupations; all other occupations are considered "working class" in this analysis.

70. David A. Cotter, Joan M. Hermsen, and Reeve Vanneman, "Gender Inequality at Work," *The American People: Census 2000* (New York: Russell Sage Foundation / Washington, D.C.: Population Reference Bureau, 2004); see also Paula England, "The Gender Revolution: Uneven and Stalled," *Gender and Society* 24, no. 2 (2010): 149–66; Ariane Hegewisch, Hannah Liepmann, Jeffrey Hayes, and Heidi Hartmann, "Separate and Not Equal? Gender Segregation in the Labor Market and the Gender Wage Gap," Briefing Paper C377 (Washington, D.C.: Institute for Women's Policy Research, 2010).

71. Ruth Milkman and Eileen Appelbaum, *Unfinished Business: Paid Family Leave in California and the Future of U.S. Work-Family Policy* (Ithaca, N.Y.: Cornell University Press, 2013).

72. Leslie McCall, "What Does Class Inequality among Women Look Like? A Comparison with Men and Families, 1970 to 2000," in *Social Class: How Does It Work?* edited by Annette Lareau and Dalton Conley (New York: Russell Sage Foundation, 2008), 309.

73. On the contrast in working hours between women of different classes, see Jerry A. Jacobs and Kathleen Gerson, *The Time Divide: Work, Family and Gender Inequality* (Cambridge: Harvard University Press, 2004). On intensive mothering and its relationship to

social class reproduction, see Sharon Hays, *The Cultural Contradictions of Motherhood* (New Haven, Conn.: Yale University Press, 1996); Annette Lareau, *Unequal Childhoods: Class, Race, and Family Life* (Berkeley: University of California Press, 2003); and "An hereditary Meritocracy," *Economist*, January 24–30, 2015, 17–20.

74. Gary Burtless, "Effects of Growing Wage Disparities and Changing Family Composition on the U.S. Income Distribution," *European Economic Review* 43 (1999): 853–65; June Carbone and Naomi Chan, *Marriage Markets: How Inequality is Remaking the American Family* (New York: Oxford University Press, 2014); McCall, "Class Inequality"; Sarah Damaske, *For the Family? How Class and Gender Shape Women's Work* (New York: Oxford University Press, 2011).

Index

RUTH MILKMAN is Distinguished Professor of Sociology at the CUNY Graduate Center. Her books include *L.A. Story: Immigrant Workers and the Future of the U.S. Labor Movement* and *Gender at Work: The Dynamics of Job Segregation by Sex during World War II*. She is the 2016 president of the American Sociological Association.

The Working Class in American History